# CUBAN
## LITERATURE
## IN THE AGE OF
# BLACK
## INSURRECTION

### MANZANO, PLÁCIDO, AND AFRO-LATINO RELIGION

## MATTHEW PETTWAY

UNIVERSITY PRESS OF MISSISSIPPI / JACKSON

The University Press of Mississippi is the scholarly publishing agency of
the Mississippi Institutions of Higher Learning: Alcorn State University,
Delta State University, Jackson State University, Mississippi State University,
Mississippi University for Women, Mississippi Valley State University,
University of Mississippi, and University of Southern Mississippi.

www.upress.state.ms.us

The University Press of Mississippi is a member of
the Association of University Presses.

First printing 2020
∞

Library of Congress Cataloging-in-Publication Data

Names: Pettway, Matthew, author.
Title: Cuban literature in the age of black insurrection : Manzano,
Plácido, and Afro-Latino religion / Matthew Pettway.
Other titles: Caribbean studies series (Jackson, Miss.)
Description: Jackson : University Press of Mississippi, 2019. | Series:
Caribbean studies series | Includes bibliographical references and index.
Identifiers: LCCN 2019034312 (print) | LCCN 2019034313 (ebook) | ISBN
9781496824967 (hardback) | ISBN 9781496825018 (trade paperback) | ISBN
9781496824981 (epub) | ISBN 9781496824974 (epub) | ISBN 9781496825001
(pdf) | ISBN 9781496824998 (pdf)
Subjects: LCSH: Manzano, Juan Francisco, 1797–1854. | Plácido, 1809–1844.
| Cuban literature—Black authors—History and criticism. | Cuban
literature—19th century—History and criticism. | Cuban
literature—Religious aspects.
Classification: LCC PQ7377 .P48 2019 (print) | LCC PQ7377 (ebook) | DDC
860.9/896097291—dc23
LC record available at https://lccn.loc.gov/2019034312
LC ebook record available at https://lccn.loc.gov/2019034313

British Library Cataloging-in-Publication Data available

*To Timothy, my lost brother.*
*A poetic genius, and a gentle man who lost the battle*
*with the words teeming in his head.*

# CONTENTS

# ACKNOWLEDGMENTS

Writing this book was an odyssey of inexplicable proportions. It represented seven years of contemplation, hand-wringing, frustrations, further research, and, of course, rewriting. Research on any project is a thorny matter; it must be directed by logic and proven methodologies, but it is always informed by instinct. To unearth Afro-Latin American colonial literature, I followed improbable leads, traversed obscure tunnels, assembled fragments of the past, and *spoke* when the text was silent. This project led me to eight different archives in the United States and Cuba. It demanded the interpretation and translation of rare Spanish-language manuscripts, books, and colonial era documentation. But it would have been inconceivable without the moral, intellectual, and emotional support of countless people. I want to acknowledge a cherished group of Cuban scholars, ritual priests, cultural experts, activists, and artists that not only introduced me to their world but also helped to navigate it.

I am deeply indebted to Daisy Cué Fernández for bringing her formidable intellect and resources to bear in a series of conversations that lasted nearly a decade. I owe a heartfelt thanks to Tomasito Fernández Robaina, a giant in Afro-Cuban Studies, a friend, and a generous soul that welcomed me in his home and his intellectual community on several occasions. Tomasito, my students will never forget the classes you taught at your home in Havana in 2012. You are a gatekeeper who enabled me to gain access to irreplaceable manuscripts at the Biblioteca Nacional José Martí after my long hiatus from the island. I am forever in your debt. I deeply grateful to Roberto Zurbano, who has been a collaborator, a co-conspirator and, most of all, my Cuban brother. Daisy Rubiera Castillo has expanded the notion of the possible for black Cuban women with her vision, determination, and unassailable sense of self-love. I also want to recognize Henry Heredia at Centro Juan Marinello, who sponsored me and promoted critical projects on Afro-Cuban studies on and off the island. I am grateful to Henry for his bilingualism and his lasting influence on my students. A special thanks to the members of the Cuban rap group Hermanazos, who bridged the past with the present by preserving African-inspired spirituality in their lyrics.

Special thanks to *difunto* Tata-Nganga Andriol Stivens Portuondo of the religious community in Santiago de Cuba for welcoming me into his *cabildo*.

There are few librarians equal to Yasnay Cuesta Álvarez. Yasnay opened the doors of the Instituto de Literatura y Lingüística to me, and she exhumed black Cuban materials that were often in fragments and in varying stages of decay. This unearthing of materials in print is a crucial contribution to the rewriting of the history of Latin American literature. I also want to recognize the Cuban research staff at the Archivo Nacional de Cuba, Archivo Histórico Provincial de Camagüey, Biblioteca Nacional de Cuba, Biblioteca Julio Antonio Mella, Instituto de Literatura Lingüística and the Oficina del Historiador de la Ciudad de La Habana. This book would not have been possible without the Houghton Library at Harvard University and the Sterling Memorial Library at Yale University.

A special thanks to Bates College for generously supporting my research travel to Cuba and my archival work at Harvard. I want to acknowledge the affection and loyalty of my colleagues at Bates College. I am grateful to Sue Houchins and Baltasar Fra-Molinero for engaging me in conversations about the rituals and rites of the Catholic priesthood. Your insight, acumen, and penchant for complexity were monumental when writing early drafts of journal articles that would inform the completion of the manuscript. Collaborating with Val Carnegie on a study-abroad trip to Cuba made way for conversations that I am still processing today. A special thanks to Therí Pickens for being an intellectual co-conspirator, a supportive colleague amidst great uncertainty, and, most of all, for being my friend. Steadfast.

Thank you to the University of Kansas for naming me the Langston Hughes Visiting Professor and for crafting an intellectual environment where I was able to blossom. The former Langston Hughes Visiting Professors Maryemma Graham, Randal Jelks, Edgar Tidwell, and Clarence Lang became great colleagues; together we explored the political parallels and religious divergences between black Cuban and African American authors. I want to recognize Randal Jelks for encouraging me to narrativize my authors' stories and to present them in a language that is cognitively appealing and emotionally compelling. I also owe a debt of gratitude to Junot Díaz, whom I met at the University of Kansas. Junot sensed what motivated my research, and his response to my first two journal articles helped me to reimagine the significance of African spirituality in Cuban modernity.

A special thanks to the College of Charleston for supporting my research in its latter stages at the University of North Carolina at Chapel Hill. Likewise, I am grateful to the University of South Alabama for funding the production costs of my book.

María Mudrovcic at Michigan State University was the most incisive and constructive reader of my work in the early years. Her hermeneutical suspicions and commitment to intellectual brilliance were invaluable. I am grateful to the members of the African Atlantic Research Team for providing me with an early paradigm for rethinking the world we inhabit through the lens of African-inspired religion. Our travels in Santiago de Cuba and Accra—both in the ivory tower and on *dem streets*—showed me how cultural ethnography informs erudite literary practice. Jualynne Dodson has taught me more about religions of African inspiration than most books; her commitment to black Diaspora and the power embedded in her pedagogy are contagious.

My intellectual family traverses the United Sates and includes many in the Caribbean. Over the years, this family has encompassed historians, anthropologists, sociologists, and literary scholars of all stripes. Aisha Finch, Fannie Rushing, and Joseph Dorsey are a brilliant triumvirate of Caribbeanist historians whose enlightening conversation enabled me to situate my authors within the historical vicissitudes of nineteenth-century Cuba.

I do not know where this project would be without the steadfast support of Antonio Tillis. We walked together in Charleston, Seville, Santo Domingo, and Accra, and in myriad other towns and cities. Your gentle guidance and exemplary conduct have been a model for me. Thank you for showing up when I least expected it but needed your encouragement the most. A special thanks to Jerome Branche for reading an earlier draft of the manuscript and encouraging me to further develop my ideas and argumentation. I want to recognize Kameelah Martin for helping me to think through how African ideas of spirit and cosmos encode themselves *differently* throughout African diasporic literatures. I am grateful to Jossianna Arroyo Martínez and César Salgado for hosting me at the University of Texas at Austin and providing a constructive and productive space to workshop an early iteration of my book. I am thankful to John Harfouch for his steadfast support during the lean years and for his feedback on key parts of this book. I am eternally grateful to Devyn Spence Benson and Tracey Benson for making their home into a constructive space for black radical thinking. A special thanks to Godfrey Gibbison, Ramona La Roche, and Tara Bynum for listening to early presentations of my ideas and providing critique, constructive feedback and support.

Lastly, Kenya Conaway has been a friend like no other; she is a confidant, a sister, and a fierce ally. My gratitude is heartfelt, and our friendship is eternal.

# PREFATORY NOTE ON RACIAL TERMINOLOGY

Racial terminology is often convoluted; it presents complexities for the author and for her or his readership. This book is no exception. Although scientists have proven that race is not a biological category, race must be acknowledged as a social reality, a historical formation whose meanings are articulated in the symbolic language of culture and differ over time and space. I have made use of racial terminology in a manner that reflects the racial categories of colonial Cuba in order to reproduce the historical moment as accurately as possible. In so doing, I acknowledge the precedent set by historians Verena Martínez-Alier, Ada Ferrer, and Aisha Finch. I have endeavored to do so even while rejecting the racist logic that informs Spanish American cultural discourse. This is a difficult thing to achieve. One must probe representations of race as well as skin color hierarchies in the colonial Caribbean to understand the ways in which they have informed one another. Skin color hierarchies are known as pigmentocracy: a political order granting socioeconomic privileges based on the relative fairness of the skin and a professed proximity to whiteness. In *Cuban Literature in the Age of Black Insurrection*, I have examined race and pigmentocracy in nineteenth-century Cuba. Throughout the book, I refer to people of African descent—regardless of their hue—as African or African descendants and to those of European ancestry as white. I have preferred the contemporary usage whenever possible; as such, Spanish Caribbean racial labels are common throughout. The terms *negro* (black), *mulato, pardo* (mixed race or mulatto), *chinito* (offspring from a black and a mulatto), or *cuarterón* (quadroon) appear throughout the book to convey how racial terms are demonstrative of the procurement (or loss) of cultural power in Spanish colonial societies. The malleability of these terms and their inconsistent usage, sometimes in reference to the same person, may create confusion. I acknowledge the nuances embedded in the language of pigmentocracy, and I have endeavored to bring those nuances to light, whenever possible.

## A Brief Note on Original Spanish-Language Sources

Gabriel de la Concepción Valdés (also known as Plácido) and Juan Francisco Manzano belong to an impressive tradition of African-descended autodidacticism, encompassing Anglophone and Hispanophone writers across the globe. Throughout the book, I have reproduced Plácido's and Manzano's poetry, autobiographical writings, letters, and court documents without the use of "[sic]." In Latin, *sic* means "intentionally so written," and typically it appears italicized in brackets right after an error. Because Manzano's and Plácido's writings were an idiosyncratic expression of autodidactic genius, I believe conventional usage of [sic] would be impractical in this case. The repeated use of [sic] would be cumbersome and unsightly for the reader.

Manzano's autobiography and Plácido's statement to the military commission also present challenges of their own. I have quoted from William Luis's transcription of Manzano's autobiography throughout the book (though in a few instances, I include my own transcriptions.) The original autobiographical manuscript is in the possession of the Biblioteca Nacional José Martí in Havana. William Luis employed a series of useful symbols to demystify an otherwise impenetrable text. Brackets indicate that someone has introduced a change to the original line. Words that are scratched out appear in regular lettering and those that were added in bold letters. Luis uses curly brackets {} to indicate there are words written above the line in the manuscript. Again, words that are scratched out appear in typical lettering, and what was added to the manuscript is in bold print. Empty brackets [] represent illegible words appearing in the original text. Lastly, in the original autobiography, there are words and letters underlined. William Luis reproduced the underlining of those words/letters as they appeared in the original.[1]

I have reproduced fragments of Plácido's 1844 statement to the military commission in this book. The entire eleventh-hour appeal—which Plácido deployed to save his life—appears in Daisy Cué Fernández's book *Plácido: El poeta conspirador* and in her article "Plácido y la Conspiración de la Escalera." I have relied on both texts for the purposes of this book.[2] Daisy Cué copied verbatim Manuel Sanguily's 1885 transcription of Plácido's statement to the military tribunal. Sanguily capitalized clauses and sentences within the statement that were of particular interest to him as a researcher. Consequently, the transcription is replete with clauses and sentences in uppercase that do not conform to the norms of Spanish orthography. Daisy Cué respected Sanguily's transcription, and I have reproduced the poet's statement to the military tribunal as it appears in Cué's scholarship.

# CUBAN LITERATURE IN THE AGE OF BLACK INSURRECTION

## CHAPTER ONE

# The Introduction

Ser negro es vivir improvisando.

A BLACK CUBAN SAYING

I know that I know that I know.
Epistemological certitude

MY GRANDMOTHER

On August 16, 1844, a Spanish newspaper rejoiced in the "peace and tranquility" of the American continent whose "virgin and innocent country" had defeated a dangerous conspiracy against the queen. *El Laberinto* named one conspirator: Gabriel de la Concepción Valdés, a Cuban poet known as Plácido. Plácido was portrayed as "a celebrated poet, a sublime genius in whose veins flow both African and European blood."[1] The exposé aroused emotion in its Madrid readership, referring to the "vast continent where our brothers of America [reside]," and it depicted Spanish readers as sympathizers whose hearts were torn to pieces by "the most crushing pain." Furthermore, the newspaper exclaimed, "the tears well up in our eyes and the soul empathizes when speaking of that unhappy scene." The "unhappy scene" was a euphemism for antislavery insurgencies that threatened to abolish the slave regime in Cuba and deprive Her Majesty of extraordinary wealth.[2] This was the conspiracy in which Plácido was implicated. Although the author of the article didn't doubt Plácido's culpability, he approached his subject with a grave sense of ambivalence, not unlike other contemporaries. He observed that readers might condemn Plácido to death on the one hand, even as they unlocked his prison cell on the other.

Curiously, the author did not name the charges brought against Plácido, rather he described a litany of poems that his "brilliant and audacious imagination" had conjured up. Among these was the sonnet "El juramento" (The Oath), wherein Plácido swore to defile his vestments with the blood of queen.

In the shadow of a towering tree
That stands at the end of an ample valley
There is a fount that bids you
Drink its pure and silvery water

There I went by my duty called
And making an altar of the hardened earth
Before the sacred code of life,
My hands extended, I have sworn an oath.

To be the eternal enemy of the tyrant,
If it is possible, to tarnish my vestments,
With his detestable blood, by my hand

Shedding it with repeated blows
And dying at the hands of an executioner,
If need be, to break the yoke (Plácido qtd. in Cué, *Plácido: El poeta* 87–88)

Plácido's power resided in his pen. "El juramento" was a counterhegemonic poem for three reasons: it swore an oath of secrecy among blacks, it professed a sacred code of life, and it prophesied the execution of the queen. Plácido believed in the intrinsic power of language, the power of words to transform the outcome of events and to prophesy against empire. He produced Janus-faced poetry that affirmed loyalty to the Catholic Church even while undermining its doctrinal premises with African-inspired ideas of spirit and cosmos. In "El juramento," Plácido resignified religious tropes steeped in Spanish Catholic history: the altar, the divine calling, and the oath of fidelity. In the first two stanzas, the prospective insurgent is invited to a shaded area beneath a tree, where he proceeds to make an altar of "the hardened earth." Plácido constructed an altar of his own; a ritual object he fashioned outside the cathedral walls and without the interference of Catholic priests. Plácido's altar did not sanctify the Eucharist; instead, *his* altar revered the sacredness of the natural world. In contradistinction to Catholicism, the African-inspired altar is "sacred space" (Dodson 62), an edifice for remembering the dead that is consecrated for sacrifice to African divine spirits and ancestors (Millet 7; Cabrera 287).

But the meanings, contours, and function of the altar are determined by the religious tradition in question. Plácido's altar of "hardened earth" is reminiscent of a Bakongo Cuban conception of the natural world, particularly the forested wilderness as a sanctuary for communion with African divine spirits and ancestors. Lydia Cabrera affirmed that forests possess everything black Cubans require for their "magic . . . and their well-being" (15). Cabrera's informants expounded on that theme explaining, "The *ceiba* tree is an altar to *palo monte* practitioners" that deposit sacred items beneath the tree to absorb "the virtue of its shadow" (166). In Plácido's poem, the tree is not an altar per se, but its sacred silhouette creates space for insurgents to swear oaths of vengeance against slave society. Plácido's altar beckoned a religio-political order where African descendants might reject Spanish colonialism and subvert the political authority of the Spanish Catholic Church. The nature metaphors—the tree and hardened earth—are important because they establish Cuba, not Spain, as Plácido's fatherland.

Oaths inhabit the intersection between religion and politics (Prodi qtd. in Agamben 1); they constitute a social and political covenant between diverse interlocutors within a given polity. Giorgio Agamben points out that political crises arise when either party disregards or dishonors the oath they have sworn (Philo qtd. in Agamben 21). Plácido's oath "to tarnish, my vestments / With his detestable blood" was a revolutionary speech act articulated in a subtle but formidable African-Cuban religious discourse. The emerging antislavery aesthetic in Plácido's poetry constituted what Edward Said described as "a systematic conversion of the power relationship between the controller and the controlled" (16). But Plácido was not the only Cuban writer to incorporate an African spiritual subtext in literature, nor was he the only one to provoke the queen's wrath with seditious writings.

In May 1844 Plácido and his accomplice Manzano sat in dark and dreadful prisons awaiting trial for their alleged involvement in what the Spanish government described as "the conspiracy devised by people of color . . . to exterminate . . . the white population."[3] Plácido and Juan Francisco Manzano did not enjoy the anonymity that may have protected their spoken-word counterparts from political persecution and arrest. Forty years following the triumph of the only revolution engineered by enslaved persons, the Spanish dreaded that Cuba, too, might become black and African, in a word *Haitian*. The military government scoured the free population of color in search of the movement's intellectual leaders, and a small, though culturally significant, African-descended artisan and professional class fell under suspicion as agents and agitators of conspiracy. The authorities charged Manzano with aiding and abetting a conspiracy to abolish slavery and depose the regime. But the charges levied against Plácido were far more severe. Gabriel de la Concepción Valdés was convicted of being the president, mastermind, and recruiter of an insidious plot to exterminate the white inhabitants and to institute a republic of blacks and mulattoes on the island. Though Manzano would survive the gruesome ordeal on June 28, 1844, colonial authorities executed Plácido on charges of treason, having him shot in the back.

The authorities not only questioned Plácido and Manzano's secretive meetings, hidden communiqués, and travel plans but also interrogated them about writing seditious literature. The government inquest about a "pohetica alusiva a planes contrarios a la tranquilidad y seguridad de esta Isla" (poetics alluding to plans contrary to the tranquility and security of the Island) (Friol 207) bespoke a concerted effort to define the poetics of conspiracy. The Spanish government's suspicions about seditious literature reflect the pervasive abolitionist atmosphere of the 1830s. In 1833 Britain abolished slavery in the Anglophone Caribbean and in 1835 pressured Spain to consent to yet another antislave-trade treaty (Paquette 92, 132). Perhaps of even greater consequence, slave insurrections throughout Cuba had become frequent roughly ten years prior to the detention of Manzano and Plácido in 1844 (Midlo Hall 56).[4] The Spanish government employed all manner of surveillance, interrogation, and torture to discover who had instigated "the conspiracy of the people of color" and, perhaps more importantly, to determine the intellectual character of an emerging black Cuban literary tradition.

The charges levied against Plácido and Manzano were indicative of white anxieties about African-descended writers as the architects of discourse. How could writers with no formal humanistic training, no military expertise to speak of, and no experience in the diplomatic corps pose a political threat to one of the greatest empires in the world? What subversive writing practices did Plácido and Manzano employ in their poetry and prose? What role did religious discourse play in the creation of anticolonial literature? And what did they hope to accomplish by writing against the Spanish Empire? This book analyzes what Eugene Genovese termed a "revolution in consciousness" that the Haitian Revolution ignited. Blacks throughout the African Diaspora encrypted antislavery ideology in literature, in their quotidian behaviors, and even in plantation uprisings.[5]

My central claim is that Manzano and Plácido portrayed African-inspired spirituality beneath the surface of Hispano-Catholic aesthetics, which, in effect, transformed early Cuban literature into an instrument of black liberation. I argue that Manzano and Plácido seized upon images of the Virgin Mary and Catholic saints, and resignified Neoclassical and Romantic tropes to conceal the African-inspired ritual subtext they had relied upon to procure myriad modalities of freedom. Although much of their writing touched upon uncontroversial motifs, including the pastoral idyll, unrequited love, and celebratory verse in honor of a wealthy patronage, their politically motivated portrayal of religion often subverted the Catholic traditions they claimed to represent. Plácido and Manzano did not envision emancipation through the lens of a Catholic doctrine that extolled redemptive suffering as a means to salvation. Rather, they relied on a spirituality of African inspiration in order to procure the power necessary to liberate themselves. Their depiction of African-inspired spirituality masqueraded as folk Catholicism. Because the government censored all literature, and black poets relied on the social legitimacy that the Church afforded them, Manzano and Plácido could not set the terms of debate. Yet, for all its power over language and liturgy, the Church could neither define nor control the

African-Cuban cultural lens, nor could it govern African-descended sensibilities about spirit presence, revelation, and ritual powers. I define the African-Cuban cultural lens as a dichromatic paradigm, an inclusive worldview where multiple religious epistemologies coexist and intermingle in the colonial environment.

Plácido and Manzano introduced African ideas of spirit and cosmos into a nascent Cuban literary tradition in the early nineteenth century. In a manner consistent with Michel Foucault's theory on discourse analysis, they incorporated African-inspired spirituality within the official religious discourse (216). Manzano and Plácido managed, on occasion, to avert the censorship regime, because their transculturated colonial literature affirmed and negated religious meanings at the same time. Consequently, they eluded Spanish censorship of religious writings that contradicted the Holy Faith. But the censorship administration and the Catholic Church were not the only threats to their literary imagination. Plácido and Manzano relied on tightknit units of white Cuban writers to publish their literature. Domingo del Monte was the leading Cuban humanist and he exerted considerable influence over the direction of early Cuban literature. Del Monte was a reformer who feared that the growing African population in Cuba might foment rebellion and, eventually, imperil his dream of white Creole self-governance (Fernández de Castro ed. 144–145). Del Monte endorsed reformist literature that critiqued Cuban slavery in hopes of abolishing the Atlantic slave trade. And he collaborated with Manzano and Plácido in furtherance of his political project, but they did not always share similar objectives. Despite what some critics have claimed, del Monte was not an abolitionist. In fact, del Monte dreaded the abolition of slavery, because he assumed abolition would imperil his person and his profits, and eventually threaten "the existence of my race" (M. Miller 426; Branche, *Colonialism* 129). Del Monte's literary coterie produced black characters as romanticized victims of slavery, never rebellious maroons that defied their subjugation (Barreda 44–45). Anselmo Suárez y Romero's novel *Francisco* and Félix Tanco y Bosmeniel's *Petrona y Rosalía* promoted a form of Catholicism that neither emancipated the *slaves* nor empowered them to liberate themselves.[6] In the main, white intelligentsia precluded African spiritual practices from their construction of Cuban national culture. As Cuban scholar Eduardo Torres Cuevas writes, "Catholicism became the ideological expression and the unifying factor of Creole identity" (90). Domingo del Monte was an avowed Catholic who was unsympathetic to the cultural values within African-inspired religious culture. Del Monte struggled to wrest creative control from Plácido and Manzano in order to yield propaganda that might further the interests of white society.

Manzano and Plácido's writings alluding to African ideas of spirit and cosmos constitute what I have termed *transculturated colonial literature*, that is, intercultural texts that emerged as an aesthetic response to the discursive prohibitions of the Catholic Church, the censorship administration, and del Monte's literary circle. I posit transculturated colonial literature as a theoretical lens for probing self-dissembling texts existing within an intervening space, situated on the periphery yet palatable to a metropolitan readership. (I will expound on this theory later in the chapter.) Plácido and Manzano portrayed Bakongo and Yoruba cosmologies (West Central and West African belief systems respectively) in euphemisms that subverted Catholic doctrine and at the same time created space for continuous revelation from the spirit world. Manzano and Plácido's literature questioned the authority of the Catholic Church, even though they had pledged loyalty to the one true religion. Furthermore, Manzano produced the only known slave autobiography in Spanish American cultural history, and he published the earliest example of black Cuban theatrical work. Manzano ultimately became an antislavery intellectual comparable to his counterpart Plácido. Plácido published revolutionary poetry that defined liberty as the divine right of Cubans, and he assailed the queen as an illegitimate ruler on the throne.

Juan Francisco Manzano and Gabriel de la Concepción Valdés were the most radical poets of African descent in nineteenth-century Cuba, producing an extensive body of work even as the slave aristocracy reached the height of its power.[7] Manzano was born into slavery in Havana in 1797 and didn't achieve emancipation until 1836; but his contemporary Plácido was born free in Havana in 1809. Plácido and Manzano published more than seven hundred poems between 1821 and 1844.[8] Though much of their poetry appeared in the white Cuban press, they also circulated unpublished manuscripts within clandestine dissident networks.

Both poets gained recognition from white literati; but they also affirmed a sense of cultural belonging within black and mulatto communities, whose antislavery worldview was informed by African-inspired spiritual practices and beliefs. Plácido and Manzano negotiated an ostensible contradiction of values and political loyalties because they wrote about Catholicism—the official religion of the Spanish Empire—even though their literature engaged its supposed antithesis: African spirituality. The Spanish government promoted Catholic doctrines to delegitimize African spirituality and to malign its power, so that no black political project would emerge as an alternative to the system of white supremacy. Plácido's and Manzano's transculturated representations of the sacred occupied a radical political terrain that critiqued slave labor and undermined Church authority while working within its strictures.

To summarize the findings of Joan Bristol, enslaved Africans and other colonial Spanish Americans did not draw a firm line of demarcation between different religious practices ("Church, Africans" 203). In the Spanish Caribbean, there was no black clergy comparable to the array of Protestant preachers in the United States in the second half of the eighteenth century. And Spanish authorities forbade blacks to be priests in the Spanish Caribbean with precious few exceptions (S. C. Drake 28; Andrews, *Afro-Latin America* 12, 44; Pettway, "The Altar, the Oath" 20).[9] The Catholic Church in nineteenth-century Cuba lacked evangelical zeal, and priests made fewer efforts to convert enslaved Africans than earlier generations had done with indigenous Mesoamericans (Madden 104–106; Rivera Pagán 25). Consequently, an Afro-Latino Creole culture emerged throughout Latin America and the Caribbean that revered Catholic clerics and African priests and priestesses alike (S.C. Drake 20).

Free blacks and mulattoes that aspired to leadership in their communities had to acquire *sacred authority* within the parameters of the Church, but they also accessed African-inspired spiritual power that held sway among a black Cuban counterpublic. Historian Vincent Brown defines "sacred authority" as the appropriation of African or European symbolic practices that contain social and spiritual power and may be harnessed to achieve political might (24, 34). This did not mean that Afro-Latino Caribbean elites rejected Catholicism, but rather that they negotiated their relationship to the local clergy even as they preserved a belief in African-inspired spirituality. African Americans' cultural and political relationship to Protestantism, however, was vastly different. This was especially true for a small literate Christian elite in the antebellum United States for whom the Bible was critical to the articulation of an emancipation theology.

The Christian redemptive narrative was at the core of African American Protestantism in the antebellum period. Black Protestant intellectuals—some in favor of antislavery revolts and some opposed to such uprisings—crafted a theology based on the Protestant "open Bible" tradition, where congregants and clergy alike exercised their right to interpret sacred text for themselves (S. C. Drake 48). African American exegesis emboldened prominent thinkers such as David Walker—who in 1829 wrote his incendiary *Appeal to the Colored Citizens of the World, Particular and Very Expressly, to Those of the United States of America*—to defy derogatory white interpretations of the Bible (S. C. Drake 44–45, 48). Comparable to Barbadian freemason Prince Hall, Walker linked biblical prophecy about Ethiopia with the contemporary black struggle against slavery (S. C. Drake 45; Ferrer, *Freedom's Mirror* 307). With Bible in hand, black Protestant preachers—some literate and others semiliterate—refuted the Hamitic myth that alleged slavery was a divine curse on black people. Rather, black Protestants reasoned that God would bring an end to slavery one way or another. "Negro folk theologians" preached of a glorious African past, even naming their churches for the African continent or for the ancient kingdom of Abyssinia, an archaic word for Ethiopia (S. C. Drake 48). But the black Protestant vision of Africa had little in common with Afro-Latino Caribbean writers Plácido and Manzano. African Americans and some Afro-Caribbeans believed in the prophetic word of God and in the inevitability of divine judgment. But while black American Protestant leaders turned to the Bible as a source of moral authority, Afro-Latinos appropriated the symbols of Catholic legitimacy and invested them with radical meanings born of an African-Atlantic religious culture.

For black American Protestants, Africa was a continent in need of redemption, redemption at the hands of Protestant Christianity (S. C. Drake 52; Washington 8).[10] Black Protestant writers—such as Olaudah Equiano and Martin Delany—rejected African-inspired spiritual practices as heathenism and embraced Christianity as a *civilized* rationale for black freedom (Martin, "Hoodoo Ladies" 120–121). But the condemnation of African-inspired spirituality among elites did not mean that the black folk in the United States had abandoned the efficacy of such practices (Martin, *Conjuring Moments* 55–56). Manzano and Plácido were formative in the invention of Cuban literature, and they constituted part of an African diasporic antislavery tradition that Olaudah Equiano, Phillis Wheatley, David Walker, Mary Prince, Frederick Douglass, and Martin Delany constructed in the Caribbean, England, and the United States. But Plácido and Manzano's reclamation of African-inspired spirituality, not as witchcraft but rather as epistemology, constituted an early decolonial critique within diasporic literatures that promoted a different kind of *black* freedom, one that was neither defined nor delimited by white Creole control.

Cuban writers of African descent navigated two worlds and traversed cultural boundaries. Collaboration with white authors ensured their work would be published, and careful coalitions with members of the clergy enhanced their sense of respectability. The white intelligentsia monopolized a fledging Cuban press for fifty years prior to the founding of the black press in 1842.[11] But dialogue with the Church and white reformists would never help Manzano and Plácido procure the power necessary to achieve the liberation of African-descended people. Though they benefited from elite affiliations, they did not relinquish a sense of belonging in black and mulatto communities in Havana and Matanzas. African descendants—both enslaved and free—premised their antislavery worldview on their shared experience of racialization in Cuban slave society, and they frequently envisaged freedom through the lens of West and West Central African–inspired spiritualties. Despite their dissimilar social origins, Plácido and Manzano collaborated aesthetically and politically. They conversed about the racial politics of colonial Cuba, they exchanged unpublished manuscripts with each other, and they wrote on common themes. Plácido and Manzano contributed to an antislavery aesthetic premised on an African Atlantic religious belief structure. My research reveals that Manzano and Plácido had three primary objectives in mind. They wrote literature invoking African-inspired spirituality as an alternative to the universality of Catholic doctrine, they fomented interaction with the spirit world, and they harnessed the power of ritual in a broader struggle against slavery. A brief discussion of African Atlantic religion will make Plácido and Manzano's engagement with African-inspired spirituality more legible.

Sylvia Frey explains that African Atlantic religions are systems of belief defined by the principle of "continuous creation." The Atlantic slave trade triggered unprecedented violence in Africa and on the high seas, and it caused innumerable ruptures in ethnic identity that made the principle of "continuous creation" a requisite feature of these religions. Societies like Cuba and Brazil that received an unceasing supply of new captives into the nineteenth century developed lasting connections between autochthonous African ethnic beliefs and Luso-Hispanic Catholicism. The frequent transformations within African Atlantic religions produced "multilayered" ritual practices that comingled African beliefs with Catholic symbols and narrative, thus forming a new tapestry of religious performance. African Atlantic religions developed throughout the diaspora in three successive historical periods. Frey describes these three historical periods as follows. The first stage occurred in Africa from ancient times until circa 1500, when indigenous religions, early Christianity, and Islam flourished. In the second stage, Africans were transported to the Western Hemisphere, and they became part of the advent of the Luso-Hispanic Catholic world circa 1500–1700. In the final historical period, circa 1700 well into the nineteenth century, Africans in Latin America endured religious transformations that were produced by the massive importation of captives to the region (Frey 153, 164). African Atlantic religion is characterized by inspiration, malleability, and novelty, as opposed to traditions defined by an immutable African cultural past. Anthropologist Todd Ochoa theorizes that "African-inspired" spirituality is "a hinge between the past and the future" that adopts an improvisational approach to the often sober relationship between the distant historical past and an uncertain future. Inspiration articulates its power to create in a given moment; thus, "African-inspired" spirituality cannot be defined exclusively as a creative response to suffering or merely understood as a futile attempt to retrieve the African past (8). I will use *African Atlantic religion* and *African-inspired spirituality* interchangeably throughout the book. The African Atlantic religious transformations that interest me here emerged in the late eighteenth and early nineteenth centuries.

The Cuban antislavery aesthetic was born with the *libro de pinturas* (book of drawings) of José Antonio Aponte, a free black Cuban militiaman that organized an insurgency against slavery and Spanish colonialism in 1812. Aponte's *libro de pinturas* used an array of military and religious symbolism to depict African men embroiled in a righteous struggle against whites to eradicate slavery. (The *libro de pinturas* has never been recovered.) But Aponte's heterogeneous book of drawings also portrayed the metaphysical dimensions of his war against slavery. Aponte represented Our Lady of Remedies (Virgen de Remedios) as his patron saint in an uprising to end Spanish colonial rule in Cuba. The Virgen de Remedios was the patroness that Mexicans had beseeched in support of black Cuban battalions fighting the British siege of Havana in

1762. Aponte's antislavery aesthetic consists of three essential qualities that are significant for understanding Manzano and Plácido's work. These are: The Virgin Mary and Catholic saints laboring in the interest of black freedom, Greco-Roman deities invested with new meaning, and African-inspired spirituality as a source of power in colonial texts (Ferrer, *Freedom's Mirror* 296, 311).[12] Aponte's book of drawings differed from Plácido and Manzano's poetry/prose because he privileged visual imagery and symbols over the wordplay and double entendre common to literary language. Notwithstanding the dissimilarity, Plácido and Manzano also appropriated Catholic symbols of sacred authority and commissioned them in the interest of black freedom. Comparable to Aponte (and his accomplices), Manzano and Plácido's inconspicuous representations of African-inspired spirituality bespoke an epistemology endowed with emancipatory potential. Aponte's, Plácido's, and Manzano's texts were informed by the principle of "continuous creation" inherent in African Atlantic religions. In effect, Plácido and Manzano's antislavery aesthetic—emerging some twenty-four years after José Antonio Aponte had been executed—was also a creation of the African Atlantic.

### *African Cuban Literati in Ascendance*: The Literary Exploits of Manzano and Plácido

Juan Francisco Manzano was born into slavery in Havana in 1797, raised on a Matanzas sugar plantation, and socialized into Spanish Catholicism as well as African-inspired religious culture. Manzano escaped the Matanzas plantation circa 1817 and fled to Havana, putting an end to the psychosexual abuse of his enslaver. In Havana, Manzano taught himself to read and write while serving in the households of Don Tello Mantilla and María de la Luz de Zayas. Manzano became acquainted with white Cuban reformer and Indianist writer Ignacio Valdés Machuca, who orchestrated the publication of his first compilation, *Poesías líricas*. The publication of *Poesías líricas* in 1821 was an unparalleled feat, because it became the first collection of Cuban verse published by anyone, black or white. *Flores pasageras*, his second book of poetry, came out in 1830. After the publication of two compilations, Valdés Machuca introduced Manzano to Domingo del Monte at some point in the 1830s, and del Monte became the poet's editor (Friol 195–196).[13] Domingo del Monte was the most prominent humanist and literary critic in early nineteenth-century Cuba.[14] Del Monte's family—the Alfonso-Aldama-Madam clan—managed an enormous slave-owning and slave-trading enterprise that exploited African captives on sugar plantations in order to amass considerable wealth. Domingo del Monte personally owned one hundred enslaved persons on a nine-hundred-acre estate. His sizable wealth positioned him to build the institutional framework of a reformist Catholic literary culture in Cuba (Branche, *Colonialism* 129–130). In 1836, at the behest of his benefactor Domingo del Monte, Juan Francisco

Manzano finished writing the only known autobiographical account of slavery in Spanish America.[15]

Manzano's letters to del Monte dating from 1835 reveal that both men had entered into an unspoken pact: white reformists would purchase the poet's freedom if he wrote an intimate account of his life as a *slave*.[16] Del Monte requested the slave narrative as propaganda to condemn the brutality of slavery and, consequently, put an end to the slave trade, which had already changed the demographics of the island. However, del Monte also wanted to ensure the whiteness and "future prosperity" of the island once the slave trade had been abolished. But Manzano ascribed to a worldview that was antithetical to the political interests of Domingo del Monte. Manzano labored to transform the aesthetic object into an instrument of emancipation: a freedom narrative that would not only secure his manumission but also enable him to reconstitute his family that had been torn asunder by slavery. Manzano appealed to the French Revolution's *Declaration of the Rights of Man and of Citizens* to portray himself as a good Catholic and a Man of Reason in the letters he wrote to del Monte. Though he relied on the respectability that his mulatto-Catholic image afforded him, his literature seldom beseeched the Christian God for redemption but rather sought to procure the power necessary to emancipate himself. Manzano conjured the power of African divine spirits (*mpungos* and *orishas*)—dissembled as Catholic saints—to escape the Matanzas sugar plantation circa 1817. Manzano's use of Catholic saints and, on occasion, Greco-Roman deities enabled him to allude to African divine spirits in his autobiography and in some poetry in ways that were indecipherable to his white readership. But this camouflage also ensured their legibility for his black and mulatto interlocutors. However, once Manzano handed over the autobiography to be published, del Monte's circle denied him any editorial control. Anselmo Suárez y Romero, a member of the del Monte group, reconfigured the manuscript, and Irish abolitionist Richard Robert Madden effaced the religious character of the narrative, removing language that Protestants might have deemed superstitious. Madden translated the slave narrative and published it in England in 1840 after he had removed the author's surname. Then, Madden further intervened.

Richard Robert Madden did not publish the first antislavery poem Manzano wrote, "The Absent Slave Woman" (1823), because he wanted to cultivate an image of the respectable *slave poet* in Europe. In "The Absent Slave Woman," Manzano assumed a female voice that pleaded with her captor not to destroy her marital union with her black husband. Though the poem's meaning is heavily cloaked in metaphor, Manzano implied that the slave owner intended to rape the captive black woman. It is no surprise, then, that Madden did not include this poem in his 1840 publication of Manzano's work, because the erotic subtext might have disturbed his Victorian readership and undermined the abolitionist cause. Madden's refusal to publish "The Absent Slave Woman" meant that this poignant critique of racialized sexual violence—and by extension, Manzano's reputation as a radical antislavery writer—would be virtually unknown to readers for nearly 170 years after Manzano wrote it. "The Poet's Vision: Composed on a Sugar Plantation" was another unpublished antislavery poem; but it was not part of the dossier of Manzano's work that Madden carried to London. "The Poet's Vision" is a protracted narrative poem consisting of 386 lines of verse where Manzano employed the dream sequence as a portal for contact with the spirit world. In "The Poet's Vision," Venus—the Roman goddess of female beauty—appeared to Manzano on the planation with a strategy to rescue him from his *locus horrendous.*[17]

Far from a genteel exchange, Manzano's collaboration with Madden and del Monte (and other elites) was more like a protracted struggle over what could and could not be said, an entrenched battle over the cultural lens that black and mulatto writers used to navigate the colonial world.

Although Plácido enjoyed *legal* freedoms that Manzano would not procure until age thirty-nine, he also navigated a white-dominated literary scene where Creoles such as Domingo del Monte promoted a notion of freedom centered on national independence that would ultimately lead to the abolition of the slave trade without undermining white political power.

Plácido was born legally free in Havana in 1809 of a Spanish mother and a mixed-race father said to be one-eighth African (quadroon). At his birth, Plácido was abandoned to the Casa de Beneficencia y Maternidad de la Habana, a Catholic orphanage, but his father rescued him from the orphanage, and his black grandmother reared him, presumably in the extramural black and mulatto neighborhoods of the capital. Plácido's baptismal records described him as *al parecer blanco* (white in appearance), but despite the privilege associated with his whitish complexion, he put down roots in the black community and affirmed his African-inspired religious culture by participating in African Cuban religious ceremonies.[18] Plácido received meager instruction in Havana until 1821, when he briefly studied drawing. Two years later, he began to work as a typographer at the prestigious printing press of José Severino Boloña. Because whites erected legal barriers to deny blacks and mulattoes access to formal education, Plácido received only modest humanistic instruction. However, African-descended teachers in Havana tutored Plácido, and he studied in the Colegio de Belén, an important parochial school on the outskirts of the capital city. Both factors left an indelible mark on his poetic production. And although he did not publish until 1834—more than ten years after his counterpart Juan Francisco Manzano—he became the most prolific poet and renowned improvisator throughout the island. There is no other Cuban poet, black or white, that published more than Plácido in the nineteenth century. In merely ten years, he wrote, extemporized, and published nearly seven hundred poems and distributed them in several compilations and newspapers all over Cuba. Plácido's first known publication was a pithy appraisal of an Italian opera that came out in *Diario de la Habana* in 1834.[19] And in the same year, Plácido debuted his virtuosity reciting "La siempreviva," an ode he had dedicated to Francisco Martínez de la Rosa, a liberal Spanish poet and government minister.

Plácido alluded to an emancipatory project in its nascency in his ode to Martínez de la Rosa. And Plácido applauded the liberalism of queen regent María Cristina. María Cristina had assumed the regency in 1833, after her husband King Fernando VII died, and she governed Spain as proxy for her young daughter, Isabel (born 1830). But three years later the political landscape shifted for Cuban liberals. Though María Cristina had enacted a liberal constitution in Spain in 1836, she refused to extend those same freedoms to what remained of her Latin American colonies (Fischer 102–103). María Cristina reasoned that freedom of any kind was anathema to the maintenance of power within a slave colony. Moreover, the decisive military victory of African rebels in the Haitian Revolution (1791–1804) astounded the Spanish crown, and the royals dreaded that an ascendant class of free blacks might ignite such an insurrection and ultimately achieve power over the whites. But Madrid's refusal to bestow freedom on its black/mulatto subjects, and its unlawful participation in the slave trade, further emboldened Plácido to subvert the symbolic order through poetry that condemned tyranny and championed the cause of liberty.[20]

Plácido took aim at the monarchy he had once admired, and his poetry challenged the institutional authority of the Church he had often exalted. Perhaps his most fearless attacks on Queen Isabel II are embodied in the poems "In the Proclamation of Isabel II" (also referred to as "The Spirit of Padilla"), "The Prophecy from Cuba to Spain," "Havana Liberty!," and "The Oath," to name but a few. It is remarkable that Plácido managed to publish such incendiary work, because his calls for "liberty" and his criticism of the queen transgressed the boundaries of polite discourse and violated the censorship rules. Notwithstanding his immense popularity as a published author, Plácido achieved a far greater feat as a spoken-word poet, because improvisation enabled him to evade government censorship and to impart politically sensitive—even revolutionary ideas—within an urban and rural African-descended public.

Gabriel de la Concepción Valdés published every conceivable poetic genre, and he experimented with highbrow and popular forms. Plácido debuted four books of poetry in his lifetime: *Poesías* (1838), *El veguero* (1841, 1842), *Poesías escogidas* (1842), and *El hijo de maldición* (1843). The broad dissemination of his work in newspapers such as *El Eco de Villa Clara*, *El Pasatiempo*, and *Correo de Trinidad* are testimony to the aesthetic and thematic appeal of his poetry. Plácido's immense body of work reveals a range of aesthetic choices from Neoclassicism to Romanticism. Though his mélange of literary styles resists classification, there are at least four identifiable categories: satire, poems of political protest, popular fables, and religious poetry alluding to African-inspired spirituality. This book examines Plácido's racial satire and religious poetry as furtive interventions into official discourses on race and religion. Plácido critiqued the notion that whiteness was a symbol of cultural purity and social refinement, and he also defied Catholicism as the arbiter of universal truth.

Plácido's satire depicted slave society as a structure marked by depravity, but it did so with the ambivalence of laughter as not to infringe on the sensibilities of the authoritarian regime. Some of Plácido's notable parodies are "The Man and the Canary," "Get Somebody Else to Believe That!," "What an Angry Bull!," "Let Him Tell That to His Grandmother," "If Arcino Says to Everyone," "Don't Play Around, You'll Get Me Wet," "A *Curro*'s Reply," and "The Thug." Plácido undressed power with laughter, and he disparaged alcoholism, fraud, and usury. But I am mainly interested in Plácido's caricature of the mulatto desire to become white and how he reclaimed Africa as the ancestral home of persons purported to be *mulato*. Plácido critiqued pigmentocracy—social hierarchy based on skin color—by humorously engaging internecine battles over light skin privilege in communities of African descent. Plácido and Manzano's intervention into the discourse on race and religion symbolized a grave danger to the colonial regime that censored all printed materials in order to deter the dissemination of radical ideas about liberty. But perhaps even more impressive than their individual bodies of work was their decision to collaborate creatively to achieve political ends.

Manzano and Plácido became acquainted in Havana circa 1839, an encounter that would spur an artistic and political collaboration that made them enemies of the state. When Manzano met Plácido, both writers were swiftly approaching the pinnacle of their literary careers, and their political importance was in ascendance. Plácido had issued *Poesías* in Matanzas in 1838, and after completing his autobiography, Manzano was exploring new prospects for his career, including the creation of an authentic Cuban novel. Ever since his debut in praise of Spanish liberalism, Plácido had adopted a far more acerbic tone, and his political meaning became uncompromisingly clear. Plácido made an exceptional claim: he maintained that Cuban subjects to the Spanish crown had a divine right to liberty. In 1838 he published "The Spirit of Padilla," a poem that condemned the queen as a bloodthirsty tyrant. Juan de Padilla was a sixteenth-century Spaniard that led the *comunero* uprising in Toledo in 1520 against absolute monarchy (Fischer 101). Government reaction was swift, and the authorities imprisoned Plácido for writing subversive literature. "The Spirit of Padilla" represented an aesthetic shift for the author, because Plácido engaged spiritual imagery to voice revolutionary dissent. Plácido conjured Padilla as ancestral spirit; Padilla addressed the poet by name, and as ancestor he named the presence of another spirit, a wonderful goddess called LIBERTY (Valdés, "*Plácido: Gabriel de la Concepción*" 647). Spanish government suspicions were such that the governor of Matanzas, García Oña, forbade Plácido to travel throughout the island without his consent. And although Manzano's tenor was less severe, in 1838 he also began to address the problem of black freedom as the primary concern of his literary work.

Manzano published the most remarkable poem of his career, "A Dream: For My Second Brother," in the *Álbum* in 1838, nearly two years after del Monte's literary circle had purchased his manumission. Manzano dedicated "A Dream" to Florencio, his younger brother who remained on the Matanzas sugar plantation twenty-one years after the poet's escape to Havana. He relied on the poem to make his brother's fate known and to advocate for his emancipation. Manzano situated the poem in the cultural interstices of colonial Cuba, brilliantly appropriating a great variety of Romantic tropes to reimagine freedom through a distinctly African-Cuban cultural lens. Manzano alluded to African-inspired spirituality through the dream sequence and he evoked ancestral memory in a moment of political crisis. In Spanish Romanticism, the dream sequence is unencumbered by logic, existing outside of time and space; it is always open, in constant metamorphosis and, as such, dreams are spaces where the spirit world may exist. Likewise, African spirituality perceived dreams as spaces were spirit revelation might ensue. John Thornton points out that in the sixteenth and seventeenth centuries, spirit revelation in Africa included dreams, augury, visions, and spirit possession of humans, animals and inanimate objects (Thornton, *Africa and Africans* 239). In the "New World," dreams continued to be a medium for spirit revelation from the dead for practitioners of Bakongo-inspired practices in Cuba (Dodson 19, 55). This is significant because in "A Dream" and in "The Spirit of Padilla" Manzano and Plácido's visions inflame their passions to pursue liberty for an *enslaved* Cuban nation. In other words, liberty is a divine right, and Spain had deprived Cubans of African descent of that right. Though the spiritual subtext may have been undecipherable to Manzano and Plácido's white readership, it would most certainly have been culturally resonant with blacks and mulattoes aware that the British had abolished slavery in their Caribbean colonies.

Manzano introduced himself to Plácido in 1839 at a cockfight in Havana, and they kindled a friendship in which they often dined, imbibed brandy, and discussed poetry at length (Friol 192, 198). Manzano was conversant with Plácido's poetry and well aware of his notoriety, yet he pursued a friendship with him. They shared a common interest in writing antislavery poetry that challenged the political status quo. In 1840 Manzano's work achieved international acclaim when R. R. Madden published an English translation of his antislavery poetry and autobiography in London, *Poems by a Slave in the Island of Cuba, Recently Liberated; Translated from the Spanish, by R. R. Madden*. Although Manzano was a cause célèbre in his own right—after the publication of "Havana Liberty!" and "The Oath" in 1840—Plácido was by far the most prominent revolutionary writer on the island. Plácido and Manzano conferred about rhetorical strategies

and they began to develop an antislavery aesthetic that would disrupt and subvert Spanish Catholic cultural hegemony.

## Spanish Catholicism, Race and Black Redemption in Colonial Cuba

Manzano and Plácido's challenge to Spanish Catholic supremacy raises questions about how the Church perceived the material realities of African slavery while advocating for the religious redemption of black souls. Was black
redemption by way of Catholicism possible if such redemption did not also
entail the emancipation of the body from slavery? How did the Church envisage the black body? And how did Catholicism construct the body of Christ as a
salvific figure in a society where religious conversion did not ensure ownership
of one's own body?

Centuries before slavery became synonymous with blackness in the "New
World," Church fathers had already sanctioned the practice. Saint Thomas
Aquinas (1225–1274) defended slavery as part of the governing structure of the
natural world. But Aquinas acknowledged that slavery caused human agony
and had not existed in the state of nature. In some regard, Aquinas's views on
slavery seem remarkably close to the beliefs held by the white Latin American
slave-owning aristocracy about enslaved Africans. Aquinas, too, considered
slaves to be assets. He wrote "a slave is his master's chattel in matters superadded
to nature but in natural things all are equal." Aquinas defended the master/
slave relationship even as he espoused a belief in monogenesis and in the principle of human equality before God. However, Aquinas's views diverged from
those of colonial Latin American slaveholders in an important way; when he
wrote in the thirteenth century, Europeans had not yet invented the idea of race
(Davis 94–96). In fact, Africans were not the only slaves in late fifteenth-century
Europe; light-skinned Muslims and white Slavs were also among the groups
that could be lawfully enslaved (Rivera Pagán 185–186). Racial ideology transformed the Catholic rationale for slavery when an ascendant Portugal inaugurated the Atlantic slave trade in the 1440s.

Scholars have attributed the ideological framework that transformed
European views on slavery to Portuguese chronicler, Gomes Eanes de Zurara,
who published *Crónica dos feitos de Guiné* in 1453. Zurara's portrayal of Africans
was as distorted as it was prescriptive. Zurara equated Africans with animals; he
depicted them as naked creatures bereft of reason and industriousness, without proper shelter, and living "in a bestial sloth." He advanced an ethnocentric
idea that African culture represented a "much greater captivity" than European
Christian government (Branche, *Colonialism* 42). Zurara inaugurated a discourse on blackness inflected by Aristotle's ideas that nature endowed certain
people with remarkable physical strength but little-to-no mental acuity. His

1453 chronicle honoring the exploits of Portuguese slave traders alluded to Saint Thomas Aquinas's judgment that Catholics were justified in making war on nonbelievers that resisted evangelization (Branche, *Colonialism* 42–43). Zurara's ideological framework presented an additional rationale for the enslavement of Africans: divine punishment for sin. European Catholics claimed the *right* to take Moroccans captive by virtue of their Muslim faith, and they enslaved sub-Saharan Africans because they were said to be the descendants of Noah's errant son, Ham. In the Hebrew Old Testament, Noah curses Ham for looking upon his father's nakedness. Zurara explained the Hamitic myth thus: "the curse which, after the Deluge, Noah laid upon his son Cain [*sic*] . . . that his race should be subject to all the other races of the world" (Zurara qtd. in Branche, *Colonialism* 43). In effect, the Hamitic myth meant that Africans were born into the original sin of Noah's perverse son and were, by nature, impure and in need of redemption. In Zurara's tergiversated logic, Africans' intrinsic sinfulness and bestiality justified their captivity in perpetuity. The significance of Zurara's chronicle notwithstanding, ultimately the Vatican delivered the most powerful rationale for Christian domination and for the religious conversion of Africans.

African slavery in medieval Catholic theology was not an arcane philosophical question, but rather a pressing political matter. As early as 1436, the Vatican granted Portugal dominion over non-Christian West African territories. In theory the pope bequeathed ownership of African territories to Portugal, commissioned the Portuguese to propagate the Holy Faith, and, most importantly, granted them the authority to enslave (Rivera Pagán 194).[21] The fifteenth-century papal bulls that sanctioned Portugal to enslave West Africans and granted Spain authority in the Americas were momentous because they birthed a world in which decisions about Africans and indigenous peoples would be made in their absence and without their consent.

In 1493 Pope Alexander VI endowed Isabel and Fernando—the Catholic monarchs of Castile and Aragón—with divine authority to subdue "barbarous nations" and bring them to the apostolic faith. The divine right to conquer and convert persons presumed to be *savages*, in a sustained and systematic fashion, became the legal and theological foundation for Spanish political authority in Latin America (Rivera Pagán 29–30) as it had been for Portuguese slave trading in West Africa. Pope Alexander VI, a Spaniard by birth, decreed the following regarding the relationship between conquest and conversion in the *Inter caetera* (1493):

> Among other works acceptable to the Divine Majesty and according to our own hearts' desire, this certainly is the most important, that the Catholic faith and Christian religion, especially in this our time, may in all places be exalted, amplified, and enlarged whereby the health of souls may be procured, and the barbarous nations subdued and brought to the faith . . . (Rivera Pagán 29).

The *Inter caetera* inextricably linked the expansion of Catholicism to the growth of the Spanish Empire. The pope's claims over lands he had never seen and peoples whose languages he could not fathom might seem rather absurd at first glance. But Luis N. Rivera explains that the Church designated the pope as the Vicar of Christ (*Vicarius Christi*), and it adhered to a medieval doctrine, which, in theory, conceded him supreme authority on earth, *dominus totius orbis* (lord of the entire world) (26–27). Impassioned by his own sense of "desire," a word brimming with material and metaphysical ambitions, Pope Alexander VI justified the procurement of souls through violent, even catastrophic means.[22] The Catholic mandate to ensure the "health of souls" was a universal directive that neither demanded nor required the knowledge or consent of the conquered.[23] Rivera explains the politics of Catholic missionary work thus: "The Christian religion becomes the official ideology for imperial expansion" (25). Papal decrees afforded moral legitimacy to what Rivera called the Catholic monarchs' violent "transaction[s]" (29) in Latin America and the Caribbean. The papacy legitimized otherwise unlawful acts, providing them a moral veneer that assuaged the conscience of priests and soldiers alike. The Catholic discourse on the problem of slavery was a profoundly labyrinthine and contradictory one, asserting on the one hand a desire to fulfill divine will and on the other a craven lust for earthly riches.

Catholic theological musings about African slavery tackled a critical paradox: how could the Catholic Church justify the ritualized violence of empire and, at the same time, maintain the mantle of moral authority? Clerics often wrestled with this conundrum by defending their right to redeem pagan souls from eternal damnation. In essence, eternal salvation was infinitely more precious than the ephemeral and tenuous realities of black freedom. Catholic theology taught that the black body was destined to suffer so that the *souls of black folk* might enjoy heavenly freedom. Catholic theologians seldom questioned the enslavement of Africans in a politically persuasive manner. Much to the contrary, the Church and ecclesiastical organizations owned slaves (Rivera Pagán 182); and most Spanish and Portuguese clerics embraced a logic that defended the right to enslave Africans. Clerics simply took issue with the legality of the methods of enslavement (Bristol, "The Church, Africans" 200; Rivera Pagán 189). When ecclesiastics did defend African humanity, they did so to promote the religious conversion of enslaved persons, which, in effect, fomented the institutional growth and power of the Church (Olsen, *Slavery* 61, 87). The ideological rationale for African slavery was the European mission *supposedly* to civilize Africans; and this civilizing mission could be achieved only if Africans and their descendants abandoned their original belief systems for Catholicism.

Gomes de Zurara's 1453 chronicle introduced racial ideology into the epistemological fabric of Catholic religious conversion. Well into the nineteenth century, the theological rationale for African slavery produced *black* as an unprotected category and claimed that African slavery was the will of the Christian God. Portugal and Spain renamed a panoply of African ethnic difference and ascribed members of myriad ethnic groups the generic category of *negro*. As Jerome Branche points out, *negro*—the Spanish word for "black"—meant "he who has no political significance" (*Colonialism* 140). Thus, the power to enslave permitted Europeans "to name, define and categorize" Africans in ways that transformed mahogany skin into a permanent sign of an imagined inferiority. Spanish and Portuguese colonies constructed the subpersonhood of Africans and their descendants as intrinsic negative difference premised on their status as "saleable beings" (Branche, *Colonialism* 2, 95). The racialization of the enslaved individual as black had two functions: it defined whiteness as the absence of contamination, and it invented blackness as the nadir of degradation in cultural, religious, and juridical frameworks (Branche, *Colonialism* 87). Gomes de Zurara's ideological framework for blackness endured in colonial Spanish America. Jesuit priest Alonso de Sandoval (1577–1652)—remembered for his missionary work among Africans in Cartagena de las Indias—embraced the Hamitic myth. Like Zurara and countless others, Sandoval also believed that blackness was a metaphysical sign of Africans' transgressions against God (Olsen, *Slavery* 23, 85). For Sandoval, the purported blackness of the African soul could be purified and become metaphorically white through salvation in Christ (Olsen, *Slavery* 87). In this way, the Spanish Catholic Church managed to present itself as God's charitable servant, thus preserving claims to moral authority.

Catholic notions of black redemption in colonial Cuba did not ensure the emancipation of the body. Catholics believed the body was impure, decadent flesh but that the spirit could be refined and the soul could be saved from hellfire (Barreras 149). Alonso de Sandoval invoked this body/soul dichotomy that revered the spirit realm over and against the obscenity of the natural world. But in order to convince Africans of their need for redemption, catechists had to persuade them of their sinfulness. The Havana Diocese underscored original sin, venial sin, and mortal sin to dissuade Africans from revering their ancestors and to indoctrinate them in the Christian redemptive narrative (Barreras 61, 80). Redemption was the central tenet of the Catholic ideology of religious conversion for non-Hispanicized Africans and black Cubans because it accentuated the sinful nature of the *slave*. Baptism alone cured original sin, a transgression against God that all persons were thought to have inherited from Adam and Eve, the legendary first man and woman. Likewise, as an example of manipulative wordplay, the diocese claimed that baptism was necessary to convert sinful Africans from "the Devil's slave[s]" (esclavo del Diablo) into "son[s] of God" (hijo de Dios) (Barreras 142–143). Regarding the baptism of Africans, Sandoval wrote, "Aunque a la vista son negros, pueden tener la candidez y blancura, que dà la sangre de Christo a quien se lava con ella" (Although they are black to the eye, they can have the innocence and whiteness that Christ's blood gives to one who is washed in it) (Olsen, *Slavery* 84–85). Spanish Catholicism imposed upon Africans a new theory of the world; a theory where phenotypical blackness was a symbol of their transgression against a God that had sanctioned their enslavement in order to save them.

Catholicism was the official religion of the colony from 1512 to 1898 and exercised a major organizational and social role in the Spanish conquest of Cuba. The influence of the Church was such that each town was named and "placed under the protection of a saint, a path of the Virgin, or other religious figure" (Cros Sandoval 19–21).

Manzano was born in Cuba, not in Africa, but his baptism revealed that catechists had a similar set of concerns when instructing Cuban blacks/mulattoes in the Holy Faith. Comparable to religious instruction for Africans, the priesthood also instructed household servants in the doctrine of original sin. But for Manzano, theories of black redemption that did not emancipate the physical body could never engender a true sense of freedom for him. The Church perceived the body of Jesus Christ as a white body whose sacrificial blood purified the blackness of the African (and Afro-Latin American) soul. Baptism *saved* Manzano from sin and damnation and, metaphorically speaking, baptism whitened his soul and redeemed him from the African religion of his ancestors. Catholicism also *saved* Plácido from sin and eternal condemnation. And as a free mulatto, salvation paid important social dividends because it ensured Plácido a sense of belonging in a respectable cultural community that the Church had sanctioned. Blacks and mulattoes that embraced Catholic norms were afforded privileges, and they created "an accepted public sphere" that unacculturated Africans (known as *bozales*) could not access (Landers 145). African descendants that were legally free benefited socially by marrying in the Church, attending mass, and participating in patronage networks with the local parish (Landers 41–42, 44). Manzano and Plácido were baptized in the Church, and they enjoyed the privileges of Catholic community. But their poetry and prose suggest that "the innocence and whiteness" that clerics like Alonso de Sandoval had promised were a mere fallacy. Catholic dogma about black redemption would not liberate the African-descended body. And for all its ceremonial and symbolic power, baptism could not redeem Plácido and Manzano from the condemnation of blackness that slavery had produced in Cuban society.

## The African Cultural Archive, the *Cabildo*, and Religious Transculturation in Colonial Cuba

The number of Africans transported to Cuba in the early nineteenth century is nothing short of staggering. Between 1801 and 1850, the Atlantic slave trade brought approximately 547,000 African captives to Cuba, an astounding number of dislocated persons that exceeded the volume of any other place in the Western Hemisphere, except Brazil (Finch, *Rethinking* 23). Historians cannot specify how many persons of any given African ethnicity were imported to Cuba, but they have proven that captives were brought from the Upper Guinea Coast, West Africa, West Central Africa, and even Southeast Africa. From 1806 to 1845, the largest African groups in Cuba were ascribed the following *nombres de nación* (nation names): *congos*, *carabalís*, *gangás*, and *lucumís*. These geographic identifiers were not African ethnic insignia per se, but rather signaled the point of embarkation (Finch, *Rethinking* 24–25). Africans that survived the transatlantic genocide of epic proportions—those not swallowed whole by what Derek Walcott terms *the gray vault*—struggled to reconstitute (and if possible preserve) ancestral belief systems from the fragments that remained. Enslaved persons' apparent acceptance of Christianity did not imply their abandonment of African-inspired belief systems. African captives carried their concepts about spirit and cosmos with them, but upon arrival in a racialized plantation society they had to adapt their understandings of the spirit world to the dreadful realities of the slave colony. The exponential growth of slave trafficking in Cuba— even after Spain had endorsed treaties with Great Britain to end the importation of slaves—meant that Manzano and Plácido would have had plentiful contact with an African cultural archive whether in the city or in the countryside.

Plácido's and Manzano's direct African ancestors are unknown, because the transatlantic trade that brought millions of captives to American shores ruptured African ethnic continuity and often disintegrated family systems. So, I am speaking of an African heritage that may or may not reflect the particular culture that Plácido's and Manzano's grandparents (or great-grandparents) professed. Rather, I am talking about a cultural milieu, an ethos and a set of informal and formal understandings about the spiritual realm that informed how Africans and their descendants traversed the slave colony. For instance, Manzano lived on a Matanzas sugar plantation for a considerable part of his childhood and into adolescence. On average, there were ninety-six African captives on sugar plantations to every four Cuban-born laborers (Fraginals, "Africa in Cuba" 193). The preponderance of Africans on Cuban plantations meant that there would have been West African and/or West Central African ritual connoisseurs living in the slave huts and in the barracks. By probing Manzano's cultural landscape and his literature, I infer some ideas about his contact with an African-inspired belief structure. Manzano alluded to African-inspired principles regarding the spirit world in his autobiography when he composed "cuentos de encantamiento" (sorcery tales) and performed them for the other slaves, and when he spoke about his dread of "cosa mala" (evil forces) (Manzano, *Autobiografía* 305, 308). Although Manzano was a Catholicized domestic, his mistress chastised him by sending him to the field, where his contact with Africans would have been much greater (Manzano, *Autobiografía* 330). A belief in spirit presence and the fear of malevolent forces are recurrent themes not only in his autobiography but also in his poetry. Likewise, Manzano portrayed

ritual in a manner that evoked West Central African beliefs about the vital
force within mortal remains that can be harnessed to make things happen in
the natural world. In the poem "Un sueño a mi segundo hermano" (A Dream:
For My Second Brother), he pays homage to "los miserable restos" (the miserable remains) of his parents (Manzano, *Autobiografía* 120), and in "La visión
del poeta compuesta en un ingenio de fabricar azúcar" (The Poet's Vision:
Composed on a Sugar Plantation), he conjures the mortal remains of his father
to perform a cleansing ritual. Even if we allow for poetic license, these poems
are consistent with the Bakongo-inspired belief structure, where bones, skulls,
and skeletons are ritual objects that enable practitioners to commune with the
invisible powers of the spirit world (S. Johnson 91). Manzano's depictions of
human remains are indicative of his relationship to African-descended Cuban
religious communities. However, silences in the written record—his literature
and in government trial records—complicate what is knowable about the full
breadth of Manzano's familiarity with African-inspired beliefs.

Plácido's knowledge of an African cultural archive in Havana and Matanzas
is far more legible in the historical record than that of his contemporary.
Plácido immersed himself in all manner of African Atlantic religious culture.
He attended the African-oriented Epiphany festivities in Matanzas on January
6, where African *cabildos* commanded public space, parading pirouetting
masked dancers through the streets with great provocation and symbolism
(Cué, *Plácido: El poeta* 299). Catholics commemorated the birth of the Christ
Child on Epiphany (Three Kings Day). But Africans turned the Christian holiday to their uses. Religious brotherhoods chanted in African languages, pranced
about, and gestured provocatively; and, most importantly they performed the
"monotonous tones" (Ortiz, *Los Cabildos y la fiesta* 27) of consciousness-altering African drums (Andrews, *Afro-Latin America* 28–29). African-inspired
performativity was a source of aesthetic inspiration for Plácido as his poems
"El diablito" (The Little Devil), "A la Virgen de Rosario" (To Our Lady of the
Rosary), and "Mi no sé que ha richo" (Me Don't Know What I've Said) bear
out. But Plácido was more than a curious spectator; he regularly participated
in saints' feast days and partook in African-descended religious communities
(Cué, "Plácido y la conspiración" 197, 199–200). Eyewitness accounts describe
*fiestas de santos* as religiously transculturated rituals. One eyewitness recalled,
"Ellos decían san Juan, pero era *Oggún*. *Oggún* es el dios de la guerra. En esos
años era el más conocido en la zona." (They said San Juan, but it was Oggún.
Oggún is the god of war. In those years, he was best known in the area) (Barnet,
*Cimarrón: Historia* 83). Blacks played drums and fed African divine spirits
disguised as Catholic saints in *fiestas de santos*. That Plácido—a light-skinned
mulatto—compromised his social privilege to involve himself in (and write
about) African rituals proves his belief in African ideas about spirit and cosmos.

Plácido and Manzano inhabited a colonial world defined by religious multiplicity. African-descended persons embraced a pluralistic approach to the spirit world, and, as such, they juxtaposed Spanish Catholicism with Bakongo and Yoruba cosmologies in an uneasy, yet enduring dialogue. Since Catholicism was premised on a hegemonic set of doctrines, free and enslaved blacks were forbidden to openly practice African-inspired spirituality. But the ethnohistoric record throughout the colonial Caribbean and Latin America suggests that they may have been less interested in religious purity and more concerned with ritual efficacy.[24] St. Clair Drake explains this phenomenon in Haiti and Brazil thus: "The emerging Creole culture institutionalized the high status of two sets of holy persons, equally revered. There were priests and monks and nuns predominately white. [ . . . ] But there were also black priests and priestesses that 'knew' the other gods of Africa" (20). African-descended writers faced a serious conundrum: how might they legitimize their authority in black communities when slave society denied them political power? It is my contention that the sacred realm provided a symbolic language for negotiating and pursuing the authority they desired. Manzano and Plácido's antislavery aesthetic did not amount to an indiscriminate rejection of Catholicism; rather, they intermingled Catholic imagery and narrative with Bakongo and Yoruba spiritual practices so that they might achieve *sacred authority* within their own communities. Vincent Brown defines "sacred authority" as the appropriation of African or European symbolic practices that contain social and spiritual power and may be harnessed to achieve political might (24–24, 34).

Manzano and Plácido utilized Catholicism for their own purposes; they sought to construct an edifice of authority that would be intimately linked with the transcendent. Both writers sought to procure power through supernatural means by appropriating whatever symbolic practices they deemed efficacious: prayers to the Virgin Mary or Catholic saints, oaths of fidelity, making the sign of the cross, and prophecy. Spanish Catholicism was a permeable belief structure, notwithstanding its emphasis on the good/evil binary and the dogma of original sin. For instance, the Church claimed that Africans and their descendants were guilty of original sin. But instead of instructing Africans to pray to Jesus Christ, slave catechism commended them to the Virgin Mary so that she might beseech God for their forgiveness. Slave catechists taught that the Virgin Mary might act as an intercessor with God the Father, as the passage below explains.

> If we pray the Ave Maria with a good heart, the Virgin looks upon us with a good visage, and speaks to God on our behalf. She is our patroness, she asks God to forgive our sins, to give us a good death, and to carry us to Heaven, and God does not cover his ears. (Barreras, 141)

The implication was that God might not forgive sins if the faithful did not implore the Virgin Mary for mercy. Nonetheless, Catholics held that Jesus Christ had sacrificed himself to make the forgiveness of sin possible. Slave catechism portrayed Jesus as the suffering Lamb and the universal Redeemer that would condemn any person that did not submit to Church authority (Barreras, 64–65). But colonial Cubans revered the Virgin, a trend that emerged in medieval Mediterranean Catholicism and took root in popular black and white religious circles on the island (Elena Díaz 96; Cros Sandoval 20). The emphasis on Mary as the Mother of God who interceded for her wayward children was comparable to some aspects of West African belief systems. Yoruba spiritual practices and Spanish Catholic doctrine share some important principles in their respective cultural ethoi. Among these are a belief in a Supreme Being, contact with spirits of the dead, spirit possession, a pervasive belief in sorcery (coercive power), making offerings to divine intermediaries, the maintenance of personal altars, and the emphasis on ritual (Cros Sandoval 39–40). The diocese of Havana introduced the Virgin as an intercessor for Africans in the mid-eighteenth century; but this doctrine did not have the desired effect. Rather, the emphasis on the Virgin Mary as mediator resonated with West African principles about divine spirits as intermediaries that convey personal messages to God and command natural phenomena.

Different from Catholic saints, Yoruba *orishas* embody natural phenomena such as lightning, rivers, and the sea; and the Supreme Being endowed *orishas* with the authority to harness the powers of nature for either good or evil. Such power over nature enables the *orishas* to act independently of Olodumare, the Yoruba name for Creator (Cros Sandoval 39, 181).[25] Similarly, African divine spirits do not personify either good or evil. Rather, they exemplify the uneasy relationship between positive and negative forces, since there cannot be peace without strife, and there is no safety without danger (Bolívar 36, 40). Spanish Catholicism imposed a liturgy on Africans that effectively enabled them to conceal their reverence for their own divine spirits behind the facade of the Virgin Mary. And such concealment became an impetus for religious transculturation in colonial Havana.

Clerics adopted diverse approaches to proselytizing Africans, some significantly less doctrinaire than others. The bishop of Havana, José Agustín Morell de Santa Cruz (1694–1768), attempted to convert African religious brotherhoods, known as *cabildos*, to Christianity through a deliberate but gradual process. Upon his arrival in Havana from Central America in the mid-eighteenth century, the bishop was astonished by the preponderance of African-inspired beliefs and practices in the *cabildos*, describing the scene thus: "fue tan excesivo el tropel de sus negocios e impertinencias" (their horde of activities and indiscretions were so excessive) (del Carmen Barcia 66). He likened the music and dances of their religious processions to little more than drunken revelry. But instead of suppressing African religio-cultural expressions, in 1755 Morell de Santa Cruz attempted to progressively reform them. The Bishop administered the sacrament of confirmation, prayed the Rosary before an image of the Virgin Mary, taught the confreres to do penitence, and admonished them to abide by Catholic doctrine (del Carmen Barcia 66–69). The bishop tolerated a degree of religious amalgamation in hopes that contradictions would dissipate as Africans learned the gospel. But as Roger Bastide explains, Africans adhered to an inclusive religious logic because African cosmologies are paradoxical knowledge systems that embrace conceptual conundrums and defy austere classifications. African captives constituted a vast ethnic amalgamation of persons that engaged their own cosmologies, that is, "a certain concept of the universe and the place of man within it" (Wyatt MacGaffey qtd. in Apter, 149).[26] Cosmology is somewhat akin to grammar rules for native speakers of any given language; it is presupposed by its adherents, internalized, and codified in social practice. In this way African cosmologies posed a challenge to the logic of European philosophy that is based on the principle of noncontradiction (Bastide qtd. in D. Brown, *Santería* 127).

Morell de Santa Cruz critiqued the preponderance of African-inspired practices and beliefs in Havana, which posed a threat to the Church's universal claims to sacred authority. African brotherhoods displayed images of their divine spirits publicly in religious processions until successive colonial administrations forbade the use of African-inspired images (del Carmen Barcia 170). The prohibition was such that colonial black Cubans did not even mention African spirits in their final testaments. Religious repression created a cult of secrecy, so that when Africans requested burial vestments for Saint Francis and the Virgin of the Mercedes, historian María del Carmen Barcia says, in truth, they were referring to Orula and Obatalá. But she cites a rare exception to this rule: an African insurrectionist "quien al ser interrogado sobre si creía en un dios supremo respondió afirmativamente y dio el nombre de Olorun" (who having been interrogated about whether or not he believed in a supreme god responded in the affirmative and gave the name Olorun) (170). The *cabildos* appropriated Catholic saints, seized upon their social legitimacy, and fused Christian images with the sacred meanings of West African and West Central African religious thought (del Carmen Barcia 180, 184–186). In this way, the saints acquired the qualities of the Yoruba *orishas*, the Dahomeyan *vodun*, the Fon-Ewe *loas*, and the Bakongo *mpungos*.

Cultural history confirms that these processes of religious transculturation within western Cuban *cabildos* not only had begun but had also coalesced into distinguishable patterns of worship articulated in the symbolic language of Catholicism nearly half a century before Juan Francisco Manzano was born, in 1797. The religious interactions between Spanish Catholics and Africans acquired an unpredictability marked by improvisation and subterfuge. Such an environment is best described as what Mary Louise Pratt calls "contact zones," colonial spaces wherein disparate cultural groups—who had been historically and geographically apart—were brought into zones of encounter where ongoing interactions marked by coercion, deep-seated inequality, and enduring conflict take place. The contact zone creates the conditions for transculturation (*Imperial Eyes* 6).

Fernando Ortiz conceived the theory of transculturation in *Contrapunteo cubano de tabaco y azúcar* (1940) to problematize Melville Herskovits's notion of acculturation, which described the almost complete disappearance of one's native culture and assimilation to the dominant one.[27] Ortiz claimed that acculturation effaced the active role of the oppressed in the formation of national culture (254, 260). He defined transculturation as a process whereby Europeans, indigenous persons, and Africans created a third cultural space through their sustained reciprocal yet unequal interactions in the colonial era. Ortiz envisaged Cuban culture as the result of multifaceted processes of geographic and cultural uprooting, several dislocations, forced adjustments to new landscapes, the forfeiture of one's autochthonous culture, and the imposition of the dominant one that resulted in what he termed *transculturación* (*Contrapunteo* 254). Transculturation provides highly plausible explanations with regard to how culture is produced within colonial environments in the course of sustained reciprocal interactions and selectivity: so as to avow that the conquest of the Other is never fully realized. The description of Cuban national culture as an amalgamation of African, Iberian, and Amerindian contributions permitted Ortiz to rewrite his earlier works *Los negros brujos* (1906) and *Los negros esclavos* (1916), whose deterministic posture had denigrated African Cuban culture as a malignant stain on the social fabric. Nearly three decades later, *transculturación* provided a conceptual framework for reimagining Cuba even as it effectively overlooked a protracted history of white racial domination. In what follows, I use the theory of transculturation to contemplate African cosmology in the Cuban colonial setting.

In sixteenth- and seventeenth-century Cuba, Bantu-speaking Africans from the Kongo kingdom or neighboring vassal states featured prominently as the human cargo that Portuguese slave traders transported to Luso-Hispanic colonies. The Bakongo were the most culturally and religiously cohesive of the many African groups carried to Cuba in the first two centuries of Spanish colonialism (Dodson 27–28). The kingdom of the Kongo was the preeminent political force in West Central Africa from the mid-fifteenth century until the mid-seventeenth century (Young 26). The Bakongo enjoyed a broad sphere of religious and political influence that covered a large expanse of West Central Africa, including present-day Gabon, Angola, Congo, and the Democratic Republic of Congo (Finch, *Rethinking* 25). Due to their early arrival in substantial numbers, the Bakongo—who shared a common set of languages and cultural perspectives

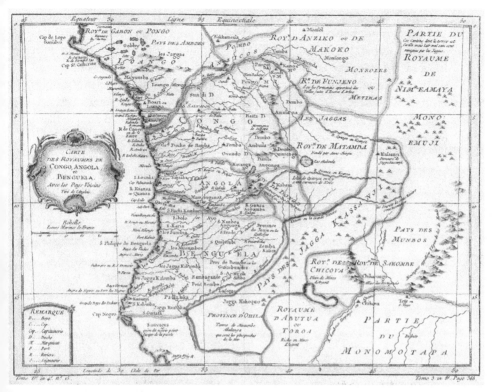

The kingdom of the Kongo and Portugal entered into a series of commercial treaties promoting trade in elaborate Kongolese fabrics, copper, and captives.

about spirit and cosmos—became influential in cultural terms among the other African ethnicities present in eastern Cuba (Dodson 28–29).

Scholars generally concur that most Africans sent to Cuba through the Atlantic slave trade were either Kikongo-speakers or persons that understood Kikongo, the lingua franca in the Kongo-Angolan region. And in the nineteenth century—the historical period that interests us here—slave traders carried more individuals from West Central Africa to Cuba than from any other region on the continent. Though these Africans hailed from multitudinous ethnic groups and political entities, they shared common understandings about the cosmos and the spirit world (Finch, *Rethinking* 25).

Bakongo cosmology and its diasporic derivatives do not place emphasis on divine spirits as in Yoruba cosmology (Thompson 106–107); instead, they privilege the *nganga* as the axis of ritual practice (Figarola 25, 31). Dodson writes that in Bakongo-inspired traditions the *nganga* has three meanings: it is a cauldron filled with sacred material objects, an incorporeal being, or a powerful devotee of the tradition (89). Devotees harness the energies of mortal remains and objects from the natural world in rituals designed to change the outcome of events (Ochoa 158). Bakongo cosmology was based on notions of continuity and equilibrium between the spiritual and material realms, the deceased and the living. Robert Farris Thompson writes that the indestructibility of the spirit was a sacred principle among the Bakongo, for whom "the sun, in its rising and setting, is a sign of this cycle, and death is merely a transition in this process of change" (108). Traditional Kongolese architecture, art, and some royal ceremonies were patterned on a persistent quest for equilibrium and centeredness. Mbanza Kongo—the historic capital of the Bakongo–Kikongo group (located in modern Angola)—was sited at the crest of a hill. The placement of the capital city reflected the idea that the world is a mountain that sits above the land of the dead, known in Kikongo as *mpemba*. The inextricable union between the mirrored physical and ethereal worlds in Bakongo spirituality means that humans are at all times connected to the world of the departed (Thompson 106). In Cuba, the Bakongo-inspired religion is known as *palo monte/palo mayombe*. Bakongo and Yoruba cosmologies did not survive the Middle Passage as unbroken knowledge systems. Rather, Africans relied upon whatever fragments of Yoruba, Bakongo, and other belief structures were available to them to navigate the dangers of the Cuban social world.[28]

Scholarly debates about the religious transculturation of Catholic saints with Yoruba *orishas* in Cuban *regla de ocha* have described the Catholic saints either as a convenient facade for the *orishas* or as some sort of religious hybridity. David Brown's research suggests that "gods, saints, and pantheons" do not readily conform to austere classificatory schemes but rather, as Andrew Apter has said, these entities lend themselves to ambiguity and "slippage" (*Santería* 127). What I have been referring to as African-inspired spirituality has a history of continuity marked by significant ruptures, interference, reformulations, and manifold negotiations among practitioners. As Brown has adequately shown in his work, priestly councils negotiated, sustained, and even restructured Yoruba-inspired (*lucumí*) religion (*Santería* 160–161).

Ritual objects were also essential to the transculturated practices of Africans in Cuba, as evidenced in the interrogation of Juan Nepomuceno Prieto, leader of the Cabildo Lucumí Gronces in the early 1800s. The authorities found in his possession "a rag doll with a bag of herbs to make prayers that promote health [ . . . ] the largest doll . . . is Changó, which is the same as saying King or Saint Barbara, they worship him as a god" (del Carmen Barcia 180). Nepomuceno's *cabildo* practiced Yoruba-inspired healing rituals, which by the time of the interrogation had clearly transculturated St. Barbara with the mighty Yoruba warrior spirit, *Changó*. But the processes of religious transculturation evident within the "*lucumí*" *cabildo* not only constituted Catholic and Yoruba symbols but also Bakongo ritual fragments: "the skull of a man covered by a gourd and beneath that, on the floor, [was] a cauldron with many bones and an elephant tooth" (del Carmen Barcia 179–180). The description of Nepomuceno's

An illustration of Mbanza Kongo, the capital city of the kingdom of the Kongo from Olfert Dapper's *Description of Africa* (1670), German edition.

effects suggests that he may have possessed an *nganga*, the most sacred item in Bakongo-inspired religion. In this instance, *nganga* indubitably refers to a cauldron of sacred objects that Nepomuceno invoked to command the obedience of spirits of deceased persons, which is one of the central tenets of Bakongo-inspired religion in the Caribbean.

This is important because it demonstrates that the *Cabildo Lucumí* Gronces not only transculturated Yoruba cosmology with Roman Catholicism but also amalgamated Bakongo cosmology into a complex, multidimensional ritual. Thus, del Carmen Barcia's archival work suggests that Nepomuceno adopted the central tenets of two different African cosmologies: the Yoruba liturgical emphasis on *orishas* and a Bakongo preference for coercive power through the ritual use of the *nganga*. Cuban maroon Esteban Montejo, who escaped a plantation in Las Villas in the 1860s, noted that black Cubans often viewed the Yoruba and Bakongo belief systems as diametrically opposed to each other. Montejo mused, "La diferencia entre el congo y el lucumí es que el congo resuelve, pero el lucumí adivina" (The difference between the *congo* and the *lucumí* is that the *congo* resolves [problems] and the *lucumí* divines) (Barnet, *Biography* 38). Thus, Montejo explained the different uses of ritual among enslaved Africans. Yoruba-speaking Africans were commonly known for contacting the spirit world in an effort to unravel mysteries, while Africans that hailed from the Kongo-Angola region relied on ritual to bring pestilence and death to their enemies' doorstep. But the early nineteenth century co-presence of Yoruba and Bakongo cosmologies in Juan Nepomuceno's *lucumí cabildo* suggests that African brotherhoods embraced a both/and approach regarding disparate bodies of religious knowledge. *Cabildos* were situated at the cross-roads where the production of innovative religio-cultural meaning took place. In what follows, I posit *transculturated colonial literature* as a theoretical lens for probing similar processes of transculturation in the early Cuban literature of Manzano and Plácido.

### Reading the *Poetics of Freedom* in Manzano's and Plácido's Transculturated Colonial Literature

What Manzano and Plácido did with early Cuban literature was nothing short of radical. Manzano and Plácido were members of a black counterpublic in ascendance, and they understood that creative control was a proxy for political power. A counterpublic is a community of interlocutors within a subculture that constitutes itself in opposition to the true centers of power (Dalleo 4–5). The black counterpublic in colonial Cuba was composed of artisans, musicians, dancers, painters, and most notably poets that articulated the political and cultural aspirations of an African-descended demographic majority. I disagree with one critic that argued that the Caribbean counterpublic manifested "entirely in nonliterary forms" (Pettway, "Sacred Ways" 42–43). However, when the black counterpublic did publish, they often conveyed their political ideas in a symbolic language immersed in ambiguity, subtlety, and misdirection. The censorship administration defined what constituted permissible speech and canonical beliefs; and they granted legitimacy to proslavery viewpoints while rejecting antislavery ideas as inadmissible, sacrilegious, or even treasonous. Colonial state institutions such as the Catholic Church and the censorship administration harnessed their powers to avert what Michel Foucault considered chance appearances of discourse and to decide which ideas abide within the true (Foucault 216).[29] I theorize that Plácido and Manzano forged *transculturated colonial literature* in a discursive crucible wherein the Catholic Church, the censorship administration, and the political ambitions of Domingo del Monte's literary circle converged to thwart the exercise of creative control. Transculturated colonial literature emerged as an aesthetic response to the notion that the Catholic Church was the arbiter of what Father Varela called "true religion" (*Cartas* 85–86). In what follows I propose a method for deciphering the transculturation of Catholicism with Bakongo and Yoruba-inspired belief structures in Manzano and Plácido's writings.

Domingo del Monte assembled gatherings of eminent white male authors: José de la Luz y Caballero, José Jacinto Milanés, Anselmo Suárez y Romero, Félix Tanco y Bosmeniel, and Cirilo Villaverde. These male-centered *tertulias* excluded talented women like Gertrudis Gómez de Avellaneda, who published a Romantic abolitionist novel, *Sab* (1841), in Spain. These men were disciples of abolitionist Félix Varela—a Catholic priest and professor at the Colegio-Seminario de San Carlos—and they were sympathetic with Varela's 1823 critique of slavery and absolute monarchy.[30] Though there was no sense of political unanimity among white intelligentsia, the major thinkers hoped to create a reformist Catholic society that would be politically liberal and culturally *mestizo*, imbued with picturesque minutiae from the black population (Luis, *Literary Bondage* 40). White reformers pursued a concept of freedom that would eliminate the absolute monarchy but leave white Creole domination of blacks firmly in place. They desired political representation and sought to end censorship, institute free trade policies, and even eradicate the slave trade (Finch, *Rethinking* 117). But they rejected the notion that freedom could be achieved only through radical racial equality. Nevertheless, Captain General Miguel Tacón delivered major setbacks to del Monte's reform agenda when he dissolved the Cuban Academy of Literature in 1833 and closed the *Revista Bimestre Cubana* a year later (Luis, *Literary Bondage* 34). In the shadow of a defunct literary academy, Cuban literature went underground. Del Monte turned to Juan Francisco Manzano in 1834 for creative inspiration and antislavery propaganda, and he also tried to exploit Plácido's incendiary verses to incite an uprising that might overthrow Spanish rule.

Between 1834 and 1840, Domingo del Monte promoted the abolition of the African slave trade, and in 1839—like Francisco de Arango y Parreño before him—del Monte proposed that European immigrants work the cane fields in order to restore the numeric predominance of whites on the island (Fernández de Castro 144–145). Del Monte reasoned that a white majority would make Cuban self-governance feasible and that the arrival of fewer Africans would make Haitian-style revolution less probable. Del Monte embraced all manner of schemes to achieve white self-governance: he collaborated with British consul David Turnbull, an ardent abolitionist, to end Spanish rule; and he quietly endorsed annexation to the United States as a southern slave state (Finch, *Rethinking* 127). But since del Monte was a prominent humanist, literature was his most formidable way of doing politics.[31] Del Monte's literary group appropriated Manzano's autobiography as an ethnography, and they exploited the manuscript to produce early Cuban fiction. Critics rightly regard Manzano's autobiographical relation as the birth of Cuban narrative.[32] Anselmo Suárez y Romero's novel *Francisco*, and Félix Tanco y Bosmeniel's *Petrona y Rosalía*, depicted slave characters as frail victims and domesticated Negroes that were incapable of insurgency and desperately in need of Christian salvation. The misappropriation of Manzano's autobiography documents the theft of black cultural labor by white intelligentsia bent on pursuing its own political interests and preserving its power. Because Plácido was legally free and was immensely popular among the lower classes, del Monte attempted to utilize his lyrical talents to disrupt Spanish rule in Cuba.

Del Monte's exploitation of Plácido, however, was more complicated and nuanced. Because Plácido enjoyed a greater degree of freedom, he was not as vulnerable to the artistic misappropriation that Manzano struggled against. Del Monte sought to render Plácido an agent provocateur that would write seditious poetry to rouse political sentiment among people of color and ignite a Cuban rebellion in such a way as to invest political power in white Creole hands rather than embolden black militancy (Cué, *Plácido: El poeta* 299). Del Monte struggled to wrest creative control from Plácido to that end. But like his literary collaborator Manzano, Plácido had other ideas about the best use of his aesthetic materials.

Manzano and Plácido wrote in a manner that enabled them to profess Catholicism without eschewing the knowledge and the rituals of African cosmologies. Their writings did not succumb entirely to the ecumenical claims of the Catholic Church. *Pluriversality* is a domain in which many worlds can coexist, not the imposition of a presumably universal concept of knowledge, but rather an entanglement of cosmologies. Walter Mignolo seeks to build structures of knowledge that emerged from the experience of humiliation and marginalization of oppressed peoples (Mignolo, "Delinking" 492). Mignolo cites Aníbal Quijano's assertion that "epistemic decolonization is necessary to make possible and move toward a truly intercultural communication; to an exchange of experiences and significations as the foundation of an-other rationality" (Quijano qtd. in Mignolo 499).

Pluriversality is a concept that emerged from the Zapatista liberation movement. Pluriversality engages dialogue as a strategy for ethno-racial communities in pursuit of "intercultural communication." When dialogue transcends ethnic difference, "inter-epistemic communication" emerges so that individuals may engage the knowledge claims their interlocutors profess. Pluriversality is a decolonial terrain that discards the assumed universality of any particular worldview; instead the "pluriverse" embraces disparate knowledge systems (Mignolo, "Delinking" 499, 453).[33] This method is apropos for understanding the processes of religious transculturation within Manzano's and Plácido's writings, because the entanglement of cosmologies implies that the Catholic concept of the universe, which by definition relies on the principle of exclusivity, is brought into dialogue with African bodies of knowledge that may contradict or even supplant its claims to supremacy. In Spanish America pluriversality became a way for African-descended writers to affirm other worldviews, draw on other epistemologies and, pursue paths to freedom that their oppressors did not understand and could not control.

The entanglement of Catholic symbols and African cosmologies becomes legible in Plácido's and Manzano's work if we examine the paradigm within their literature that the Church would have deemed superstitious. The Church defined superstition (also known as *hechicería*) as an aberration of otherwise customary religious practices; superstition was either occasioned by ignorance of established doctrines or, in the most egregious cases, the product of deceit (Palmié, *Wizards* 229; Varela y Morales, *Cartas* 86). Superstition deviated from *true* religion, but it was not the same as *brujería* (witchcraft), because *brujería* implied the intent to do harm and to carry out anti-Christian conspiracy. Father Félix Varela inveighed against superstition in *Cartas a Elpidio sobre la impiedad, la superstición, el fanatismo en sus relaciones con la sociedad* (1838).[34] Varela argued that superstition represented a threat to the hegemony of the Catholic Church, and he referred to superstitious individuals as "enemigos de la autoridad divina" (enemies of divine authority) (*Cartas* 85–86). I quote from *Cartas a Elpidio* to explore Varela's conception of divine authority:

> In the nations where the only true religion has been established, which is Catholicism, her divine origin demands there be only one divine modus operandi. And this cannot be found in the vicissitudes, limitations and whims of human understanding; the principle of authority is fundamental. (Varela y Morales, *Cartas* 85).

Father Varela perceived the struggle between superstition and "true religion" as a contest of wills, a fight for the hearts and minds of the Cuban public. Varela not only contended that Catholicism was the one true religion but also maintained that there was a canonical set of practices and beliefs that true Catholics were beholden to. Not every set of beliefs or rituals warranted the imprimatur of the Church. For Father Varela, the unilateral authority of the Church to define Cuban religious life was in danger. Writing from exile in New York, he mused, "En una palabra, confunden los católicos con los supersticiosos" (In a word, they conflate Catholics with superstitious persons) (Varela y Morales, *Cartas* 86). Varela erected a Manichean divide between religion and superstition among the lower social classes in Cuba where it didn't exist. His defense of "the principle of [ecclesiastical] authority" is reminiscent of Foucault's "rules of *exclusion*" by which institutions and disciplines vie to control the definition and methods of knowledge production (original emphasis, Foucault 216).

I believe superstitious practices represented more than a political challenge to ecclesiastical authority; superstition constituted an epistemological threat to the broad terrain of religious knowledge that the Church governed. If we consider the characteristics Varela ascribed to superstitious individuals, it becomes evident that they constituted a threat to the notion of universal religious truth. In *Cartas a Elpidio*, he observed that the *supersticiosos* endeavored to "para erigirse en oráculo o para abusar de la verdadera autoridad hasta el punto de hacerla ridícula y atribuirle, como los falsos profetas, sentencias y hechos que la sabiduría divina detesta y condena." (in order to erect themselves as oracles perhaps to abuse true authority to the point of mocking it or attributing to it, as false prophets [would], maxims and deeds that divine authority detests and condemns) (Varela, *Cartas* 86). Varela did not regard superstitious individuals as unenlightened believers. Much to the contrary, he insisted that superstitious people had proclaimed themselves oracles, which were vessels for contact with the otherworld. In Ancient Greece, an oracle was a person through whom the gods were believed to convey hidden messages. Varela's choice of language is revealing. He regarded *supersticiosos* as individuals who had deliberately concocted a set of beliefs and practices that differed from the Church and even defied its authority. By arguing that superstitious people knowingly practiced aberrant beliefs, Father Varela was able to ascribe to them knowledge and intent, thus making them answerable for their actions. The presbyter accused the oracle of being a "false prophet," not because of his ignorance of the spirit realm, but rather because the oracle constituted an alternative source of knowledge and sacred authority that the priesthood could not conceivably control. Plácido and Manzano erected a similar edifice of sacred authority in their literature that alluded to African-Cuban ideas of spirit and cosmos.

I identify a corpus of religious beliefs that Félix Varela regarded as an aberration; because a brief analysis of these beliefs will enable the reader to decode Manzano's and Plácido's representation of African-inspired spirituality. Father Varela identified three forms of superstition that plagued Cuban society: the emphasis on miraculous saints, the abundance of spirit apparitions, and premonitory dreams.

> People reach a point where they acquire a propensity to believe everything miraculous and to find divine authority in all matter, and to shield themselves with it, even to commit the gravest crimes. This is the origin of the numerous miracles that the common people believe and that the Church has not sanctioned and cannot corroborate, and the apparitions that many misled persons after being deceived themselves, deceive the unthinking masses. (Varela y Morales, *Cartas* 86–87).

Varela protested that Cuban popular culture had become enamored with the marvelous and miraculous and that divine authority was said to inhabit all things. The purported miracles were so numerous—and for Varela of dubious merit—that the Catholic Church could not substantiate they had actually taken place (Varela y Morales, *Cartas* 86–87). Father Varela condemned premonitory dreams, apparitions, and mystical battles between Catholic saints as "un verdadero sacrilegio" (a true sacrilege); but he did not attribute these peculiar (and even criminal) belief systems to any particular ethno-racial community in Cuba. Varela apparently observed a pervasive tendency among Cubans of European and African descent to construct alternative sources of religious knowledge and power. As I pointed out earlier, popular Catholicism and Yoruba-inspired religion featured some similarities: knowledge of spirit apparitions, a pervasive belief in coercive power (also known as sorcery), an emphasis on ritual, and the practice of making offerings to divine intermediaries (Cros Sandoval 38–40). Despite its pervasiveness among different ethnicities in late colonial Cuba, Catholics (and Protestants) racialized the discourse on superstition. This process of Othering began in the early colonial period. Spanish, Portuguese, Dutch, French, and English colonists reduced an array of Amerindian and African religious practices to a racialized assortment of premodern nonsense (J. Drake 2). By the nineteenth century, superstition was defined as an antimodern set of practices that muddled the lines between knowledge and gibberish, shamans and physicians, fallacy and faith (Román 221, 223, 234). All of this is important, because the spirituality that Varela deemed "superstitious"—the belief in miraculous saints, the abundance of spirit apparitions and premonitory dreams—was the hallmark of Plácido's and Manzano's transculturated colonial literature.

Manzano and Plácido defied what I have termed Varela's *imagined dichotomy* between "true religion" and superstition, because they amalgamated Catholicism with African cosmologies in their poetry and prose. The Catholic Church and the censorship administration engaged in a protracted struggle with white Creoles and African descendants to determine who would control image and myth. African Cuban colonial writers adopted an interepistemic a priori as their creative point of departure. Plácido and Manzano bridged the chasm between African cosmologies and Catholicism (in popular and orthodox practices), since they acknowledged both as disparate epistemological and aesthetic practices based on divergent claims to knowledge. Such a pluriversal approach enabled them to engage the doctrines of sin/repentance and the divinity of Christ and the Holy Trinity without relinquishing the memory of their African ancestors. Transculturated colonial literature makes legible what anthropologist Stephan Palmié called "a culturally specific mode of knowledge production" (*Wizards* 201) embedded in otherwise conventional texts. It is not the medium—Spanish sonnets, elegies, or odes—that disrupts the aesthetic rule, but rather the substance of the utterance itself, which, I believe, solicits an improvisational reading based on circumstance, context, and rhetorical gestures.

I engage this body of work as a sort of "literary archeology" to borrow a phrase from Toni Morrison (Morrison qtd. in Sharpe xi). Jenny Sharpe explains that Morrison relied on historical knowledge and an "imaginative recreation of the past" to write great works of fiction like her novel *Beloved* (Morrison qtd. in Sharpe xi). But I perceive archaeology as apropos for the unearthing of black Cuban texts characterized by double-voicing, ostensible contradictions, silences, and the subversive use of Catholic, Romantic, and Neoclassical symbology. I locate, excavate, and recover voices that have been *disappeared.* This book is literary analysis and part cultural history; so, I too am "piecing together a world that exists only in the archives" (Sharpe xi). To exhume an Afro-Latino religious presence in the colonial Caribbean, I employ an array of conceptual tools that are equal to the task: Pratt's contact zone theory and autoethnography, Ortiz's transculturation, and Sylvia Frey's work on African Atlantic religion.

Mary Louise Pratt defined autoethnographic literature as oral or written texts that colonized peoples produced in response to dominant metropolitan representations of themselves. Autoethnographic texts appropriate the idioms of the colonizer and dialogue with divergent readerships: the dominant culture and their own cultural communities (*Imperial Eyes* 7). Pratt applied auto-ethnography to seventeenth-century Peru, where Quechua persons appeared at the center of a Christian world ("Transculturation" 27, 34–35). But for the purposes of this book, I have revised autoethnography in order to develop a theory that has resonance in the Cuban colonial situation where African cosmologies permeated social space, and African Cuban ritual functioned as an alternative system of control with emancipatory promise for black writers. Pratt maintained that Felipe Guamán Poma de Ayala's 1613 letter to the Spanish monarch addressed dual readerships, contested metropolitan representations of natives, and was informed by Andean cosmology. Inca autoethnography was a vital component of the transculturated letter, but Guamán Poma imagined "a Christian world with Andean rather than European peoples at the centre of it" ("Transculturation" 27, 34–35). Though Manzano and Plácido juxtaposed Catholicism with African-inspired spirituality, their transculturated texts performed a different religious politics. Plácido and Manzano situated black characters at the center of an African Atlantic cosmological order where Yoruba- and Bakongo-inspired beliefs were the foundation upon which emancipation would be procured. Black Cuban autoethnography was more than a revision of the Catholic narrative; rather, it was a *pluriversal* endeavor to produce a discourse capable of mending ruptures with the ancestral past so that African-descended liberation might become achievable.

I support my claim with a few illustrations. Plácido and Manzano alluded to African-inspired spirituality by invoking paths to the Virgin Mary and to specific Catholic saints that blacks had transculturated with African divine spirits (Yoruba *orishas* and Bakongo *mpungos*). A few examples will suffice. Manzano did not credit the clemency of the Christian God for his escape from the plantation; rather, he boasted that Saint Anthony—whom blacks had equated with Elegguá and Mundo Lucero, the spirit of the crossroads—had made his escape possible. And Plácido addressed his sonnet "The Virgin of the Rosary" to African religious brotherhoods in Matanzas, known as *cabildos*, for whom the Virgin of the Rosary was Dadá, the royal sister of the Changó warrior spirit in the Yoruba pantheon. Phantasms permeated the spiritual geography of Manzano's autobiography, and Plácido warned against the nuisance of angry spirits in his poem "Ghosts, Spirits and Witches." Similarly, dreams and visions were sources of spiritual revelation in Plácido's indigenous-themed poem "To the Mountain Pan," and they guided Manzano in the Romantic poem "A Dream: For My Second Brother." This is what Mary Louise Pratt calls the intercultural nature of writing in the contact zone (*Imperial Eyes* 4) in that symbols and images may mean one thing to a white Catholic readership even as they allude to something altogether different for the African-descended interlocutor. I am theorizing that Manzano and Plácido contributed to an antislavery aesthetic in its nascency that camouflaged the presence of African ideas about spirit and cosmos; these transculturated ideas constituted an alternative source of sacred authority that disrupted Catholic claims to universality. On occasion, Manzano and Plácido managed to avert censorship because their writings negotiated with the dominant discourse on religion by affirming and negating meanings at same time. Plácido and Manzano posed a danger to the maintenance of colonial power because they circulated manuscripts in dissident communities, and their improvised rhymes effectively evaded the censorship regime altogether. Notwithstanding government authority over official discourses on race and religion, the colonial state could not determine the full measure of Manzano's and Plácido's political influence in Havana and Matanzas.

## Constructing *A New Critical Approach* to Plácido and Manzano

Critics often regard Gabriel de la Concepción Valdés and Juan Francisco Manzano as assimilationist writers that divorced themselves from African culture as a necessary concession to the white Catholic literary establishment in Cuba. As *mulatos* in a stratified pigmentocracy, Manzano's and Plácido's racial identities are often conflated with their cultural and religious reality. Critical approaches to the poetry and testimonial literature of Juan Francisco Manzano address some of the primary concerns of slave narrative research: black writer as assimilationist, literacy as an instrument of enslaved resistance, and black authorship as a problem of authenticity. Ever since Cuban critic Ramón Guirao reencountered Manzano in *Bohemia* in 1934, three trends in Manzano scholarship have emerged: the African Cuban poet as an assimilated *slave*, the enslaved writer as the agent of literary resistance, and, more recently, a renewed interest in the 1840 English translation of the slave narrative not as evidence of Richard Madden's manipulation of subaltern voice, but rather as a transatlantic collaboration. The construction of a mulatto self-portrait in the autobiographical relation of Juan Francisco Manzano has sustained the attention of literary critics for more than three decades. Scholars that examined Manzano as a mulatto poet construed his literary work as a concession to the Hispano-Catholic symbolic order, an assimilationist gesture and a negation of blackness that constituted a rupture with Africa. Thus, mulatto identity was a construct that situated Manzano in the interstices and enabled him to acquire highbrow culture in order to procure his manumission. Until the late 1990s, this interpretative approach—mulatto personhood as deculturation—was the dominant trend in the scholarship on Manzano's poetry and testimonial literature.

Literary scholars Adriana Lewis Galanes and William Luis made monumental contributions to the study of Juan Francisco Manzano. In 1991 Galanes's pioneering book *Poesías de J. F. Manzano, esclavo en la isla de Cuba* uncovered Manzano's antislavery poems in the National Library of Madrid and presented them for the first time to a modern scholarly public. Some of these poems had never before been published. Preeminent scholar William Luis later reissued some of these poems in 1994 and also uncovered new antislavery poetry after conducting archival research at Yale University. Their pioneering research reshaped the possibilities for critical analysis, so that in addition to his slave narrative, his poetry might also be read as a critique of the slave regime. Again in 2007, Luis offered a revised edition of Manzano's poetry, letters, and slave narrative that includes a transcription of the original manuscript of Manzano's slave narrative, simply entitled *la verdadera istoria de mi vida* (the true story of my life). Throughout this book, I cite from Luis's transcription as well as from my own record of the original manuscript.

In his seminal work *Literary Bondage: Slavery in Cuban Narrative* (1990), William Luis studies the trajectory of the representation of slavery in Cuban literature, from Juan Francisco Manzano's 1835 slave narrative to *Graveyard of the Angels*, a late twentieth-century novel by Reinaldo Arenas. Luis demonstrates that Manzano's account was a testimonial blueprint for the fiction produced by white literati. But he sees Manzano as an assimilationist that appropriated literary discourse and discarded an African frame of reference as a necessary concession to white aesthetics (65). Sylvia Molloy and Miriam DeCosta-Willis also read Manzano's subject formation as an inexorable process of deculturation. Whereas Molloy describes the poet's pursuit of literacy as an act of mimicry in search of a "*master* image" ("From Serf to Self" 416), DeCosta-Willis's emphasis on racial identity leads her to conclude that Manzano was a "tragic mulatto," a social misfit, bereft of cultural affinity in either black or white communities (9, 11). In "From Serf to Self: The Autobiography of Juan Francisco Manzano," Molloy does not see lyrical genius in Manzano but mimicry instead, because—as she insists—his poetic "I" is modeled on the voice of the white master and is devoid of "personal confessions or reflections on slavery" (414). Molloy misreads Manzano's reliance on mnemonic techniques as the absence of written language, thus rendering illegible the repository of knowledge embedded in African Cuban oral tradition. She did not perform a close reading of poetry, and her emphasis on mimesis leads her to conclude that without autobiography—where the author "writes himself down [ . . . ] as a black man and a slave" (416)—selfhood might be unattainable.

The examination of Manzano as a deculturated individual conflates his reputed racial identity with his cultural worldview. In "'*Mulato entre negros*' (y blancos): Writing, Race, the Antislavery Question, and Juan Francisco Manzano's *Autobiografía*," Jerome Branche examines the mulatto image as a means to social power within colonial pigmentocracy and as a way to win the sympathies of a white readership. Branche is concerned with a mulatto racial politics that enabled Manzano to disidentify with blackness, disdain blacks as a subgroup, and reproduce the discursive power of an imagined, yet unattainable whiteness (77–79). Branche writes that "[the] self-promotional rhetoric of the autobiography," foregrounds the mulatto as a rational individual even while condemning most black captives on the plantation to anonymity (78–79). Branche provides a more historicized analysis than DeCosta-Willis's Romantic notion of Manzano's descent from self to cipher (9). And he concludes that in the fallout of the 1844 antislavery movement, Manzano's white patron seemed to dismiss him as just another black man. Manzano's fall from grace reduced him to "the status of *negro* (in the sense of 'he who has no political significance')" (84). Ifeoma Nwankwo agrees with Branche to a certain extent, and she identifies Manzano's racial separateness as a disidentification with blackness (189). Nonetheless, Nwankwo doesn't believe Manzano's racial persona was unambiguous, because though he disidentified with blackness, he maintained affective bonds with "los negros" (200). In effect, she avers that Manzano should not be read as a self-loathing creature that advocated mulatto racial superiority (201–202).

Literacy as an instrument of enslaved resistance is a critical approach that decenters Manzano's racial persona in order to privilege the rhetorical trappings of the author. This trend in Manzano criticism has made a significant contribution, because its emphasis on the theoretical and critical dimensions of autobiography and poetry reorients interpretative efforts away from an apparent fixation with pathology. Sonia Labrador-Rodríguez, Luis A. Jiménez, and Marilyn Miller examine slave literacy and the subsequent production of the written text, as the acquisition of knowledge heretofore denied, knowledge that Manzano appropriated in order to defy slavery and to construct his own literary voice. Although they identify the mulatto persona in Manzano's testimonial literature, they stress the author's mechanisms of narrative control: the creation of explicit silences, thematic repetition, and nonlinear temporality alongside an insistence on the self-conscious gaze.

Labrador-Rodríguez and Marilyn Miller suggest that by acquiring literacy, Manzano ruptured the white Creole monopoly on knowledge upon which the slaveholder's power relied (Labrador-Rodríguez 21; Miller, "Rebeldía narrativa" 425). Labrador-Rodríguez furthers this line of reasoning by arguing that the written word enables Manzano to disabuse his readership of an inhumane concept of the enslaved, and, furthermore, it transforms him into an "intellectual" that is "superior" in knowledge to his white contemporaries (23). While Labrador-Rodríguez and Miller conceive knowledge in strictly Eurocentric terms, Jiménez gestures toward the presence of peripheral knowledge in

Manzano's texts. His work compares Manzano's slave narrative (1835) with Frederick Douglass's *Autobiography* (1845), reading these accounts as "linguistic events" in a hemispheric context (48). Both narrators harness the discursive privilege reputed to the authorial function, but their "speakerly" texts "intimate forms of the oral traditions to be found in African (American and Latin American) literature" (51). Literary criticism on Plácido has often concentrated on his racial identity and his involvement in the 1844 antislavery movement.

Sibylle Fischer's book *Modernity Disavowed: Haiti and the Cultures of Slavery in the Age of Revolution* sees Plácido's awkward and imprecise treatment of neoclassical imagery as literature that neither submits to the rigor mandated by aesthetic law nor deposes it (91). Fischer reads Plácido's poetry through the lens of Julia Kristeva's theory of the abject. In her formulation, Plácido's poems represented a revolting expulsion that defied order and violated the demarcation between highbrow and lowbrow culture, thus menacing a nascent white Cuban literary institution (90). Although her book does not examine Plácido through the lens of racial solidarity, she does insist that the poet's work is a repudiation of white Creole nationalism that would eviscerate Haitian revolutionary antislavery from any prospective national project (105). Others have also engaged Plácido as cultural symbol and historical personage by placing emphasis on what his literature might reveal about his racial politics.

In *Black Cosmopolitanism: Racial Consciousness and Transnational Identity in the Nineteenth-Century Americas*, Ifeoma Nwankwo has shown that subsequent to Plácido's execution as the chief conspirator of the 1844 movement, the Cuban government and US and European abolitionists ascribed to him a diasporic racial consciousness that transcended his nationalist sentiment (87). Even if the colonial state denied his Cubanness altogether, certain abolitionists celebrated his putative *blackness* and nationalism concurrently (87).[35] Nwankwo's study is among the most comprehensive with regard to Plácido's racial representations, providing an analysis of the sentimental verse, the liberal-minded political poems, and his odes in ostensible praise of the monarch. She concludes that earlier biographers were not misguided to portray the poet's literature as illustrative of a broad notion of racial solidarity among persons of African descent (112–113). Moreover, Nwankwo reads Plácido as a nationalist zealot who symbolically engaged the liberatory aspirations of oppressed nations (205–206). Nwankwo's study of race, however, is without an analysis of Plácido's satirical poetry, which critiques whiteness ideology. Sybille Fischer and Ifeoma Nwankwo contribute significantly to the scholarship on Plácido by engaging aesthetics and race in a concerted effort to decipher a political project with emancipatory promise. While their books provide reasonable explanations for the ostensible incongruity in Plácido's work, they are inconclusive with regard to his alleged involvement in the 1844 conspiracy, thus leaving numerous questions unanswered.

I am indebted to Cuban scholar Daisy Cué Fernández's groundbreaking book *Plácido: El poeta conspirador*, which is a painstaking analysis of archival documentation, correspondence, and poetry that corroborates Plácido's involvement in the 1844 conspiracy. Cué demonstrates that Plácido was the conscious representative of African-descended people that were "savagely oppressed by Spanish colonialism." The author acknowledges that Plácido was a voice for blacks and mulattoes, but she does not identity him politically with blackness. Cué confines Plácido to a national political arena, nearly silences Haitian "radical antislavery," and is cautious not to claim that the poet was in solidarity with subjugated nations worldwide (250). In this regard, Cué's scholarship is squarely grounded within the Cuban racial imaginary, so that Plácido is rendered a tragic mulatto of sorts whose cultural *mestizaje* finds clear expression in his lyrical work. Akin to other critics, Daisy Cué also discerns the presence of a political project in Plácido's sonnets, fables, *romances, letrillas*, odes, and elegies. Cué concurs with historian Robert Paquette that Plácido was not the chief conspirator of the 1844 movement but did engage as a propagandist and courier (102; Paquette 257, 259).[36]

*Cuban Literature in the Age of Black Insurrection* contributes to the field of Latin American studies in several ways. This is the first book-length study of Juan Francisco Manzano and Gabriel de la Concepción Valdés, perhaps the most important writers of African descent in colonial Spanish American history. Moreover, my emphasis on African-inspired spirituality as a source of knowledge and a means to sacred authority for black Cuban writers contributes to our understanding of Manzano and Plácido not as mere imitators but as aesthetic and political innovators. Finally, by reworking theories of transculturation from the angle of African religious epistemology, I seek to demonstrate that some of the processes of social transformation that cultural anthropologists have examined were also at work in literature in ways heretofore unknown.

This book represents a paradigm shift in our thinking about black writers in colonial Latin America because it analyzes how they reconstructed *Africa* in America through an epistemological engagement with Bakongo- and Yoruba-inspired spiritualties. It is an African Atlantic system of religious knowledge—not the strictures of Catholic doctrine—that provided Plácido and Manzano with the tools, both political and metaphysical, to conceive what African-descended liberation might look like. This book is a radical departure from earlier scholarship that analyzed Plácido and Manzano through the lens of mimicry as peripheral figures within an elite humanistic tradition. That tendency in Afro-Hispanic criticism has effectively divorced African-descended writers from all things African, especially diasporic spirituality.[37] I acknowledge that Manzano and Plácido displayed a sense of simultaneity in their relationship with the Catholic Church and black ritual communities. They negotiated meaning and claimed membership in both places at the same time. But I disagree with critics that perceived the authors as archetypical *mulatos* because of their mixed ancestry, hence rendering them ambivalent persons that assimilated to metropolitan culture and repudiated their African religious heritage. This body of critical work granted white Creoles the mantle of reform because they had advocated gradual slave abolition, but it silenced the racial politics of black authors that had fought (and died) for radical racial equality. *Cuban Literature in the Age of Black Insurrection* rectifies that imbalance by arguing that African Cuban religious multiplicity and simultaneity did not mean that black writers were ambivalent about their relationship to African Atlantic religion.

Cuban debates about the definition of freedom and selfhood were never the exclusive domain of the white Creole elite.[38] While the appropriation and destruction of African bodies for profit defined the Caribbean as a violent site of modernity, the political activity of black religious brotherhoods, ever-increasing insurrections, and African Atlantic religion were emblematic of an emancipation articulated through the lens of African religious epistemology. *Cuban Literature in the Age of Black Insurrection* shows that African-descended interventions in larger debates about liberty and subjectivity situated Cuba at the center of an alternative modernity, defined not only by rational thought but by its supposed antithesis, African tradition. I believe that the representation of African-inspired spirituality has been illegible to most readers because critics have used the wrong metrics—particularly the lens of cultural mimicry—to examine its presence. *Cuban Literature in the Age of Black Insurrection* contributes to the fields of Latin American studies, Hispanic Cultural Studies, religious studies, Cuban and Caribbean history, and Africana studies by suggesting a paradigm shift for the way scholars analyze Afro-Latin American colonial literature.

## CHAPTER TWO

# Católico a mi manera
## Christianizing Juan Francisco Manzano

bistionme de ropa fina y detras de
la bolante me condujo otra vez al pueblo
y en servisio ya yo era un objeto conosido pr.
El chinito o el mulatico de la Mar.

JUAN FRANCISCO MANZANO

And use without consent of the used is abuse.

AUDRE LORDE

### In Pursuit of a *Promised Freedom*

In 1835 Juan Francisco Manzano—one of Cuba's most prominent African-descended colonial poets—embarked upon writing what he termed *la verdadera istoria de mi vida* (the true story of my life).[1] Manzano entered into a secret pact with literary patron Domingo del Monte: del Monte would purchase Manzano's freedom if he agreed to write a provocative, yet intimate account of his life as a *slave*. Though wary of the public scrutiny this would entail, Manzano began to write the book that would ultimately secure his freedom. Manzano's autobiography was the product of considerable intellectual and psychological labor, but it was also a disjointed narrative that defied any real sense of chronology, lacked grammatical order, and was chock-full of silences and double entendres.[2] In many ways Manzano's autobiography might have been indecipherable to del Monte's coterie of white reformists that had requested an ethnographic account of Cuban slavery. Del Monte wanted Manzano to depict the horrors of slavery in order to condemn the Atlantic slave trade, which by 1827, had already made Africans and their Cuban descendants the numeric majority on the island (Knight 22). Furthermore, del Monte was the most prominent Cuban humanist, and he sought a literary prototype that might give Cuban fiction a national character of its own. But del Monte got more than he had bargained for. Manzano's autobiography was illegible not only because he had conceived it in the oral register (Luis, "Juan Francisco Manzano" 34) but also because his narrative comprised a peculiar sense of religious multiplicity that promoted Catholicism—the official religion of the Spanish Empire—even as it created space for African-inspired spirituality. The Church regarded African spirituality as the antithesis of the Holy Faith, an "abomination," a mishmash of savage practices that only religious conversion could remedy (Barcia, *Los Ilustres apellidos* 68–69). But the colonial government did not censor religious literature based on a desire for doctrinal purity; rather, censorship was a means to maintain social order and prevent antislavery uprising. Spain regarded the religious practices of Africans and some African descendants as a potential source of social disruption and insurrection (Palmié, *Wizards* 228). Thus, when Manzano created an African-inspired spiritual subtext in his autobiography, he was gesturing toward another audience, a black Cuban readership that didn't gain access to his manuscript until nearly a century later.[3]

What del Monte intended as propaganda to reverse demographic trends and thwart the *africanización* of Cuba, Manzano fashioned into a groundbreaking slave autobiography. As William Luis correctly points out, Manzano's autobiography became the cornerstone of an emerging Cuban narrative tradition (*Literary Bondage* 39). Consequently, the genesis of Cuban literature is the examination of the master/slave relationship (Arrufat qtd. in Arroyo Martínez, *Travestimos* 70).

Manzano's autobiography was a coming-of-age narrative, a Cuban bildungsroman about how he navigated the vicissitudes of racial slavery even as he maintained a belief in family and transformed himself into a literary writer against all odds. Manzano's narrative is the only self-authored account of Spanish American slavery known to exist. Irish abolitionist Richard Robert Madden translated Manzano's memoirs into English and published them in London in 1840. Hence, Manzano's Cuban slave narrative preceded the work of black American abolitionists Frederick Douglass (*Narrative of the Life of Frederick Douglass, an American Slave* [1845]) and William Wells Brown (*Narrative of William W. Brown, a Fugitive Slave. Written by Himself* [1847]). That Manzano published his autobiography in 1840 is important, because unlike other authors of slave narrative, he did not abjure African spirituality as a deterrent to civilization and moral progress. Neither did he argue that Catholicism was a prerequisite for black liberation. Nonetheless, the Church is very present in Manzano's story. Indeed, the holy sacrament of baptism is the first significant religious act in the autobiography, and Manzano recounted the personal value of religious relics that his family owned and priestly sermons that he had memorized by heart (Manzano, *Autobiografía* 300–301, 333).

This chapter explores a series of questions that have yet to be examined. How did Manzano appeal to *imitatio Christi* (imitation of Christ) as a rhetorical strategy for representing the *slave* as a human being? What role did Spanish Catholicism play in Manzano's efforts to construct an African-descended persona that had never existed in the brief history of Cuban letters? Likewise, what was the political relationship between the image of the good Catholic (*buen católico*) and the mulatto house slave in Manzano's autobiographical relation? I am interested in Manzano's autobiography, poetry, and letters to del Monte as a window into the perpetual act of becoming. Manzano's slave narrative revealed how colonialism functioned in slave societies. Catholic priests baptized Africans into the Church in order to assimilate them into Cuban society as persons defined by a religious doctrine of racial difference. Catholicism imposed a set of doctrines that required proselytes to categorically reject other belief systems (Midlo Hall 32–34). And as the offspring of enslaved household servants, Manzano was particularly susceptible to the ideological influence that Catholicism wielded over domestic bondsmen. I am arguing that Manzano benefited from the privileges that the Catholic Church and his status as a mulatto afforded him, but that he became doubtful of the power of Catholicism to emancipate him.

Scholars have attributed *The Imitation of Christ* (*imitatio Christi*) to Thomas à Kempis, who disseminated the concept in the fifteenth century through the publication of devotional literature.[4] Thomas à Kempis joined the Brethren of Common Life in 1392 and was ordained in 1413. The Brethren of Common Life devoted themselves to caring for the infirm and to doing charitable work among the poor; but they also studied the scriptures and copied religious books. Thomas à Kempis spent his monastic life at Mount Saint Agnes in Zwolle, Holland (Zelyck 77). He is most remembered for *The Imitation of Christ*, a four-part devotional that was printed in 1472 and has been translated into fifty languages. The writings of à Kempis epitomized the *devotio moderna* (modern devotion) (Zelyck 77), a late fourteenth-century reformist movement within medieval Catholicism.[5] *Devotio moderna* accentuated the importance of holy living, it instructed the faithful to meditate on the agonies of Christ, and it advocated that priests and laity alike pursue religious knowledge (Zelyck 77). *The Imitation of Christ* described believers as contemptible creatures that were "unworthy of divine solace and deserving of much tribulation" (à Kempis qtd. in Zelyck 79). Thomas à Kempis described the Catholic as an "unworthy sinner who [is] but dust and ashes" and characterized the faithful as a subordinate lot: "[that] are inferior to all others" (à Kempis qtd. in Zelyck 79). Contemptibility was central to à Kempis's doctrine of mortification, that is, the denial of vital passions and appetites through abstinence or self-inflicted pain or discomfort.[6] Thomas à Kempis highlighted the importance of Christian discipleship, and he commended abnegation as a way to identify with Jesus's sufferings and achieve "perfect mortification" (Zelyck 81). For à Kempis mortification was spiritual progress for believers because self-inflicted pain enabled them to achieve sinlessness (Zelyck 83–84).

Since the thirteenth century, Spanish slave law articulated an ambiguous, even paradoxical concept of slavery: slavery was "the most vile thing in the world," but it was not without legal justification (Twinam 85). The medieval Spanish legislation known as the *Siete Partidas* (1256–1265) established parameters for colonial Spanish American slave codes. The *Siete Partidas* defined the *slave* as a member of the master's family that should be integrated into a broader Catholic community. Medieval law also acknowledged the right of slaves to pursue their freedom by purchase or other means. At least in theory, medieval Spanish law conceded that "all the creatures of the earth love and desire liberty" (Twinam 85, 122). The notion that *slaves* were members of their masters' families resonated with Manzano's situation in early nineteenth-century Cuba.

Manzano emulated the humility and mercy of Christ throughout his autobiography in order to humanize himself in the eyes of a white Catholic readership. Manzano regarded himself as a *manso cordero* (meek lamb) who by the force of circumstances transformed himself into a roaring *leon* (lion) (Manzano, *Autobiografía* 311–312). He even acknowledged human suffering as an act of piety that would bring God nigh in one of his letters to Domingo del Monte. But if suffering for the Holy Faith condemned him to a life of perpetual slavery, Manzano would have to search for spiritual resources cut from another cloth. Manzano transformed himself from "faithful slave" (esclavo fiel)—as he once described himself—into "la criatura mas despresia" (the most despicable creature imaginable) (Manzano, *Autobiografía* 333). Such a radical transformation meant that Manzano had embraced an antislavery worldview and had become cognizant of the religious doctrines that held him in bondage. Notwithstanding historical precedent or Spanish legal theory, Manzano's mistresses rendered him property that could be disposed of as according to their whims. I argue that Manzano fought to redeem his body from the person/property duality that racial slavery inflicted upon Africans and their descendants. But in order to redeem his body from slavery, Manzano had to wrest control of the symbolic practices—both racial and religious—that Cuban slave society wielded over him. Slave traders captured millions of men, women, and children on the African continent, marched them to the sea, and transported them to the Western Hemisphere in some 36,000 voyages.[7] But they could not hold those bodies in captivity unless they also stole their minds. Manzano struggled to unshackle his mind, for it was the *theft of the mind* that made the African-descended body compliant to the dictates of white supremacy.

## Catholicism and the Making of a *Mulato*

Manzano situated his birth family at the heart of his autobiography. Manzano's mother, María de Pilar, emerged as a central figure in his life story; she was the matriarch and the source of familial origins, and he ascribed to her a symbolic significance. The first lines almost read as a novel: "Entre las escojidas fue una M$^a$. del Pilar Manzano, mi madre, q$^e$. del servisio de la mano de la S$^{ra}$. Marqueza Justiz en su mayor edad, [] era una de las criadas de *distinsion* o de *estimasion* o de *razon* como quiera q$^e$. se llame" (among the chosen was one María del Pilar Manzano, my mother, who [was] handmaiden to Marchioness Justiz in her old age, [] she was one of the servants of *distinction* or *esteem* or of *reason* however you want to describe it) (Manzano, *Autobiografía* 299). Manzano's choice of words—underlined in his original manuscript—sets his mother apart not only from the plantation field workers but also from all the other domestic servants. It is noteworthy that Manzano never referred to his mother as a *slave*, though she certainly was, but rather as an esteemed servant (*criada*) of a "good-natured mistress" (*bondadosisima señora*) (Manzano, *Autobiografía* 302). María de Pilar was the black matriarch that anchored Manzano's narrative. Naturally, María de Pilar's standing also afforded her son a favored status on the plantation. Manzano's description of his mother as the Marchioness's distinguished servant and as a woman of "*reason*" not only signaled her position within the household but also negated the mammy stereotype (*nodriza*) of the black wetnurse as contented servant, loyal to a fault and more eager to serve the white family than her own. Manzano inverted the symbolic order by attributing rationality to a black woman that had been denied the faculty of reason based on gender, race, and condition of servitude. In his representation, María de Pilar is a rational subject, and she is the foremother of an African Cuban family structure. Manzano began the slow but deliberate process of deconstructing the person/property duality inherent in Cuban slave society.

But Manzano could not deny the power dynamics within the big house where his mother had no legal authority over her progeny, and the very notion of black family was antithetical to the profit motive of the slavery system. In "Mama's Baby, Papa's Maybe: An American Grammar Book," Hortense Spillers explains that the Atlantic slave trade denied female captives gender specificity, and since they were deemed chattel, they had no legal right to offspring (75–76). Spillers elaborates on the historical-juridical problem of kinship for enslaved persons in the African Diaspora:

> It is that order that forces "family" to modify itself when it does not mean family of the "master," or dominant enclave. It is this rhetorical and symbolic move that declares primacy over any other human and social claim, and in that political order of things, "kin," just as gender formation, has no decisive legal or social efficacy.

> [...]

> Certainly if "kinship" were possible, the property relations would be undermined, since the offspring would then "belong" to a mother and a father. In the system that Douglas articulates, genetic reproduction becomes, then, not an

elaboration of the life principle in its cultural overlap, but an extension of the boundaries of proliferating properties. (Spillers 75)

The concept of family, or in Latin American Spanish *buena familia*, is equated with the white patriarchal ideal that "declares primacy" over black Cuban claims to kinship, autonomy, and mutual support. Separating the black mother from her offspring is a recurring theme in the slave narrative: Manzano writes, "mi ama la S$^{ra.}$ Marqueza Justi[z], ya señora de edad, me tomo como un genero de entretenimiento y disen q$^e$. mas estaba en sus brasos q$^e$. en los de mi madre" (my mistress The Lady Marchioness Justiz, who was well on in years, took me as a some sort of amusement and they say I was in her arms more than those of my mother) (Luis, ed. 300). Though Manzano makes no explicit mention of race in this pithy portrayal of his early childhood, he does demonstrate the power of race in social practice by depicting himself through his mistress's lens as a mere object for her amusement. The author reveals that the power of the mistress's gaze displaced María de Pilar's parental authority because the white gaze was predicated on legal discourse and the ever-present threat of violence.

The Marchioness permitted María de Pilar to marry Manzano's father, Toribio de Castro, a harpist who was also the chief manservant. María de Pilar's and Toribio de Castro's social position meant that Manzano spent an inordinate amount of time with his mistress, with whom he enjoyed French operas, attended mass, and frequented the theater. When he was six, his owners even permitted Trinidad de Zayas, his baptismal godmother, to provide him some schooling (Manzano, *Autobiografía* 300–301). The Marchioness's vigilance toward the young child was palpable, for she deemed him "el niño de su bejez" (the child of her old age) and required him to eat at her feet (Manzano, *Autobiografía* 300, 304).

> Da. Joaquina q$^e$. me trataba como a un niño ella me bestia peinaba y cuidaba de q$^e$. no me rosase con los otros negritos de la misma mesa como en tiempo de señora la Marqueza Justis se me daba mi plato q$^e$. comia a los pies de mi señora La Marqueza de [p] Pr. A. toda esta epoca la pasaba yo lejos de mis padres [mas cuando ellos supieron q$^e$. estaba al serbisio de mi señora de esta epoca a la de [] de mi []] cuando yo tenia dose años (Manzano, *Autobiografía* 304)

(Doña Joaquina treated me like a child, she dressed me, combed my hair and saw to it that I did not mingle with the other little black children at the same table. As in the times of the Marchioness Justiz, she served me my food [and] I ate at the feet of my mistress the Marchioness of Prado Ameno. I spent this entire era far from my parents [but when they found out that I was at the service of my mistress in this period, I was 12 years old])

Doña Beatriz's daughter, Prado Ameno, would continue the dishonorable act of domestication by feeding Manzano as one would a pet after her mother died. But Manzano communicated something more in this passage. He deliberately linked the conferral of special treatment in the slaveholder's household with the construction of his mulatto racial identity. Doña Joaquina dressed the young boy, he ate at the feet of his mistresses, and he was forbidden from playing with the other *black* children. When his mistresses forbade him to play with the "otros negritos" (other black children), she uttered a contradictory statement that acknowledged Manzano's blackness even while purposely disidentifying him from his black peers and, by extension, from the enslaved black community at large. Saidiya Hartman's preoccupation with the enactment of violence, terror, and pleasure upon the captive body explores slavery in the antebellum United States as socio-juridical practice that constituted the slave in incongruent terms as both property and person (80). Hartman describes this "dual invocation of the slave" as a mechanism by which the white slaveholder patterned relationships on a perverse web of reciprocity in which the enslaved experienced both intimacy and domination in an arrangement that denied them consent and legitimated violence against them (80). Manzano's white mistresses treated the young boy as a docile house pet, while his biological parents lingered on the sideline as bystanders who only later discovered that he had returned to Matanzas.

Manzano relished these privileges as a young boy, even boasting that Doña Beatriz forbade that his birth father subject him to corporal punishment. He wrote, "Ocurrió una vez q $^e$. estando yo muy majadero me sacudió mi padre *pero* resio; *supolo mi* señora y fue lo bastante p$^{a.}$ q$^e$. no lo quisiera ver en muchos dias, hasta q$^e$. a istansia de su confesor, el padre Moya, Religioso de S$^n$. Fran.$^{co}$ le [bo] bolvió su grasia . . ." (On one occasion [because] I was acting so foolishly that my father shook me up so hard that when my mistress found out that was enough for her to refuse to see him [Manzano's father] for several days. Until, at the request of her confesor, Father Moya, a Franciscan priest, she let him back into her good graces) (Manzano, *Autobiografía* 301). Father Moya intervened on Doña Beatriz's behalf to reprimand Toribio de Castro and remind him that only the slave owner had the authority to strike the young child. Thus, the Franciscan friar performed his ecclesiastical duties by reiterating what Hortense Spillers has demonstrated in another context. Manzano did not belong to the man that sired him but rather to the woman that owned him. That the marchioness turned to the priest to reprimand Manzano's father also means that Manzano, symbolically speaking, was property of the Catholic Church, whose duty it was to inculcate a submissive worldview in black converts. In fact, Manzano's first references to religion of any kind in the autobiography describe his attendance at Catholic mass and his baptism as a small child.

The story of Manzano's baptism is a window into Spanish Catholic acculturation designed to extinguish African cultural histories and supplant African ethnic identities with pejorative racial categories. Manzano was born into slavery in Havana in 1797, and his parents—María de Pilar and Toribio de Castro—were Cuban-born Creoles. Manzano was a second-generation Cuban, and his family maintained some African cultural knowledge in the form of proverbs and a belief in the ethereal presence of the dead (Manzano, *Autobiografía* 311, 318). We do not know if Manzano was knowledgeable of his family's African ethnic past. But if he was, he suppressed such knowledge in order to exemplify the good Catholic and garner sympathy from a white readership.

Manzano conveyed a sense of belonging within his mistress's family at this juncture in his childhood. But this sense of belonging did not liberate him from his object status within the white Cuban imagination. I analyze his baptism into the Catholic Church in conjunction with Doña Beatriz's notion of the young Manzano as "genero de entretenimiento" (some sort of amusement) (Manzano, *Autobiografía* 300). Manzano's description of his baptism is so elaborate it is worth quoting at length:

> pasando p$^r$. otros p$^r$. menores ocurridos en los dias q$^e$. debia resivir el bautismo me señiré unicamente a lo agradable pues {**ahora**}voi corriendo una serie de felicidades {**por un jardin de bellisimas flores**}. Fui embuelto {alli llevaron} a la iglesia en el faldellin con que se bautizó la Sr$^a$. D$^a$. Beatris de Cárdenas y Manzano selebrandose con Arpa, q$^e$. la tocaba mi padre p$^r$. música {**con**} clarinete y flauta: quiso mi señora marcar este dia con uno de sus rasgos de generosidad con {**coartando**} aber coartado a mis padres *dejandolos* en trescientos pesos a cada uno y yo devi ser algo mas feliz; pero pase. (original emphasis) (Manzano, *Autobiografía* 301–302)

> {**mas**} aquella bondadosisima señora fuente inagotable de grasias le bolvio a renobar un documento en darle libre {**ofresiendole la libertad del**} el otro vientre nasiese lo q$^e$. nasiese y nasieron mellisos baron y embra ubo en esto unas diferensias mas lo terminante del documento iso q$^e$. un tribunal diese livertad a los dos p$^r$. q$^e$. ambos formaron un bientre la embra vive con este motivo. (original emphasis; Luis, ed. 302)

> (Passing over other details that occurred in the days in which I was to be baptized; I will only abbreviate the pleasurable **now**. I'll run through a series of felicities {**through a garden of beautiful flowers**}. I was wrapped [they carried me] to the church in the baptismal gown in which Señora Doña Beatriz de Cárdenas y Manzano was baptized celebrating with the Harp, that my father played as a musician with clarinet and flute: my mistress wanted to mark this day with her characteristic generosity by {fixing the price} having fixed the price on my parents for 300 pesos each and I must have been somewhat happy; but let's continue.)

(**But** that most generous mistress inexhaustible fount of gratitude again renewed a document granting freedom {**offering liberty**} to the next child to be born whatever it was. And twins were born male and female there were some differences in this but the point of the document was that a court granted them both liberty because both were of the same womb, the female child lives because of this.)

Manzano's baptism was a felicitous moment for his mistress, a performance of religious belonging that ensured him membership in the divine Catholic family even though it reiterated his slave status. Manzano explained his religious formation in sequential order: his mistress carried him to mass, and he committed catechism and the sermons of Luis de Granada to memory. Finally, Doña Beatriz had him baptized in her gown. The sequence of events was important not only because it inducted him into the Holy Faith but also because it bespoke the significance of ceremony and ritual in the proselytism of Africans and their descendants. The author did not present himself as a reformed *savage* rescued by the European "civilizing mission," as black North American poet Phillis Wheatley had exclaimed in her late eighteenth-century poem "On Being Brought From AFRICA to AMERICA" (Carretta ed. 13).[8] Rather, he concocted a romantic account of his baptism as cause célèbre, an event so important that it entailed celebratory music of its own.

The Spanish slave code of 1789 mandated that Africans be instructed in Church doctrines and baptized as a means of social control (Knight 124–125). But in this episode, the narrator's tone does not admit coercion or captivity, but rather celebration. Doña Beatriz acted as maternal proxy: she chose suitable baptismal vestments, had Toribio de Castro perform music, and, as an act of largesse, set the purchase price for both of the child's parents. In addition, she pledged to grant liberty to María de Pilar's future offspring (Manzano, *Autobiografía* 302). Though Manzano characterized these acts as the bountiful generosity of a kind mistress, the subtext again signals the subpersonhood of his entire family. Doña Beatriz did not manumit his parents, which would have enabled them to direct their own affairs, perhaps by purchasing their son's liberty. On the contrary, she freed children yet to be born who would not be detrimental to the profit motive. In these passages the white gaze reiterates the concept of African-descended person as chattel and dependent child. Doña Beatriz's act of largesse in granting freedom to María de Pilar's children could be seen as an act of violence, a dismembering of the African-descended family if the children were separated from their parents. But the purpose of Manzano's baptism becomes even clearer if we look at the catechism that the Diocese of Havana commissioned for the religious instruction of unacculturated enslaved Africans.

In 1796, a year before Manzano was born, the Diocese of Havana authorized the *Explicación de la doctrina cristiana acomodada a la capacidad de los negros bozales* (Explication of Christian Doctrine Adapted to the Aptitude of non-Hispanicized Blacks). The catechism, which was reprinted in 1818 and again in 1823, was most certainly in use when the young Manzano was baptized around age ten (Manzano, *Autobiografía* 301–302). The Diocese wanted to persuade Africans to abandon their religious philosophies and to assume the core tenets of the Catholic faith. To that end, the Church emphasized the following doctrines: the omnipotence of God, the indivisibility of the Holy Trinity, the nature and degree of sin, and baptism as the redemption of the soul. But the bishop did not neglect to introduce the Virgin Mary as the Mother of God. The Church taught that the Virgin Mary was a patroness to the enslaved and downtrodden and that she interceded on behalf of African converts that had committed sin (Barreras 141). The text reads thus: "nos mira la Vírgen con buena cara, y jabla à Dios por nosotros, es nuestra madrina, le pide á Dios que nos perdone nuestros pecados" (the Virgin looks upon us with a good visage, and speaks to God on our behalf. She is our patroness, she asks God to forgive our sins) (Barreras 141). There was a logic to this. Redemption from sin through Jesus Christ is the central tenet of Catholicism. But in African notions of the cosmos, individuals who had committed offenses against the ancestors had to make amends in order to restore harmony to those relationships (Awolalu 279, 283–284, 286). So, clergymen believed that if they could persuade Africans that sin was an offense against the biblical God that imperiled them in the afterlife, then Africans would become contrite and beseech the Virgin Mary to pray to God to redeem their sins. For if sin is an offense against God, there must be some way for sinners to cleanse themselves of all blemishes (Barreras 140). The Diocese emphasized original sin, venial sin, and mortal sin to dissuade Africans from revering their ancestors and to indoctrinate them in the Catholic redemptive narrative (80). Though Manzano was born in Cuba not in Africa, his baptism into the Catholic Church revealed a similar set of concerns: like non-Hispanicized blacks (*bozales*), the priesthood also instructed household servants in the doctrine of original sin.

Redemption was the central tenet of the Catholic ideology of religious conversion for non-Hispanicized Africans and black Cubans, because it emphasized the sinful nature of the *slave*. Baptism alone cured original sin, a transgression against God that all persons were thought to have inherited from Adam and Eve, the mythical first man and woman. Furthermore, as an example of manipulative wordplay, the Diocese claimed that baptism was necessary to convert sinful Africans from "the Devil's slave[s]" (esclavo del Diablo) into "hijo de Dios" (son[s] of God) (142–143). The Church conflated African religious culture with slavery to sin, original sin and mortal sin to be precise, which produced a justification for European enslavement of blacks as a means to redeem their souls from eternal damnation. The Cuban priesthood was certainly not alone in the perverse opinion that blackness was a somatic sign of moral depravity. Catholic theology had long held that the phenotypical blackness of African peoples was derivative of Noah's errant son Ham, who is portrayed in Hebrew

Scripture (Olsen, *Slavery* 23). Racial ideology was inextricably woven into the epistemological fabric of Catholic religious conversion. Jesuit missionary Alonso de Sandoval—remembered for his proselytism among Africans in sixteenth-century Cartagena de las Indias—argued that once baptized, Africans would be redeemed from blackness, and their souls would be endowed with the innocence of whiteness (Olsen, *Slavery* 23, 85). Margaret Olsen explains Sandoval's viewpoint regarding the imagined relationship between blackness and sin:

> This project obliges him to transform for his reader a seemingly bewildering myriad of African physiological, cultural and linguistic manifestations into an endless potential for redemption. Blackness, for example, is identified as an apparently bizarre phenomenon present in Africa that Sandoval links to historical sin, but at the same time it is represented as enormous opportunity for spiritual illumination: the black that can be whitened, darkness illuminated. (Olsen, *Slavery* 23)

Sandoval's position regarding blackness as an inherently sinful state of being resonated with the Cuban priesthood as late as the nineteenth century, even if one was not a Jesuit. Baptism was not simply salvation from original sin but, perhaps more importantly, salvation from blackness itself.

A closer look at the rhetorical structure of the 1796 catechism further explains the racial ideology of Catholic religious conversion in colonial Cuba.

> Quien gobierna la Iglesia en nombre de nuestro Señor Jesucristo es el Papa. Si señores, el Papa, y porque la gobierna, se llama, y es tambien la cabeza de la Iglesia. Pongan ustedes cuidado, para saber bien esto, que es preciso saberlo. La cabeza de este Ingenio es su amo; pero quien gobierna el Ingenio (porque su amo lo ha puesto aquí, para que lo gobierne) es el Mayoral: y por eso el Mayoral es y se llama tambien la cabeza del Ingenio. Pues lo mismo: el Papa es cabeza de la Iglesia porque nuestro Señor Jesucristo crucificado lo ha puesto para que la gobierne. El que gobierna el Igenio se llama *Mayoral;* el Papa que gobierna la Iglesia se llama *Vicario* de Jesucristo. Cuando el Mayoral manda una cosa su amo la manda, y cuando el Papa manda una cosa, Jesucristo la manda, y como el que no jace lo que manda el Mayoral, no cumple con su obligacion, y merece lo que castigue Dios (original emphasis) (Barreras 85–86).

(He that governs the Church in the name of our Lord Jesus Christ is the pope. Yes sirs, the pope, and because he governs, he is called, and he is the head of the Church. Be careful, to know this well, it is required to know this. The head of this sugar plantation is your master; but he that governs the sugar plantation (because your master has placed him here to govern) is the Overseer. And for that reason, the Overseer is and is also called the head of the sugar plantation. It is also so: [that] the pope is the head of the Church because our Lord Jesus

Christ crucified has placed him there so that he might govern. He that governs
the sugar plantation is the *Overseer* and the pope that governs the Church is the
*Vicar* of Christ. When the Overseer orders you to do something your master
commands you, and when the pope orders something, Jesus Christ mandates
it, and he that does not fulfill what the Overseer commands does not fulfill his
duty, and is deserving of God's punishment.)

The Catholic Church redefined the cosmological order for Africans and their
descendants in theory, though not always in practice. Africans believed in a
Supreme Being, in divine spirits that governed natural phenomena, and in powerful ancestors and spirits of the departed that might be harnessed to effect
change in the material world (Mbiti 31–33, 75–76, 81–83, 88). The ideology of
Catholic religious conversion disrupted African cosmology and imposed a new
hierarchy: the pope was the head of the Church, the master was the head of the
plantation, and the overseer was the legitimate representative of the master's
power, a power sanctioned by God himself. The 1796 slave catechism posited
hierarchy as part of the divine order where race and religion were entangled in
the construction of colonial systems of meaning. The key concept is governance
throughout the passage I have cited. The Spanish verb *gobernar* appears seven
times in the text, and in every instance it means to administer the affairs, to
control and rule over a body of religious converts that are subject to the authority of the Catholic Church. The slave catechism relied on the presumption of
universal authority to justify the Overseer's power on the plantation, using the
verb *gobernar* in reference to both of them. In effect, the Overseer emerged as
an individual of greater consequence to the slave than the plantation owner
himself: "The head of this sugar plantation is your master; but the Overseer
(because your master has placed him here to govern) is he who administers.
And for that reason, the Overseer is also called the head of the plantation." The
Overseer is mentioned more than the slaveholder. The slaveholder legitimated
the Overseer's authority, but it was the Overseer—the *mayoral* was always a
white male hired hand (Pichardo y Tapia, *Diccionario provincial de voces* 177)—
that "administers."[9] The power to *administer* this carceral landscape was the
power to abuse enslaved persons with religious (and often political) impunity.
In effect, Spanish Catholicism modeled the slave plantation on the Catholic
Church itself. Therefore, all power and authority was vested in the pope, who
was the Vicar of Christ, and his deputy and political representative on the plantation was the Overseer. If the slave did not comply with "su obligacion" (his
obligation[s]), "merece lo que castigue Dios," (he deserves however God chooses
to punish him) (Barreras 86). Far from articulating a doctrine of redemption
from the wicked snares of slavery, Spanish Catholicism justified black slavery in
the strongest terms possible as the perfect will of the Christian God.

In this regard, Manzano's baptism was more than a reenactment of Church
authority; baptism was a decisive step in the process of racializing him. Doña

Beatriz, not the priest, presided over the christening of her *mulatico*, her little mulatto boy. Manzano's baptism was designed to rupture the potentially subversive power of African-inspired spirituality (Midlo Hall 32–34), but his mistress also baptized him to ensure his loyalty to the interests of the slaveholding class.

Manzano's father was also present at his son's baptism. Toribio de Castro had preferential status within the household, and he performed domestic duties pursuant to his racial condition as a mulatto manservant: he was a musician and a tailor. Doña Beatriz designated Toribio de Castro to perform festive music in honor of his son's religious ceremony. Other sources corroborate the relationship between the priesthood and black domestic servants on Cuban plantations. In Miguel Barnet's *Biografía de un cimarrón* (1966), former Cuban maroon Esteban Montejo described the slave barracks and the big house as divergent and incompatible spheres of religious practice. Montejo said the *esclavos domésticos* (domestic slaves) absorbed catechism and learned Cristian prayers, unlike the field workers that had almost no contact with the priests and virtually no understanding of Christian doctrines. Montejo portrayed a sociocultural chasm between unacculturated field workers devoted to African-inspired spirituality and Hispanicized domestics for whom Catholicism was legitimate dogma (Barnet, *Cimarrón: Historia* 39–40).

> La otra religion era la católica. Ésa la introducían los curas, que por nada del mundo entraban a los barracones de la esclavitud. [...] Eran tan serios que hasta había negros que los seguían al pie de la letra. [...] Se aprendían el catecismo y se lo leían a los demás. Con todas las palabras y las oraciones. Estos negros eran esclavos domésticos, y se reunían con los otros esclavos, los del campo, en los bateyes. Venían siendo como mesajeros de los curas. La verdad es que yo jamás me aprendí esa doctrina porque no entendía nada. Yo creo que los domésticos tampoco, aunque como eran tan finos y bien tratados, se hacían los cristianos (Barnet, *Cimarrón: Historia* 39–40).

> (The other religion was the Catholic one. The priest introduced that [religion], that for nothing in the world could enter the slave barracks. [...] They were so serious that there were even blacks that followed them to the letter. [...] They learned the catechism and read it to everyone else. With all the words and the prayers. These blacks were domestic slaves and they met with the other slaves, the field workers, in the outbuildings of the sugar refinery. They came as messengers of the priests. But the truth is I never learned this doctrine because I didn't understand anything. I don't think the domestics did either, but because they were so refined and well treated, they pretended to be Christians.[10])

In a sense, Montejo corroborated Manzano's description of his early life. The mistress ordered that Manzano be taught catechism and that he be baptized, presumably like her other domestic servants. Manzano's prodigious memory enabled him not only to absorb catechism but also to memorize most of the sermons of Renaissance Spanish priest Fray Luis de Granada (1504–1588) by age ten. In fact, Manzano's Christian poetry demonstrated not only an understanding of doctrines but also an uncanny ability to question their dictates. Manzano's exposure to Catholicism didn't preclude his interactions with African-inspired spiritual practices (as we shall see later); neither did it prevent from him from selectively using what he had absorbed from the Holy Faith.

The Marchioness Justiz de Santa Ana certainly considered herself a devout Catholic. And she insisted that enslaved domestic servants—that had intimate contact with her family—be instructed in the Catholic faith to secure the sanctity and security of her home. Manzano's description of her death is telling. He wrote, "me llebaron al fondo de la casa donde estaban las demas criadas enlutadas en la noche toda la negrada {de la asienda} sollosando resaron el rosario yo lloraba a mares y me separaron entregandome a mi padre" (they carried me to the back of the house where all the domestic slaves mournful in the night, all the blacks {on the plantation} wept and prayed the rosary. I wept profusely and they separated me and handed me to my father) (Manzano, *Autobiografía* 303). That the enslaved community prayed the rosary in memoriam further implies that Doña Beatriz placed much emphasis on the sacraments and other rites of the Catholic faith. However, we do not know whether the African community prayed to the Virgin Mary as the priesthood understood her or if their devotion was to a transculturated notion of the Virgin as an African divine spirit (*orisha*, *mpungo*). Whatever the case, there is reason to believe that Manzano's father viewed his son's baptism as a way to integrate him into the symbolic order where Catholicism enjoyed an unquestioned hegemony and mulattoes relished a higher social status than blacks.

Rather than simply assuming a mulatto identity for his white readership, Manzano insisted that his slave mistresses and his father had shaped his emerging identity. Manzano recalled an instance where his father forbade him to cavort with the other black children on the plantation. To demonstrate the ideological link between Catholic religious conversion and racialization, I cite the passage below.

mi padre era algo altivo y nunca permitio no solo corrillos en su casa pero ni q$^e$. sus hijos jugasen con lo negritos de la asienda; mi madre vivia con él y sus hijos p$^r$. lo q$^e$. no eramos muy bien queridos (Luis, ed. 339)

(My father was somewhat haughty and not only would he never allow little Creoles in his house but neither would he let his children play with the other little blacks on the plantation. My mother lived with him and his children for which we were not well liked.)

Manzano's father was not only present in his life but he was also an agent of acculturation. Manzano maintained that his father defended pigmentocracy: a political order that affords socioeconomic privilege based on the relative lightness of the skin and perceived proximity to whiteness. Manzano adopted a remarkably critical tone toward his father; he even called him "altivo," or haughty, because he forbade any of his children to socialize with the other black youths on the estate. Manzano apparently faulted his father (and perhaps his mistresses) for this social distance from *los negros*, explaining that Toribio de Castro had hindered his offspring from playing with the other black children. (Manzano's father apparently had had children with another woman, hence the phrasing, "his children".) Though on another occasion Manzano says that his father's presence sometimes shielded him from physical and emotional abuse, he also revealed that theirs was not an affectionate bond (Manzano, *Autobiografía* 306). Toribio de Castro's racial attitude may be explained if we consider that he was a *pardo* (a mixed-race person often of black and white parentage [Madden 39]) whose father may have been a white slaveholder. The details of Toribio de Castro's parentage remain unclear. Still, there is no doubt that Manzano's early experiences shaped his self-concept as a Roman Catholic and a "mulato y entre negros" ([a] mulatto among blacks) (Friol 194; Manzano, *Autobiografía* 339), as he would later describe himself.

Racial and religious acculturation was more than a convenient facade to convince slaveholders and overseers that blacks were true converts to Catholicism. The degree to which persons of African descent assimilated to Hispano-Catholic norms depended in large part on how they were positioned within a given colonial society. African descendants that were legally free were more likely to receive social privilege if they married in the Church, attended mass and participated in patronage networks with the local parish (Landers 41–42, 44). Enslaved servants also forged a relationship to white power that might garner them certain privileges, but these favors were contingent upon whether or not they were perceived as nonthreatening *slaves*. In colonial Latin America, acculturation implied what Ifeoma Nwankwo has termed a "disidentifiation with Blacks" (193) and a rejection of Africanity in all its forms, particularly religious. Spain and Portugal renamed a panoply of African ethnic difference and assigned members of myriad ethnic groups the generic category of *negro*. As Jerome Branche points out, *negro*—the Spanish word for "black"—signified "he who has no political significance" (140). Hence, the path to political significance in colonial society was paved with a need to gain socio-cultural distance from slavery and sin by disidentifying with blackness and accepting Christianity, in essence, by striving for an unattainable whiteness.

Survival was the foremost concern of enslaved persons whatever their socioeconomic position within slave society. Toribio de Castro's embrace of colorism must be understood in that context. Caribbean pigmentocracy separated blacks and mulattoes into discrete races, and mulattoes were constituted as an interstitial category in an inevitable march toward Hispano-Catholic racial and cultural normativity. In fact, the desire for whitening was so pervasive in communities of African descent that Vera Kutzinski explains that nineteenth-century merchants advertised whitening agents to black Cubans (Kutzinski, *Sugar's Secrets* 59). Though the mulatto was afforded a higher place within Latin American pigmentocracies than black men and women, the racial epithet *mulato* has its origins in deterministic ideas about animal breeding. The term *mulatto* is derived from the word *mule* and is reminiscent of white North American debates that questioned the humanity of black persons (*Black Women Novelists*, Christian qtd. in Mejía-López 36).

In Manzano's narrative, the African-descended paternal figure reclaimed a sort of personhood grounded in heteronormative notions of masculinity. Though Manzano never claimed to have had an affectionate bond with his father, he strove to preserve his father's legacy by describing him as a man of honor. As Branche so eloquently explains, the Luso-Hispanic symbolic order denied enslaved Africans and their progeny *honra*, since the enslaved "symbolized the limit point of degradation and, in social terms, the opposite of honor" (95). The following passages demonstrate the significance of honor in Manzano's narrative strategy.

> desde la edad de tres a catorse años la alegria y viveza de mi genio lo parlero de mis lavios llamados pico de oro se trocó todo en sierta melancolia q$^e$. se me iso con el tiempo caracteristica . . .
>
> [ . . . ]
>
> Tendria yo unos quinse o dies y seis años cuando fue llebado a Matanzas otra vez abrasé a mis padres y a mis hermanos y conosí a los q$^e$. nasieron despues de mi, el cararte seco y la horradez de mi padre como estaba siempre a la vista me asian pasar una vida algo mas llevadera no sufria los orribles y continuos azotes ni los golpes de mano q$^e$. p$^r$. lo regular sufre un muchacho lejos de algun doliente suyo aun que siempre mis infelices cachetes y narices estaban . . . (Manzano, *Autobiografía* 306)
>
> (From age thirteen or fourteen the joy and liveliness of my temperament the talkativeness of my lips, known as the Golden Bill, turned into a certain melancholy that within time became characteristic . . .
>
> [ . . . ]
>
> I must have been fifteen or sixteen years old when I was once again brought to Matanzas. Again, I embraced my parents and my siblings and I met those that

were born after me, the sullen temperament and the honor of my father, since I was always in his sight, made certain that I experienced a somewhat more tolerable life. I did not suffer the horrible and persistent whippings, or the slaps that a boy who is far removed from his relatives suffers, although the miserable slaps in the face and the broken nose were always [with me] . . . )

Manzano implies that being made to accompany his mistress to the capital not only demonstrated that his parents had no lawful authority over him but also left him in a precarious state where he might be abused. The mulatto boy (as he was often described) lived a precarious existence because he was set apart from the other black children yet made to endure the same (or perhaps a worse) fate. The symbolic order did not allow Manzano to consign his father *honra*, a concept rooted in early modern and Renaissance Spain and based on notions of legitimate birth, nobility, and whiteness (Branche, *Colonialism* 83). As an enslaved man, Toribio de Castro was bereft of socio-racial legitimacy and symbolic power, and as long as be remained in bondage as a nonwhite, he would never be able to acquire them. But Manzano did not derive his notion of honor from the Hispano-Catholic archetype. Rather, his father was honorable because he afforded Manzano protection and inculcated strength within him as a bulwark against the hostility of white domination. Though he could not end the physical and psychological mistreatment, Toribio de Castro did provide Juan Francisco more than a semblance of safety, because the frequency and intensity of the abuse subsided. The narrative singles out the father figure as protector and attributes his actions to African-descended notions of honor. Such an ethics of black Cuban masculinity resurfaced in *Cantos del esclavo* (1879) (*Songs of Slave*) by José del Carmen Díaz, another enslaved black writer who addressed the problem of white male sexual violence against black women but also constructed explicit silences in his poetry to safeguard black female honor (Pettway, "Black Femininity" 25–26). By attributing honor to Toribio de Castro, Manzano negated the subpersonhood that might feminize his father and render him a nonentity within colonial society.

### *Myth* of the Mulatto Slave: Juan Francisco Manzano's Broken Body

Juan Francisco Manzano's affinity for literature did not begin with the Spanish scribal tradition, because improvisation was the origin of his poetry and short stories. Besides the love poetry he dedicated to Seraphina, a pretty black girl, he also improvised tales of sorcery for the children, and *décimas* for the elder handmaidens of the plantation community (Manzano, *Autobiografía* 304, 307–308). But Manzano's mistress thought his status as the "Golden Bill" imperiled her project of socialization, and she forbade anyone in the household to speak to him. Manzano's narrative is emphatic about how the Marchioness of Prado Ameno sought to silence self-expression in his early adolescence.

solo cuando me podia juntar con los niños les desia muchos versos y le contaba cuentos de encantamientos q$^e$ yo componia de memoria [ . . . ] mi ama qe. no me perdia de vista ni aun dormiendo p$^r$. q$^e$. hasta soñaba conmigo ubo de penetrar algo me isieron repetir un cuento una noche de imbierno rodeado de muchos niños y [] criadas, y ella se mantenia oculta en otro cuarto detras unas persianas o romanas; al dia siguien [ . . . ] me pusieron una grande mordaza . . . (Manzano, *Autobiografía* 308)

(Only when I could meet with the children I recited many verses to them and I told them many sorcery tales that I composed from memory [ . . . ] My mistress, who never lost sight of me, not even while sleeping because she even dreamt of me, was going to penetrate into the matter somehow. They made me repeat a short story one winter night surrounded by several children and [] handmaidens, and she hid herself in another room behind Venetian blinds or curtains; and the subsequent day [ . . . ] they gagged me . . . )

The Marchioness arranged the mise-en-scène, quietly gathered the necessary audience and incited the young Manzano to perform. Prado Ameno was both present and absent, so that though Manzano did not see her, he remained within her purview. The recitation was a caricature, because the Marchioness did not intend to celebrate but rather to quell his nascent self-expression. Julio Ramos argues that Manzano's captors punished him whenever they discovered him telling stories, reciting poetry, or otherwise exercising rhetorical eloquence. Ramos concludes that enslaved people's capacity for mimicry produced an anxiety in slaveholders; it nurtured their suspicions that black people's rhetorical expression was not passive mimicry. The rhetorical resemblance between slaveholders and their captives imperiled the perception of difference between masters and slaves ("La ley es otra" 319–320).

Prado Ameno's desire to "penetrate into the matter somehow" demonstrates that her authority reproduced the hegemonic violence of white masculinity so that she might govern what Manzano did and, perhaps more importantly, what he said. Marilyn Miller writes that the emergence of Manzano's literary voice—appearing initially as improvised poetry—disrupted the imagined dichotomy of master/slave, the enunciative power of the written/spoken discourse, and the silence consigned to domesticated African bodies. It is not mimicry of the master but the presence of "original voice" and the possibility that Manzano might learn to read that imperiled the mistress's power over the household ("Rebeldía narrativa" 424–425). But there is something more to the knowledge that Manzano's improvisations represented. If the mistress sought to silence Manzano's tales of sorcery—and the passage implies as much— then Prado Ameno's broader concern was to preserve her authority over what Orlando Patterson has termed the "appropriate symbolic instruments" of slave regimes (37). Patterson says that slaveholders' power required "extracoercive support," an authority derived from the master's command of the symbolic order (37). By penetrating into the cultural content of African Cuban short stories (perhaps fictionalized), the mistress not only sought to silence Manzano but to suppress a religio-cultural discourse that might subvert the order of things. Prado Ameno sought to maintain unquestioned control of the symbolic realm.

The narrative is imbued with a heightened sense of sartorial and somatic violence that Patterson termed "the ritual of enslavement" but I have preferred to designate as a ritual of racialization. The ritual of enslavement is a multiphase process that entailed: a symbolic rejection of kinship, a renaming of the captive, the imposition of an observable mark of servitude, and incorporation into the master's household (52).[11] But having been born into slavery, Manzano found himself in an amorphous space, an inchoate state of being. Despite his parents' relative powerlessness, he maintained affective ties to biological kin, and Prado Ameno refused to assign him a household function that might have integrated him into the domestic sphere. He forever remained what Patterson has termed the "permanent enemy on the inside" (39) and the mistress seemed to prefer him that way. Prado Ameno's description of Manzano as the *mas malo* (the worst one) was incompatible with his self-concept but was consistent with the property/person duality that enabled slave society to deny him free will even while assigning him criminal intent (Hartman 80). There are three incidents that demonstrate this point: Manzano's arrest by the commissioner, the public outfitting of his body upon his return to the big house from the field, and a conversation he had with a free black servant about racial degradation. Manzano was placed under arrest after having fled the plantation to escape the wrath of the overseer. Five days after the adolescent took refuge in el Conde de Jibacoa's residence, the slave patrol was dispatched to the house, seized him, tied his arms and carried him off to the public jail in Matanzas. Later, a young white man— probably a *guajiro* (landless white peasant)—returned him to the El Molino plantation by force. Instead of flogging Manzano upon return, they subjected him to ridicule by dressing him as a field worker, shaving his head, and removing his shoes (Manzano, *Autobiografía* 330).[12] The abrupt change in his sartorial profile demonstrated the precariousness of his situation and underscored that, like all other enslaved persons, Manzano had lost his own body.

Prado Ameno required Manzano to work on the sugar plantation for nine days as chastisement for his short-lived escape; then she sent for him.[13]

estube allí como nueve dias en los trabajos de la finca y una mañana q$^e$. vino a almorzar mi S$^{ra}$. me mandó buscar bistionme de ropa fina y detras de la bolante me condujo otra vez al pueblo y en servisio ya yo era un objeto conosido p$^r$. el chinito o el mulatico de la Mar. todos me preguntaban q$^e$. abia sido aquello y me abochornaba satisfacer a tanto curioso (Manzano, *Autobiografía* 330)

(I was there nine days [doing] fieldwork and one morning when my mistress came to have lunch, she sent for me. They dressed me in fine clothing and behind the wheel they drove me to town and in service I was already the object known as the Little Chinamen or the Marchioness' little mulatto. Everyone asked me what that was about and it shamed me to satisfy such curiosity)

Manzano's status as a *mulatico* (a little mulatto) in Matanzas was wrought with arbitrary violence and disgrace; effrontery that spurned nostalgia for what he recalled as "las delisias de unos amos jovenes y amables" (the delights of youthful kind masters) whose "aire de cortesano" (courtly airs) rewarded his loyal service (Manzano, *Autobiografía* 330). Though his perception of the master/ slave relationship would change radically later in adolescence, at this juncture Manzano understood himself as a *mulato* who wanted to live in harmony with beneficent masters. The urban/rural divide in his autobiography reproduced the civilization/barbarism dichotomy inherent in nineteenth-century Latin American national discourse. But that discursive commonplace is complicated by the poets' engagement with African-inspired spirituality throughout the relation. (I examine Manzano's representation of African-inspired spirituality in chapter four.) I do not think that Manzano's work with black field hands signified a true loss of status in the symbolic order that his mistress ascribed to, but rather that Prado Ameno understood blackness—regardless of hue—as a sense of nothingness and degradation. Manzano's notion of mulatto identity contradicted his mistress's insistence on brutal objectification, or what Frederick Douglass termed "the exercise of irresponsible power" (43). The mistress punished her "object known as the Little Mulatto" to remind the adolescent that, as Patterson says, "without the master [ . . . ] the slave does not exist" (46).[14] Prado Ameno must have reasoned that Manzano was a cipher but not an outcast. His aggrieved body represented a necessary fiction about black Cuban masculinity, a symbolic castration and violent feminization that rendered him both fragile girl child and roguish Negro.

Manzano invited his readers to view him through the prism of those that held existential power over him. The floating signifiers *chinito* and *mulatico de la Mar* are markers of indeterminacy, part of that necessary fiction that Hortense Spillers termed "a locus of confounded identities" (65). In other words, Prado Ameno sought to (re)make Manzano into whatever the occasion called for. *Chinito* not only denotes the sexual union of black and mulatto persons— an apt descriptor of the author's racial admixture—but it is also a racial epithet that makes whiteness inaccessible by signaling several generations of *saltatrás* (marrying down).

Es de admirarse q<sup>e</sup>. mi señora no pudiese estar sin mí 10 dias seguidos así era
q<sup>e</sup>. mis prisiones jamas pasaban de 11 a 12 dias pintandome siempre como el

mas malo de todos los nasidos *en* el molino de donde desia q$^e$. yo era criollo
esto era otro genero de mortificasion q$^e$. yo tenia (original emphasis, Manzano,
*Autobiografía* 334–335).

(It's astonishing that my mistress could not be without me for ten days in a row,
that's why my detention never endured for more than eleven or twelve days.
Describing me always as the worst one ever born on the sugar plantation, where
it was said that I was Creole, that was another sort of mortification for me.)

Manzano's assertion about the fixity of the African-descended male stereotype accurately portrayed the panoptic gaze: "depicting me always as the worst
one ever born on the sugar plantation" (Manzano, *Autobiografía* 334–335).[15]
The author acknowledged the relationship between language, representation
and the symbolic order. Unlike the epithets *chinito* and *mulatico de la Mar*,
*criollo*—an expression that labeled captive offspring as subhuman—does not
set the author apart from the black masses but is rather an erasure of light-
skinned privilege because it equated him with blackness.[16] We know nothing of
Manzano's phenotype. No physical descriptions of Manzano have surfaced, and
there were no portraits of him produced during his lifetime. In colonial Cuba,
racial labels were applied inconsistently, and the legal color ascribed to African
descendants at birth did not always coincide with their physical appearance.
But whatever his skin color, Cuban officials said that African ancestry was "the
mark of slavery which has descended from his parents" (Martínez Alier 74–75).
Manzano's rejection of the defamatory term *criollo* is resonant with his father's
admonition not to play "con lo negritos de la asienda" (with the little blacks
on the plantation). Toribio de Castro referred to black children as "corrillos"—
the same term that slaveholders used—and he forbade them to enter his abode
(Manzano, *Autobiografía* 339). Prado Ameno not only evaded responsibility for
her actions by promoting the myth of black criminality but also caricatured
Manzano's cherished notion of selfhood. The use of floating racial signifiers
enabled his mistress to assign an illusory sense of privilege and withdraw it at
will. But Prado Ameno's sense of ownership over the onomastic domain also
extended to a psychosexual dynamic upon which her authority relied. The
obsessive attention lavished on Manzano's admittedly frail body was further
aggravated when the colonial administrator committed the ultimate act of degradation: penetrative assault.

apenas me vi solo en aquel lugar cuando todos los muertos me paresia q$^e$. se
[leval] levantaban y q$^e$. vagaban p$^r$. todo lo largo de el salon [ . . . ] no bien
avia empesado a aclarar cuando sentí correr el serrojo entra un contra mayoral
seguido del arminstrador me sacan una tabla parada a un orcon q$^e$. sostiene
el colgadiso un maso de cujes con sincuenta de ellos beo al pie de la tabla el

administrador embuelto en su capote dise debajo del pañuelo q$^e$. le tapaba la boca con una voz ronca amarra mis manos se atan como las de Jesucristo se me carga y meto los pies en las dos aberturas q$^e$. tiene tambien mís pies se atan ¡oh Dios! corramos un belo p$^r$. el resto de esta exena mi sangre se ha derramado yo perdí el sentido . . . (Manzano, *Autobiografía* 321)

(I saw myself alone in that place when all the spirits of the dead it seemed to me rose up and roamed all throughout the room [ . . . ] It had hardly begun to grow light when I heard the door bolt slide a contra mayoral enters followed by the administrator they take out a plank intended for me which was attached to a gibbet from which hung a bunch of hooks, about fifty of them at the foot of the plank I see the administrator wrapped in his cape from under his scarf he tells the others in a rough voice to gag me they bind my hands tie them up like Jesus Christ's they pick me up and put my feet in the two openings [of the stocks] and also tie my feet Oh God! let us draw a veil over the rest of this scene my blood has poured out I lost consciousness.)[17]

A sequential reconstruction of events is imperative. Ergo, the relation: Manzano's mistress condemned him to the stocks for crushing a geranium, they broke his nose, and a colonial administrator (an immigrant from Saint Domingue) confined him to the stocks in a desolate infirmary on the San Miguel plantation imbued with the presence of meandering spirits of the deceased.[18] What Manzano construed as the torment of maleficent spirits devolved into a nightmarish rape scenario when two men forced him onto a wooden plank, "tied his hands like those of Jesus Christ," fastened his feet in the stocks and bound them further as to render his body vulnerable to penetration (Manzano, *Autobiografía* 321). Lorna Williams draws attention to silences embedded in the passage as authorial self-assertion, and Susan Willis believes the sudden shift from imperfect to present tense is indicative of a trauma experienced anew (qtd. in Ellis 431). But Ellis reads silence as the absence of language, the rupture of a discursive thread produced by traumatic sexual experience, which he surmises may have occurred more than once (431). But there is more to be said about this obscure matter.

The rhetorical veil that Manzano used to evade the prurient gaze of his readership safeguarded the body even as it divulged the secret. The tête-à-tête between the *contramayoral* (black slave driver), the administrator, and Manzano made the infirmary into homoerotic space where the small degree of bodily integrity that remained could be wrested away. The metaphor of the suffering Christ not only identified the enslaved with the Lamb of God—a theme that would resurface in his poetry—but also conjured up the image of the Roman cross, not as a sacred symbol but rather an instrument of torture. If the arms were extended and fastened to the wooden board, then the supine body is exposed to the male gaze and all its instrumentality. Draped in a cloak with a handkerchief covering his "deep voice," the administrator emerged as the plantation patriarch whose limitless authority over the African-descended male body allowed him to feminize the *girl child* by performing the lowest act of degradation imaginable. Abnegated in tears, embraced by his mother, and afflicted by hemorrhaging, Manzano's body had been broken; he was virtually condemned to social death. What the author relates after this incident maybe as telling as the violation itself. Manzano recalled, "o pocos mas q$^e$. se levantó mi S$^{ra}$. fue su primera diligensia imponerse de si se me avia tratado bien el arministrador q$^e$. la esperaba me llamó y me le presentó, me preguntó si queria otra vez tomar unas ojas de su geranio" (a little later my mistress awoke and her first diligence was to take it upon herself to see if the administrator had treated me fittingly. I waited for her, she called for me and I presented myself before her, she asked me if I might want to take another geranium leaf . . . ) (Manzano, *Autobiografía* 321). Manzano's narrative sequence did more than implicate Prado Ameno in the crime; it afforded her masculinity and thus transformed her into the symbolic agent of rape.

Manzano was a marked man. Mulattoness should have afforded him a greater measure of worthiness, and his apparent affinity for Hispano-Catholic culture should have secured his place within the colonial pigmentocracy. If the author's dialogue with the free household servant is any indication, blacks and mulattoes on the plantation also thought that "the little mulatto" was unduly degraded and despised.

> cuando la gente estaba en misa me llamó un criado libre de la casa y estando a solas con él me dijo; hombre q$^e$. tu no tienes berguenza p$^a$. estar pasando tanto trabajos cualquiera negro bozal está mejor tratado q$^e$. tú, un mulatico fino con tantas abilidades como tú al momento hallará quien lo compre p$^r$. este estilo me abló mucho rato (Manzano, *Autobiografía* 338)

> (When people were away at mass, a free house servant called me and being alone with him, he told me; man aren't you ashamed of being put through so much? Any African slave is better treated than you. A fine little mulatto with such aptitude like yourself could find someone to purchase him in an instant. He talked to me in that way for quite a while.)

The conversation about skin color, social position, and the price of captive bodies revealed the symbolic dichotomy and economic implications of the black/mulatto divide. The *disgrace* that the freeborn servant referred to was not so much about physical brutality as it was about the indignity that Manzano's mulatto self-image had endured. In this way, I believe that the servant's advice to flee Matanzas, make a detailed account of the mistreatment to the captain general, and thereby secure freedom (or find a new owner), may also be read as an endeavor to redeem a degenerated sense of self. Although it is discontinuous and disjointed, Manzano's autobiography is a remarkably reiterative account. At the mere sight of Don Saturnino mounted on a horse—an image infused with phallic implications—Manzano's body quivered with sexual trauma, "un temblor general cundió todo mi cuerpo y atacandome un dolor de cabeza apenas me podia baler" (a great trembling extended across my entire body and a headache seized me so that I could scarcely stand) (Manzano, *Autobiografía* 338–339). A breakdown in the corporal schema signaled violence untold and bespoke Manzano's struggle to assert masculinity in the course of an existential crisis. The mere image of the administrator provoked memories of Manzano's public incarceration. The author reimagined his body bound like a delinquent, outfitted in the attire of fieldworkers, and head shorn upon his release from the Matanzas public jail. As Manzano says, "en aquel momento determiné mi fuga" (in that moment I determined my escape), because without parents, siblings, or even relatives, he saw himself "en una palabra mulato y entre negros" (in a word [as] [a] mulatto among blacks) (Manzano, *Autobiografía* 339).

## Crying Out to a *Silent God*: The Jeremiad in Manzano's Catholic Poetry

In 1835, more than ten years after achieving some measure of celebrity, Manzano reminisced about how he had taught himself to read and write. Manzano described his autodidactic process in the slave narrative that Domingo del Monte had requested of him. But for the meager instruction that Manzano's baptismal godmother provided him, Manzano received no formal humanistic training. Spanish American slave codes prohibited enslaved Africans and Afro-Latin Americans from pursuing a formal education (Luis, "Juan Francisco Manzano" 33). And Prado Ameno had gone to great lengths, even resorting to violence to prevent Manzano from concocting short stories and improvising poetry. Manzano explained that as he developed the talent to compose verse, his enslavers forbade him to learn to read and write.

> yo tenia dose años ya abia compuesto muchas desimas de memorias causa p$^r$. q$^e$. mis padrinos no querian q$^e$. aprendiese a escribir. pero yo las dictaba de memorias en particular a una joven morena llamáda Serafina cuyas cartas en desimas mantenian una correspondensia amorosa (Manzano, *Autobiografía* 304).

> (I was twelve years old [and] I had already composed many *décimas* from memory, which is why my godparents didn't want me to learn to write. But I dictated them from memory mostly to a young black girl called Seraphina whose letters in *décimas* maintained an amorous correspondence [with me].)

Manzano's autodidacticism was marked by an abiding interest in composing verse and telling stories, for which he found an engaged and participatory audience on the plantation and in the big house. A pretty young black girl named Seraphina became Manzano's muse; she was an adolescent object of affection, and she inspired him to improvise *décimas*.[19] The *décima espinela* is a stanza of ten octosyllabic verses that can be traced to fifteenth-century Iberia, where it was known as *la copla real*. The *copla real* originated in Portugal but is also recited in France. Spanish poet and musician Vicente Espinela established a new formula for the *copla real* and published his *Diversas rimas* in 1591. His late sixteenth-century publication introduced the *décima* into Renaissance Spanish literature (Orta Ruiz 7, 12–13). Manzano's godparents reasoned that his genius for improvising poetry would inevitably lead him to learn to read and write. The marchioness's family had introduced the young Manzano to Western European culture: they had taken him to French operas and to the theater, and he had often attended mass. His baptismal godmother even provided him some schooling at age six (Manzano, *Autobiografía* 300–301). But they forbade him to learn to read and write, because they knew that literacy in the hands of a captive would endow him with dangerous forms of knowledge, with foreign ideas about liberty, and most of all, with the power of discourse.

Manzano sought to bridge the gap between the spoken word and written discourse. Manzano was a second-generation Cuban of African descent for whom Spanish was "mi idioma" (my language) (Manzano, *Autobiografía* 335). Manzano did not have access to precolonial African writing systems such as the Nsibidi script of Calabar, Nigeria, that Africans adapted to the Cuban environment when the Abakuá male initiation society was founded in Regla in 1836 (I. Miller 13–14, 41). Consequently, written Spanish was among the most powerful arrows in Manzano's quiver. Oral practices relied on memory, recitation, various formulae of repetition, and gestural language to preserve and transmit cultural knowledge and assert political meaning. Manzano wrote in the oral register; he wrote the same way that he spoke. Certain passages from the autobiographical manuscript bear out the intimate relationship between oral and written language. William Luis points out that Manzano confused *c* with *s*, *l* with *r*, *g* with *jota*, and *v* with *b* because there was a little distance between the spoken and written word for him. Domingo del Monte edited Manzano's poetry, and though some of his changes were cosmetic, other interventions modified the original meaning (Luis, "Juan Francisco Manzano" 34). Consequently, Luis argues that Manzano lost control of his literature when it went from spoken-word improvisation to written discourse (Luis, "Juan Francisco Manzano" 40). But I propose that rather than relinquishing control of his written work, Manzano leveraged as much creative control as he could, because creative control was a proxy for political power. My reading of Manzano's religious poetry suggests that he was unwilling to wait on the Lord, so to speak, because he disbelieved that the Christian God would redeem him from slavery. Such poetry is evidence of Manzano's struggle for creative control. I develop this argument further in chapter four, which examines African-inspired ideas of spirit and cosmos.

Memorization and mnemonic devices were sure-fire techniques for Manzano to teach himself to read and write. The mnemonic devices of African-descended and Spanish oral traditions enabled Manzano to remember volumes of material: poems he had improvised and stories he had composed. He even boasted that he possessed a notebook of verses in his memory: "yo me com-plasia bajo la guasima [qe] cuyas raises formaba una espesie de pedestal al q^e. pescaba en componer algunos versos de memoria y todos eran siempre triste los cuales no escrivia pr. ignorar este ramo pr. esto siempre tenia un cuaderno de versos en la memoria y a cualquier cosa improvísaba . . ." (I took pleasure beneath the *guásima* tree whose roots formed a sort of pedestal where I went fishing [and] composed verses from memory. [These verses] were always sad; I did not write them down because I was unfamiliar with that practice. That's why I had a notebook of verses in memory and I improvised about all sorts of things) (Manzano, *Autobiografía* 307–308). Jossianna Arroyo Martínez describes Manzano as a mulatto Cuban poet situated between two bodies of knowledge: one determined by Afro-Caribbean oral practices and another codified in Western literary traditions (Arroyo Martínez, *Travestismos* 66). Manzano explained that his memory was a catalogue of cultural materials that enabled him to cultivate popular forms of literature like the *décima* prior to mastering the written word.

Manzano also put his capacity for memorization to use in order to learn Catholic doctrine and African ideas of spirit and cosmos. He learned the sermons of Fray Luis de Granada, the *décima*, and classical European rhetoric, as well as African Cuban proverbs and sorcery tales (Manzano, *Autobiografía* 301, 307–308, 318, 326). (I explore the significance of sorcery tales as part of Manzano's African Cuban religious repertoire in chapter 4.) Manzano demystifies his process of autodidacticism in the following passages from the autobiography.

nos benimos a la Habana y se me dejó con el S^{or}. D^{n}. Nicolas que me queria no como a esclavo sino como a hijo

[ . . . ]

lo queria sin tamaño; . . . le preparaba antes de todo la mesa sillon y libros p^{a}. entregarse al estudio me fui identificando de tal modo con sus costumbres q^{e}. empese yo tambien a darme estudios, la poesia en todos los tramites de mi vida me suministraba versos analogos a mi situasion ya prozpera ya adversa, tomaba sus libros de retorica me ponia mi leccion de memoria la aprendia como el papagallo . . . (Manzano, *Autobiografía* 325–326)

[ . . . ]

hay sierta identidad entre su letra y la mia contentisimo con mi logrado intento me pasaba desde las sinco hasta las dies ejersitando la mano en letras . . . (Manzano, *Autobiografía* 326)

(We came to Havana and they left me with Mr. Don Nicolás that loved me not like a slave but as a son

[ . . . ]

I loved him without measure; [ . . . ] More than anything else I prepared [his] entire table, his armchair and books so that he could devote himself to study. I began to identify myself with his customs to the extent that I, too, began to devote myself to study. Poetry in all of the stages of my life provided me verses that that were analogous to my situation whether prosperous or adverse. I took his books of rhetoric and gave myself lessons from memory, learning it like a parrot.

There is a certain relationship between his handwriting and mine. Very happy with my achievement, I practiced my handwriting from five until ten at night.)

Manzano was deliberate, even calculating, when he taught himself to read and write. He identified with the habits of Nicolás de Cárdenas y Manzano, the president of la Sección de Educación de la Sociedad Económica de Amigos del País (the Havana Economic Society). Manzano's mother was a wetnurse to the young Nicolás. Juan Francisco Manzano had known Cárdenas y Manzano since childhood, and their master/slave relationship was not defined by physical violence. Even so, Cárdenas y Manzano was paternalistic in his dealings with Juan Francisco. Manzano took refuge in Havana away from his abusive mistress, the Marchioness of Prado Ameno. In Havana, Manzano cultivated his talent for versification and learned to write standard Neoclassical and Romantic poetry. Havana afforded Manzano aesthetic and political opportunities that were indispensable for transforming himself into an antislavery intellectual with transatlantic appeal.

In the final section of this chapter, I explore Manzano's poetic engagement with the Catholic concept of God. Manzano's religious poetry was a jeremiad that critiqued the failure of Catholicism to redeem the black body from the slave plantation. Nonetheless, redemption emerged as an important theme in

"Oda a La Religión" (Ode to Religion), "A Jesús en la cruz" (To Jesus on the Cross) and "A la esclava ausente" (To the Absent Slave Woman). "Oda a La Religión" and "A Jesús en la cruz" perform three discursive functions: they denounce the affliction of the enslaved, they portray the author as a devout Catholic, and they address the official religion with suitable reverence. "Oda a La Religión" appeared in *Diario de la Habana* in 1831, and in most respects it was a poem honoring God the Father, the Holy Trinity, and the Virgin Mary in accordance with Church doctrine. But Manzano's familiarity with the sermons of Fray Luis de Granada (Manzano, *Autobiografía* 301) created space for an intimate encounter with God.

Cuando triste levanto
El alma tierna do el dolor reposa,
Y con vista llorosa
A Dios me eleva, desde el bajo suelo
Rápido subo en alentado vuelo.

Y en éxtasis profundo
El alma siento de mi ser huyendo,
Que a su Hacedor rindiendo . . .

Olvida los fugaces devaneos,
y sólo a Dios consagra sus deseos. (Manzano, *Esclavo poeta* 188)

(When sad I raise
The tender soul where suffering lies
And with tearful visage
To God I am lifted from the lowly earth
Swiftly I rise in cherished flight.

In profound ecstasy
The soul I feel fleeing my being
Yielding to its Maker . . .

Forget idle pursuits,
And to God alone consecrate your desires)

"Oda a La Religión" is among the first representations of black personhood in Cuban poetry depicting slavery. Manzano restored sentience to the captive body by abandoning the flesh for its symbolic antithesis, the Christian soul. The grief-stricken, yet tender spirit of the African-descended subject is liberated from the constraints of a tortured body and ascends to commune with his

Maker in "éxtasis profundo" (profound ecstasy). Manzano's tears are not evidence of contrition; rather, they prove his apparent devotion to the "Religión Cristiana" (the Christian Religion). The poet has neglected "devaneos" (idle pursuits) and consecrated his desires to the Almighty. Manzano's first two stanzas are illustrative of his desire for an intimate, perhaps even mystical connection with God, a yearning to transcend consciousness and, with it, to transcend his life as an enslaved man.

Mysticism can be defined as a direct and intimate union with God that circumvents the conscious mind.[20] In sixteenth-century Spain, mystics theorized that physical, emotional, or psychic suffering could bring God nigh. In Spanish mysticism suffering manifested not only as a willingness to experience pain when wronged by others, but also as a need to inflict pain upon oneself as an act of discipline. For instance, mystics practiced self-castigation, sleep deprivation, and kneeling upon iron spikes; they refused to speak to family members, and they bound their hands with horsehair in order to bruise them. Among the most famous mystics were Carmelites San Juan de la Cruz and Teresa de Ávila who mortified their bodies in hopes of drawing near to God (Flynn 257–258, 260). But Manzano did not pursue pain in a quest to know God; pain and humiliation were quotidian experiences for the African-descended captive whose mother and father had already died by 1831. Among prominent sixteenth-century Spanish ministers, Fray Luis de Granada merits attention, because Manzano memorized his sermons as a child.

Fray Luis de Granada (Friar Louis of Granada) was born in Granada, Spain, in 1504, the same year that Isabel I, queen of Castile, died. Luis de Granada was born Luis de Sarria to a poor Galician family; his father died when he was five years old. At age twenty-one, Luis de Granada entered the Dominican monastery in Santa Cruz of Granada. He studied in the Colegio de San Gregorio in Valladolid (Huerga 27). Fray Luis exhorted commoners to a life of piety and service to Christ; and he penned his sermons in Spanish, not Latin, so they might understand him (J. Moore 316). Luis de Granada's influence extended beyond Spain into the Hispanophone Caribbean and South America. Rolena Adorno points out that Guamán Poma de Ayala—a seventeenth-century Quechan writer—cited Fray Luis de Granada's *Memorial de la vida cristiana* six times in his *Nueva corónica y buen gobierno* (57). A brief foray into Luis de Granada's ideas about prayer will help to clarify his influence on Manzano's religious poetry. Below, I cite from his *Libro de oración y meditación* (Book of Prayer and Meditation).

Oracion es subir el ánima sobre sí, y sobre todo lo criado, y juntarse con Dios, y engolfarse en aquel piélago de infinita suavidad y amor. Oracion es salir el ánima á recibir á Dios cuando viene á ella, y traerlo á sí como á su nido, y aposentarlo en sí como en su templo, y allí poseerlo, y amarlo, y gozarlo. Oracion es estar el ánima en presencia de Dios, y Dios en presencia della, mirando él á ella, con ojos de misericordia, y ella á él con ojos de humildad; la cual vista es de mayor virtud y fecundidad que la de todos los aspectos de las estrellas y planetas del cielo (Luis de Granada, *Obras* 161).

(Prayer is raising the soul above itself, and above all creation, and to join with God, and to become engulfed in that ocean of infinite kindness and love. Prayer is leaving the soul to receive God when he comes, and bring him to your nest, to make him at home as if he were in his temple, and in that temple to possess him, to love him, and to enjoy him. Prayer is when the soul is in the presence of God, and God in the presence of the soul, he looks upon the soul with merciful eyes, and the soul gazes at him with humility; such a gaze is more virtuous and fecund then all of the celestial stars and planets.)

In the *Book of Prayer and Meditation*, Fray Luis de Granada described prayer as levitation, as lifting one's soul above all creation to become one with God. Union with the Christian God unraveled a series of spiritual potentialities: the soul could "become engulfed" in "infinite kindness and love," and the devout could encounter God directly. The Spanish expression "engolfarse en piélago" (to become engulfed in that ocean) implies an expanse, a sea of *agape* love whose divine resources cannot be exhausted. Such language depicts the Christian God as the embodiment of love; as the antithesis of the *deus otiosus* that abandoned humanity after bringing the world into existence.[21] For Luis de Granada, God is not only present but also active in the material world. The believer's body is a temple where he may enjoy God and even possess him. The Spanish verb *poseer* has erotic undertones. *Poseer* (to possesses) means to consummate or make perfect an amorous relationship through sexual intercourse. It is coitus that makes the marital union complete, thus perfecting it in the eyes of the Church. Luis de Granada's writings imply an erotic encounter between God and man; to achieve the perfect union with God, one must pierce deep into his being. Even so, devout Catholics had certain obligations if they were to "receive God when he comes." The aforementioned passage explained that devotees had to display humility when their souls were in the presence of God. If Catholics expressed humility before God, God would look upon them with merciful eyes.

Luis de Granada's influence on "Oda a La Religión" manifests in Manzano's emphasis on levitation, the soul, and the rejection of "idle pursuits." The poetic "I" raises his tearful visage to God as his soul ascends to heaven, leaving his tormented body. As Julio Ramos states, Manzano refashioned himself as a sentimental subject, and his self-portrait deconstructed the image of the slave as "un fardo que no siente" (an unfeeling thing). For Ramos, Manzano mastered the language of subjectivity in the melancholy of lyricism (314). Manzano mused: "The soul I feel fleeing my being / Yielding to its Maker." The first couple of stanzas underscore the importance of feeling as part of religious experience. Manzano surrenders his soul to his Creator and in that way privileges the spiritual realm and the experience of God above and beyond the pleasures of the created world. In many respects Luis de Granada's ideas about prayer as an intimate union with God must have appealed to Manzano, who sought to achieve freedom from a multitude of sufferings. Even though Manzano abandoned "idle pursuits," "Oda a La Religión" suggests that God had not yet looked upon him with mercy, because he had not redeemed him from slavery.

Cuban slavery is the subtext of "Oda a La Religión." Manzano adopted the slavery-to-freedom narrative of biblical Israel as an analogy for the subjugation of Cubans of African descent. As in the book of Exodus, the Old Testament God delivers his chosen people from slavery and guides them into the promised land, where they are free to worship him. Manzano relished the idea of spiritual union with God, comparable to the intimacy that Fray Luis de Granada described, but his immediate political concern was emancipation from slavery.

En niebla sepultado
El pueblo de Israel te suspiraba,
Cuando ya se inspiraba
A tu poder el triunfo destinado
Y en la sangre teñida del cordero
Se alzó tu manto por el orbe entero. (Manzano, *Esclavo poeta* 189)

(Obscured in fog
The people of Israel yearned,
Once inspired
By your power [that] predestined triumph
And in the bloodstained lamb
Your canopy raised up [over] the entire globe.)

Manzano's engagement with the Old and New Testaments signal that blood sacrifice—either animal sacrifice or that of Christ crucified—makes salvation possible. In the antebellum United States, enslaved African Americans often linked the captivity of the ancient Israelites to their own plight and struggled for the day that God would deliver his chosen people. Lawrence Levine says that African American spirituals were the product of "improvisational communal consciousness" that forged new songs from "pre-existing bits of old songs" with novel tunes and lyrics. In this way, they made use of what they knew of Old Testament accounts to construct a narrative about their own liberation (23, 29). David Howard-Pitney says the African American jeremiad was a rhetorical variant of the Puritans' lament, and it forewarned white society of the divine verdict to befall them if slavery was not abolished. Fredrick Douglass's invective, for example, condemned slavery as the desecration of the US democratic ideal (49–50). Plácido, a free African-descended poet, had more in common with the African American jeremiad than Manzano. Plácido prophesied condemnation for the Spanish Empire if the Queen did not liberate Cuba. The vitriol of his most revolutionary poems, "El juramento" (The Oath), "La profecía de Cuba a España" (The Prophecy from Cuba to Spain), and "¡Habaneros Libertad!" (Havana Liberty!) bear this out. But Manzano's jeremiad in poetry represented a struggle with the Christian God himself, where the inaction of the divine Father embittered the poet held in perpetual bondage. The rhetorical shift from sacred rapture to ardent protest is borne out in two verses: "Por qué me deja do el pecado nace / y no contigo que a la gloria pase" (Why do you leave me where sin is born / And not carry me with you up to Glory?) (Manzano, *Esclavo poeta* 190). Manzano reimagined his relationship to the Christian God through Fray Luis de Granada's sermons, but the intimacy he achieved did not ensure freedom from slavery.

Juan Francisco Manzano critiqued the Christian redemptive narrative in "La Esclava ausente" (The Absent Slave Woman), an 1823 poem wherein the author assumed the voice of an enslaved Afro-Caribbean woman. "La esclava ausente" was published posthumously; it remained virtually unavailable to readers for nearly 171 years after it was written. In 1991 Adriana Lewis Galanes uncovered Manzano's antislavery poetry in the National Library of Madrid, presenting it for the first time to a modern scholarly public. William Luis later reissued some of these poems in 1994 and also published other antislavery poetry after conducting archival research at Yale University. Galanes mused that Manzano may have adopted a feminine persona in "La esclava ausente" for dramatic effect or that his female lover may have written the poem herself (102–103). But Moroccan critic Abdeslam Azougarh resolved that literary conundrum when he determined that the poem constituted part of a dossier of writings that Domingo del Monte delivered to Richard Robert Madden for publication in England (36–37). Madden did not include this poem in his 1840 translation of the autobiography, in all likelihood because the erotic subtext might have disquieted the Victorian readership he sought to persuade and effectively threaten the abolitionist cause.

In my view, Manzano employed the black female character in "La esclava ausente" to give voice to the pain, shame, and powerlessness that he experienced when he was raped on the Matanzas plantation. Manzano assumed the voice of an enslaved black female whose Christian love relationship with her male partner was imperiled by the owner's decree to separate the couple. The poem is a sui generis depiction of the black Catholic subject whose conception of love is erotic yet sacred, chaste but passionate. The black female persona commands discursive space, crafting an appeal to the white slaveholder that leaves him no room for rejoinder, riposte, or revenge. Manzano ascribed an eroticism to the female speaker that was largely absent in his work and was anathema to virginal notions of the white female body epitomized by the Iberian cult of the Virgin Mary (Marianism). The anonymous black character gives language to her love: variously described as "amor más puro" (the purest love), "verdadero amor" (true love), "amar tiernamente" (tenderly love), "deseos" (desires), "ardor de tu fuego" (the ardor of your fire), and perhaps most cogently as "esta llama que me alienta" (this flame that invigorates) (Manzano, *Autobiografía* 170, 172). If it were not for the poetic allusion to holy matrimony—that is, "dos almas finas" (two fine souls) that "La muerte sola dividirlos puede" (death alone can divide them)—the erotic appeal of the captive woman might be deemed an impurity (Manzano, *Autobiografía* 170–171).

Manzano's depiction of the enslaved body as a gendered domain gave voice to what Lorna Williams referred to as "the unspeakable" in early Cuban narrative (20). That colonial slave codes forbade slaveholders to sell African women into prostitution was proof that white men raped enslaved black women. Consequently, the ameliorative measures of the *Código Negro Español* (1789) were designed to chastise slaveholders who raped black women or prostituted them (Shepherd 43).[22] The fictive black woman in "La esclava ausente" implies that the justification for white male authority rested within a legal framework that was cloaked in violence.

Pues todos los placeres se acibaran
Cuando la dulce libertad no media . . .
¿Qué pudo un juramento firme, eterno?
¿Qué la constancia y fe; qué la firmeza
Si de un poder *el bárbaro precepto*
Tenaz hoy burla todas tus promesas? (original emphasis, Manzano,
    *Autobiografía* 171)

[ . . . ]

Esta mano, este pecho, este mi todo
Es de mi bien: mi boca lo confiesa.
Déjame unir a él, que así lo exigen
Religión, amor, naturaleza.
Si la suerte te ha hecho *Señor mío,*
¿Son por ventura tuya mis potencias?
Si en tu poder, hoy tienes mi albedrío,
Esta mi vida y alma a caso es vuestra? . . . (original emphasis; Manzano,
    *Autobiografía* 172–173)

(But all the pleasures are embittered
When liberty does not intercede . . .

What might a vow firm and eternal do?
What of steadfastness and faith; what of firmness
If the power of *the barbarous precept*
Tenaciously mocks all your vows?

[ ... ]

This hand, this bosom, this is my all
It is my well-being: my mouth professes thus.
Let me be united to him, as
Religion, Love, Nature commands.
If fate has made you *my Lord*,
Are my powers conceivably yours?
If in your power, today you have my will,
Is my life and soul also yours?)

The black Cuban woman dramatizes a dispute between two men, the man she loves and the man who owns her legally. The slaveholder's illicit desire for his black chambermaid made a mockery of holy matrimony, because his power to compel her imperiled a relationship that enjoyed the sanction of the Church. In 1804 the Spanish crown mandated rural estates to purchase African women alone as captives to correct the gender imbalance on plantations; but those measures were never enforced (Finch, "Scandalous" 112, 114, 127). The slave codes of 1789 and 1842 mandated protections for the nuclear family and for expectant mothers as well as adequate shelter for family units (Finch, "Scandalous" 114, 115). But Manzano insisted that the intrinsic contradictions of the *bárbaro precepto* (barbarous precept) made the fulfillment of marital vows impossible for women of African descent. The "constancia y fe" (constancy and faith) of "un juramento firme, eterno" (a firm and eternal vow) (Manzano, *Autobiografía* 171) could not negate white male property rights. The bird in flight is an Afrodiasporic freedom symbol, an enviable creature that although incapable of reason enjoys a greater measure of liberty than the enslaved woman. This recurring trope—which also appeared in "Un sueño. A mi segundo hermano," "La visión del poeta," and in the autobiography—appropriated the bird as a metaphor for freedom. The bird is "Sueltos de leyes (para mí tan duras!)" (Loose from laws (so harsh to me!). The black captive woman does not make claims to the much-heralded ameliorative measures of Spanish law; rather, she appeals to "el derecho de amar" (The right to love) as a "principio inviolable" (inviolable principle) of the divine natural order (Manzano, *Autobiografía* 171–172).

The black woman's claims to her own body and to the irreversible laws of nature depict religious personhood as a sacred covenant between husband and wife, divine love and erotic desire, and women and nature. Since the black woman exercises rhetorical force, she is able to collapse the dichotomy between the sacred and the profane in Catholicism and claim free will, in spite of her physical captivity. The emphasis on black sentience and desire suggests that although she is enslaved, the female persona exercises what Omise'eke Natasha Tinsley has termed "erotic autonomy." The Afro-Caribbean woman intervenes into an otherwise exploitative history of sexual labor in plantation societies (20). Her religious devotion and righteousness notwithstanding, the Christian God does not redeem the enslaved female from "sufrir sus tormentos me condenan" (suffering those torments that condemn me) (Manzano, *Autobiografía* 174).

In 1841 "A Jesús en la cruz" appeared on Good Friday in *Diario de la Habana* alongside other poems with similar titles: "La muerte de Jesus" by Ramón Vélez and "A la muerte de Jesus" by F. Orgaz. "A Jesús en la cruz" is comparable to the passion poems that Ramón Vélez and F. Orgaz composed, with one important caveat. Manzano transformed an ode to the suffering Christ into a jeremiad much like his other religious poetry. In "A Jesús en la cruz," the people of Israel again intone praises to the Christian God. The blood sacrifice of Christ crucified is the fulfillment of prophetic tradition, and it is a necessary atonement for human transgressions. Manzano wrote: "Asi cuanto llena á el mundo todo / Con tu muerte y pasion fue redimido, / El hombre de las garras arrancado / Del infernal poder ya no es perdido" (In that way the whole world is filled. / By your death and passion was redeemed, / Man from the claws snatched / Of hellish power he is no longer adrift).[23] But as in "Oda a La Religión," the Omnipotent Christian God does not redeem the African-descended poet from the "infernal poder" (hellish power) of slave society. Manzano's post-manumission vision in "A Jesús en la cruz" is a dystopia.

Y porque queda piedra sobre piedra
Cuando te privan de vital aliento!. . . . .
¡Por qué la muerte tu piedad no arredra
Cuando se emplaza tan terrible intento!. . . . .
¡Por qué dócil y fácil cual la yedra
A quien arrolla en su torrente el viento.
Te dejas abatir de gente impia
A quien solo tu aliento abrasaria!

[ . . . ]

Signo de redencion, emblema mudo
De caridad, é inagotable fuente,
Donde encuentra el cristiano cuanto pudo
De su inmensa hacedor su escelsa mente;
A tí por siempre indisoluble nudo

Me lleve unido, y el amor ardiente
Con que probaste al hombre tu ternura
Mis juicios guie á tu eterna ventura.[24]

(And why does stone lie upon stone
When they deprive you of life-giving breath!.....
Why doesn't your piety frighten Death
When they consign such terrible intent?!.....
Why docile and defenseless like the ivy plant
Which is strewn by torrential winds.
You let yourself be overcome by irreverent people
Whom your very breath would scorch!

[ . . . ]

Sign of redemption, mute symbol
Of charity, and infinite fountain,
Where Christians find all that they can
From their immense Creator, the sublime mind;
To you the always indestructible bond
Take me joined together, and the ardent love
With which you proved to Man your tenderness
My judgment shows the way to your eternal felicity.)

The Son of God is not a redemptive figure in this poem; rather, Manzano portrayed Jesus Christ as a vacuous symbol, unable or perhaps unwilling to rescue black Cubans from slavery. Such a statement might be deemed heretical if not for the lyrical play on words. Christ is a symbol of charity that does not protest crucifixion at the hands of Roman soldiers. But his silence might also imply an unmerciful response to the cries of black misery. Manzano employed nature metaphors (such as the ivy plant) commonly associated with femininity to depict crucifixion as a violation of masculinity. Christ is "dócil y fácil como la yedra" (docile and defenseless like the ivy plant). Rather than portraying the blood of Christ for its sacred and redemptive qualities, Manzano suggested that Christ crucified lay prostrate like the ivy. As Liza Bakewell points out, blood and guts are a symbol of sacrifice in Spanish America, as evidenced by the blood of Christ and that of war heroes (174). Perhaps most appallingly, Christ was submissive in the face of physical violence and permitted other men to humiliate him. These humiliations were comparable to that which Manzano had grieved in his flesh. What drove Manzano's lyrical protest was the collapse of his own corporeal schema and the multiple ways in which slavery had deprived of him cultural power both symbolic and real.

In a letter addressed to Domingo del Monte dating from October 16, 1834, Manzano articulated a belief that suffering was good for the soul. He wrote:

> . . . mucho suspiro pero me consuelo cuando considero que Dios me ha dado las desgrasias, y tambien una alma que me ase superior a algunos que sin el menor cuidado se rien de mi. (Manzano, *Obras* 78).

> (I yearn for many things, but I console myself when I consider that God has given me this disgrace, and also a soul that makes me superior to others that without the slightest care mock me.)

In the 1834 letter, Manzano contended that his perseverance in the face of disgrace attested to the superiority of his Christian soul. And though this letter does not mention Christ by name, the implication is clear. As I have already established, suffering was an unavoidable part of Manzano's life as an enslaved person of African descent. But Manzano's "soul that makes me superior," which enabled him to endure suffering mustn't be confused with a desire to suffer for Christ, as an expression of the *imitatio Christi* of Spanish mysticism. Manzano reasoned that del Monte, and perhaps some of his white critics, might acknowledge his humanity if he could persuade them that his soul was comparable to that of Christ. Thus, his self-image as an enslaved poet struggling justly for his freedom was of great importance to him. In another letter to del Monte dating from 1835, Manzano wrote: "mi esposa ni sm. me amaran si yo no fuera hombre de bien" (neither my wife nor Your Grace would love me if I were not a good man) (Manzano, *Obras* 87). The expression "good man" reveals Manzano's rhetorical need to convince his white readership (and, apparently, his wife) of his blamelessness. But there is no evidence that he believed that self-inflicted pain was a desirable state of being, which—as Spanish mystics claimed—would enable believers to circumvent the conscious mind and commune in ecstasy with God. Simone Weil, a modern French mystic, explained the problem of suffering thus: "the extreme greatness of Christianity lies in the fact that it does not seek a supernatural remedy for suffering, but a supernatural use for suffering" (Flynn, "Spiritual Uses" 258). Such a mystical theology of suffering was untenable, perhaps even absurd, to Manzano. After all, Manzano's adolescence was brimming with memories of turbulence, uncertainty, and pain: he suffered thrashings, he was placed in the stocks and in the slave infirmary, and his mistress even starved him. Remaining on the plantation meant inflicting pain upon himself. For Manzano freedom constituted the absence of suffering. Therefore, Manzano's escape from the slave labor camp circa 1817 represented his rejection of suffering as a path to intimate knowledge about God.

Manzano did not romanticize the crucifixion as did José Jacinto Milanés's "En la muerte de nuestro Señor Jesucristo" (In the Death of Our Lord Jesus

Christ), where the poetic "I" is moved to contrition because of his sins (Milanés 349).[25] But for Manzano, the death of Christ did not prompt a penitent response. Manzano's disavowal of Christ crucified represented a rupture with the docility of the good mulatto slave and is resonant with a transformation in his self-image that had occurred nearly thirty years prior.

Manzano labored to redeem himself from the girl child/roguish Negro dichotomy that his mistress had imposed upon him. He was in search of a new sort of African-descended masculinity. By identifying as a Catholic house slave, Manzano had attempted to escape a sense of nothingness. But the mulatto Catholic self-image had failed him. So, Manzano strove to articulate this new sense of self through the idiom of masculinity. I think "A Jesús en la cruz" is an allusion to the slave narrative where crucifixion becomes analogous with physical abuse, public humiliation, and even sexual assault. In a word, crucifixion meant the loss of masculinity. With his hands and feet fastened to a wooden plank, Jesus Christ was a passive man on the cross. Christ crucified was reminiscent of the moment when Manzano was utterly powerless and the administrator raped him. But whereas Christ's blood redeemed humanity from sin and transformed him into a heroic figure, Manzano's bleeding connoted weakness and moral degradation.

Manzano asserted his masculinity in three ways: he defended his mother vigorously, he fled the plantation to save himself (and salvage what remained of his honor), and he labored to secure his brother's freedom. Manzano disavowed the Lamb of God, and he embraced the Lion of the Tribe of Judah, which signaled a rupture in the narrative of the faithful *slave*, because the author forsook crucified Christ as an appropriate symbol for his affliction. Manzano recalled the violence inflicted upon his mother when she tried to spare him yet another whipping at the hands of the overseers.

S^or. Silbestre q^e. era el nombre del joben malloral este condusiendome p^a. el sepo se encontró con mi madre q^e. siguiendo los impulsos de su corazon vino a acabar de colmar mis infortunios ella al berme quiso preguntarme q^e. abia hecho cuando el malloral imponiendole silensio se lo quiso estorbar [ . . . ] lebanto la mano y dió a mi madre con el manatí este golpe lo yo sentí mi corazon dar un grito y convertirme de manso cordero en un leon todo fue una cosa [ . . . ] y me le tiré en sima con dientes y manos cuantas patadas manatiazos y de mas golpes q^e. llebé se puede considerar y mi madre y yo fuimos condusidos y puesto en un mismo lugar . . . (Manzano, *Autobiografía* 311–312).

(Mr. Silvestre, which was the name of the young overseer that was carrying me off to the stocks [when] I encountered my mother who following the impulses of her heart, came to put an end to my misfortune. Seeing me, she wanted to ask what I had done when the overseer imposing silence, wanted to hinder her [ . . . ] He raised his hand and struck my mother with the whip. That whipping

I felt in my heart crying out and being transformed from meek lamb to a lion that was everything [ . . . ] I leaped on top of him with my teeth and fists and kicking and more blows than you can imagine. And my mother and I were both carried off and put in the same place.)

This is an especially appalling scene, since María de Pilar—a much-respected domestic servant—had never before the death of her husband been beaten. I believe the shift in gender roles explains the intensity, immediacy, and violence of Manzano's response. For Manzano, the adolescent, the defense of María de Pilar was a vindication of what remained of the familial arrangement. By defending his widowed mother, Manzano acted as a surrogate for his deceased father and as a would-be protector of his younger brothers Florencio and Fernando (Manzano, *Autobiografía* 314). The text portrays the Christ as a paradox: he is both conquering lion and meek lamb. This moment constitutes a rhetorical shift for the author, a rupture with Christian martyrdom that expected slaves to suffer without providing them a viable path to redemption. Manzano's words in the slave narrative are far removed from the June 1835 letter where he insisted that del Monte "consideradme un martir y allareis que los infinitos azotes que ha mutilado mis carnes [ . . . ] jamas embiliseran a vuestro afectisimo siervo" (consider me a martyr; and you will find that the infinite lashes that have mutilated my flesh [ . . . ] never tarnished your fond servant) (Manzano, *Autobiografía* 215). If we consider that Manzano maintained written correspondence with del Monte while writing his slave narrative, then another reading surfaces. Though Christian martyrdom was no longer the metaphor of Manzano's emancipatory struggle, it remained a useful idiom to convince his benefactor that he was worthy of mercy. However, the restoration of mutilated flesh—language imbued with religious and erotic meaning—would be inconceivable unless the poet procured the power to emancipate himself. Subsequent to his mother's demise, the faithful mulatto persona was no longer a viable construct, "desde el momento en qe. perdí la alhagueña ilusion de mi esperanza ya no era un esclavo fiel me combertí de manso cordero en la criatura mas despresia [ . . . ] solo meditaba en mi fuga" (from the moment I lost the promising illusion of my hope, I was no longer a faithful slave. I was converted from meek lamb into the most despicable creature imaginable . . .) (Manzano, *Autobiografía* 333). Manzano's repudiation of Christian redemption through blood sacrifice, long suffering and meekness created space for him to construct a sense of self rooted in principles of defiance, self-assertion, and familial responsibility.

## Conclusion

Juan Francisco Manzano's Catholic poetry exposed the racial confines of the Christian redemption narrative. Even if Manzano professed allegiance

to the Church under interrogation in 1844 for his involvement in an anticolonial movement, his poetry and autobiography challenged the sacred tenets
of blood sacrifice and redemptive suffering. In "A Jesús en la cruz" and "Oda a
La Religión," blood sacrifice does not redeem the African-descended subject,
because Christianity does not liberate the captive body from a society "where
sin is born." Christ crucified represented a loss of agency and virility likened
only to feminization. In 1841 Manzano was a prominent member of the free
black literati; thus, the injured and bludgeoned body of Christ crucified was a
countersign to the emancipatory politics he embraced. Crucifixion was more
than a rhetorical device for the author; it constituted a violation, an assault of
a different sort that might mortify and vanquish the resolve of enslaved black
men. I have tried to demonstrate that the Lamb to Lion transformation did
not signify salvation for Manzano, but rather represented a sustained effort to
procure power to liberate himself. This counter-signification of identity represented a departure from biblical martyrdom, where the Hebrew captive awaited
redemption at the hands of an Omnipotent God.

The black woman in "La esclava ausente" (1823) is a metaphor, and she was
one of the first depiction of black religious subjectivity in Cuban literary history. Within the sacred confines of marital union, Manzano endowed the fictive
woman with sexual desire so that hetero-eroticism might bespeak the enduring
conflict between the body as vessel and the body as chattel. Religious subjectivity is unbound by the spirit/flesh dichotomy intrinsic to Catholic dogma so
that the black woman exists in harmony with nature and carnal desire. Church
dogma imagined the body as an unclean thing, predisposed to filth and perver-
sion and in desperate need of atonement to become a vessel of the Holy Spirit.
But Christian doctrine about the flesh—particularly dogma regarding black
flesh—legitimized the degradation and perpetual enslavement of Africans.
The black woman reclaims the divinity of dark flesh by collapsing the dichotomy. Perhaps the most brilliant thing about "La esclava ausente" is its ability
to explore Audre Lorde's distinction between the erotic and the pornographic:
"But pornography is a direct denial of the power of the erotic; for it represents
the suppression of true feeling. Pornography emphasizes sensation without
feeling" (54). I read Manzano's oak tree metaphor in this light. The oak tree
was double entendre; it represented the constancy of a decade of wedded bliss
that was ruptured by the phallic metaphor, its second and somewhat absconded
meaning. Ironically, the metaphor is unstable, because the hardening of the tree
suggests disparate realities: it is a symbol for the erect penis of the slave master
and an analogy for the black woman's resistance to rape, which Manzano appro-
priately coded as "all violence." Reminiscent of the poet himself, the bonds-
woman "with vigor resists all violence" in a rhetorical confrontation with the
slaveholder to preserve the rights that "Religion, Love and Nature" assure her
(Manzano, *Autobiografía* 172–173).

Manzano's investment in mulatto identity politics could not liberate him from blackness. Manzano entered into crisis because the slaveholder imposed every act of violence imaginable to make him into her little mulatto. In *Black Skin, White Masks*, Frantz Fanon asserts that the Caribbean mulatto not only disdains blackness but also professes whiteness to "save the race" and sever himself from the collective dark body (45–47, 55). Moreover, Manzano rejected Christ crucified because the martyr concept would not empower black liberation. The colonial state constructed a system of white supremacy premised on the racism of medieval Spain so that blackness would yield to white hegemony. In order to emancipate himself, Manzano would have to mend a fractured self with religio-cultural resources cut from another cloth.

## CHAPTER THREE

# Myth of the Christian Poet

The Death, Resurrection, and Redemption of Plácido

> . . . palabras hinchadas, resonantes, disparatadas,
> huecas—¡palabras, palabras, palabras!—siendo lo
> peor que a menudo ignora su significado.
>
> MANUEL SANGUILY'S CRITIQUE OF PLÁCIDO'S POETRY

## The History of a Literary Controversy

In 1894 Manuel Sanguily disputed the aesthetic merit of Cuba's most prolific poet: Gabriel de la Concepción Valdés (also known as Plácido). Sanguily questioned Plácido's place in an emerging Cuban literary tradition by degrading his rhymes as simple, grammatically unsound, and bereft of political ideas. He decried the popular image of Plácido as "The Cuban Pindar," whose "Homeric" verse crowned him as a black poet concerned with the destiny of the enslaved and downtrodden ("Un improvisador cubano" 161, 166).[1] In fact, as far as Sanguily was concerned, Plácido wasn't *black* at all. Sanguily's essays in *Hojas literarias* refuted Plácido's putative blackness by reminding his readership that the poet was born of a Spanish woman in 1809 that had given birth to a fair-skinned mulatto. In Sanguily's version of events, Plácido had disregarded the predicament of black Cubans, he had relished life as a mulatto, and he had never condemned the institution of slavery ("Otra vez Plácido" 188). Sanguily attributed broad public admiration of the poet to a general ignorance of literary conventions and credited Plácido's fame to his untimely death at the hands of Spanish authorities in 1844. Sanguily insisted that Plácido was a tragic mulatto whose execution at the hands of the colonial government—not the debatable merit of his poetry—justified an otherwise indefensible martyrdom ("Un improvisador cubano" 160). With precious few exceptions, Sanguily regarded Plácido's poems as illogical, hollow, nonsense language worthy of ridicule ("Un improvisador cubano" 161, 166).[2]

A marble statue of Plácido in Matanzas by Cuban sculptor Rodulfo Tardo.

Manuel Sanguily was a formidable orator and affluent white landowner who
served as an officer in the Ten Years War for Cuban Independence (Paquette 5).
Sanguily bristled at a black Cuban newspaper's portrayal of Plácido as an illustrious national figure and, above all else, as "EL IDOLO DE LOS CUBANOS
NEGROS" (THE IDOL OF BLACK CUBANS) (Sanguily, "Otra vez Plácido"
187).[3] Cuban debates about Plácido typically reproduced long-standing animosi-
ties between blacks and whites. Black Cubans demanded that a statue be erected
in commemoration of Plácido (Paquette 4), and they admonished whites not
to tarnish "*el nombre glorioso de Plácido*" (the glorious name of Plácido), which
they likened to that of Sanguily's mentor José de la Luz y Caballero (Sanguily,
"Otra vez Plácido" 187, original emphasis,).[4] For many black Cubans, Plácido
was a proto-martyr of Cuban independence, and an intellectual whose opposition to the proslavery regime in 1844 was justified (Horrego Estuch, *Juan
Gualberto* 71). The impassioned debate between Sanguily and the black newspaper *La Igualdad* proved that half a century after the government had executed
Plácido, his literature continued to be disputed terrain upon which black and
white intellectuals sought to define Cuban culture from rival vantage points.

It is no wonder that critics have wrestled with Plácido's legacy, often espousing competing narratives to illustrate his significance within Cuban cultural history. When the Spanish government executed Plácido in 1844 as the architect of
"la conspiracion proyectada por la gente de color . . . para el esterminio . . . de

poblacion blanca" (the conspiracy devised by people of color . . . to exterminate
. . . the white population), his racial politics and religious loyalties became a
point of contention among historians.[5] The military tribunal not only convicted
Plácido of conspiring to depose the regime but also condemned him for an
unspeakable crime: the utter annihilation of the white race. Plácido's conspiracy
was regarded as a crime against the natural order of things. The execution notice
published in Matanzas the day Plácido was put to death asserted as much:

> Gabriel de la Concepcion Valdes conocido por Plácido [ . . . ] convencidos del
> horrendo crímen de conspiracion contra la raza blanca, promoviendo rebeli-
> ones en las dotaciones de algunas fincas, con el pernicioso objeto de disolver la
> debida sumision que en todas ellas ha reinado siempre.[6]

> (Gabriel de la Concepción Valdés known as Plácido [ . . . ] persuaded of the
> horrendous crime of conspiracy against the white race, promoting rebellions
> among the blacks on certain plantations with the pernicious objective of dis-
> solving the rightful submission that has always governed all plantations.)

Plácido provoked antislavery insurrections on a number of plantations in
order to, as the government narrative claimed, dissolve "the rightful submission that has always governed them." Africans would destroy their white masters and become sovereigns of their own destinies. Plácido's ignominious past
and his execution on charges of racial conspiracy negated his public persona as
a mulatto that had happily assimilated into Hispano-Catholic literary culture.
Scholars have grappled with this very conundrum for more than a century. Why
would the mulatto writer refuse to assimilate into the white supremacist order
that favored individuals of a lighter hue? And what would motivate him to
identify so closely with the plight of enslaved blacks, and to risk his life to institute an African-descended governing structure in the tradition of the Haitian
Revolution (1791–1804)? That Plácido was a person of African and European
ancestry who performed multiple religious customs and weaved in and out of
black and white society may explain the enduring debate regarding his legacy.

Plácido was born Diego Gabriel de la Concepción Valdés in Havana, Cuba,
in 1809 to a Spanish mother and a mixed-race father said to be a person of
one-quarter African ancestry (quadroon) (Horrego Estuch, *Plácido: el poeta*
71). Plácido was abandoned at birth and left at the Casa de Beneficencia y
Maternidad de la Habana (House of Beneficence and Motherhood), a Catholic
orphanage. The presbyter baptized him as an infant, and according to some
biographers, the child was given the priest's surname, Valdés. Although he
was a person of named and claimed African ancestry, Plácido's baptismal
records described him as *al parecer blanco*, that is, white in appearance (Cué,
*Plácido: El poeta* 15, 18–19). Notwithstanding the social value ascribed to his

whitish complexion, Plácido did not pass for white. Some sources claim that Diego Ferrer Matoso, Plácido's father, rescued him from the Catholic orphanage so that the child's black grandmother might raise him (Cué, *Plácido: El poeta* 18; Hostos 213, Nwankwo 97). Plácido grew up in Havana within African-descended communities, presumably in the extramural neighborhoods of the early nineteenth century, where he set down social, cultural, and religious roots. Little is known of his father, Diego Ferrer Matoso, except that as a hairdresser, he was part of an emergent free urban professional class. Ferrer Matoso apparently played a nominal role in rearing his son. But Plácido's mother, Concepción Vázquez, was a Spanish woman with whom the poet maintained a strong familial bond well into adulthood.[7] Though he did not publish until 1834—more than ten years after his counterpart Juan Francisco Manzano—Plácido became the most prolific poet and celebrated improvisator throughout the island. There is no other Cuban poet, black or white, that published more than Plácido in the nineteenth century. In merely ten years, he wrote, extemporized, and published nearly seven hundred poems and disseminated them in several compilations and newspapers all over Cuba. I engage something that critics have struggled to resolve for well over a century: Plácido's racial politics and his relationship to the Catholic Church.

Plácido composed a body of work that is difficult to classify or otherwise define. Though he often wrote on uncontroversial themes—such as sentimental poetry, the pastoral idyll, and celebratory verse in honor of his wealthy patronage—his political poems were anticolonial, and that poetry has complicated his standing in Cuban cultural history. This presents a series of questions for his observers. Which of Plácido's poems is the reader to believe: odes to the queen of Spain or revolutionary poems decrying tyranny? Do we privilege poems in praise of white aristocrats or should we focus on racial satire that lampoons a desire to become white in African-descended communities? Which are a truer reflection of the poet's worldview: *cantos* in honor of the Catholic Church or poetry that insinuates African Cuban ritual? If read without critical distance—as I believe was the case with Sanguily—Plácido's nearly seven hundred poems give the appearance of a disjointed mishmash best relegated to an inglorious past. But as a black Cuban poet in a slave colony, Plácido had to contend with the symbolic practices of Hispano-Catholic society.

One critic has remarked that Plácido and Manzano's publication of romantic poetry about Afro-Caribbean women represented the introduction of a subversive aesthetic in Caribbean literature (Williams, *Charcoal* 24–25). While this aesthetic innovation was significant, Plácido's love poems intimate very little about his racial identity and will not be treated here.[8] To be sure, racial self-portraiture is infrequent in Plácido's poetry, letters, and court testimony that I have been made privy to. Not until his arrest in 1844 as an alleged conspirator did Plácido claim belonging—at least in writing—to the *clase de pardos y morenos* (class of free blacks and mulattoes). Plácido maintained that he was a mulatto in order to disassociate himself from enslaved blacks that had implicated him in the insurgency (Cué, *Plácido: El poeta* 311–312). Besides, he needed to garner favor with the military regime in an eleventh-hour effort to save himself. Plácido performed his racial and religious identity on a stage of someone else's making. Comparable to other colonized authors, he negotiated the space between black writer as intellectual and black writer as sycophant. Jill Lane explains that there is little difference between imitation and creation, because both rely on the success or failure of a given performance (13). Performance theory contends that racial and gendered identities are the products of actions that were intended to produce a series of effects in the social world. Performative acts consolidate an impression about identity (Butler). Consequently, racial identities may be considered real or be spurned as mimicry depending upon the audience in attendance, the stage in question, and the anticipated outcome of the performance.

Plácido practiced Catholicism and he published poems attesting to his faith. Plácido was baptized as an infant, he attended mass, he presumably married in the Church, and he received the last rites on his death bed. But his Catholic poetry did not represent the sum total of his religious identity. (African-inspired spirituality as a subtext in his poetry is examined in chapter five.) Plácido produced art under the aegis of an authoritarian regime that censored literature contradicting the Holy Faith.[9] On occasion, he wrote sacred poetry to divert attention from his political activities. Consequently, I analyze his religious poetry as a statement of faith as well as a performance of respectability that ensured he remained in good standing with the priesthood. In this chapter, I contrast Plácido's religious poetry with his racial satire to analyze the competing narratives that emerge within his body of work. Plácido deconstructed whiteness ideology in his caricature of the mulatto that wants to be white. But even as he critiqued the ideology of white supremacy, he praised the sanctity of the Catholic Church. In fact, Plácido proved reluctant to critique the Church. His silence regarding Catholic racial ideology is significant, because Catholic theology labeled Africans "slaves of the Devil" (Barreras, 142–143) and defended slavery as a means to salvation (Rivera-Pagán 28–29). Therefore, I contend that his Catholic self-portrait was largely a politically motivated representation that persuaded his biographers to embrace an otherwise revolutionary figure in early stages of Cuban canon formation.

### White in Appearance Alone: The Making and Unmaking of a Mulatto Poet

Nearly two decades before Plácido appeared on the Cuban literary scene, blackface performance had already taken theatergoers by storm. Cuban blackface known as *teatro bufo* became the most popular theatrical genre in nineteenth-century Cuba (R. Moore 26). The pejorative representation of black men as boorish, uncouth, and reckless buffoons was the work of white authors that promoted the notion of *black as object*.[10] In 1812 Cuban actor Francisco Covarrubias (1775–1850) performed *El negrito* (The Little Black), the first minstrel show on the island. Covarrubias's first minstrel show was a "dialogue between negritos" that purported to represent how Africans sang and danced in their own countries (Lane 29). Covarrubias adapted the *sainete*—a one-act comic sketch popular in Spain and Latin America in the late 1700s—to entertain the Havana public (Lane 24). And his work gave birth to impersonators. The white Cuban actor continued to perform in blackface throughout his fifty-year career in the idiosyncratic Spanish spoken by captive Africans known as *bozal*. *Bozal* also means "muzzle" in Spanish, and it was a term designating recently arrived Africans that had not been acculturated into Hispano-Catholic slave society. In 1815 Covarrubias performed another blackface show, entitled *El desengaño feliz o el negrito* (The Happy Realization or the Little Black) (Lane 29). Covarrubias's black buffoon character had deep ideological origins in Spanish Renaissance and Baroque theater.

The earliest black characters in European literature appeared in Spain and Portugal, but these comic portrayals did not mention African slavery as a historical reality (Fra-Molinero "Los negros como figura" 9). Comedy was a vehicle for anti-black sentiment in Renaissance theater of the sixteenth and seventeenth centuries. Spanish playwrights portrayed black characters in absurd scenarios that degraded their humanity and subordinated them to whites in physical, moral, ontological, and even intellectual terms. Some African-descended characters attempted to eliminate their mahogany hue and, in this way, expunged themselves from the cultural and historical record. Black skin was an insurmountable social barrier; blackness constituted the lowest point imaginable in Renaissance Spain, and it was equated with slavery. Lope de Vega's drama *La Dragontea* (1598) was an exception to the rule, because his depiction of maroon characters reflected African resistance to slavery in colonial Spanish America (Fra-Molinero, "Los negros como figura" 9, 11). In effect, humor was the most valuable ideological arrow in the Spanish quiver, because humor is insidious, blithe, and fleeting. But the broader social meanings embedded in antiblack comedic performances had an enduring legacy in the Spanish Caribbean.

Cuban minstrelsy was unique in Latin America; no other Spanish- or Portuguese-speaking country, with the possible exception of Argentina, produced anything remotely similar (R. Moore "26). Though none of Covarrubias's works remain, his disciples exploited a full range of black stereotypes in popular theater (Barreda 23). Among them, Galician playwright Bartolomé José Crespo y Borbón (1811–1871)—famously known by the pseudonym "Creto Gangá"—has been credited with producing vernacular theater that promoted an array of black characters: the graceful black woman, the little black "professor," the African native, and the picturesque man from the mangrove swamp (Barreda

23). José Crespo y Borbón launched his minstrel performances in the heyday of early Cuban narrative production, 1838–1840 (Lane 31).

Crespo y Borbón began minstrel shows in 1838, and published his first black-face character in 1839, long after Covarrubias's 1812 debut. Crespo y Borbón's work was not imitative of Covarrubias's style (Lane 29, 31–32). Rather, he invented a fictive African author named Creto Gangá as his rhetorical vehicle for social critique. Crespo y Borbón's minstrelsy provided linguistic portraits of his subjects and phonetic spellings to suggest vocal intonation. His invention of an ahistorical African character with the *gangá* ethnonym was presumably intended to lend authenticity to his racial fantasy. Jesús Guanche writes that the *gangá* were not a specific African ethnicity; rather, the term referred to captives from an extensive stretch of the upper Guinea coast comprising the modern African nations of Guinea, Sierra Leone, Liberia, and the coastal regions of Ivory Coast (71–76) that had been brought to Cuba to labor in the interest of white wealth production. Such captives represented multiple ethnic groups and spoke myriad non-Bantu languages (Guanche 66). Alessandra Basso Ortiz concurs with Guanche that Sierra Leone and Liberia represent the geographic region where the so-called *gangá* originated, but she discounts Guinea and Ivory Coast (63). Historians paint a dynamic portrait of the *gangás* that contradicts the fictive African of Crespo y Borbón's imagination. In Cuba the *gangá* were frequently involved in antislavery resistance, and they were implicated in the 1844 antislavery movement. The historical record mentions *gangás* who acted as ritual priests, harnessed sacred powers to dominate the spirits of others, and acquired natural elements to combat the slaveholding aristocracy (Finch, *Rethinking* 311–312, 465, 431; Midlo Hall 58). In fact, the military tribunal condemned eleven different individuals identified with the ethnonym *gangá* for conspiratorial activities in the town of Bainoa.[11] Crespo y Borbón's strawman was a gross distortion of the *gangá* tradition of antislavery resistance.

Jill Lane explains the performance of the *bozal* character in depth:

> The bozal verse provides the poem's comic value. The poem manages to disguise the outright parody of the African's inability to speak Spanish "properly" by appealing to the truth-value of costumbrista representational techniques. Couching the appearance of the African character in a familiar costumbrista description, that descriptive detail in turn lends credibility to the written representation of spoken bozal. Pasqual's odd speech pattern is presented as simply a true record of what the gentleman-author happened to hear (the sad accent that "wounded" the aural landscape) while indulging in the fragrant pleasures of the countryside. (Lane 34)

Lane writes that Crespo y Borbón's blackface relied on the representational techniques of *costumbrismo* to convince white spectators of the authenticity of the character's speech, his overstated mannerisms, and supposedly deficient intellect. *Costumbrismo* is, according to Lane, "any description—literary, visual, or embodied—of a particular social or cultural custom that gives attention to realist detail" (21). Representations of the black male in vernacular theater were not innocuous portrayals of social foibles, but rather a hegemonic statement about the perception of colonized black men as powerless.

But even as the Galician author was performing *sainetes*, Plácido and Manzano were becoming acquainted and had begun to confer about how they might write poetry in the interest of black freedom (Friol 192, 198). Manzano had finished the *Autobiografía* and submitted it to Domingo del Monte by 1836. And, for the next few years, Anselmo Suárez y Romero and Félix Tanco y Bosmeniel authored reformist novels in order to hasten the abolition of the Atlantic slave trade and to persuade the white public that a growing African population posed a threat to the balance of power (Luis, *Literary Bondage* 4, 30). However, government censorship prevented the publication of all the del Monte novels until 1880, when Suárez y Romero's *Francisco* saw the light of day. The other novels were not published in Cuba until the twentieth century (Luis, *Literary Bondage* 1, 4). So, reformist literature did not enter the public sphere until after the Spanish government had initiated the process of gradual slave abolition. Plácido's racial satire on the one hand, and minstrelsy on the other, filled the discursive void in Cuba and competed for the public imagination.

Plácido launched his career in the racialized atmosphere of the 1830s; but as a person of African descent, he did not possess the discursive freedom to defy minstrelsy openly. So, he adopted satire as a vehicle for racial commentary, where he addressed the social purchase of whiteness among mulattoes who denied their African lineage. Plácido was a poet of the people. His improvisations, *décimas*, *fábulas*, and *letrillas* spoke to lower-class black and white Cubans without formal access to written practices of literacy. His parody relied on memorable refrains, Cuban argot, and a disarming capacity to evoke laughter in his audiences. Plácido recited and extemporized poetry at weddings, soirées, and baptisms, and at newborn celebrations for local elites ("Prólogo," xviii–xix). Moreover, he was intimately familiar with African-inspired expressive culture. Plácido attended saints' feast days on several occasions, and he participated in carnival performances in Matanzas. He was conversant in the cast of carnival characters, especially the African Cuban masquerade that conjured laughter from a population that was unenlightened about its spiritual meaning.

If African-descended writers were to find a place in the emerging literary canon of the late nineteenth century, they had to be perceived as apolitical, appreciated for their artistry, not their agency. For Plácido to exist within a national Parnassus, he could not be *black*. Blackness signified negative difference (Branche, *Colonialism* 2); it was the antithesis of whiteness and was inextricably equated with servility, indolence, and irrationality. Africa was the origin

of blackness, which, according to Jesuit priest Alonso de Sandoval's racist perceptions, languished in a woeful absence of culture and civilization and in need
of Christian sanctification (Olsen, *Slavery* 23, 85). But there was an even worse
problem: if Plácido were deemed black, Haitian antislavery ideology would be
the immediate referent for white Cuban readers. As Sibylle Fischer has shown, if
Plácido were *black*, the literary establishment might be implicated in antislavery
ideology, which promised to abolish the institution where Cuban wealth had
originated and to destroy the racial ideology that justified it (105, 276). Haitian
antislavery ideology threatened Spanish Caribbean colonies, because Africans
had vanquished the French, emancipated themselves from slavery, and established an independent black republic only miles from Cuban shores. Moreover,
the Imperial Constitution of Haiti decreed in 1805, a year after independence,
denied whites property rights on Haitian soil and declared all Haitian citizens
*black*, regardless of their hue (Fischer 276). The Haitian Revolution merged
black racial identity with African Atlantic spirituality to invent a new symbolic
order. By making this connection, Haitians advised that the black nation was
a means to defeat white supremacy and to abolish the nefarious institutions it
had spawned (Fischer 276).

   If Plácido were to be canonized, he would have to be remembered as a *mestizo*, not simply in racial but also cultural terms, so that *mestizaje* (racial/culture
admixture) rather than African ancestry might define him. Plácido's biographers did not speak to his phenotype in order to deny his African ancestors.
Rather, his biographers (and some of his contemporaries) sought to diminish the symbolic significance of his ancestral past. The debate about Plácido's
position in Cuban literature has often addressed his physiognomy to classify
him racially, describe his temperament, and most importantly, determine his
political proclivities. Seeing as there is no reliable portraiture of Plácido, Cuban
scholars have relied on his contemporaries' recollections to reconstruct how
he might have looked (Cué, *Plácido: El poeta* 34–35, 44).[12] In the main, such
descriptions rely on typical racial signifiers—the hair, the angle of the nose,
the lips, and skin color—to construct depictions premised on his proximity to
whiteness. Whereas Plácido's contemporaries (and some of his biographers)
regarded him as nearly white, José Buscaglia Salgado considered Plácido as a
"physically unrepresentable" subject, an individual that epitomized "the very
color of ambiguity" (222). Buscaglia-Salgado did not measure the mulatto in
terms of his proximity to whiteness but rather in terms of the mulatto's capacity
to erode the legitimacy of the black/white dichotomy.

   In *Undoing Empire*, Buscaglia-Salgado theorizes that the mulatto was an
unstable terrain of shifting meanings and social uncertainties. The mulatto
emerged in the Iberian contact zone where medieval Europeans and Arab and
African Muslims resided. Buscaglia-Salgado maintains that the mulatto defies
the European ideal by achieving what José Lezama Lima called "the practice of

the counterconquest" (184). For him, the mulatto is "the very prankster of the imago, always escaping reduction and definition" (xvii). The Caribbean mulatto is neither black nor white; he is "the master of the in-between . . . a gatekeeper of sorts" and "a mediator" between masters and slaves on plantations (185). In what follows I analyze how Plácido's white contemporaries portrayed him, and I contemplate Buscaglia-Salgado's view of "the mulatto world" (184) in light of Plácido's racial parody disparaging mulatto identity. The competing portraits of the poet constitute a narrative wherein the African-descended male body is reduced to a disputed terrain of colonial racial politics.[13]

Ramón Vélez Herrera—a leading figure in the Indianist literary movement and a close acquaintance of Plácido—described him thus:

> Plácido era de estatura regular, muy delgado, un si es no encorvado, de color blanco pálido, pelo apasado y ojos vivísimos y ardientes. Vestía con mucho desaliño, jamás usó corbata ni chaleco, no solo por lo despreocupado de su carácter, sino por su extraordinaria pobreza. (Cué, *Plácido: El poeta* 35)

> (Plácido was of regular height, very thin, not hunchbacked, of a pale white color, nappy hair and lively and fiery eyes. He dressed with much modesty, never wearing a tie or a sport coat, not only because of his carefree nature but also due to his extraordinary poverty.)[14]

Velez's racial portrait situates the poet between black and white, European and African parentage, so that his body straddles the fence residing in the social interstices. The description is neither laudatory nor particularly offensive; rather, it adopts an ostensibly neutral tone. Plácido's baptismal records described him as *al parecer blanco*, that is, white in appearance (Cué, *Plácido: El poeta* 15), and Velez's description seems to substantiate the record with one important difference: the poet's "nappy hair." Clearly, Plácido's tightly coiled locks are his albatross, a stubborn reminder of African phenotypes.

The sisters of prominent Cuban writers José Jacinto and Federico Milanés, who knew Plácido personally, painted a far more descriptive portrait, tinged with erotic subtleties:

> Su cara era angosta y aguileña sin acabar en barba aguda ni señársele hueso ni de pómulos ni de las mandíbulas. Sus ojos hermosos de color negro, la nariz recta, la boca pequeña y los labios delgados formaban de su cara un conjunto agradable a primera vista y que continuaba persistiendo hasta darle la belleza de un bien parecido.

> Su pelo era lacio y con las vueltas ya imperceptibles del que tiene ascendientes africanos después de varios cruzamientos. Lo llevaba largo con la vuelta

sobre las orejas como entonces se usaba y atrás las puntas se ensortijaban en una melena. [ . . . ]

Su color era trigueño pero rosado. Su voz era de plata. Los rasgos finos de su cara pueden compararse a los de la de Enrique Piñeyro (Cué, *Plácido: El poeta* 41).

(His face was long, thin and narrow not ending in a pointy chin and without gaunt jaws or cheekbones. His beautiful dark eyes, his straight nose, his small mouth and his thin lips made for a pleasant overall look at first sight which endowed him with the beauty of a good-looking man.

His hair was straight with the hardly noticeable curls that African descendants have after much admixture. He wore it long around his ears as was the custom back then and in the back of his head, the ends curled up tightly in a mane of hair [ . . . ]

His skin was wheat-colored but rosy. His voice was silvery. The refined features of his countenance can be compared with those of Enrique Piñeyro.)

The Milanés sisters depict a handsome mulatto with a yellowish-brown or rosy, wheat-colored complexion, wavy but not coarse hair, and an elongated, straight nose culminating in a Grecian profile. His is a "delicate mouth" with slender lips that utter incisive yet eloquent verse. From their heteronormative viewpoint, beauty is the sum and harmony of European features. The racial portraits of the Milanés sisters and Sebastián Alfredo de Morales establish a clear relationship between Plácido's near-white appearance, his social status, and cultural attainment. From an erotic white female perspective, Plácido is not black; rather, he is a nearly white mulatto, a *pardo* to be admired and desired, albeit in secret.

Plácido biographer and personal confidant, Sebastián Alfredo de Morales, provided a description comparable to that of the Milanés sisters, but his political project was more pronounced. Morales's description was integral to his 1886 edition of Plácido's complete works, which includes a portrait of a man with alabaster skin, a small mouth, and a Grecian profile. Morales maintained that a Spanish painter from Cádiz had sketched this spontaneous drawing of the poet. And he insisted that the drawing was the only extant illustration of Plácido, though other such drawings existed (Cué, *Plácido: El Poeta* 31–33). Morales canonized the image of a nearly white Plácido that endures in the public imagination to this day.[15]

Gabriel de la Concepción Valdés o Plácido el poeta, era de regular estatura, delgado de cuerpo; musculación seca, si bien contorneada; color pálido terso luciente como el del ámbar [ . . . ] cabeza proporcionada; pelo esponjado, mas no retorcido [ . . . ] frente espaciosa, tersa y convexa con anchas entradas; rostro oval, cejas sutiles y rasgadas; ojos negros, pequeños y vivos, con mirada de

Dueling portraits of Plácido. The Dubrocq portrait (left) is the image that comes closest to Plácido's likeness. However, the portrait that Sebastián Alfredo Morales published (right) in 1886 is more commonly known. Morales depicted Plácido with a Grecian profile, and he canonized him as an almost-white writer.

águila, altiva y escudriñadora; nariz perfilada, pequeña y de tipo griego; boca delicada, contraída [ . . . ] labios delgados; expresión simpática y juvenil [ . . . ] dentadura pequeña, sana y pareja.

[ . . . ] voz argentina, palabra elocuente e incisiva [ . . . ] su traje, si bien modesto y muy pobre, era siempre aseado (Cué, *Plácido: El poeta* 36-37).

(Gabriel de la Concepción Valdés or Plácido the Poet, was of regular height, slender body; slight musculature, well built; of a smooth pale shiny amber-like color [ . . . ] a proportionately sized head; spongy but not curly hair [ . . . ] a wide, smooth and prominent forehead with a wide receding hairline; oval-shaped face with subtle and almond-shaped eyebrows; dark, small and lively eyes, with an eagle's gaze, haughty and scrutinizing; a small but elongated Grecian nose, a fine delicate mouth; [ . . . ] thin lips; a kind and youthful expression [ . . . ] small, healthy and straight teeth.

[ . . . ] a silvery voice, eloquent and incisive words [ . . . ] his clothing was very modest and very meager, [but] always tidy.)[16]

Morales and the Milanés sisters apparently quarreled with Velez's claims regarding Plácido's skin color and hair texture. They did not portray Plácido as a classic *jabao* with ashen skin and wooly hair; instead their racial portraits placed emphasis on his "refined features," that is, the straight nose and delicate mouth. Perhaps the most effective trope in Morales's repertoire was the "Grecian nose," which consolidated the impression that despite his African ancestry, Plácido was not far removed from the European aesthetic ideal. Likewise, Morales and the Milanés sisters repudiated Velez's statement about the poet's coarse wooly mane because it was inconsistent with Mediterranean conceptions of male beauty.

Nineteenth-century depictions of Plácido are deeply ambivalent representations of the African-descended male body that privilege the poet's nearly white status. Africa is accounted for, yet contained. Plácido's contemporaries diminished the significance of Africa as a wellspring of Plácido's cultural origins. Africa is present but not as a symbol that would define the poet phenotypically or culturally. The absence of blackness or any referent whatsoever to Africa legitimizes the racialized body, so that the nonwhite poet is endowed with limited purchase of whiteness. Jerome Branche writes that whiteness assumed an unprecedented institutional and discursive power in colonial Spanish America, so that persons deemed anything but white were blemished with an "ugly stain," an allusion to miscegenation and unorthodox cultural and religious practices. Cuban society inherited Renaissance notions of *honra*, which was reserved for persons of legitimate birth with verifiable claims to nobility and an immaculate white lineage (*Colonialism* 83–85). In effect, Plácido's biographers aim to legitimize him by cleansing the dishonorable blemishes owing to the low circumstances of his birth. *Mestizaje* is not a sign of impurity and degradation, but rather an imaginary step on a path toward (an unattainable) social whiteness. But as Homi Bhabha writes, "colonial mimicry is the desire for a reformed, recognizable Other, as a subject of a difference that is almost the same, but not quite," (86) in other words not quite white. Such depictions of Plácido are incongruent with the image he had of himself. Nonetheless, these portrayals set a precedent for the racial in-betweenness that some twentieth-century critics imputed to Plácido.

Cuban criticism in the twentieth century also labeled Gabriel de la Concepción Valdés an almost-white poet who did not address black cultural and political themes. The conflation of racial and cultural identities distanced Plácido from his black counterparts in the colonial era, thus designating him as a cultural outsider. There are voluminous articles written in Spanish on the poet, but for obvious reasons I will treat only a few here.[17] In *The Black Protagonist in the Cuban Novel*, Pedro Barreda describes Plácido as a mixed-race troubadour whose lightly hued skin all but allowed him to pass for white in colonial society. For Barreda, Plácido's poetic work is largely devoid of the critical exposition of "the black point of view," because race does not figure prominently (17). Fernández de Castro's perspective is comparable to that of Barreda.

In a similar line of reasoning, de Castro supposes that Plácido might have been perceived as a poor white artisan had his black grandmother not raised him. His recognition of Plácido's lyrical talent is tempered by a strident critique of his poems. De Castro is silent on romantic poetry that gestures toward an Afro-Caribbean female aesthetic and says nothing of the poet's innovative racial satire. Moreover, he is dismissive of the odes that Plácido wrote to the queen of Spain and to prominent white Cubans. De Castro concurs with Domingo del Monte that Plácido's poems were bereft of social critique (Fernández de Castro 170–71). On the other hand, Mary Cruz does consider racial representation in a few poems, but she asserts incorrectly that the poet was not influenced by black musical and poetic traditions and that he was unfamiliar with its social institutions or mythology. In reality, Cruz's reading of Plácido is dictated by his epidermic condition, which rendered any socio-cultural affiliations with blackness impossible (81). Cruz's use of the word *black* to signify African-inspired culture reproduces Cuban racial demarcations black/mulatto, slave/free, and civilized/uncivilized. In my view, the near unavailability of Plácido's complete works explains, at least in part, the paucity of criticism on the black theme in his poems. As is the case with the poet's depictions of African-inspired spirituality, Daisy Cué Fernández points out that the race-themed poetry has been excluded from all Cuban anthologies with the exception of Emilio Ballagas (Cué, *Plácido: El poeta* 225–26, 232).

Plácido conveyed his racial politics through the prism of humor, and his satire represented a radical departure from the stereotype of *pardo* mimicry. *Pardos* were persons of direct African and European ancestry. Colonial stereotypes maintained that *pardos* exhibited a certain polarity: either they would do anything to impersonate white people or they fervently resented them (Nwankwo 38, 222). Plácido's satire defies the logic of *pardo* stereotypes because his satirical work decenters whiteness as a Cuban cultural ideal. His parody invested the dark body with new racial meaning, it deconstructed the chasm between African *bozales* and mulattoes, and it enabled the poet to conceive a racial identity grounded in a common African ancestry. These poems constitute a political project that chisels away at colonial racial hierarchy meant to nullify African Cuban political power. In the satirical poetry that I analyze below, Plácido disparages mulatto characters for denying their African heredity. "Que se lo cuente a su abuela" (Let Him Tell That to His Grandmother), "Si a todos Arcino dices" (If Arcino Says to Everyone), and "¡Oh . . .! no juegue, que me moja" (Don't Play Around You'll Get Me Wet) portray three mulatto characters that do their utmost to pass for white.

The first three stanzas of "Que se lo cuente a su abuela" admonish gentlemen that feigned great learning and deride an uncomely woman that claims to have once been beautiful. Though these characters are presumably white, the initial stanzas say nothing about race. The popular refrain after each stanza is

"Let him tell that to his grandmother," thus insinuating the laughability of their assertions. Plácido's most important character is Don Longino, a mulatto who appears in the final stanza. Don Longino not only disassociates from Africa but goes as far as to proclaim noble European descent to purify his blood in the sphere of public opinion.

> Siempre exclama Don Longino
> —<<Soy de sangre noble y pura,>>
> Con una pasión más dura
> Que cáscara de tocino,
> Y con su rostro cetrino
> Que africana estirpe indica,
> Alucinado publica
> Ser de excelsa parentela!
> *Que se lo cuente a su abuela.* (original emphasis; Valdés, *Plácido, Gabriel de la Concepción* 482)

> (Don Longino always exclaims
> —<<I am of noble and pure blood,>>
> With nappy hair that is tougher
> Than the rind of bacon,
> And with a high-yellow countenance
> That bespeaks African heritage
> Deluded he publicly claims
> To be of proud parentage!
> *Let him tell that to his grandmother.*)[18]

Plácido underscores his character's choice of language: "Siempre exclama Don Longino / <<Soy de sangre noble y pura,>>" (Don Longino always exclaims /—"I am of noble and pure blood) (Valdés, *Plácido, Gabriel de la Concepción* 482). The word *always* serves two functions: It is a reiteration of Don Longino's claims to whiteness and—when read aloud—it adds to the comic effect of the piece. Don Longino's claim to whiteness is couched within a pseudoscientific discourse that defined race as the transmission of hereditary traits through blood (Martínez Alier 6, 15).[19] Colonial racial discourse notwithstanding, Don Longino's physical features refute his apocryphal claims to racial purity, because coarse hair and sallow skin were signifiers of African ancestry in slave society. Said another way, Don Longino has a touch of the brush.

But Don Longino has claimed not only whiteness but nobility and an hon-orific title as well. However laughable, his edifice of racial privilege relies on the knowledge of genealogy, the denial of undesirable ancestors, and the dis-missal of the black matriarch. In slave society, free persons of African descent sought to divorce themselves from the humiliation, pain, and infamy of slavery and its inextricable correlation with blackness. As the dispute between free mulattoes Uribe and Pimienta in Cirilo Villaverde's *Cecilia Valdés* (1882) bears out, the struggle to use the title of *don* was more than a matter of semantics, since the honorific title might ensure high standing, if not in white society, then certainly within African-descended communities (Villaverde 206). Titles of nobility were reserved for white propertied elites (Knight 232), so any suggestion that Don Longino might not be white would also imperil his claims to noble birth and impugn his right to the title of *don* (Branche, *Colonialism* 91). If we read the aforementioned racial portraits of Plácido in the aggregate, then it becomes clear that Don Longino and the poet have much in common; they are *trigueños* with wheat-colored skin and coarse, thick tightly coiled hair. The comical refrain, "Let him tell that to his grandmother" is endowed with new meaning in the final stanza, because Don Longino keeps the black matriarch in the kitchen to safeguard his claims to whiteness. I would like to further Plácido's reputation as a literary pioneer since these poems appear to be the first example of racial satire critiquing whiteness in the history of Hispanophone Caribbean literatures. The template that Plácido provided became a leitmotif in the Spanish Caribbean where it emerged in Dominican poet Juan Antonio Alix's, 1883 piece "El negro tras de la oreja" (Black behind the Ears) and Puerto Rican Fortunato Vizcarrondo's *negrista* poem "¿Y tu agüela a'onde ejtá?" (And Your Grandmamma, Where Is She?) (1942).

"¡Oh . . .! no juegue, que me moja" and "Si a todos Arcino dices" also ridicule the denial of African ancestry as a means to ascend the socio-racial ladder. In what follows, I quote selected stanzas from both poems.

*Al que mentiras arroja*
*Como agua por azotea,*
*Le diré cuando lo vea:*
*<<¡Oh . . .! no juegue, que me moja.>>*

Atencion: salgo de casa
Con Juan, hallo á Don Marcelo,
Hombre tan largo de pelo
Que hasta el bigote le pasa.
—¿Porqué se unta con tanta grasa?
—Para que no se le encoja.
¡Oh . . .! No juegue, que me moja. (Valdés, *Plácido, Gabriel de la Concepción*
    482)

(To he that hurls lies
Like water from the rooftop

When I see him, I'll say:
<<*Oh . . .! Don't play around; you'll get me wet.*>>

Consider this: I leave home
With Juan, I run into Don Marcelo,
A man with hair so long
That it passes his moustache.
—Why does he grease it so much?
—So that it doesn't shrivel up.
*Oh . . .! Don't play around; you'll get my hair wet.*)

<Si a todos, Arcino, dices
que son de baja ralea,
cuando tienen a Guinea
en el pelo y las narices.

Debes confesar, Arcino,
que es desatino probado,
siendo de vidrio el tejado
tirar piedras al vecino.     (Valdés, "Si a todos" 149)

(If Arcino says to everyone
that they are from the lower castes,
when they possess Guinea
in their hair and in their nostrils.

Arcino, you should confess
its proven nonsense,
to throw stones at your neighbor
when the roof is made of glass.)[20]

Although each character description differs from the other, hair texture functions as the cultural signifier of racial difference in all three poems. In effect,
the mulattoes' tightly coiled tresses render their denial of African heritage
demonstrably false. Plácido seemed to be laughing at himself—some described
his wooly hair as "nappy"—even as he ridiculed these male characters in the
court of public opinion. One can imagine Plácido making such a comic gesture
at a cockfight (where he met Manzano), after concluding the prescribed ritual
at a saints' feast day celebration or within the African cultural atmosphere of
carnival in Matanzas. Collective laughter taunts mulattoes as impostors without excluding them from the community to which they rightly belong. The
amusing refrain "Don't play around you'll get me wet" is double entendre that

admonishes persons making disingenuous claims to social prestige and ridicules the fact that Don Marcelo straightens his wooly hair.[21]

Again, I think Plácido's use of the honorific title *don* is derisive not because persons of African descent didn't aspire to such prestigious titles, but because Don Marcelo's social ascension is based on a fictive genealogy. The length of and fastidious attention to hair styling was considered a sign of effeminacy in men, thus granting the poet yet another motive for mockery. Cuban presbyter José Agustín Caballero criticized male effeminacy in a 1791 article he published in *El Papel Periódico de la Havana,* entitled "Critical Letter to the Man-Woman." The cleric described such men as effeminate: "¿Quién podrá contener la risa cuando vé a un hombre barbado gastar la mayor parte de una mañana en peinarse . . .? [ . . . ] Ellos representan el papel de Gallos entre las Mujeres y de Gallinas entre los Hombres, al paso de que estos merecen la compasión, cuando de aquellas el desprecio" (Who can contain his laughter when he sees a bearded man waste the better part of the morning combing his hair . . .? [ . . . ] They play Roosters among Women and Hens among Men, so that they deserve the pity of men and the scorn of women) (González Pagés 70–71). Caballero mocked the "Man-Woman," who presumably wore long hair, as an aberration from Church-sanctioned gender norms. The presbyter policed the boundaries of Cuban masculinity when he implied that the well-groomed gentleman might be sexually transgressive. Caballero's rooster/hen dichotomy was a metaphor for the power differential between sexual partners who perform active and passive roles in the bedroom. If we follow Caballero's reasoning to its logical conclusion, men who are fastidiously groomed are effeminate creatures who may be dominant among women but are sexually submissive to other men. Though Plácido's gendered critique doesn't impugn the sexuality of Don Marcelo, his criticism of the mulatto's lengthy hair certainly leaves his masculinity in doubt.

Much like Don Longino and Marcelo, Arcino also denies his African origins, and instead of identifying as a *pardo* or a mulatto, he professes to be white. Though his hair and nostrils are African, Arcino struggles to escape the social stigma of his racial origins by identifying with the Spanish colonizer and projecting an attitude of "whiter than thou" in conversation with other persons of African descent. Daisy Cué observes that Plácido's criticism of Arcino is particularly harsh because Arcino's denial of African heritage is marked by a note of condescension (*Plácido: El Poeta* 227). Arcino's contemptuous attitude toward African descendants of a darker hue has a deep history in Luso-Hispanic modes of racial representation. Black characters in Renaissance theater sought desperately to eliminate blackness on physical and metaphysical levels. Metaphysically, the removal of blackness had religious benefits, but this process of self-erasure also rendered the black presence in the historical record nearly imperceptible (Fra-Molinero, "Los negros como figura" 10–11).

Don Marcelo, Don Longino, and Arcino could not conceivably pass as white in Cuban society without a general acquiescence to their assertions of whiteness. Arguably, there are two things at play for Plácido's characters: mulatto self-concept and the broader epistemology of ignorance that makes racial passing possible. In *The Racial Contract* (1997), Charles Mills argues:

> [O]n matters related to race, the Racial Contract prescribes for its signatories an inverted epistemology, an epistemology of ignorance, a particular pattern of localized and global cognitive dysfunctions (which are psychologically and socially functional), producing the ironic outcome that whites will in general be unable to understand the world they themselves have made (qtd. in Sullivan and Tuana eds. 2).

In colonial Cuba, Europeans were not the only persons to partake in such a willful "cognitive dysfunctions." Plácido's poetry signals that mulatto communities actively engaged what Mills terms an "inverted epistemology," a way of knowing the social world that amounts to an active *not-knowing* coupled with a deliberate negation of otherwise provable facts. Victor Goldgel does not examine passing in nineteenth-century Cuban literature as a practice of deceit, but rather as an alternative relationship to truth and representation. Goldgel calls this "an active not knowing which ranges from civil inattention and tactful reserve to hypocrisy and unconscious disavowal" (Goldgel 129). Goldgel dismisses traditional definitions of passing, where an authentic identity is masked by an apocryphal one, that is, a black person pretends to be white. Rather, Goldgel suggests that racial passing in nineteenth-century Cuba involved self-deception, individual hypocrisy and, lastly, the disavowal of verifiable facts (Goldgel 130–131). Visibility and knowability do not always converge in the phenotypes of light-skinned African descendants (Goldgel 139). But in the case of Plácido's characters, not knowing is an art and a science that some Cubans of African descent exerted when it best suited their interests. Plácido, however, refused to play along. His parody of mulatto men that pass for white disrupts the epistemology of ignorance and points out contradictions in their painstaking performance of white identity.

Plácido's satirical characters exemplify an internalized sense of racial and cultural inferiority, for they have fallen victim to what Fanon termed the "myth of the Negro" (*Black Skin*, 117). In *Black Skin, White Masks* (1952), Frantz Fanon's painful semiautobiographical account, the white gaze misrepresents blacks as "savages, brutes, [and] illiterates" (117). Fanon brilliantly describes the man of African descent as an individual "who cannot escape his body" (*Black Skin* 65). I have cited Fanon at length below:

> In the Antilles there was also that little gulf that exists among the almost-white, the mulatto, and the nigger. But I was satisfied with an intellectual understanding of these differences. It was not really dramatic. And then....

And then the occasion arose when I had to meet the white man's eyes. An unfamiliar weight burdened me. The real world challenged my claims. In the white world the man of color encounters difficulties in the development of his bodily schema. Consciousness of the body is solely a negating activity.

[ . . . ]

I was responsible at the same time for my body, for my race, for my ancestors. I subjected myself to an objective examination, I discovered my blackness, my ethnic characteristics; and I was battered down by tom-toms, cannibalism, intellectual deficiency, fetishism, racial defects, slave-ships, and above all else, above all: "Sho' good eatin'." (*Black Skin* 110, 112)

Plácido insisted that the real tragedy of the *mulato* was not his failure to become white, but rather his desire to be white. Fanon differs with Buscaglia Salgado's theory of the mulatto world. Rather than view the mulatto as someone "always escaping reduction and definition" (Buscaglia Salgado xv), Fanon contends that to inhabit an African-descended body is to be held to account for one's African ancestors (*Black Skin* 110, 112). Fanon argues that Caribbean pigmentocracy crumbles under careful examination, because white society scrutinizes nonwhite people, such as almost-white individuals, mulattoes, and blacks, for their attachments to African cultural history and spirituality. The white gaze revels in the indignities of enslavement and black subjugation. So, the fair-skinned African descendant is simply unable to escape aesthetic judgments about his physical appearance, or intellectual and cultural attainments. The *mestizo* cannot wish away a torrent of assumptions about his character that have more to do with stereotypes than with historical reality. Don Longino, Marcelo, and Arcino do their utmost to escape Fanon's "zone of non-being" (*Black Skin* 8), that infertile space of insignificance where the black man is a nonentity irreversibly condemned to subpersonhood. In such a formulation, to be black is to be a *slave*.

Conversely, Plácido's parody of mulatto men that passed for white is remarkable, because he did not genuflect before the white aesthetic, nor did he seek to placate a white readership by disparaging blackness. Indeed, Plácido writes against the ideology of whiteness at a time when a petite *literatus* availed itself of literature to foment Hispano-Catholic values in a society numerically dominated by enslaved and free persons of African descent. Plácido used satire and wit to deconstruct Cuban racial hierarchies and to construct a racial identity that positioned *la raza de color* (people of color) in relation to Africa rather than in opposition to the continent.

Vera Kutzinski is among the few critics who have studied Plácido's racial satire referring to the problem in somewhat benign language as a "cultural anxiety over ancestry" and reading "Que se lo cuente a su abuela" as a critique of the unbridled hypocrisy of colonial society ("Unseasonal Flowers" 155, 157).

Kutzinski correctly analyzes *mestizaje* through the lens of white patrician Francisco Arango y Parreño, who imagined a scenario wherein black would yield to white and prevent the *africanización* (read: Haiti) of Cuban society (*Sugar's Secrets* 31). This is an accurate but insufficient critique, because it says nothing of Plácido's racial politics. Plácido's racial satire, in my view, refers to what Branche terms "whiteness" as "an object of purchase," something akin to the *cédulas de gracias al sacar*, that the crown administered in eighteenth-century Spanish America to grant privileges to persons otherwise denied them due to African and/or indigenous origins (*Colonialism* 89). For such characters, there is but one destiny: the erasure of blackness and acquiescence to the dominant ideology of whiteness. In 1784 the *Código Negro Carolino* (Spanish Negro Code) enumerated four racial categories or "spheres" that originated with a black individual and, over successive generations of admixture with Europeans, produced a white moral subject. The racial categories were the following: *pardo* (brown), *tercerón* (terceroon), *cuarterón* (quadroon), and *mestizo* (nearly white). Miscegenation was a social good that would *mejorar la raza* (better the race) and improve the moral character of individuals that achieved ever-increasing degrees of whiteness (Buscaglia Salgado 191–192).

Plácido's critique of whiteness not only was a departure from *pardo* mimicry but also subverted a Cuban racial hierarchy that Spanish authorities had designed to cause a rift between African descendants. Spanish American colonies were structured on a *régimen de castas* (caste system), a system of racial stratification that afforded the white population a broad array of economic, social, and political privileges. George Reid Andrews explains that, "by dividing American society into racial estates and encouraging antagonism among them, the crown reduced the likelihood of its subjects' uniting to contest royal rule" ("Spanish American Independence" 113–114). I read these poems as seditious materials not because they advocate deposing the queen but because they gnaw away at the discursive structure Spain (and white Creole society) relied upon to avert intra-ethnic unity that might produce a black Cuban polity.

Plácido's satires were merely a fraction of his oeuvre, but they managed to give voice to a new racial imagination wherein African descendants would not claim social advantage based on phenotypical differences. Even if these poems do not eliminate Caribbean pigmentocracy, they do contest the negation of Africa among mulattoes. There were political consequences for Plácido's repudiation of the whiteness doctrine, because as an African descendant with light skin, he was expected to align himself with whites as a means to improve his socio-racial standing. Plácido's social and cultural investments in black communities were also evidenced by his choice of romantic partners. Mulattoes often chose white female partners or married mulatto women to better the race, but the poet fell madly in love with Rafaela, a beautiful free black woman with a dark mahogany skin. Their plans to marry, however, never came to fruition. In 1833 Havana was stricken with a cholera epidemic, and Rafaela soon fell victim to the illness. Plácido dedicated several elegies to "Fela"; calling her his "dulce morena" (sweet dark woman) and "[la] mitad de mi alma" (the other half of my soul) (Valdés, *Plácido, Gabriel de la Concepción* 504). His elegiac poetry to Fela are his only poems praising the allure and charm of mahogany-hued Afro-Caribbean women (Cué, *Plácido: El poeta* 21). In November 1842 Plácido married María Gila Morales Poveda, a free black woman and daughter of Pilar Poveda and Doroteo Morales. And for this *saltatrás* (marrying down), Plácido suffered the critique of his contemporaries (Finch, *Rethinking* 120). Moreover, his wife's family had strong antislavery convictions. The government later implicated his mother-in-law, Pilar Poveda, for aiding and abetting would-be insurgents in the 1844 movement (Deschamps Chapeaux, *El Negro en la economía* 181–182).[22] Plácido was not "unrepresentable," as Buscaglia Salgado suggests, because despite his *mestizaje*, Africa was the basis for his racial identity. Buscaglia Salgado misreads Plácido's racial politics, because he neglects the poet's racial parody. While Plácido's satires do not make explicit claims to blackness, they do position his racial identity within the African lineage of his paternal ancestors. In the following, I compare Plácido's religious self-portrait with the tragic mulatto trope that Cuban critics constructed to disassociate him from Haitian antislavery ideology.

## Plácido as a Lamb to the Slaughter

Africans and their descendants could neither remove nor dilute their ebony color: physiologically speaking, "Aethiopum lavare" (washing of the Ethiopian) was impossible. "Aethiopum lavare" was a common trope in Renaissance Spain premised on an Old Testament verse in the book of Jeremiah: "'Can the blacke More change his skin? Or the leopard his spots?" As Kim Hall explains, "To wash an Ethiop/blackamoor is to labor in vain" (Hall qtd. in Olsen, *Slavery* 86–87). Blackness was a phenotypical problem, but it also constituted a religious dilemma and a moral predicament for Spanish Catholics. Catholics argued that Africans were born into the original sin of Noah's perverse son Ham and, by nature, were impure and in need of redemption (Branche, *Colonialism* 43). Spanish playwrights addressed pervasive anxieties about blackness by transforming their black protagonists into white characters. But the fictional white-washing of black flesh was inadequate: black people had to be sanctified. In Spanish dramas, black sinners became white saints so that the heavenly hosts might embrace them for eternity. Such was the case in Lope de Vega's *El prodigio de Etiopía* and *El Santo negro Rosambuco* (Fra-Molinero, "Los negros como figura" 10–11).[23] The condemnation of blackness depicted in Renaissance writing was also a central tenet of Catholic theology in colonial Spanish America.

Jesuit priest Alonso de Sandoval reasoned that if the leopard could not change his spots, he could at least purify his soul (Olsen, *Slavery* 86–87). Sandoval advocated for the spiritual redemption of the souls of black folks arguing in *De Instauranda æthiopum Salute* (1627), "aunque a la vista son negros, pueden tener la candidez y blancura, que dà la sangre de Christo a quien se lava con ella." (Although they are black to the eye, they can have the innocence and whiteness that Christ's blood gives to one who is washed in it [Olsen, *Slavery* 84–85]). Sandoval insisted that God did not disparage Africans for their pigmentation, "porque jamas Dios desprecia colores, sino precia almas para subirlas al colmo de los bienes espirituales" (because God never disdains colors, but rather values souls to lift them to the peak of spiritual riches) (Olsen, *Slavery* 83).[24] Sandoval's belief that the blood of Christ could cleanse the black man's soul has implications for my treatment of Plácido's sacred poetry.

If Plácido wasn't seduced by the promise of white privilege, how could Cuban critics redeem his *soul* and absorb him into an otherwise white literary canon? Plácido's redemption acquired a symbolic meaning for his biographers that insisted he was neither an apolitical author who spewed "nonsense," as Sanguily had charged ("Un improvisador cubano" 161, 166), nor a revolutionary, as the government contended.[25] I analyze Francisco Calcagno, Sebastián Alfredo de Morales and Jorge Castellanos' construction of Plácido as a lamb to the slaughter, a tragic yet innocent mulatto who revealed courage under fire. I argue that the image of Plácido the blameless Catholic emerged from a myopic reading of his sacred poetry. My analysis bears out that Plácido's devotion to *La Religión* afforded a sense of respectability for a poet of ignoble birth, but it did not necessarily signify deference to God and the queen.

Plácido's sacred poetry varies in form and content, and I classify it as commemorative verse, poems about the Passion of the Christ, prison poems, and writings that appeal to Afro-Caribbean religious sensibilities. Plácido's first publication—a piece of literary criticism—appeared in *el Diario de la Habana* in 1834. But he inaugurated his career in *La Aurora de Matanzas* two years later, publishing resurrection poems and laudatory verse in honor of the Spanish crown. Matanzas was the hub of a burgeoning freeborn professional elite, and the city became the focal point of Plácido's literary and conspiratorial activities. Plácido dedicated four poems to Matanzas parish priest Dr. Don Manuel Francisco García that provide an insightful though fragmentary record of his relationship to the clerical elite.[26] Within this collection of nine religious texts, five poems emerge that either portray the magnificence of the Messiah or memorialize the construction of the Matanzas Parochial Church.[27] One such sonnet heaps a great deal of praise on Father Manuel Francisco García. The first stanza immortalizes Father García alongside Dominican priest Bartolomé de las Casas (1484–1566) and Cuban bishop Juan José Díaz de Espada (1756–1832). Here are the final six lines of the poem.

> Disfruta el lauro que te dá la historia,
> De la casa de Dios, ministro santo;

Y cuando vueles á la eterna gloria,
De cada boca escucharás un canto,
Siendo de la virtud sublime ejemplo,
Y en cada corazón tendrás un templo (Valdés, *Plácido: Poesías completas* 23).

(Relish the laurel that history confers on you
From the House of God, holy minister;
And when you ascend to eternal glory,
From each mouth, you will hear a song,
Being a sublime exemplar of virtue
And in each heart, you will have a temple).

Father García is regarded as an immaculate soul, a virtuous creature that presents Christ to his inviolate bride. The priest ascends to the heavenly hosts like Jesus Christ before him. Father García shepherds his flock, and he consecrates each heart so that there is "a temple" within believers. Plácido not only applauded the priest, but he also enshrined the "holy minister" as an "exemplar of virtue" in the annals of Catholic religious history.

Plácido's poem commending the positioning of the first stone of the nave of the Matanzas Church also reads as an ode to Father Manuel Francisco García, as the first seven lines bear out.

Salve, pastor benéfico y humano,
Que ensanchas el redil dó las ovejas
Con rostro humilde y corazon cristiano,
Himnos entonan llenos de alegría
Al rey de reyes que el Empíreo mora,
Al que la corte celestial adora,
Al Dios, hijo del hombre y de María. (Valdés, *Plácido, Gabriel de la Concepción* 610–611)

(Hail, beneficent and human shepherd,
That increases the fold where the sheep [reside]
With humble visage and a Christian heart
They intone joyful hymns
To the King of Kings that dwells in the Empyrean,
Whom the celestial court adores,
To God, son of man and of Mary)

Plácido lauded the parish priest as a "beneficent and human shepherd" with "humble visage and [a] Christian heart." He likened the cleric to Moses's brother Aaron: "Hoy que un nuevo Aaron humilde / bautiza tu santa casa" (Today a new humble Aaron / Consecrates your holy dwelling) (Valdés, *Plácido, Gabriel de la Concepción* 613). The temple is a sacred metaphor for the Catholic Church and for the consecrated heart of believers. The parish priest has christened both temples and made them into hallowed dwellings of the Lord.[28] In the poem, Father García epitomizes the *imitatio Christi*, that is, the unimpeachable imitation of the Christ.[29] On the whole, such literature is clichéd, uninspired, and devoid of personal sentiment, lending credence to Sanguily's charge that Plácido was little more than an opportunist and a sycophant who garnered favor with whoever might be of use. But Plácido had deep political reasons for genuflecting before the parish priest.

Manuel Francisco García represented the intellectual and religious interests of the western Cuban elite. The Catholic Church assigned priests to cities and towns and located parishes where there were significant white populations (Knight 107), and the expansion of sugar production in the region brought about growth in the captive African population. García's construction of the parochial church and the role he played as founder of the Matanzas Faculty of Philosophy of the University of Havana (Valdés, *Plácido, Gabriel de la Concepción* 668), are emblematic of the wealth created by the exploitation of African labor and the material progress it produced for Creole society. Naturally, the poetry Plácido dedicated to the parish priest is silent on this matter, proffering no critique of the Church's complicity in slavery. But Father García's role in the Faculty of Philosophy was further proof of the Church's monopoly on the very nature and definition of knowledge.

Although the law did not subject free blacks and mulattoes to bondage, Spanish legal codes did exert control over their quotidian pursuits. Colonial legislation sought to delineate and structure the political possibilities of free-born African descendants. Legislation forbade free blacks and mulattoes to possess firearms, required they carry licenses attesting to their freedom, sought to regulate their public appearance, and required them to have white patrons (Knight 124). Plácido maintained an important relationship with Matanzas parish priest Manuel Francisco García, upon whose protection he relied (Calcagno 100). The Holy Office of the Spanish Inquisition, whose mission was to maintain "an order secured through culture" (Palmié, *Wizards* 228), never took root in Cuba. But I believe Plácido's religious poetry demonstrated an awareness of the Inquisitorial mandate and functioned as an effort to garner legitimacy in the public sphere where African Cuban spirituality was under assault by Christian proselytism.

Plácido's poetry about the death and resurrection of Jesus Christ can be read as a putative statement of doctrine. The poems reflect dogma regarding sinful humanity, the need for repentance, redemption, and the preeminence of the Christian God.[30] Jesus is enshrined as the Messiah and the Redeemer, an afflicted yet resurrected Savior, whose epic triumph over death and the grave is celebrated by all of nature. Death is the dreadful yet awe-inspiring theme of these poems that draw attention to divine suffering caused by human transgression. Published in 1836 (and again in 1838) in *La Aurora de Matanzas*, "Muerte de Jesucristo" (Death of Jesus Christ) is a requiem for the fallen Messiah. As in Scripture, the first two stanzas portray the death of Christ as an event that reverberates throughout nature: the sky becomes dark, lightning strikes, the stones break open, the rivers cease to flow, the birds refuse to sing, and even the dead rise. The third and fourth stanzas portray the suffering of Christ for a contemptible world.

> Cuando en el monte Gólgota sagrado
> Dice el Dios-Hombre con dolor profundo:
> <<Cúmplase, Padre, em mí vuestro mandato>>
> Y á la rabia de un pueblo furibundo,
> Inocente, sangriento y enclavado,
> Muere en la cruz el Salvador del mundo. (Valdés, *Plácido, Gabriel de la Concepción* 31)

> (When on the sacred Mount of Golgotha
> With profound pain the God-Man says
> <<Father, may your will be done>>
> And for the rage of an infuriated people,
> Innocent, bloodied and nailed,
> The Savior of the world dies.)

Christ submits to the will of God the Father, surrendering his life to cleanse the iniquities of wretched humanity. The sharp distinction between "an infuriated people" and an "Innocent, [and] bloodied" Savior convinces the reader of the moral superiority of the Godhead. The Cuban people, whatever their station in life may be, are unworthy—though desperately in need—of redemption. The central tenets of Plácido's poems about the Passion of the Christ were humility and self-abnegation, and they bespoke the qualities that the priesthood required of black and mulatto proselytes. Plácido makes himself into a worthy subject in these poems, for he performed the grace and humility the Church expected of him.

"Muerte del Redentor" (Death of the Redeemer) (1839, 1841) is a narrative poem where the crucifixion atones for sin again and alters natural phenomena within the material world. Plácido also published this poem in honor of Father García. Jesus is likened to God the Father in both poems, but there is a notable difference. In "Muerte del Redentor," Jesus is "Hijo en carne de Dios" (Son in the flesh of God), and the "Hijo de Dios Padre" (Son of God the Father) (Valdés, *Plácido, Gabriel de la Concepción* 606–608), whereas in "Muerte de Jesucristo" Jesus is rendered "Dios-Hombre" (God-Man) (Valdés, *Plácido:*

*Poesías completas* 31). Although endowed with unparalleled redemptive power, the Christ figure submits to the Father, since the poet refers to him as the Son. Such a designation conforms to Catholic doctrine, which maintains that God the Father is the ultimate patriarch. The poetic persona in both texts identifies Jesus as the self-sacrificial Son of God, in that way embracing the apostolic yet paradoxical view of the Church that Jesus possessed the contradictory qualities of the divine and the human.

Perhaps what is most remarkable is that Plácido suggested that colonial authorities persecuted him in a manner comparable to Jesus Christ at the hands of the Roman Empire. Under constant surveillance and imminent threat of search and seizure, Plácido's body was on trial. The nearly white status some critics and contemporaries ascribed to him was a myth born of the romanticization of the mulatto as a subject in medias res. Prior to 1844 Plácido was arrested on three separate occasions for seditious writing, for closely associating with other mulattoes who had also fallen under suspicion, and for conspiring against whites (Cué, *Plácido: El poeta* 86, 89). The authorities detained him in 1838 for "La sombra de Padilla" (The Shadow of Padilla), a protest poem that admonished the queen of Spain to heed Cuban cries for liberty (Horrego Estuch, *Plácido: el poeta* 70–71). Subsequent arrests, interrogations, and lengthy detentions in 1839, in Villa Clara, and once more in 1843, while returning from Cienfuegos represent a consistent pattern of government suspicion. Colonial authorities so feared Gabriel de la Concepción Valdés that they forbade him to travel throughout the island without the consent of Matanzas governor García Oña (Cué, *Plácido: El poeta* 88). As a rule, the prison poems refer to literature that Plácido wrote shortly before his execution and smuggled out of prison. Nonetheless, I am referring to poems Plácido wrote in prison before 1844, that embody a subtle but significant shift in the political tone of his Catholic poetry, and signal resistance and social protest: "A la muerte de Cristo" (To the Death of Christ), "La resurrección" (The Resurrection), and two relatively unknown poems, "Mi Prisión" (My Imprisonment) and "A Lince, desde la prisión" (To Lince, from Prison).

Plácido composed poetry while imprisoned in Trinidad, which later appeared in *La Aurora de Matanzas*. He sought to accomplish paradoxical but equally important objectives: reassure his broad readership of his allegiance to the Holy Faith even while conveying a sense of resolve to his supporters.[31] The government incarcerated Plácido to supress a discourse that was contrary to the maintenance of power, something censorship had failed to do. The authorities suppressed Plácido's ideas throughout his brief career; this culminated in his execution, which is the ultimate act of silencing. But when Plácido smuggled poems to the outside world from prison, he effectively circumvented censorship. Moreover, he managed to employ Catholic discourse to create a space where he might contest his own captivity.[32] Even if it was customary for Cuban poets to write about the Passion of the Christ during Holy Week, "A la muerte de Cristo" (To the Death of Christ) and "La resurrección" (The Resurrection) are peculiar, in view of the fact that they were written from prison by an African-descended poet accused of conspiracy against the white race (Valdés, *Plácido, poeta, y mártir* 150). First, let us examine the typical features of these poems.

"A la muerte de Cristo" and "La resurrección" are characteristic of commem-orative literature that venerates the crucifixion and resurrection of the Messiah. "A la muerte de Cristo" (1843) is a fire-and-brimstone poem about treacher-ous and brutal humanity, desperately in need, even if unworthy, of redemption. The Christian God is the ultimate Creator and judge: "Destructor de Sodoma" ([the] Destroyer of Sodom) "Hacdeor Supremo" (Supreme Maker), and "Rey de los reyes" (King of Kings). The wrathful deity of the Hebraic tradition is likened to the New Testament God, a holy and sacred father demanding righ-teousness but—much to the astonishment of the poet—also predisposed to sacrifice for the redemption of wayward man (Valdés, *Plácido, poeta, y mártir* 149–150). "La resurrección" (1843) adopts an exultant tone that venerates the rebirth of Jesus Christ from the dead as a glorious conqueror.[33] The resurrec-tion of Jesus Christ is triumph over evil, death, and the grave, but the premier glory is reserved not for the Son but for the Father. Plácido wrote in a patri-archal voice so that Mary the mother of Jesus and Mary Magdalene did not figure prominently. Female biblical characters were mere beneficiaries of patri-archal benevolence, not agents of their own redemption or active in the salva-tion of others. Plácido's androcentric path to the divine was incongruent with the emphasis many Cubans placed on the Virgin Mary, a trend that emerged in medieval Mediterranean Catholicism and took root in popular religious practice on the island (Elena Díaz 96). Among African peoples, the Catholic pantheon of saints and paths to the Virgin Mary provided a rubric of religious legitimacy for the concealment of non-Christian beliefs (Cros Sandoval 41, 53). Without the Virgin Mary and the saints, the sacred is confined to knowledge of God the Father and the Son, thus rendering alternative paths to the divine unat-tainable. In subsequent chapters, I address how Plácido's representations of the Virgin Mary and the saints privilege popular ritual practices over dogma, thus empowering the improvisational proclivities of the subject and creating space for Afro-Caribbean spirituality.

The prison poems indisputably represent the passion of the Christ, but they also play on the doctrine of sin and repentance to condemn the "crímenes" (crimes) of the colonial order. Below, are three stanzas from "A la muerte de Cristo."

Tanto es verdad, que la infernal malicia
Raza de maldición reina entre nos!
Quién extraña en los hombres la injusticia
Si supieron usarla hasta con Dios?
[ . . . ]

Un falso amigo te vende
Y del pueblo entre la turba,
Ante un débil juez pareces
Que te sentencia sin culpa.
[. . . .]


Pero tú, Señor, en breve
Alzarás la frente fúlgida
Y ellos bajarán envueltos
En crímenes a la tumba. (Valdés, *Plácido, poeta, y mártir* 149)


(It is truly infernal malevolence
The cursed race that reigns among us
Who is astonished by the injustice of mankind
If mankind knew how to exercise malice against God?
[. . . .]


A false friend betrays you
And from the people among the horde,
You appear before a feeble judge
That condemns you without fault.
[. . . .]


But soon you, Lord,
You will raise your immaculate brow
And enveloped in their crimes
They will descend into the tomb.)

Plácido introduced the notion of racial difference in a poem commemorating the Passion of the Christ. A false friend betrays "The Redeemer of the Universe" and subjects him to violence at the hands of an irreverent horde. However, the biblical portrait of sinful humanity is racialized, depicted as "aquesta estirpe impura" (that impure lineage) and "Raza de maldición reina entre nos" ([The] cursed race that reigns among us) (Valdés, *Plácido, poeta, y mártir* 149). Race is a pejorative signifier in colonial discourse assigning hypodescent to persons of named or claimed African ancestry. But the meaning of the word is modified in the immediate context of this poem as a textual strategy that condemns white hegemony. There is no doubt that *the cursed race* is the white race that "reigns" over an ever-expanding population of African captives and their Cuban-born descendants, so that the poet justifiably avows: "Y ellos bajarán envueltos / En crímenes a la tumba" (And enveloped in their crimes / They will descend into the tomb) (Valdés, *Plácido, poeta, y mártir* 149). Plácido's denunciation of white racial politics resignifies Cuban slave society as an unclean horde unable to escape the impending judgment. In this instance, race does not constitute a phenotypical condition but rather signals a moral pathology. Impurity denotes immorality; it is a sign of the moral degradation of white Cubans who sin against the Christian God by enslaving Africans. Remarkably, Plácido is transformed from sycophant into a subversive religious subject with a counterhegemonic project of racial equality.

In an ode to Sebastián Alfredo de Morales entitled, "A Lince, desde la prisión" (To Lince, from Prison), Plácido refers to his white confidant as an exception to the *engañosa raza*, the deceitful race. Plácido divested whiteness of its representational power so that persons of named and claimed European ancestry might lose their hierarchical standing as Christian inhabitants of "the ever-faithful isle."[34] The poet likened his imprisonment to the tribulations of the Christ, since his arrest resulted from an anonymous source, a Judas of sorts that betrayed his trust and informed the governor of Trinidad of conspiratorial activity.[35] Like Manzano's autobiography, Plácido inverted moral categories by comparing himself with Jesus, the Lamb to the slaughter. I do not believe the cross is merely a liturgical device in these prison poems, but rather a rhetorical one that affords a sense of morality to Plácido's strident critique of whiteness.

Plácido was accused of colluding to ignite a race war on Cuban soil, but he maintained a defiant and dismissive tone in "Mi prisión," a poem dedicated to his second spouse, María Gila Morales Poveda. "Mi prisión" is by far the boldest poem regarding his incarceration in Trinidad.[36] Plácido portrayed military confinement as a crucible for the Christian soul, which is refined like gold so that the poet boasts: "Pray to God always / That every four months / I would be behind bars for two" (Valdés, *Plácido, poeta, y mártir* 152). In a stroke of Romanticism, Plácido portrays himself as a Christian captive, a suffering sojourner who was wrongfully accused and detained. Conspicuously absent from this poem, however, is a refutation of the explosive charges brought against him: incitement to rebellion and race war. The poet's rejoinder is an avowal of patriotism: "Así mientras se averigua / Si soy inocente, o no, / Me ensayo para ser útil / A la patria que es mi primor" (And so while they examine / If I am innocent or not / I endeavor to be of use to the fatherland / Which is my darling) (Valdés, *Plácido, poeta, y mártir* 151). Nationalist discourse represents the African-descended poet as a noble and dutiful soul whose true loyalty is not to black people but to *la patria*, the Cuban fatherland. In 1844 such a line of reasoning resurfaced in the poet's eleventh-hour plea to the president of the Military Commission in Matanzas, but to no avail. Plácido exclaimed, "porque colocado (permítame VS. decirlo) a una altura de civilización que ellos no alcanzan, estoy resuelto a cumplir con los deberes que me imponen la naturaleza, la humanidad y mi patria" (because I am situated (If Your Grace will allow me to say it) at the height of civilization they have not reached, I am resolved to fulfill the duties that nature, humanity and my country require of me" (Cué, *Plácido: El poeta* 304).

Fischer reads Plácido's political poems in their precise historical context, suggesting that praise for the queen regent María Cristina reflected a general sense of enthusiasm in Cuba regarding her enactment of a liberal constitution in 1836. Her reading of the poem "La Ambarina: En los días de S. M. la Reina Gobernadora" (In the Days of Her Majesty the Regent Queen) is instructive. Soon after the enactment of the liberal constitution, the monarchy made clear that Spain would be governed by one set of laws, and the plantation colony by another. Fischer reasons that Plácido's euphoric praise devolved into scorn since "the agent of liberty has become the oppressor" (102–103). Furthermore, she correctly points out that white Cubans and liberal Spaniards sought to resolve the problem of the "universality of liberty" by placing severe limitations along geopolitical/color lines (104). Comparable to black insurgent José Antonio Aponte, Plácido's politics also disrupted his cultural significance in Cuban society. The articulation of Plácido's racial politics in "Mi prisión," "A Lince, desde la prisión," "A la muerte de Cristo," and the satire I have examined deconstructs the premises of whiteness doctrine that claims a privilege based on an imagined moral, religious, and racial pulchritude. Plácido's project was radical (and therefore dangerous) because he incorporated the race question into contemporary debates on liberalism so that whiteness ceased to be what Jerome Branche has termed a "metaphor for the absence of contamination" (*Colonialism* 87). The words "Guinea" and "African lineage" in his satires not only gestured toward the black grandmother in the kitchen, so to speak, but also reminded the reader that white power derived from the Spanish American slave regime that performed violence in discourse and in social practices. Thus, free blacks and mulattoes could not liberate themselves by becoming white, but rather their freedom depended on a sustained connection with African ancestors. Nevertheless, Cuban scholars desired a less offensive Plácido, a mild *mestizo* writer with undisputed loyalties to the Catholic Church who fit neatly into the narrative of Christian martyrdom.

Francisco Calcagno was a white abolitionist and novelist from the sugarproducing town of Güines, whose book *Poetas de color* (1887) depicted Plácido as a Christian martyr who suffered violence in what constituted "la mancha más negra de nuestra historia política y literaria" (the darkest stain on our political and literary history) (7, 24). Calcagno cited Plácido's final letter to his wife María Gila Morales Poveda wherein he referred to the poet as "modelo de resignacion cristiana" (a model of Christian resignation) (24).[37] For Calcagno, Plácido was not a revolutionary, but rather a persecuted soul. His story figured among those of other "poets of color," like the well-known Juan Francisco Manzano and the nearly forgotten José del Carmen Díaz, who lived in bondage and intoned the humble cry of their Cuban lyre. Plácido's association with the downtrodden required not only complete exoneration but Christian modesty as well.

Allí, despues de oida su sentencia, el sinventura poeta que no tenia á quien volver los ojos para hallar un rostro amigo y protector, se arrojó en brazos de la Religion, y como el cisne moribundo, compuso sus mejores cantos . . . (Calcagno 22)

(After hearing the judgment against him, the ill-fated poet who had no one to look to in hopes of finding a friendly and sheltering face, threw himself into the arms of the Religion, and like a dying swan, composed his best poems . . . )

The scene reads like a passage from Romantic fiction. The poet is a forlorn victim in a calamitous moment without a friendly face to shelter him, thus hurling himself into the arms of "la Religion," personified by parish priest Manuel F. García. The denial of subjectivity invalidates the charges brought against Plácido, given that colonial authorities not only convicted him for involvement in the 1844 antislavery movement but also supposed he was the chief architect. In Calcagno's account Plácido was incapable of violence even to preserve his own life; he was the defanged mulatto who resigned himself to an unjust fate. Christian martyrdom is premised on the notion of divine calling, predestination, and the inherent tragedy of the prophetic tradition. Not only is the martyr's cause worthy of a violent death, but it is also a death that has been divinely ordained, so that Plácido has no way out.

Alfredo de Morales's 1886 edition repeats Calcagno's earlier claim that Plácido approached the firing squad with Christian resignation, but he complicates the notion of martyrdom by ascribing to him the power of prophecy. Morales released his edition of Plácido's poetry nearly two decades after Martin Delany and William Wells Brown had lionized Plácido and Manzano as black literary geniuses. Morales distanced Plácido from the black abolitionist project by constructing a near-deification of the poet that rendered him a mulatto prophet.[38] Plácido is said to have comforted a dithering friend, co-conspirator Santiago Pimienta, and to have composed his most beautiful *cantos* hours before his execution. Parish priest Manuel Francisco García's gift of a crucifix became emblematic of Plácido's own execution, since, like Christ, he was portrayed as a guiltless Lamb made to walk his own Via Dolorosa. Such a description of the final moments before execution is further dramatized when Morales not only exculpated the poet but also beatified him.

Era todo un profeta que con lira coronada de eslabones de hierro atravesaba por entre las grandes oleadas de la humanidad á la conquista de la gloria. ("El prólogo," Morales xxxvi)

(He was an absolute prophet with a lyre crowned with chains of iron walking through the great waves of humanity to the conquest of glory.)

In contradistinction to Calcagno's account of humble acquiescence, Morales's version of events resembles the righteous (and inescapable) sacrifice of the Hebraic prophets whose divine calling ends in martyrdom. But critics cannot have it both ways. In Christian scripture, the prophet-martyr is not a guiltless bystander, as Calcagno and Morales suggest. Old Testament prophets preached imminent judgment that threatened the legitimacy of political structures and complicated the maintenance of power.

Jorge Castellanos joined the chorus when he cited the work of Alfredo de Morales to assert that Plácido's ideological posture had emerged from his belief in a Christian universal order whose function was to explain everything that existed and everything that took place, even the absurd. Such a universal order meant that Plácido understood himself as *un agente del Señor*, an agent of the Lord, so that his poetry was a moral instrument of social critique and betterment (Castellanos 20–21). Once more, Plácido was positioned within Catholic orthodoxy, not only renowned as a practicing Catholic but, as Alfredo de Morales maintained, a prophet in the tradition of the Christian scriptures. This interpretation of the poet's religious-themed verse is superficial, in view of the fact that it uncritically equates the lyrical representation of a Catholic belief system with Plácido's uncomplicated and orthodox devotion to the Church's teachings. On the whole, there is little distance between reality and representation in Castellanos's analyses and no consideration of Plácido's political motives. At best, Plácido's prison poetry and correspondence are evidence of the precariousness of his position before the military commission. My research bears out (and Plácido's biographers concur) that he was a deeply religious individual. But if as Calcagno suggests Plácido turned to "La Religion" under duress, he may not have done so as an act of faithfulness, but rather to preserve his life. That is not to say that Plácido was not a Catholic; he certainly was. I do not deny that when read in aggregate Plácido's political and religious poetry lends itself to a sense of destiny, fatalism, and even prophetic authority. Nonetheless, we cannot define such religiosity in strictly Catholic terms. I demonstrate in chapter 5 that a sense of prophetic authority informed Plácido's work, but that the epistemological basis of that authority was—for the most part—African, not Christian in inspiration.

## Conclusion

Plácido's biographers and critics constructed a mulatto-Catholic persona that fit neatly into the white colonial imaginary. The colonial authorities executed him as the architect of an island-wide plot to eradicate the white race. Notwithstanding the burden of historical truth, critics rewrote Plácido's narrative as a tragic mulatto whose Christian resignation enabled him to face unjust suffering. Critics ascribed to Plácido the noble obedience of an ancient prophet, and they rendered him a defanged, pitiable Other that would be palatable to a white Cuban readership and suitable for the literary tradition. Although Plácido repudiated the notion of the mulatto escape hatch, and he pinpointed black and mulatto origins in Africa, he also underscored his relationship to the Church to ensure the publication of his literature and evade suspicions of his conspiratorial activities. Plácido's acquaintance with parish priest Manuel Francisco García proved to be a lesson in futility. Not only did Father García fail to shield Plácido from a death sentence, but he was also the very person the military tribunal assigned to read him his last rites.

> . . . auto superior de aprobacion del Escmo. Sr. Capitan General de la Isla, del dia veinte y dos del referido mes, se constituyeron en capilla en la indicada pieza, quedando entregados á los Sres. presbíteros Dr. D. Manuel Francisco García, cura párroco, [ . . . ] para su direccion espiritual . . .[39]

> ( . . . high judicial decree [with] the approval of his excellency Mr. Capitan General of the Island on the twenty-second of this month, they gathered in the chapel as indicated in this document given over to the presbyters Dr. D. Manuel Francisco García, parish priest, [ . . . ] for spiritual direction.)

Plácido and his co-conspirators gathered in the chapel before authorities handed them over to the priesthood. Among the chaplains Plácido recognized a familiar face: Father Manuel Francisco García. The military tribunal had instructed Father García to provide consolation and "spiritual direction" and assistance for those that were to be executed. Plácido's presumptive guardian proved to be more an agent of the crown than an advocate for the oppressed.

CHAPTER FOUR

# Present but Unseen
## African-Cuban Spirituality and Emancipation in the
## Literature of Juan Francisco Manzano

Cumplo, pero no obedezco.

COLONIAL SPANISH AMERICAN ADAGE

### Death of the Black Matriarch in Juan Francisco Manzano's Autobiography

Manzano's mother died without forewarning. Her sudden death orphaned Manzano and his siblings Florencio, Fernando, and María del Rosario. Even worse, Manzano didn't discover she had died until four days after her demise. His autobiography is silent about the cause of death, and we do not know why Manzano was not notified sooner. But in all likelihood, his slaveowner felt neither compunction nor obligation to give account of María de Pilar Manzano's death. Manzano was determined to ensure that his mother received proper burial though his mistress had denied him the occasion to make end-of-life decisions regarding her care. Manzano described his bereavement thus: "mi madre era lo unico q$^e$. allí tenia y esa no esistia mis lagrimas corrian con abundancia" (my mother was all I had and she no longer existed; my tears ran profusely) (Manzano, *Autobiografía* 331, 333). He made hasty funerary arrangements. And since his mother had been the chief housemaid, the marchioness gave Manzano three pesos to offer a requiem mass for her soul, also known as the Mass of Saint Gregory. María de Pilar's lengthy domestic service to Doña Beatriz and her daughter Prado Ameno meant her labor was invaluable to the maintenance of the household. Domestic servants that died were afforded similar tribute in the antebellum United States, and slaveholding families granted them proper burial (Young 178–179).

Manzano arranged to have the assistant priest (*coadjutor*) give mass for his mother's soul. Yet his profound discontent led him to purchase additional

120

masses for his late mother (Manzano, *Autobiografía* 333). Catholic burial rites were a sign of respectability for Cubans of African descent. Cuban slave labor camps extracted so much labor from black people that on many nineteenth-century plantations, slaves averaged less than seven years from the moment of their arrival. Preventable diseases, dreadful work conditions, and malnutrition cut the lives of enslaved people terribly short (Pérez 98). Such a brutal labor regime virtually deprived black lives of sacred meaning. Life was often bereft of meaning, so the enslaved community learned to consecrate death. Manzano secured additional funerary masses, which signaled his determination to wrest control of the symbolic practices with which white Cubans governed slave society. Manzano sought to put her earthly affairs in order and to secure her safe passage to the hereafter.

Manzano's demand for additional requiems signaled his knowledge of Catholic burial rites, but it also bespoke the intimacy of the mother–son relationship. Manzano was not alone in his request. Afro-Latin Americans called upon Catholic priests to administer rites on their behalf (Wade 480). This means that Afro-Latin Americans acknowledged the significance of Catholic symbolic practices and engaged them as a respected body of religious knowledge. Moreover, the following passages from Manzano's narrative shed light on the ways in which enslaved persons placed tremendous importance on the transition of loved ones from the natural world to the spirit world.

se me embotaron los todos sentimientos de gratitud y solo meditaba en mi fuga pasado algunos días bendí a un platero la manilla medio siete pesos y algunos reales p$^r$. ella y en la noche cuando dejé a mi ama en casa de las S$^{ras}$. Gomes le llevé los pesos al padre cuajutor p$^a$. misas p$^r$. mi madre y los reales fueron en belas p$^a$. las animas no tardó mucho tiempo mi señora en saber p$^r$. el mimso padre q$^e$. avia mandado desir tantas misas, preguntóme de donde tenia ese dinero mas como lo q$^e$. yo menos apresiaba p$^r$. entonces era vivir le dije sin rodeos q$^e$. bendí una manilla, quiso saber a quien mas dí palabra al platero de no desirlo me sostube disiendo q$^e$. a uno q$^e$. no conosia; pues ahora sabras p$^a$. qué nasistes me dijo tu no puedes disponer de nada sin mi consentimiento fuy preso al Molino ya era esta la tersera vez (Manzano, *Autobiografía* 333).

(All my feelings of gratitude were exhausted and I only contemplated my escape. A few days later I sold a bracelet to a silversmith for seven pesos and a couple of *reales*. At night, I left my mistress at the residence of Señor and Señora Gómez and I took the pesos to the assistant priest [to pay for] masses for my mother and the *reales* were for votive candles for souls. It was not long that my mistress found out by [speaking to] the same priest from whom I had requested several additional masses, and she asked me how I had acquired the money. My life was the thing that I least valued at that time. And I told her bluntly that I had sold a bracelet. She wanted to know to whom but I had given my word to the silversmith not to tell. So, I kept saying [I had sold it] to someone she didn't know. Well, she told me, now you'll find out why you were born. You cannot dispose of anything without my consent. I was taken prisoner to the El Molino sugar plantation. That was already the third time [that had happened].)[1]

The death of Manzano's mother marked a critical rupture in the autobiographical narrative. Manzano—who described himself as frail and small in stature—suddenly risked life and limb to ensure that his mother had transitioned properly to the spirit world (Manzano, *Autobiografía* 305, 309). Manzano sold possessions to procure additional requiems for his mother's spirit. This bespoke a religious imperative and an ethical obligation to his parents, whom he poignantly described in an 1838 poem as "Que el primer ser nos dieron" (Those that gave us our first existence) (Manzano, *El Álbum* 120). That Manzano planned these funerary masses in secret is not surprising, considering the physical and psychological brutality of his mistress. But Manzano's candid response to Prado Ameno's routine interrogation of his motives and movements constitutes an entirely new moment within the text. Comparable to Frederick Douglass, this symbolic fracas with the marchioness is Manzano's Covey moment. Douglass recounted the violent confrontation with the overseer: "This battle with Mr. Covey was the turning-point in my career as a slave. It rekindled the few expiring embers of freedom, and revived within me a sense of my own manhood" (69). Douglass rekindled what remained of his desire to be free, and he purged himself of the "cowardice" that had defined his early years (69). Manzano began to deconstruct the good-slave image subsequent to his mother's death. This transformation in self-concept eventually made freedom attainable.

I argue that Manzano acknowledged the legitimacy of Catholic burial practices, and he appealed to the power invested in the priesthood to elevate his mother's standing in the hereafter. But his deference for Catholic requiems neither constituted an indifference to African-inspired spirituality nor represented a disdain for African sources of religious power. Manzano negotiated the disparities between Catholic doctrine and African-inspired ideas about death, the afterlife, and the struggle for black freedom. In so doing, Manzano produced *transculturated colonial literature* that evoked Yoruba-inspired ideas about spirit apparitions and the power of African divine spirits, also known by Catholic saint names. Furthermore, Manzano engaged Bakongo-inspired ideas about death, ancestors, and the nature of the spirit world to pursue his brother's emancipation. Manzano's reliance on African Atlantic religions is significant because the Catholic Church condemned them as superstition that abused and eroded ecclesiastical authority. Manzano's claim to sacred authority was comparable to Father Félix Varela's critique in *Cartas a Elpidio* that superstitious Cubans had "erigirse en oráculo" (erect themselves as oracles) (86).

Manzano utilized Catholic metaphors to depict the transformation within: "desde el momento en q^e. perdí la alhagueña ilusion de mi esperanza ya no era un esclavo fiel me combertí de manso cordero en la criatura mas despresia [ . . . ] solo meditaba en mi fuga" (From the moment I lost the promising illusion of my hope, I was no longer a faithful slave. I was converted from a meek lamb into the most despicable creature imaginable [ . . . ] I only contemplated my escape) (Manzano, *Autobiografía* 333). He evoked the central paradox of Christianity to demonstrate the radical shift within his consciousness: Jesus is both sacrificial Lamb and Lion of the Tribe of Judah. Just as the biblical Christ abandoned his meek persona to become the Lion of the Tribe of Judah in the Book of Revelation, so Manzano rejected the martyrdom that slavery demanded of its captives. His rhetorical choices were deliberate. Manzano evoked a transformation within when he defended his mother, writing *me combertí* (I was converted) or *convertirme* (converting myself) (Manzano, *Autobiografía* 311–312). As in his poem "A Jesús en la Cruz," Manzano rejected the doctrine of self-sacrifice as a means to redemption. But his postmortem defense of his mother not only safeguarded her memory but also ensured that she would enter quietly into her *second existence*. In this regard, the Mass of Saint Gregory was a means to a metaphysical end.

Manzano's devotion to his mother was as real in death as it had been in life, so that the demise of the black matriarch did not mean she had ceased to *exist*. Manzano availed himself of a Catholic funerary ritual to ensure his mother's safe passage to heaven. In fact, Manzano's use of the Spanish word *animas* (Manzano, *Autobiografía* 333–334), which refers to a soul in purgatory, suggests that the St. Gregory Mass would ensure that his mother be received on high. The 1796 slave catechism describes Purgatory as one of "los cuatro calabozos" (the four dungeons) where human souls suffer different forms of separation from the Christian God (Barreras 67).

Pero el que jace pecados *veniales* (pecados chicos) ese no es menester que vaya al Infierno; pero es preciso que vaya al Purgatorio, porque eso es faltar á la cortesía á Dios. *En el Purgatorio es donde se paga todo lo que falta que pagar por los pecados, y donde se limpian las manchas que dejan en el alma los pecados porque (ya lo he dicho) ninguno que debe, ninguno que tiene que mancha entra en el Cielo. (Barreras 82–83).

(But he that commits *venial* sins (minor sins) does not deserve to go to Hell; but it is necessary that he goes to Purgatory, because this is a lack of courtesy toward God. *Purgatory is where he pays the debt of his sins, and where the blemishes that sins have left on his soul are washed away because (as I have said) no one should, no one that bears a blemish shall enter into Heaven.)

Catholics that had committed minor sins went to Purgatory; but it was an impermanent solution, a transitory space that cleansed believers of sin and rendered them without blemish. Catholic doctrine regarding redemption was unequivocal: "no one that bears a blemish shall enter into Heaven" (Barreras 83). Manzano's insistence on additional requiems for his mother's soul implies that he was uncertain of her standing with the Church. Conceivably, María de Pilar had committed venial sins before she died, or perhaps she had not confessed her sins as the priesthood mandated. We do not know for sure. Whatever the case, Manzano deemed the requiem mass a necessary ritual owing to the abrupt nature of her demise and his inability to make spiritual preparations for her departure.

The Saint Gregory Mass from fourteenth-century Europe granted Christian burial to individuals that died without confession, ensuring that they would not suffer eternal damnation. Legend has it that Pope Gregory ordered thirty masses for the soul of an Italian monk that had broken his vows of poverty, subsequently died, and had been denied Christian burial. The pope redeemed the monk soul's through intercession, and he was released from Purgatory and welcomed into heaven (Ibáñez García 8, 11). Afro-Latin Americans relied on the requiem mass ever since the early colonial period to ensure the salvation of their coreligionists. In 1632 Afro-Mexicans petitioned the local government of Tlaxcala for permission to form a religious confraternity devoted to Our Lady of the Rosary in the convent of San Francisco. Though some petitioners had apparently been born in West Africa and West Central Africa, their petition implies considerable knowledge of Church dogma. Among their objectives for forming the confraternity was their desire to bury their dead and say masses for them (Bristol, *Christians, Blasphemers* 94). In colonial Cuba, Saint Francis of Assisi was the saint most often represented in black Cuban funerary practices. Black Cubans prayed to the thirteenth-century saint more than any other divine intermediary, and they implored him to intercede for the salvation of their souls (Hevia 25).

Manzano relied on the priesthood to intercede for his mother's soul, but to properly assess his preoccupation with the afterlife we must examine his broader set of beliefs about how spirits navigated the material and spiritual worlds.

Manzano ascribed to a transculturated set of religious beliefs. He professed Catholicism, was baptized into the Church, attended mass every so often, married twice in the Church, and requested the Saint Gregory Mass when his mother died.[2] But Manzano engaged the spirit world through an African Cuban cultural lens, which, unlike Western European philosophy, is not premised on the principle of non-contradiction. His autobiography and some of his poems demonstrate that his baptism did not constitute an indiscriminate embrace of Catholic dogma, nor did it signify a rejection of African-inspired beliefs, as the clergy had intended. Manzano certainly acknowledged Catholicism as the institutionalized religion—commonly referred to as *La Religión*—but like other African descendants, he often mediated Catholicism through African-inspired notions of spirituality. Christian religious conversion—whether Catholic or Protestant in nature—did not eliminate African-inspired notions of the spirit world; rather, each system of religious belief influenced the other. Writing about enslaved Africans in South Carolina, Jason R. Young wrote the following:

> Indeed, conversion rarely entails the complete abandonment of former belief systems, nor does it imply a total embrace of new spiritual theologies. The notion of conversion as discrete movement wrongly suggests that older beliefs are too rigid to negotiate a changing spiritual environment and presumes that new belief systems are impregnable, unaffected by older notions. Instead the "new" belief system is understood largely through the context of the "old" (Young 43).

Young's characterization of how African descendants dealt selectively with Christian religious conversion is applicable to the Cuban colonial context since African cosmologies are pluriversal in nature; they do not impose a universal knowledge of the spirit world, but rather construct a domain in which many worlds may coexist (Mignolo, "Delinking" 492). It is the coexistence, even entanglement of divergent religious worlds—not necessarily the conflict between them—that first surfaces in Manzano's slave narrative.

Manzano's preoccupation with wandering spirits and his description of ethereal presence are inextricably linked to instances when his mistress had physically abused him. He recalled this shift in the narrative as "pero la verdadera istoria de mi vida empiesa desde 189 en q$^e$. empesó la fortuna a desplegarse contra mí hasta el grado de mayor encarnizamiento" (the true story of my life begins in 1809 when fate began to unfurl against me with the utmost contempt) (Manzano, *Autobiografía* 304).

> Yo tenia la cabeza llena de los cuentos de cosa mala de otros tiempos, de las almas aparesidas en este de la otra vida y de los encantamientos de los muertos, q$^e$. cuando salian un trapel de ratas asiendo ruido me paresia ver aquel sotano lleno de fantasmas y daba tanto gritos pidiendo a boses misericordia entonces se me sacaba me atormentaban con tanto fuete hasta mas no poder y se me enserraba otra vez guardandose la llave en el cuarto mismo de la S$^{ra}$. ( Manzano, *Autobiografía* 305)

> (I had my head full of tales of evil spirits from other times, of souls that appear from the other life and incantations of the dead, so that when a horde of rats were making noise it seemed to me that the cellar was full of ghosts and I screamed so much crying out for mercy. So that they took me out [and] tormented me with so many whippings until I could stand no more and they locked me away again hiding the key in the mistress's room.)

Manzano alluded to spirit apparitions in the slave narrative, when he had been beaten, shackled and abandoned to shadowy spaces such as the coal cellar or the slave infirmary. From age fourteen until his escape to Havana circa 1817, his mistress punished him sadistically for the most benign boyhood prank (Manzano, *Autobiografía* 304). The aforesaid passage recounts how Manzano was confined to a dark coal cellar adjacent to the garbage heap and brimming with deformed rats that ran over his body. His mistress denied him food and drink until he screamed out begging her for mercy. Manzano suffered acute physical pain and was under psychological duress when he began to see spirits of the deceased. In fact, the expression "me paresia ver" (it seemed to me) might provoke skepticism in readers. Though Manzano admitted that he may have confused noisy rats or a dripping faucet with spirits, the reader is not permitted to simply dismiss his account of events. Rather than engender doubt, the expression "it seemed to me"—which appears twice in the slave narrative (Manzano, *Autobiografía* 305, 321)—means that apparitions existed within a broad realm of possibilities for Manzano. The nature of the spirits Manzano portrayed in the foregoing passage is also worthy of discussion.

Manzano used five different expressions in Spanish throughout the autobiography to portray ethereal presence: "cosa mala" (evil presence/evil influence), "almas aparesidas" (the apparitions of souls), "de la otra vida" (from the other life), "los encantamientos de los muertos" (incantations of the dead), and the cultural euphemism, "fantasmas" (ghosts). The most orthodox of terms is "the apparition of souls." According to the 1796 slave catechism the soul is separated from the body after death; the soul faces divine judgment and will either be rewarded with Heaven or condemned to one of "the four dungeons" (Barreras 67, 70–71). But the notion that Manzano witnessed "almas aparecidas" implies that these Christian souls reside neither in Heaven nor Hell; rather, they wander aimlessly and exasperate the living. Manzano gestures toward popular Iberian Catholicism, which, in this regard, is comparable to Yoruba-inspired ideas about the need to propitiate spirits so that one's destiny will not be adverse (Cros Sandoval 39). But the autobiography should not be read as an unambiguous statement of Catholic doctrine regarding the destiny of the soul. Manzano's spirit sighting mentions nonmaterial beings from "otros tiempos" (other times) and "de la otra vida" (from the other life), but the text does not explain *what* life the author was referring to. What is more, "incantations of the dead" implies that Manzano may have heard the audible voices, chants, or conjuring of persons that had died on the Matanzas plantation. Whatever the case, parallels between popular Catholic beliefs and Yoruba-inspired ideas about spirits complicate any reading of the text. Manzano's portrayal of the spirit realm overlapped and entangled ideas from several bodies of religious knowledge.

Manzano's reverence for his mother's proverbs may reveal how he acquired ideas about spirit and cosmos through Cuban oral traditions. Critics have frequently disregarded his mother's appeals to her dead husband. But such invocations—which represent one of the fundamental tenets of popular Catholicism and West African/West Central African spiritualities—may also signal the epistemological origin of Manzano's belief in ethereal presence. María de Pilar beseeched her deceased husband as she grieved the rampant abuse of her son.

> . . . me llamaba «Juan» y yo le contestaba gimiendo y ella desia de fuera «hay hijo» entonses era el llamar desde la sepultura a su marido pues cuando esto ya mi padre ya abia muerto tres ocasiones en menos de dos meses me acuerdo aber visto [illegible word] repetirse esta Exena [there is a tilde on the uppercase *e*][3]

> ( . . . she used to call me «Juan» and I would answer her weeping and she would say out loud «oh son». For that reason, that was the call from the grave to her husband when this [took place] my father had already died. On three occasions in two months I recall having witnessed this scene repeat itself.)

The calling to/from the grave was her grief-stricken cry on three separate occasions, meant to resolve unsettled matters in the world of the living. Contextually, Manzano's use of the word *entonces* can be rendered "for that reason," since it implies a relationship of causation between María de Pilar's *call to/from the grave* and the need to ensure the physical and emotional well-being of her son. I interpret María de Pilar's invocation of the dead at a time of family crisis as evidence of a sustained belief in *muertos*. That Manzano's mother spoke to her departed husband Toribio de Castro suggests that she believed that human beings could contact and communicate with spirits of the deceased. María de Pilar's dialogues with her dead husband make more sense if we examine Manzano's recollection of him. Manzano characterized his father as an honorable man; he was someone with "el cararte seco y la horradez de mi padre" (the sullen temperament and the honor of my father). And Manzano felt more protected from the overseers' flagellations when he was in his father's presence. He recalled, "como estaba siempre a la vista me asian pasar una vida algo mas llevadera no sufria los orribles y continuos azotes ni los golpes de manos" (Since I was always in his sight, they made sure that I experienced a somewhat more tolerable life. I didn't suffer the persistent whippings, or the slaps) (Manzano, *Autobiografía* 306). Hence, María de Pilar's mournful *call to the grave* can be interpreted as an appeal to the spirit of her husband in "the other life" to protect his son in the same way he had when he was alive. But the slave narrative does not identify the religious tradition(s) that María de Pilar implored when making such appeals. Nevertheless, the passage does allude to a general belief in colonial Cuba that spirits of the dead occupy the natural world and may be beseeched to resolve unsettled matters.

Similarly, María de Pilar recited proverbs to reassure her son that good would triumph over evil in his prolonged struggle to end to his mistress's abuse. I am referring to a brief account where Manzano's mother shared a proverb with him after he had been beaten yet again and his life threatened: "mas puede Dios q$^e$. el demonio hijo" (God can do more than the Devil, son). Although the adage may appear to be a clear statement of biblical principle, that it was illegible to Manzano suggests that it may have been a fragment, a conundrum of sorts in need of careful analysis. Manzano decided to consult with the "criados antiguos" (old servants) and "mis mismos padrinos" (my own godparents) until they collectively arrived at a near unanimous opinion regarding the precise meaning of the proverb (Manzano, *Autobiografía* 318). But for reasons unknown to us, Manzano didn't reveal the proverb's meaning to his readers. Manzano consulted with the "criados antiguos" as one would with a council of elders endowed with cultural authority to decipher aphorisms and convey their meaning to the young. Conferring with "mis mismos padrinos" suggests that African Cuban oral traditions were an important source of knowledge for Manzano about spirit and cosmos.[4] María de Pilar's proverb did not bespeak a cosmic battle between the Christian God and his nemesis the Devil, but rather insinuated the ongoing struggle between benevolent spirits and what Manzano called *cosa mala*.

Manzano's reference to *cosa mala* in his 1836 narrative, which literally means "evil thing," bears a thematic resemblance to the ethnographic testimony of Fernando Ortiz's and Lydia Cabrera's twentieth-century black informants. Ortiz's work is useful in this instance as a catalogue of African Cuban religious argot, though his early ethnography has been critiqued for its racialized and primitivist methodology. In *Los Negros brujos* (The Black Witchdoctors) (1906) Ortiz says that *cosa mala* is synonymous with *duende*, the Spanish word for "evil spirit" in African Cuban religious practice (41). Lydia Cabrera further explored Cuban ideas about malevolence in the spirit world in her tour de force, *El monte: Igbo finda ewe orisha vititi nfinda*. Cabrera's informants characterize "la Cosa-Mala" as "maleficent, dark spirits, 'that have bad intentions'; 'all the strange people in the otherworld', phantasmal and horrible to see" that inhabit the forested wilderness (13). In Cabrera's book, *cosa mala* gestures towards Bakongo-inspired cosmology that comprehends the comportment of deceased persons according to the good or evil they exhibited during their natural lives. But, similar to the concept of *muertos*, *cosa mala* also encompasses Catholic religious meaning. Ortiz attests to the Cuban festival practice of expelling the Devil (expulsiones de los diablos or *cosa mala*), which he described as a collective removal of communal sin ("Los Cabildos y la fiesta," 55, 60). Elsewhere, Ortiz hypothesized that African rituals designed to purge malevolent forces had been amalgamated with Inquisitorial exorcisms of *la cosa mala* (qtd. in Brown, *Santería* 51). But Manzano's idea of *cosa mala* does not evoke the Christian concept of sin and repentance but rather an African-descended ethereal presence from the otherworld that has been afflicted. In this regard, Theophus Smith indicates that African spirituality is not structured on a good/evil binary, but rather that ritual experts may invoke powers to heal community members as well as to do harm to those perceived as enemies (Diakité and Hucks 46).

I do not think the author's fear of *cosa mala* was—strictly speaking—a fear of evil spirits in the Christian sense of the term, but rather a dread of the spirits of persons that had not received proper burial and, as such, might do him harm. Manzano described the slave infirmary as a holding cell for the bodies of the unburied: "solo se depositaba en él algun cadáver hasta la ora de llebar al pueblo a darle sepultura allí" (they only deposited some cadavers there until they were to be taken into town for burial) (Manzano, *Autobiografía* 321). Since Manzano's mistress sent him to an abandoned slave infirmary as punishment (Manzano, *Autobiografía* 321), it is not implausible that in such places he encountered the spirits of dead Africans.

Manzano had witnessed the horror of African cadavers strewn about the old slave infirmary without proper interment. Witnessing such horrors may have motivated him to ensure his mother's passage to the hereafter. But the days immediately following her death were plagued with intrigue and internecine battles about debts his family owed Rosa Brindis, the free mulatto woman (*parda*) that had served as a governess to his freeborn sister María de Rosario. Rosa Brindis insisted that Manzano confront his mistress every chance he got about the money she owed his family, so that he might reclaim his inheritance and settle his debts with her. Children born to enslaved Catholic parents, like Manzano, were considered legitimate offspring in Spanish American colonies. Legitimacy under inheritance law afforded the descendants of enslaved black Catholics certain protections. Enslaved persons in the Spanish Empire could legally bequeath property to their sons and daughters, and their offspring could inherit said property. The Laws of Toro (1505), made no distinctions between enslaved and free persons; neither did the law of inheritance discriminate against mulattoes or blacks. As such, persons of African descent could bequeath and inherit property under colonial law (Twinam 89).

Manzano had his own reasons for claiming his inheritance, and indeed he had already spoken to the Marchioness about that delicate, yet urgent matter. In due course, Manzano acquired the documents attesting to the debts the Marchioness owed his family, and he confronted her with them. But his mistress rebuffed him contemptuously, saying, "si estaba muy apurado p$^r$. la erensia q$^e$. si yo no sabia q$^e$. ella era eredera forsosa de sus esclavos encuanto me buelbas a abalar de la erensia te pongo donde no beas el sol ni la luna" (Aren't you rather hurried about the inheritance? [She asked] didn't I know that she was the compulsory heir of all of her slaves? And that if I spoke to her about it again she would put me where the sun doesn't shine) (Manzano, *Autobiografía* 332). When Rosa Brindis learned that Manzano had failed to obtain his inheritance, she spoke ill of the dead. Manzano described the scene thus: "al dia siguiente manifesté a Rosa lo q$^e$. avia pasado no me acuredo de lo q$^e$. dijo solo vi q$^e$. todas sus duras espresiones ivan a caer sobre las senias de mi pobre madre" (The next day I told Rosa what had happened. I do not remember what she said, only that all her harsh words were to fall upon the ashes of my poor mother) (Manzano, *Autobiografía* 332; Manzano, *The Autobiography* 119).[5] It is the ashes of Manzano's "poor mother" that concern us here, because in Bakongo-inspired burial practices human remains preserve the characteristics of the dead. Regarding the life of the dead in Bakongo-inspired traditions, Joel James Figarola wrote "porque la vida humana vivida, . . . confiere atributos y mantiene propiedades porque nada de lo ocurrido puede quitarse de lo existente; porque el muerto sigue siendo en la muerte algo equivalente . . . de lo que fue en vida" (because human life, . . . confers attributes and maintains properties because nothing that has occurred may be taken away from what exists. Because, in death, the deceased continues to be somewhat equivalent to . . . what he was in life) (42). Figarola establishes that death is a state of being where the departed continue to exist, and to preserve the virtues and defects of their personality.

Manzano made provisions for his mother's *second existence*, which demanded that he ensure her safe passage to the otherworld, and that he emancipate himself to ensure the future welfare of his siblings. But Rosa Brindis further complicated his affairs when she disparaged the dead. Manzano's indignant reaction to Brindis's "harsh words" should be read through an African Cuban cultural lens. That Manzano mentioned scornful words he could scarcely remember strongly suggests that the governess had cursed María de Pilar and that—consistent with Bakongo-inspired beliefs about death—this curse might injure her spirit.

Todd Ochoa's work on Bakongo-inspired spirituality elucidates Manzano's consternation that cruel language might injure the remains of his deceased mother. In *Society of the Dead*, Ochoa explains the polysemic nature of who/what the dead are in Bakongo-inspired spirituality.

> To help describe the proliferation of Palo's dead and the mode of understanding it implies—wherein something can be itself and its apparent opposite without contradiction—I employ the term "version." A version is a rendering of a given form that is made unique through an exercise of force that changes its direction, which turns its shape or meaning, and thus its appearance. The crucial element here is the physical relationship between force, direction and meaning. In Palo the dead have countless versions, each a sense of the other. [ . . . ] The Cuban-Kongo dead, Palo's dead, however, has no dominant entity or idea to authorize its proliferating shapes (Ochoa 14).

Todd Ochoa theorizes that in Bakongo-inspired ideas about death, the deceased not only exist in cadaveric form but also proliferate into "countless versions" of themselves, each susceptible to "an exercise of force that changes its direction" (14). Manzano's indignation with Rosa Brindis suggests that he perceived his mother's figurative ashes to contain her life force and hence to be vulnerable to malicious energies that might divert her path in the hereafter. This does not mean that the requiem Catholic mass was insignificant to Manzano; rather, his ideas about death extended beyond the reach of the slave catechism, as my reading of his poetry will bear out. Manzano's metaphorical reference to his mother's ashes would not be the last time he mentioned human remains as sacred. His poems "Un sueño: A mi segundo hermano" (A Dream: For My Second Brother) and "La visión del poeta compuesta en un ingenio de fabricar azúcar" (The Poet's Vision Composed on a Sugar Plantation) allude to the significance of skeletal remains and ashes as part and parcel of Bakongo-inspired ideas of spirit and cosmos. But even as Manzano mourned his mother with dignity, he also worked earnestly to put her earthly affairs in order, for they were, philosophically speaking, two sides of the same coin.

The death of Manzano's mother marked his transition from adolescence to adulthood, because he became responsible for settling her affairs and caring for his siblings. Toward the end of this chapter, I examine how Manzano endeavored to fulfill his mother's trust by pursuing his younger brother's freedom. Manzano could not fulfill his duties to African-descended community as long as he remained a slave, but he could not emancipate himself without collecting the debts his mistress owed his family. Indeed, the future of Manzano's family depended on his ability to settle debts.

Manzano returned to the plantation in Matanzas and identified the large chest containing his mother's effects. In the hollow of the chest, he discovered family heirlooms: fine gold jewelry, the most valuable of which were three old bracelets and two rosaries, one made of solid gold, and the other gold and coral stone, though broken and unclean. But more importantly, Manzano found a dossier of documents attesting to debts that his mistress owed him and his siblings. The sums varied from 200 to 400 pesos, and other documents testified to lesser quantities (Manzano, *Autobiografía* 331). Manzano's grandfather owned a young mare (*potranca balla de raza fina*) and dedicated the horse to his grandson, Juan Francisco. The young mare gave birth to five other horses, and Manzano's father dedicated a horse to each one of his children. Three out of those five horses also gave birth, bringing the number to eight steeds. María de Pilar and Toribio de Castro's eight horses became an independent source of wealth for them (Manzano, *Autobiografía* 332). After his mother died, the Marchioness of Prado Ameno ultimately pilfered this source of wealth, thus swelling her coffers and keeping Manzano in bondage. The Marchioness's physical and psychological abuse of Manzano was a calculated use of power, not an irrational sadistic act. Prado Ameno sought to accomplish two things by torturing Juan Francisco. She intended to break his will and prevent him from becoming an intellectual, and, moreover, she sought to ensure that he never collected the debts she owed his family. The Marchioness stole Manzano's inheritance, and in that way she denied him his legal right to *coartación*, self-purchase. Deprived of his inheritance, Manzano had to pursue emancipation through other means.

## Emancipation as Ritual of Resistance in Manzano's Autobiography

Juan Francisco Manzano suffered an existential crisis after his mother's passing. Manzano lacked the means to care for his younger siblings, and he perceived no end to the physical and psychological abuse of his enslaver. His mother had entrusted him to act as a "father" (Manzano, *Autobiografía* 322) to Florencio, Fernando, and María del Rosario; but he could not conceivably perform his ethical duties if he did not save *himself* first. Manzano described the situation thus: "perdí la alhagueña ilusion de mi esperanza" (I lost the promising illusion of my hope), and in his words, he became "la criatura mas despresia" (the most despicable creature imaginable), contemplating nothing but escape (Manzano, *Autobiografía* 333). Manzano lost illusory hope when the Marchioness refused to settle the debts she owed his family. What is more, Manzano abandoned his previously held notion that the *slave* could endure bondage if he had "unos amos jovenes y amables" (youthful and kind masters) (Manzano, *Autobiografía* 330). The good slave became a rebellious fugitive yearning to escape the plantation. Manzano's perception that he had fallen prey to evil influence (*cosa mala*) meant that the pursuit of freedom had to acquire an otherworldly dimension for him. Freedom could not be achieved without attaining power from the spirit world.

Ritual was the *axis mundi* of Manzano's religious praxis. Mircea Eliade defines *axis mundi* as "the center of the world" that functions as a connection between two cosmic spheres: heaven and earth (37). In the autobiography, Manzano performed rituals to demonstrate his intense devotion to the saints, whom he credited with his successful escape from the Matanzas plantation to the city of Havana circa 1817. Although Manzano occasionally referred to Jesus Christ and God the Father in the autobiography, he underscored his unrelenting faithfulness to the saints. On multiple occasions he appealed to spiritual intermediaries and displayed extraordinary devotion when he felt powerless before the incessant abuse of his mistress.

Pues llegaba hasta tal punto mi confianza q$^e$. pidiendo al cielo suabiase mis trabajos me pasaba casi todo el tiempo de la prima noche resando sierto numero de padrenuestros y ave marias a todos los santos de la corte celestial p$^a$. q$^e$. el dia siguiente no me fuese tan nosibo como el q$^e$. pasaba si me acontesia algunos

de mis comunes y dolorosos apremios  lo atribuia solamente a mi falta de debosion o a enojo de algun santo q$^e$. abia hechado en  olvido p$^a$. el dia siguiente . . .$^6$

(My confidence reached such a point that beseeching the heavens to lighten my
load, I spent nearly the entire early evening praying a certain number of Our
Fathers and Hail Marys to all the saints in the heavenly host so that the next
day would not be as adverse as the last. If some common and painful pressures
befell me, I only attributed them to my lack of devotion or to the anger of some
saint whom I had forgotten for the next day.)

Manzano's devotion was such that he prayed the Lord's Prayer and said Hail
Marys, calling on the Virgin and all the saints to intercede on his behalf, in
hope that they might ameliorate his day-to-day circumstances. The saints perform many functions in the slave narrative: they bear witness to Manzano's
religious commitment, they intervene on his behalf, and they afford him an
occasion to escape bondage. Manzano's relationship to the saints was premised
on reciprocity and reiteration. He theorized that the appropriate acts of reverence would persuade the saints to intervene on his behalf. But his "lack of devotion" might engender resentment and embitter them toward him. Manzano
characterized the saints as his constant companions, as dramatis personae with
subjective preferences that believers had to respect. Manzano's emphasis on
ritual—including Catholic liturgical devices such as Hail Marys and the Lord's
Prayer—demonstrates that he relied on spiritual intermediaries to convey messages to "la corte celestial" (the heavenly host). Manzano's relationship to the
saints was anything but static; as his devotion became more fervent, he became
more assertive, imploring the saints to act on his behalf.

Fionnghuala Sweeney is one of the few critics that has  tackled the issue
of non-normative religiosity in the literature of Juan Francisco  Manzano.$^7$ In
her article "Atlantic Counter Cultures and the Networked Text: Juan  Francisco
Manzano, R. R. Madden and the  Cuban Slave Narrative," she asserts that
Manzano's personal narrative emerges from within a Catholic religio-moral
context that  leaves discursive space for Afro-Caribbean ritual practice:

> The existence of hierarchies in Catholicism [ . . . ] the tendency of these same
> hierarchies not  only to mask the presence of other belief systems but also
> frequently to encourage their  absorption and continuity beneath a common
> religious umbrella; [ . . . ] and a tendency  towards mysticism and/or the non-
> rational, with an emphasis on ritual. (404)

As an example of what she calls masking (but could be  more accurately
described as transculturation), Sweeney cites the adoration of African divine
spirits through the worship of Catholic saints because "African religious belief

systems are encoded in ostensibly Catholic practices" (404). For African descendants, then, Catholic religious hierarchy and ritual provided space for the reworking of Church orthodoxy. With regard to Manzano's portrayal of spirit sightings, Sweeney says that his text is "doubly othered" since his descriptions of spirit apparitions bring to mind "creolised African religious beliefs, or at best Catholic superstition" that Protestant Anglo-Americans vehemently rejected and used in proslavery propaganda (409). Throughout Latin America and the Caribbean, persons of African descent encoded African-inspired religious beliefs in the symbolic practices of Catholicism and, the Catholic saints provided a remarkably fertile terrain for this type of transculturation.

Manzano spoke about, revered, and otherwise engaged the saints in ways very consistent with an African Atlantic pattern of ritual, reverence, and reciprocity. His belief that the saints are well disposed toward him is evidenced in the section below that picks up where the other left off.

Todavia creo q$^e$ ellos me depararon la ocasión y me custodiaron [the words *el dia* are scratched out] la noche de mi fuga de matanzas p$^a$. La Habana como beremos pues tomando el almanaque y todos los santos de aquel mes eran resados p$^r$. mi diariamente[8]

(I still believe they [the saints] afforded me the occasion and watched over me the night of my escape from Matanzas to Havana, as we shall see. Taking up the almanac, all the saints of that month were prayed to daily by me.)

Liturgical ambiguity is among the most important rhetorical devices that Manzano employed when he represented personal acts of piety. In the aforesaid passage, Manzano attributed his successful escape from the Matanzas slave labor camp to the saints. Again, the emphasis on "todos los santos" (all the saints) is so broad as to be hyperbolic; the text lends itself to a certain opacity because no Catholic saint appears by name. As the Latin saying goes, "se cuenta el milagro pero no el santo" (Tell the deed not the doer). And though Manzano does not mention any saint by name, he underscored the transformative role they played in his escape. The saints performed two duties: they offered Manzano the occasion to run away, and they secured his passage from Matanzas to Havana. (Presumably, the saints also protected the fugitive from slave-hunting parties.) Divine power made Manzano's flight from the plantation possible, but it must be noted that he ascribed that power to the saints, not the Holy Trinity. Manzano's resolute commitment to the saints invites divergent readings about the slave narrative's representation of spirituality and ritual practice.

Manzano's account of fleeing the plantation evinces a considerable familiarity with printed religious materials, as well as his fondness for one saint in particular.

Tenia yo desde bien chico la costumbre de leer cuanto era leible en mi idioma
y cuando iva p^r. la calle siempre andaba recojiendo pedasitos de papel impreso
y si estaba en verso  hasta no aprenderlo todo de memoria no resaba así sabia
la vida de todos los santos mas  milagrosos y los versos de sus resos los de
las nobena de Sn. Antonio los del trisagio en fin todos los santos. (Manzano,
*Autobiografía* 335–336)

(Ever since I was a boy I had the habit of reading everything that was legible
in my  language and when I went down the street I always went around pick-
ing up scraps of  printed paper. And if it was in verse, I did not pray it until I
had learned it by heart. In  that way, I knew the lives of all the most miraculous saints and the prayer verses of the  novena of Saint Anthony, those of the
*Trisagium*, at last, all the saints.)

Hagiographies were narratives recounting the piety, evangelical zeal, and the
miracles that Catholic saints performed; such writings were intended as instructive material for those who had received baptism. The *trisagium angelicum,* as
the Trisagion is called in Latin, is a Catholic hymn in honor of the Holy Trinity;
a reverent prayer to God the Father, God the Son, and God the Holy Spirit. The
doctrine of the Holy Trinity was a central tenet of Catholicism, as the 1796 slave
catechism bears out.

P. Y quien es la Santísima Trinidad?
R. La Santísima Trinidad es Dios Padre, Dios Hijo, Dios Espíritu Santo, tres
    personas distintas, y un solo Dios verdadero.

[ . . . ]

P. Y son tres Dioses, ó tres Todopoderosos, ó tres Criadores?
R. No es sino un solo Dios verdadero, un solo Criador, un solo Todopoderoso
    (Barreras, 49–50).

(P And who is the Blessed Trinity?
R. The Blessed Trinity is God the Father, God the Son, God the Holy Spirit,
    three discrete persons, and one true God.

[ . . . ]

P. And are there three gods, or three Almighty Gods, or three Creators?
R. No, there is but one true God, one Creator, one Almighty God.)

The slave catechism presented the Holy Trinity as a monotheistic tenet of the
faith, notwithstanding the three personae in one (Barreras 49–50). Clergymen

relied on call-and-response to instruct enslaved Africans in the dogma of the Catholic Church. But the slave catechism says little to nothing about the saints. Catholic saints appear in only one sentence, where they are described as "los santos nuestros hermanos" (our holy brothers the saints) (Barreras 112) who will accompany the obedient to Heaven. Yet this textual silence regarding the saints was atypical in popular Catholicism, and it obscured their importance within free and enslaved African-descended communities. Black and white Cubans maintained an intimate relationship with the saints, often defining them on their own terms and engaging them in rituals that served their own purposes. In fact, devotion to the saints among the Cuban lower classes was so pervasive and problematic that Father Félix Varela intervened to correct what he deemed *superstición*.

Félix Varela inveighed against superstition in *Cartas a Elpidio sobre la impiedad, la superstición, el fanatismo en sus relaciones con la sociedad* (1838) (Letters to Elpidio Concerning Impiety, Supersition, Fanaticism and its Relationship to Society).

> En los pueblos en que se halla establecida la única y verdadera religión, que es la católica, como su divino origen exige precisamente un modo divino de operar, y éste no puede hallarse en las vicisitudes, limitación y caprichos del entendimiento humano, es esencial el principio de la autoridad. (Varela, *Cartas* 85).

> No hay santo a quien no se le atribuya una multitud de portentos inauditos, y aun entra en esto cierta vanidad religiosa y competencia, procurando a veces presentar los santos como rivales y ver cuál de ellos hace más milagros (que este nombre dan a cuantas patrañas y tonterías pueden imaginarse), resultando una *batalla mística* no solo ridícula sino sacrílega, porque es un verdadero sacrilegio tratar de tal modo a los siervos de Dios que le gozan eternamente y que no pueden ser corifeos de semejantes tontos y criminales (original emphasis; Varela, *Cartas* 87).

> (In the nations where the only true religion has been established, which is Catholicism, her divine origin demands there be only one divine modus operandi. And this cannot be found in the vicissitudes, the limitations and the whims of human understanding; the principle of authority is fundamental.

> There isn't a saint to whom they do not attribute a multitude of unheard-of wonders, and there is a sort of religious vanity and competition that becomes a part of this, sometimes they try to present the saints as rivals to see which [saint] does the most miracles (this designation gives way to many lies and more foolishness than you can imagine), resulting in a *mystical battle* that is not only ridiculous but also sacrilegious. Because it is a true sacrilege to treat the

servants of God that experience him eternally in such a way. They [saints] cannot be the accomplices of such criminal and foolish individuals.)

Félix Varela crafted this statement of doctrine to preserve ecclesiastical authority. Varela premised his argument on the idea of *orbis christianus* (Rivera Pagán 35); the medieval concept of a singular world religion under the auspices of the pope. Though Varela didn't mention the ancient doctrine by name, he contended there was only one "divine" procedure for worship among Catholics. Varela reasoned that since Catholicism was the "única y verdadera religión" (only true religion), there could not be more than one means to beseech God. So, the Church assumed supremacy in all matters of doctrine. Varela asserted a belief in doctrinal purity that would, at least in theory, protect the Catholic faith from the "vicissitudes, limitations and whims of human understanding". In his estimation, the one true religion could not remain *true* if parishioners disputed priestly authority. Perhaps Varela was most disturbed by the manifold ways in which Cubans had tergiversated official doctrines regarding the saints and the nature of miracles.

Félix Varela published his treatise in Madrid in 1838, while living in exile in the United States. Varela was frustrated with the state of the Catholic Church in Cuba. And he acknowledged that Cuban spirituality had taken a turn for the miraculous. Cubans believed in the saints as mystical entities that possessed great powers and boasted an appetite for miraculous phenomena. The saints performed "unheard-of wonders." They existed in a metaphysical universe rife with conflict and rampant rivalries. Cubans were aware of these metaphysical realities—realities that Varela ignored—and they strove to appease the most miraculous saints to empower themselves. Practitioners pursued saints that would guarantee the highest returns on their investment and would triumph in "mystical battle[s]" over otherworldly foes. Colonial Cubans sought after spiritual powers that might protect them from their adversaries, ward off evil influence (*cosa mala*), and, ultimately bring them success. But Varela did not direct his criticism to any particular ethno-racial community, which suggests that Cubans of African and European descent reveled in the miraculous nature of the saints. To further contextualize the significance of the saints in the African Cuban ritual universe, I cite the curious case of Mateo Congo, an African interrogated by authorities regarding his role in the 1844 antislavery uprisings.

Mateo Congo of the Industria coffee estate testified in 1844 that "he received four pesos from the hand of the Chino Antonio, for a witchcraft item that he made with some small saints and mashed-up pumpkin seeds and wrapped them up in a piece of paper" (Finch, *Rethinking* 204). Mateo Congo buried the items to force the overseer to flee the plantation, and he hoped to replace him with another. In the ethnohistoric context of Mateo's resistance ritual, "small saints" did not mean what it would have meant for a Spanish Catholic priest. What

Mateo referred to as "small saints" were, in all likelihood, African divine spirits. Mateo Congo's affiliation with Bakongo-inspired practices—as his ethnonym Congo indicates—insinuates that those "saints" should be viewed as *mpungos*, that is, Bakongo nature spirits. Mateo Congo appropriated the Catholic saints in order to achieve a less violent situation on the plantation. His ritual of resistance is based on the same principle that Manzano practiced when he prayed to the saints. Ritual is a performance of power that unites the natural world with the spiritual realm, and if properly executed, it may ameliorate one's circumstances. Manzano appealed to Saint Anthony to secure safe passage from the Matanzas sugar plantation to Havana. Comparable to Mateo Congo who hoped to replace an abusive overseer, Manzano fled to Havana to achieve greater degrees of freedom. There, he eventually taught himself to read and write.

Manzano reasoned that the saints would perform what Varela mocked as "unheard-of wonders" if he could only distinguish the most miraculous saints from the rest and show them the requisite devotion. At one point, he even argued that his problems on the plantation were attributable to his failure to perform the appropriate acts of devotion: "si me acontesia algunos de mis comunes y dolorosos apremios lo atribuia solamente a mi falta de debosion . . ." (If some common and painful pressures befell me, I attributed them only to my lack of devotion . . . ).[9] Manzano not only *knew* that the saints were endowed with miraculous powers, and that some were mightier than others, but he also understood that devotion was the way to appease them. Manzano's knowledge of the saints clashed with that of Varela, who believed that the "vicissitudes, limitations and whims of human understanding" had given way to sacrilege and blunder and had corrupted "the one true religion." Varela was not alone in this opinion. White abolitionist Francisco Calcagno was also critical of Manzano's unorthodox religious practices. In *Poetas de Color* (1887), Calcagno opined: "Manzano era devoto, con aquella devocion mezclada de fanatismo de las personas ignorantes de su época" (Manzano was devout, that devotion mixed with the fanaticism of the ignorant people of his time) (77). Calcagno portrayed Manzano as "un ignorante manso" (a meek [and] ignorant person) (78) who practiced a form of "devotion mixed with fanaticism." Calcagno regarded Manzano as ignorant because of his "fanatismo," not his piety. Fanaticism is characterized by excessive enthusiasm and unreasoning zeal.[10] Calcagno was not critical of Manzano's faithfulness to the religion, but rather he was suspicious of the way he practiced. Again, it is Manzano's religious reasoning, his understanding of spiritual phenomena, and his zealotry that unnerved a white Catholic like Calcagno. Francisco Calcagno developed a critical view of Manzano's spirituality from reading the autobiography, fragments of which he published in *Poetas de Color*. "Mixed" is the operative word in Calcagno's phrase "devotion mixed with fanaticism," because it strongly suggests the transculturation of Catholic and African-inspired practices. Calcagno did not explicitly signal that he was referring to an African-inspired set of practices, perhaps because he wanted to safeguard Manzano's reputation. But he did regard Manzano as an excessive, misguided, and unorthodox practitioner. Even so, the charge that Manzano was "ignorant" of official doctrines does not hold up, because he received baptism, attended mass, and memorized sermons (Manzano, *Autobiografía* 300–301, 333). Manzano's proclivity to *know* "the live[s] of the most miraculous saints and the verses of their prayers" (Manzano, *Autobiografía* 335) is indicative of an African-inspired idea about appealing to coercive power that the Church had condemned. Manzano's rituals contravened Varela's "principle of authority" (*Cartas* 85), because Manzano claimed the right to conjure the saints in a way that would serve his ends.

Though the saints are protagonists in the autobiography, they did not figure prominently in Manzano's letters to Domingo del Monte, because he sought to convince his benefactor that he was a reputable Catholic. Manzano privileged his representation of God the Father in his correspondence with del Monte. Of the twelve letters Manzano wrote, del Monte received only seven, because the poet chose not to dispatch five of them (Manzano, *Autobiografía* 120). In Manzano's seven letters addressed to del Monte, the words *livertad, mi livertad,* and *la prometida livertad* (liberty, my freedom, and the promised freedom) appeared four times, and *rescate*, my rescue, appeared twice. Manzano's private communication with del Monte created space for less guarded statements concerning his fight for freedom. His use of the word *livertad* was subversive, since Manzano was a slave in a society where the use of the word *freedom* might result in his arrest.[11] Manzano's letters often attested to the tribulations that beleaguered him. In the letter dating from October 16, 1834, Manzano placed his fate in the hands of the Catholic God, not the saints.

> Si algun dia quisiere Dios que pueda ablar a smd: de serca, berá smd: que no he perdido el juisio tal vez por que no ha llegado mi ora, mucho he sufrido en mi interior, graves con las burlas que la fortuna me aja, mucho suspiro pero me consuelo cuando considero que Dios me ha dado las desgrasias, y tambien una alma que me ase superior a algunos que sin el menor cuidado se rien de mi. (Manzano, *Obras* 78)

> (If someday God permits me to speak with Your Grace: up close, Your Grace will see that I have not lost good judgment perhaps because my time has not come. I have suffered much within myself, fate's grave contempt has caused me to wither. I yearn for many things, but I console myself when I consider that God has given me this disgrace, and also a soul that makes me superior to others that without the slightest care mock me.)

Fate held Manzano's freedom in abeyance, as this poignant passage from his letter to del Monte demonstrates: "fate's grave contempt has caused me to wither." But the Christian God does not redeem him from slavery. Rather, Manzano's only consolation was his conviction that "God has given me this disgrace, and also a soul that makes me superior to others." Manzano didn't claim that his freedom would come at the hands of the Christian God anywhere in his correspondence with del Monte. The Christian God is not a redemptive figure in his poetry and prose, but rather a source of suffering that has endowed the poet with a righteous enduring soul. It is not astonishing that Manzano's letters to the man that had promised to purchase his freedom in exchange for the slave narrative are silent about the saints' powers to make his escape from Matanzas possible. The letter rejoices in the endurance of a Christian soul, which is an unambiguous adaptation of one of the New Testament's central themes.

Manzano's portrait of the divine patriarch in his letters to del Monte is reminiscent of "Oda a La Religión" (1831) and "Un sueño: A mi segundo hermano" (1838), since the Christian God does not appear in those texts as a liberator, but rather as a giver of tribulations to test the mettle of the Christian soul (Manzano, *Autobiografía* 143, 150). There is further evidence that some contemporary observers understood that when African descendants spoke of the saints, they did so investing the word with shifting and unstable meanings that signified different things to diverse readerships. Irish abolitionist Richard Robert Madden was one such observer.

Madden's 1840 English translation of Manzano's autobiography omits his frequent references to the saints, thus effacing their indispensable role in the original manuscript as purveyors of freedom from the plantation.

> . . . that I employed always part of the night praying to God to lighten my sufferings, and to preserve me from mischief on the following day, and if I did anything wrong I attributed it to my lukewarmness in prayers, or that I might have forgotten to pray; and I firmly believe that my prayers were heard, and to this I attribute the preservation of my life once, on occasion of my running away from Matanzas to Havana, as I will relate hereafter. (Manzano, *Life and Poems* 95)

In *Suite para Juan Francisco Manzano*, Roberto Friol says that Madden's translation is replete with inaccuracies, poor equivalents, and an apparent misunderstanding of the Hispano-Catholic frame of reference (36). But, as Gera Burton has shown, Madden himself was Irish Catholic, so it is more likely that he replaced the saints with God the Father in order to preclude potentially problematic interpretations of unorthodox practice, Catholic or otherwise. Madden's rewriting of the slave narrative effaces the original religious inscription, since his version reflects a Protestant ethos and faults Manzano's relationship with God for the misery he suffered. As Sweeney points out, Madden's translation of Manzano's narrative is subjected to ideological conditioning, removing language that might have been fodder for proslavery arguments about Catholicism's irrational emphasis on ritual (7). Madden's omission

POEMS

BY

A SLAVE IN THE ISLAND OF CUBA,

RECENTLY LIBERATED;

TRANSLATED FROM THE SPANISH,

BY

R. R. MADDEN, M. D.

WITH THE HISTORY OF THE

EARLY LIFE OF THE NEGRO POET,

WRITTEN BY HIMSELF;

TO WHICH ARE PREFIXED

TWO PIECES DESCRIPTIVE OF

CUBAN SLAVERY AND THE SLAVE-TRAFFIC,

BY R. R. M.

LONDON:
THOMAS WARD AND CO.,
27, PATERNOSTER ROW;
AND MAY BE HAD AT THE OFFICE OF THE BRITISH AND FOREIGN
ANTI-SLAVERY SOCIETY, 27, NEW BROAD STREET.
1840.

The 1840 English edition of Juan Francisco Manzano's autobiography. Irish abolitionist Richard Robert Madden translated the autobiography from the Spanish original and published it in London.

supports my hypothesis about the symbolic significance of the saints as a covert way to refer to African divine spirits. Catholicism did not consistitute freedom for Manzano; rather, Manzano relied on an alternative system of religious epistemology to emancipate himself.

Manzano's emphasis on ritual, whether reverence for the saints or for *muertos*, colored the way in which he engaged the spirit world. Though he prayed to the most miraculous of saints, there is a particular saint his narrative mentions by name: San Antonio (Saint Anthony). St. Anthony of Padua was a thirteenth-century Portuguese Franciscan friar much celebrated for his evangelical zeal, frequent miracles, disposition for suffering, and eagerness to achieve martyrdom in North Africa (Guerreiro 9–10, 15). Born Fernando de Bulhões in Lisbon, Portugal, toward the end of the twelfth century, he became a preacher, teacher, and expert in Christian theology upon joining the Franciscan Order in 1220 (Guerreiro 8–9). Traditionally, 1195 has been given as the year of Fernando de Bulhões's birth, but the earliest historical documents concerning the matter are ambiguous. The Catholic Church canonized Fernando de Bulhões in 1232 during the papacy of Pope Gregory (Purcell 10–11). The Church reveres Saint Anthony for his wisdom, evangelistic zeal, and virtue solidified by a Christian sense of moral clarity (Purcell 250). Persons devoted to St. Anthony of Padua consider him among the gentlest of saints. Devotees pray the novena, a nine-day series of prayers, beseeching him for protection against ill health and other problems while also asking for forgiveness.[12] In nineteenth-century colonial Cuba, as I have already shown, Africans and Cuban blacks used Catholic images as a veneer for their divine entities so that the meanings they assigned to the saints often contradicted Church dogma. Lydia Cabrera's early twentieth-century black informants confirmed the pervasive nature of this type of religious transculturation in the late colonial period. Likewise, Cabrera's informants explained the transculturation of Saint Anthony with Elegguá, the spirit of the crossroads in Yoruba cosmology.

Black Cuban religious adepts explained the relationship between Saint Anthony and Elegguá in these words:

Para adeptos de la Regla lucumí el adivino dueño de la yerba y del Monte, (de la vegetación) es Osain,—Jósai, pronunciaba Adyaí—catolizado San Anotonio Abad y San Sivestre, y una de las muchas advocaciones o "caminos" de Elégguá, Elégbara (Cabrera 70).

[ … ]

—Eshú Beleké, el niño de Atocha o Ibori que no puede tenerse en casas donde hay niños, porque se encela y los mata,—era tan travieso que en el siglo pasado no se le daba cabida en el Cabildo; ni a Mako, –ladrón,– conocido en Santa Clara por Arére-Obi-Oké, el que tiene en los brazos un Eleggua adulto, San Antonio de Padua. (Cabrera 78–79)

(For adepts of the *lucumí* Religion the fortuneteller, proprietor of herbs and of the forested wilderness (of flora), is Osain, –Jósai,—they used to pronounce it *Adyaí*—Catholicized Saint Anthony Abad and Saint Silvestre, and one of the many names or "paths" of *Elegguá, Elégbara.*

[ … ]

—*Eshú Beleké*, the child of Atocha or Ibori that cannot be in homes where there are children, because he will become jealous and kill them,—was so mischievous in the previous century that he was not allowed within the *cabildo*; neither *Mako*,—the thief—known in Santa Clara as Arére-Obi-Oké, he who has in his arms an adult *Elegguá*, Saint Anthony of Padua.)

Cabrera's informants characterized St. Anthony of Padua and St. Anthony Abad as "names or 'paths'" of *Elegguá*, the Yoruba spirit of the crossroads. By describing Saint Anthony as the "Catholicized" name for Elegguá, they tacitly acknowledged that by 1954—when Cabrera published *El monte*—the transculturative processes that Africans had initiated in the mid-eighteenth century in Havana *cabildos* had fully coalesced, so that, as Ortiz explained, transculturation produced new social meanings (*Contrapunteo* 414).[13] Del Carmen Barcia says that Saint Anthony of Padua and Saint Anthony Abad were the patron saints of two different Havana *cabildos*: the Cabildo Congo Mucamba in 1801 and the Cabildo Carabalí Viví in 1843, respectively (162). It must be noted that Africans from the Old Calabar region of Nigeria/Cameroon and persons from the Kongo-Angola region both designated Saint Anthony as their patron saint in the early and mid-nineteenth century despite differences in the respective belief structures.

Manzano's life on a Matanzas plantation peopled with African labor, and his frequent travels from Havana to Matanzas, strongly suggests that his ideas about the saints and their power to reward devotion and punish neglect were consistent with African ideas in circulation long before he was born. But Elegguá was no easy saint to please; his mischief was such that if not properly propitiated, he might become jealous and be given to violence. It is *this* Saint Anthony that Manzano had to placate so that the crossroads of potentialities might be opened to him, and make freedom possible. I believe the way in which Manzano invoked, beseeched, and placated the saints resembles the performativity characteristic of Yoruba-inspired rituals devoted to the *orishas*, where the objective is not redemption but rather empowerment. If "Oda a La Religión" is a jeremiad where Manzano suggests that the Lord has forsaken him, then saintly devotion should be viewed as a form of entreaty. Robert Farris Thompson reminds us that propitiation is vital for Yoruba-speaking adepts. Thompson explains that "the utterance of conciliatory words or acts to hardened or angered deities, entreating them to become generous and concerned at times of crisis, such as birth, death or initiation" is part and parcel of Yoruba spirituality (15). Thompson's work is apropos for my analysis because Manzano's existential crisis is marked by spiritual dislocation, physical captivity, and threats from persons that could end his life. Manzano acknowledged that his suffering was attributable to his "lack of devotion" or to the antipathy of some saint that he had neglected. In the autobiography, entreaty is more than supplication, because the author pursued reconciliation with the saints through judiciously prescribed ritual activities. It is the placation of divine fury that makes the procurement of power, or *aché*, achievable.

After his mother's precipitous death, Manzano found himself at the cross-roads; he was situated between freedom and slavery, life and death, the creative force of an emancipatory poetics or the compulsory silence of the plantation. In African cosmologies, the crossroads are envisaged as a spirit that governs the meeting of disparate worlds, linking the spirit with the flesh, and human need with divine power. In Nigeria among Yoruba-speakers, the crossroads spirit is known as Èṣù-Elegbara. Toyin Falola describes Èṣù as a divine messenger, a mediator between the Supreme Deity and humanity.

> He is the divine messenger between the Supreme Deity and the other orisa: he carries the messages of God to the orisa, and reports back to God the activities of all the orisa as well as of human beings. [ . . . ] Similarly, he acts as a media-tor between the gods and goddesses. Èṣù can spy on all activities, and he can represent the Supreme Deity (Olodumare) as his "policeman" and intelligence gatherer. Consequently, Èṣù is not location bound, but is everywhere, and at all times, supervising offerings, worship, and behavior. [ . . . ]
>
> His encounters with other gods are many, but the intent is clear: he is the ultimate trickster, divine sometimes mundane. He can ruin fellow divinities, making their power impotent, and turning the Supreme Being against them so that they come to ruin. If the divinities are afraid of Èṣù, what can humans do? ("Èṣù: The God without Boundaries" 5).

Principally, Èṣù is a divine emissary conveying messages to Olodumare, the Supreme Being in Yoruba cosmology, and to the divine spirits that govern natural phenomena. But his role as an emissary is enhanced and complicated by the fact that he reconnoiters the natural and supernatural worlds, inform-ing Olodumare of the activities of other orishas and of humans. Èṣù's ubiquity makes him especially powerful but also dangerous because his knowledge of the hidden deeds of humans and of divine spirits furnishes him with the power to frustrate their plans and bring them to ruin. Èṣù does not embody evil, but neither is he inherently good. Èṣù's Janus-faced character has resulted in a ten-dency among Christians to associate him with the Devil, the embodiment of evil in Christianity.

In *The History of the Yorubas* (1921), African missionary Samuel Johnson claimed that "Èṣù or Elegbara-Satan, the Evil One, [is] the author of all evil." Likewise, J. Olumide Lucas wrote the following on the question of evil: "Èṣù a deity who is sometimes malevolent, but whose malevolence has so preponder-ated over his beneficence that is now regarded by many as 'the Supreme Power of Evil' and the 'Prince of Darkness.'" G. J. Afolabi Ojo agrees and he writes: "Èṣù. More abstract in conception is the deity acknowledged as the supreme power of evil, evil in this sense comprising illnesses, diseases, suffering, misfor-tunes, accidents, calamities and catastrophes" (Ogungbemi 81). The Èṣù-Satan equivalency among some Nigerian scholars is not surprising; rather, such pervasive attitudes about Èṣù reflect how Christianity has restructured indigenous African approaches to the problem of evil. Falola brings clarity to the problem of Èṣù's ambivalence and speaks to the conceptual confusion that ensues when the Judeo-Christian worldview is the lens for thinking about a paradoxical character like Èṣù.

> Èṣù does not seek to destroy the bad and malevolent so that only the good and benevolent remain. Rather, Èṣù sees the positive in both forces. Èṣù, unlike the biblical Satan, does not work in opposition to God's plan for humankind. Neither does Èṣù have the mission to completely destroy. Thus, seeking his equivalence in Christianity as many have done when they compare Èṣù with the New Testament Satan is very much misguided. ("Èṣù: The God without Boundaries" 6)

Èṣù is not the embodiment of evil, and he has no conceptual parallel in Christianity. Rather, Èṣù poses a different kind of problem, because his mission is neither to destroy humanity nor to annihilate his spiritual counterparts in the Yoruba pantheon. Neither does Èṣù pursue the ultimate annihilation of evil. Falola contends that Èṣù acknowledges both good and evil as useful universal forces. Kola Abimbola further delineates how Christian and Yoruba conceptions of evil diverge. Abimbola reminds us that in Anglo-Protestant theology the Devil is the source of all evil. Satan is the antithesis of the Christian God, an entity that entices and persuades humans into improper conduct. Conversely, in Yoruba religion evil does not emanate from Èṣù, but rather from more than two hundred malevolent forces embedded within the spirit world known in the Yoruba language as *Ajogun*. Abimbola termed this understanding of maleficence within Yoruba cosmology a "poly-demonic conception of evil" (Ogungbemi 81–82).

Maureen Warner-Lewis explains the philosophical problem of good/evil in precolonial African societies beyond the cultural boundaries of the kingdoms of the Yoruba. She writes that traditional African notions of good and evil were articulated in profoundly different ways than in European Christianity. For instance, in clan-centered societies, *goodness* is understood (and is articulated) as that which enhances communal interests; whereas in Christianity goodness is a transcendent ethos contingent neither on context nor circumstance. Christianity espouses the absolute principles of humility, self-sacrifice, and forgiveness as requisites for holy living. Although Christianity posits transcendent principles of goodness, Warner-Lewis points out that this did not "preclude clerics and practitioners from infringing such precepts for ethnic, political, or personal convenience and rationalizations" (158). Manzano's perception of the problem of evil is consistent with Ambibola's notion of a "poly-demonic conception of evil." Manzano believed that he had fallen prey to malevolent forces that he referred to as *cosa mala*. As such, he evoked this dreadful notion of evil when the overseer had confined him to the abandoned San Miguel plantation full of African corpses. In this same vein, his mother recited the proverb "God can do more than the Devil" (Manzano, *Autobiografía* 305, 318) when she sought to embolden her son's quest to end the overseer's abuse and emancipate himself. Thus, Manzano and his mother pursued *goodness* for *their* clan, and they perceived the problem of evil in terms of their family's captivity and the physical cruelty they had both suffered at the hands of their enslaver. Therefore, Manzano beseeched what Otero called the "entities of the crossroads" so they might open the path for him to emancipate himself (Otero, "Èṣù at the Transatlantic Crossroads" 208).

Solimar Otero theorizes about the "entities of the crossroads" in African diasporic cultures in New Orleans, Cuba, Haiti, Brazil, and Nigeria by considering the manifold ways in which Èṣù manifests throughout the Diaspora. The Yoruba spirit Èṣù Elegbara is known as Elegguá in Cuba, Exu in Brazil, and Legba in Haiti, Benin (ancient Dahomey), and the United States. Otero avers that though the names of crossroad entities differ in African Atlantic cultures, the tracing of African cruciform signs in Haitian Vodou, Cuban *ifá*, and *palo monte/palo mayombe* transforms "an un-crossable boundary" into a borderland/*frontera*, that is, into a realm of possibility ("Èṣù at the Transatlantic Crossroads," 191–192). I cite Otero's explication of the crossroads in African diasporic religious systems extensively below.

> The transatlantic sites that Èṣù's many forms control include the meeting of the worlds between the ancestors and the living, the mundane with the divine, and the flesh with the spirit. These entities of the crossroads are thought to simultaneously intercept and allow communication between different orders of energies in a manner that reorients attention to thresholds and potentiality. In a similar manner to how the idea of borderlands/*la frontera* is understood as a zone of *mestizaje* (mixture), figures of Èṣù are linked to the breaking and remaking of unique cultural boundaries, borrowings, play and the phenomenology of ritual in these spiritual borders (Anzaldúa 1999 [1987], 21; Arrizón 2006, 83–117). On the metaphysical border these Èṣùs, police, inform, and reward in a manner that illustrates their roles as messenger deities that make us understand our precarious role of balancing fate with action. ("Èṣù at the Transatlantic Crossroads" 208)

Otero explains the crossroads as a space that enables the meeting of disparate worlds secular and sacred, natural and supernatural. The crossroads enables disparate religions to converge within common space, but the linking of these symbolic worlds, which are sometimes in political conflict with one another, is possible only because of Èṣù, the master of the crossroads. Èṣù makes and remakes these connections because he is the envoy that enables communication between different energies and entities. Otero writes, "Malevolent forces, fate, and misfortune exist in ways that have to be balanced through ritual observance of the god(s) of the crossroads" ("Èṣù at the Transatlantic Crossroads" 202). Cuban practitioners maintain that Lucero Mundo and Elegguá are "distinct entities that function in a similar manner through an Afro-Cuban transculturation" (Otero, "Èṣù at the Transatlantic Crossroads" 203). Otero's brilliant work is apropos for my reading of Manzano's invocation of Saint Anthony as Elegguá in Cuban *lucumí* or Lucero Mundo in Kongo-Cuban *palo monte*. Manzano endeavored to transform an impassable boundary—the distance between the Matanzas plantation and urban Havana—into an abundant realm of aesthetic and political possibility. And Saint Anthony was the only spirit Manzano called upon by name to cross such treacherous borders.

I contend that it was not the Catholic Saint Anthony whom Manzano sought to appease, but rather Elegguá/Lucero Mundo. Manzano's deference for the transculturated crossroads spirit is consistent with the ways that devotees evoke Èṣù throughout the African Diaspora. Falola explains that in Yorubaland "he [Èṣù] cannot be cast in a subordinate position, even when he carries messages on their [other *orishas'*] behalf to the Supreme Deity." And "the first salutation" is made to Èṣù in most ritual ceremonies ("Èṣù: The God without Boundaries" 4). Likewise, Otero explains that in Cuban *palo monte*, priests draw the Kongo-Cuban cosmograms, called *firmas*, to Lucero Mundo, then sketch those of other divine spirits. The same pattern emerges in Vodou, where Legba receives the first sacred cosmograms ("Èṣù at the Transatlantic Crossroads" 203). I do not mean to suggest that Manzano drew Kongo-Cuban cosmograms before performing his rituals. I have seen no evidence of this in Manzano's poetry or prose; neither have I come across any such references in the trial record for the 1844 antislavery movement. Rather, I contend that Manzano engaged Saint Anthony in a manner that is very consistent with the African ethnohistoric record not only in colonial Cuba but also throughout the Diaspora. Though the narrative never mentions Elegguá by name, the African-descended author engaged Saint Anthony in a way that is inconsistent with Saint Anthony himself, but characteristic of qualities ascribed to Elegguá.

Manzano invoked Elegguá/Lucero Mundo and granted him primacy in his ritual of emancipation because he needed the power that the crossroads spirit provides in order to liberate himself. Thompson's ideas about the power phenomenon—both definitional and anthropological in nature—are imperative to my reading. For Thompson, *àshe* is defined as "spiritual command," "the power-to-make-things-happen," so that the Supreme Being is the quintessence of a divine light, which is also rendered accessible to humankind (5). Although they do not possess the absolute power of Creator, African divine spirits, like

Elegguá, are the embodiment of *àshe* (*aché* in Cuban Spanish) (5) for they command myriad natural phenomena and, if called upon, may intervene in the material world through spirit possession or ritual activity. Orunmila is the divine spirit that guides human communication with the spirit world, but no communication can occur without the help of Èṣù. Èṣù and Orunmila work in unison because Èṣù is the messenger that delivers the *aché*, or required spiritual force, to complete any ceremony or ritual (Otero, "Èṣù at the Transatlantic Crossroads" 207). Thus, attaining *aché* was critical to Manzano's escape from the plantation, for it might turn the scales in his favor, counteract the power of *cosa mala*, and open a conduit to freedom.

Manzano's attempt to appease the wrath of "the saints"—Saint Anthony chief among them—implied a belief in the paradoxical nature of divine entities, something incompatible with Church doctrine but consistent with Yoruba-inspired conceptions of the spirit world. Moreover, there is a correlation between the San Antonio figure and Manzano's pursuit of freedom within the narrative. In his poetry, correspondence, and narrative, Manzano employs *fate* not only as a conventional trope but also as a metaphor for the uncertain outcome of spiritual warfare. Manzano's letters to Domingo del Monte and his slave narrative reveal a certain angst regarding *la fortuna* (fate), a frequent trope in Spanish Romanticism. If read alongside the author's relationship to Saint Anthony, however, the Romantic notion of *la fortuna* is divested of its normative meaning. Fate held the poet in contempt, it made him an object of mockery and scorn, so that, as he told del Monte in an 1834 letter, he should bear "un baso de lagrimas que derramar a los pies de la fortuna" (a goblet of tears to wail at destiny's feet) (Manzano, *Obras* 80). Manzano's description of destiny as "el arbitro de las cosas" (the arbiter of things) (Manzano, *Obras* 80) in the aforesaid letter makes *la fortuna* comparable to his conception of the saints. Fate is a literary trope and an agent of uncertainty that has brought many more calamities than blessings upon Manzano.

In Manzano's liturgy, San-Antonio-Elegguá embodied the Yoruba conception of destiny, individual chance, and uncertainty in the quotidian struggle to survive and prosper. He was a paradoxical figure, empowered to open or close the crossroads, and he had to be placated lest the poet's destiny be adverse. Cuban scholar Rómulo Lachatañeré challenged Ortiz's criminological lens in the book *Los negros brujos* (1906), which lent scientific credence to popular perceptions that African Cuban religiosity was a mishmash of primitive superstitions that imperiled civilization. Lachatañeré exposed Ortiz's methodological problems and argued that African-inspired spirituality constituted a coherent system of practices pursuant to its own logic. Moreover, Lachatañeré renamed Yoruba-inspired religion *santería*, or worship of the saints, to do away with Ortiz's racialized idiom, witchcraft (*brujería*) ("Las Creencias religiosas de los afrocubanos" 197). Lachatañeré describes Elegguá as the owner of the crossroads (*caminos*), which are the four corners of the universe in African cosmologies.[14] If Elegguá closes the crossroads, he impedes contact with other divine entities and may eliminate personal aspirations. Elegguá is not motivated by a transcendent notion of goodness; rather, he requires appropriate sacrifice to open the crossroads, thus enabling adepts to achieve equilibrium within the uncertainty of human existence (103). In terms of Manzano's narrative, however, San Antonio's transculturation with Elegguá may be explained by the fact that both divine personages are skilled travelers, capable of wielding extraordinary powers and alleviating personal woes.

Elegguá is a decisive factor in Manzano's successful escape. In Cuba this *orisha* is known as Elegguá-Echú, a paradoxical manifestation of the same spirit who interferes in all matters human or divine. As the proprietor of the passageway, Elegguá is the indispensable *orisha*, so that nothing is possible without his involvement (Bolívar 36). Comparable to Nigerian scholars, Natalia Bolívar explains that *orishas* do not embody the absolute concepts of good and evil. Rather, the *orishas* embody the relationship between positive energies and destructive powers since there cannot be peace without discord, and there is no safety without danger (36, 40).

Fleeing on foot from Matanzas to Havana exposed Manzano to grave dangers: possible disorientation from hunger or thirst, or even being taken into custody by slave-hunting parties.[15] Manzano entrusted the *orishas* with his passage from slavery to freedom, as the final paragraph of his autobiography indicates. Manzano described it thus: "me puse de rodillas me encomendé a los santos de mi debosion me puse el sombrero y monté cuando iva a andar p^a. retirarme de la casa" (I knelt down and I commended myself to the saints of my devotion. I put my hat on and mounted the horse when I was going to get away from the house) (Manzano, *Autobiografía* 340). Manzano's commitment to the *orishas* was so devout that he "commended" himself to them one last time before escaping the plantation. San Antonio-Elegguá—one of only two saints named in the autobiography—was the most important "[of his] saints of [his] devotion." The details of Manzano's escape are unknown, since the second part of his slave narrative was either lost or destroyed while in the possession of Ramón de Palma (Azougarh 31). Whatever the particulars of his escape, running away meant the very real possibility of death. Since Elegguá is a near-omniscient warrior spirit who possesses knowledge of Creator, of other *orishas*, and *egun* (Yoruba for "spirits of the dead") (Brown 127, 156), Manzano performed the rituals to please "God's secretary." Elegguá represents Manzano's hopes to be free and he signifies the very real possibility that he may fall into the hands of the authorities. Just as Elegguá's Janus-faced ritual objects gaze in diverging directions, the orisha may look upon Manzano with generosity and transmit his prayers to the Supreme Deity. Or an alternative scenario could emerge in which Elegguá disregarded devout prayers, provided no assistance, and left Manzano to fend for himself. For this very reason, the poet endeavored not to offend the *orishas* through a perceived lack of devotion (Manzano, *Autobiografía* 318). While the Catholic Saint Anthony is renowned for his patience and chastity, Elegguá is a provocateur that may or may not gratify the desires of his devotees (Cros Sandoval 218).

I am saying that Manzano did not pursue freedom within a Catholic conception of redemption, which implies penitence and salvation. The problem with the concept of sin in Cuban slave society is that it created a false equivalency, because it assumed the culpability of the enslaved and the slaveholder. Such doctrines render the oppressor guilty for abusing the weak, but oppressed people do not escape blame or condemnation either. They too are condemned, for their hatred of the oppressor. Whereas the word *pecado* (sin) appears in "Oda a La Religión," where Manzano lamented that the Christian God had abandoned him to a sinful world, the concept is nowhere to be found in the autobiography. Resistance through the appropriation of what was presumed to be Catholic ritual empowered Manzano to resignify the tools of the master, hence granting new meaning to Catholic prayer verses. Cros Sandoval observed that African-inspired religious practice incorporates Catholic liturgical devices such as the novena (79). The introduction of Catholic rites in Manzano's ritual space does not rule out the possibility of an African cultural frame of reference. Cuban scholar Guillermo Sierra Torres also notes that the sign of the Cross and the Lord's Prayer are an integral part of the rituals in honor of certain *orishas* (302). For a Hispano-Catholic readership, the novena and the Lord's Prayer signify Christian devotion, but they may have also spoken to the redemptive power of transculturated African-inspired ritual for black interlocutors.

The emancipatory promise of Manzano's transculturation of San Antonio with Elegguá is nowhere to be found in Delmontine reformist fiction. In the novels *Francisco*, *Cecilia Valdés*, and *Petrona y Rosalía*, the depiction of black and mulatto characters as pitiable victims of white power names the adoration of Catholic saints and the Virgin Mary as an appropriate, albeit ineffectual, act of devotion. In white antislavery fiction, reverence for the saints is a quixotic act in the hands of Romantic female protagonists Rosalía, Dorotea, and Cecilia's grandmother Seña Josefa. In these novels the Catholic saints are not agents of emancipation; rather, they perform an acculturative function. In reformist literature the Catholic saints represent the Church's power to subjugate the will of Afro-Caribbean women to resist the violence of slavery. One such example will suffice. In Suárez y Romero's *Francisco*, Dorotea is acquiescent before her mistress's mistreatment, and her entreaty to a panoply of Catholic saints also goes unheeded. Dorotea's appeal to the saints follows the psychosexual scene in which her owner, Ricardo, pleads with and threatens the enslaved woman, in due course manipulating her with false promises until she complies with his sexual desires (Suárez y Romero 8–92). The narrator describes the unremitting melancholy of Dorotea, who, deeply afflicted, kneels before the images of the saints in hopes of being reunited with Francisco, her chosen mate and the father of their child, Lutgarda. These novels signify the acculturative function of religion within white Cuban reformist fiction, because Dorotea's pleas for mercy go unheeded. Dorotea is comparable to Manzano in the coal cellar. As Frantz Fanon might say, they are mere objects in the hands of white hegemony (*Black Skin* 140), because they have lost all communicative force. Unlike Manzano, whose plea to the saints opened the crossroads for his escape from the plantation circa 1817, Dorotea does not escape her putative object status, since her enslaver refused to acknowledge the culpability of the white men who raped her and denied her manumission.

### *In Search of My Brother*: Black Family as Sacred Community in the Poetry of Juan Francisco Manzano

Juan Francisco Manzano reinvented himself as a poet in Havana nearly two decades after his escape from the slave labor camp. Manzano taught himself to read and write Spanish, much to the chagrin of his slaveholders that had forbidden his literary activities (Manzano, *Autobiografía* 304, 308). He launched his literary career with the publication of two books of Neoclassical poetry, *Flores líricas* (1821) and *Flores pasageras* (1830). In so doing he became one of the first Cuban authors to publish a collection of verse (Luis, "Introducción" 14). Nevertheless, Manzano's autobiography—which he wrote at the behest of Domingo del Monte—was his greatest feat. And even while Manzano was negotiating his own freedom, he wrote to del Monte urgently in an effort to emancipate his brother from bondage. Manzano's mother had entrusted him to care for his siblings some twenty years prior. She explained the family crisis with perspicacity: "[Juan] Juan aqui llebo el dinero de tu libertad, ya tu vez qe tu padre se ha muerto y tu vas a ser ahora el padre de tus hermanos ya no te bolberan a castigar mas" ([Juan], Juan here I carry the money for your freedom, you see that your father has already died, and you'll be a father to your siblings. They will not chastise you again) (Manzano, *Autobiografía* 322). After her husband's death, María de Pilar entrusted her eldest son to "be a father" to his siblings. But Juan Francisco had to emancipate himself first. When Manzano's mistress pilfered his inheritance, freedom became unachievable for him (Manzano, *Autobiografía* 332). Nearly twenty years later, Manzano sought to fulfill his mother's trust.

Manzano sought to reconstitute the family that slavery had torn asunder. I analyze a postscript Manzano appended to his final letter to del Monte where he implored his patron to assist his brother who remained on the plantation. Manzano's postscript was an intertext that doubled as a letter of its own, an addendum devised as an eleventh-hour appeal to ameliorate his brother's condition. Similarly, I examine a poem Manzano dedicated to his brother Florencio in 1838, "Un sueño: A mi segundo hermano" (A Dream: For My Second Brother). I argue that "Un sueño" is a vision of black brotherly love articulated in the sacred language of Bakongo cosmology. There are three motifs in "Un sueño" that merit critical attention: the dream sequence as spirit portal, the forested wilderness as a space for ritual performance, and Icarus as a metaphor for black dreams deferred. In "Un sueño" Manzano transforms himself into a bird that reveres his deceased parents, and he rescues Florencio from the slave labor camp. Similarly, "La visión del poeta compuesta en un ingenio de fabricar azúcar" (The Poet's Vision Composed on a Sugar Plantation) and "Poesías" (Poems) (1836) also portray visions and African-inspired rituals. Both poems use the dream sequence to represent the powers of spirit to transform the black subject.

On October 16, 1835, Manzano appended a postscript to his final letter to del Monte, where he discussed his brother's predicament. I cite the postscript to illustrate Manzano's sense of urgency:

> Sor D. Domingo: contando con la bondad que smd. me dispensa, le suplico me ponga la carta mañana a fin de aprovechar el lunes para embiarla el lunes por cualesquiera conducto pues cada dia que pasa va asiendo mas grave la suerte de mi hermano.

> Sor Dn Domingo, cosa de smd. pues si no ya la desgracia de mi hermano reclama su compasión, a lo menos hagalo smd: por este a quien levantó del cieno a la felicidad, y pueda su mediacion cortar las peligrosa y tristes consecuencias que pueden acarearme la colera de un amo irritado y la imprudente inrreflecion de esta criatura que guiado por mi fama que en Matanzas suena crelló allar en mi un apollo, sin conoser mi asilada impotencia en este caso: pero ya para mi [ . . . ] es mi hermano y que su equibocasion a prosedido de una esperanza que el no supo fundar bien; así espero derrame smd. todo su influjo en fabor de su criado

> J. Fr<sup>co</sup> Manzano.

> mañana a las dies airé smd me lo permite a recojer su carta (Manzano, *Obras* 90).

> (Mr. Don Domingo: relying on the goodness that Your Grace has bestowed on me, I beg of you that you send the letter tomorrow in order [that I might] make the most of Monday to send it Monday by whatever means. Because every day that passes my brother's fate becomes more dire.

> Mr. Don Domingo, Your Grace if my brother's disgrace does not spur your compassion, then at least do this for the one that you raised out of the quagmire and into happiness. And may your intercession cut away the dangerous and sad consequences that might befall me [because of] the rage of an aggravated

master and the imprudent reflection of this poor creature who guided by my
fame, which is resounding in Matanzas, thought he might find some support in
me. Without knowing of my isolated impotence in this case: but for me [ . . . ] he
is my brother and his mistake has led to a state of hopefulness that is not well
founded. For that reason, I hope that Your Grace will use all of your influence
and favor for your servant.

J. Francisco Manzano.

Tomorrow, I will go at 10 o'clock if your grace will consent for me to pick up
your letter.)

Remarkably, even as Manzano fulfilled his part of the quid pro quo to secure his
own freedom, he began to negotiate on his brother's behalf. Manzano scribbled
these words at the end of his final letter to del Monte. But these words were more
than an afterthought; they demonstrated Manzano's desire to reunite his family.
Manzano addressed del Monte with the rhetoric of noblesse oblige, appealing
to del Monte's aristocratic sensibilities and sense of racial superiority. Manzano
celebrated "the goodness that Your Grace has bestowed on me" and characterized
his patron as someone that had "raised [him] out of the quagmire and into happi-
ness." Manzano's tone is consistent throughout the seven letters that he dispatched
to del Monte through a clandestine network in Havana. Manzano's request is
quite bold, despite his rhetoric of humility. Manzano commissioned del Monte
to mediate on his brother's behalf with his former slaveholder, the Marchioness
of Prado Ameno. Manzano's message to del Monte did not mention Florencio by
name. But the postscript alluded to Florencio with the same affection Manzano
expressed for him in the autobiography. Florencio emerged in the autobiography
when Manzano suffered miserably, as the following passages bear out.

> Mi cararter se asia cada ves mas tasiturno y melancolico no hallaba consuleo
> mas q$^e$. recostado en las piernas de mi madre p$^r$. q$^e$. padre de genio seco . . . y se
> acostaba mientras mi pobre madre y mi hermano Florensio me esperaban hasta
> la ora q$^e$. yo viniera este ultimo aunque estubiera dormido luego q$^e$. yo tocaba
> la puerta y oia mi voz despertaba y venia a abrasarme senabamos y nos ivamos
> juntos a la cama . . . (Manzano, *Autobiografía* 309).

> Mi madre y yo fuimos condusidos y puesto en un mismo lugar los dos gemia-
> mos [ . . . ] mi hermano Florensio y Fernando solos lloraban en su casa el uno
> tendria [once o] dose años y el otro sinco . . . (Manzano, *Autobiografía* 312).

> (My character became more and more taciturn and melancholic. I did not find
> consolation unless I was lying on my mother's lap because of my father's dry
> character . . . and he slept while my poor mother and my brother Florencio

waited for an hour until I arrived. The latter [my brother] although he was asleep when I knocked on the door he would hear my voice and he would awake [get up and] he would embrace me, we would have dinner together and we would sleep in the same bed . . . )

(My mother and I were carried to the same place and we moaned [ . . . ] My brother[s] Florencio and Fernando would cry by themselves in their house, one was [eleven or] twelve years old and the other five years old . . . )

Manzano depicted his brother Florencio as a consoler in times of emotional and physical pain. Florencio appeared twice in the slave narrative, more than any other sibling. (Manzano also mentioned his five-year-old brother, Fernando.) In the first passage, Manzano's mother waited patiently for him to return to their *bohío* (slave hut) after his mistress had humiliated him and gagged him for composing sorcery tales (Manzano, *Autobiografía* 308–309). Florencio's sense of compassion for his older brother is palpable in the text. Whenever Florencio got word that Juan Francisco had returned, he would leap out of bed to embrace him and share a meal. Manzano used the Spanish imperfect tense to underscore the consistency in his brotherly relationship with Florencio: "mi pobre madre y mi hermano Florensio me esperaban" (my poor mother and my brother Florencio waited), "oia mi voz" (he would hear my voice), "despertaba" (he would awake), "venia a abrasarme" (he would embrace me), "senabamos" (we would have dinner together), "nos ivamos juntos a la cama" (we would sleep in the same bed). On another occasion, Manzano characterized his fraternal bond as "los indisolubles lazos del amor fraterno" (the indissoluble bonds of brotherly love) (Manzano, *Autobiografía* 314). Manzano portrayed Florencio as a sentient man of African descent capable of familial love; such commonplaces within Spanish Romanticism enabled him to resignify the enslaved black male often regarded as a brute.

Manzano sympathetically portrayed his brother Florencio in his letter to del Monte thus: "my brother's disgrace," "this poor creature," and finally, "he is my brother and his mistake has led to a state of hopefulness that is not well founded" (Manzano, *Obras* 90). Manzano's profound sense of empathy is palpable. But we do not know what Manzano wanted to achieve when he asked del Monte to intercede on his brother's behalf. How had Florencio's circumstances become "more dire"? Was Florencio—now well into his twenties—suffering at the hands of Prado Ameno? Did Manzano fear for his brother's life? Did he expect del Monte to put an end to the abuse or to mitigate Florencio's circumstances by finding him a new owner? Perhaps Manzano wanted del Monte to emancipate his brother altogether? Manzano's abbreviated memorandum obfuscates his intentions, perhaps to protect him should the letter fall into the hands of unsympathetic parties. Nonetheless, Manzano certainly anticipated a letter from del Monte that might intercede on his brother's behalf and put an end to his "disgrace." But there are several details of this fragmented narrative that remain a mystery. We do not know whether del Monte ever replied to Manzano's appeal, because del Monte's letters to Manzano did not survive (Azougarh 54). Nevertheless, the poem Manzano wrote for Florencio, "Un sueño: A mi segundo hermano," is ample evidence of a concerted effort to liberate his younger brother from the Matanzas plantation.

In 1838 Manzano published "Un sueño: A mi segundo hermano" in *El Álbum* in honor of his brother Florencio.[16] "Un sueño" is a Romantic poem recounting Manzano's struggle to liberate his younger brother from the plantation. "Un sueño" juxtaposes Romantic tropes such as the dream sequence, ascension, and magical flight with the ancient Greek god Icarus. Romanticism in Cuban literature did not emerge as a reaction to Neoclassicism, as it did in Spain. Rather, both literary movements coexisted in nineteenth-century Cuban letters (Portuondo 19). This poem was the only antislavery work Manzano published in Cuba during his lifetime. "Un sueño" is a narrative poem that reminisces about Manzano's childhood, laments the horrors of slavery, and pays reverence to his deceased parents. Imbued with a profound sense of nostalgia for family, the first two stanzas portray the cherished relationship Manzano enjoyed with his brother Florencio.

| Tú, Florencio, que sabes | Florencio, you do know |
| Las penas que padezco, | the sorrows that I grieve; |
| Cuán justas y fundadas | how, justified and understandable, |
| Martirizan mi pecho; | they torture my heart; |
| | |
| Sí, tú que en otros dias | Yes, you, who in bygone days |
| Calmabas mis tormentos, | would calm my suffering, |
| O juntas con las mias | or together with mine |
| tus lágrimas corrieron; | your tears also ran (Manzano, *El Álbum* 115).[17] |

Manzano and Florencio shared a similar relationship to the past because they were brothers bound by fraternal affection. Florencio consoled his elder brother because he had also experienced the "justified and understandable" sorrows of slavery. Manzano addressed Florencio in the second person singular to signify the intimacy of their homosocial bond. He composed the poem in the present tense because, even after manumission, the psychic wounds of slavery were too recent to be discarded. In "Un sueño," Manzano produced what is probably the most empathetic and humane image of black masculinity in Cuban colonial literature.

# UN SUEÑO.

*A MI SEGUNDO HERMANO.*

Tú, Florencio, que sabes
Las penas que padezco,
Cuán justas y fundadas
Martirizan mi pecho;

Sí, tú que en otros dias
Calmabas mis tormentos,
O juntas con las mias
Tus lágrimas corrieron;

### 116

Ay! ya que tristemente
Separados nos vemos
Cada cual por su rumbo
Nuevo mundo corriendo;

Que mis versos te lleven
Los colores de un sueño,
Cuyo principio tomo:
Escucha, estáme atento.

Confuso y agoviado,
De mil pesares lleno,
La soledad buscaba,
De los hombres huyendo.

Hácia el vecino monte,
Que de Quintana el cerro
Domina y amenaza
Los lugares internos,

### 117

Aproximeme á un bosque,
Albergue donde suelo,
Conmigo querellando,
Lamentarme en secreto.

No sé si del cansancio,
O del mismo desvelo,
Cerráronse mis ojos
A un dulce y grato sueño,

Quedando así rendido
Entre sus lazos preso;
Mas entre poco rato
Sobre mi espalda siento

De muy grandiosas plumas
Dos alas, que contemplo
Preciosas y pintadas
De mil colores bellos.

### 118

Revuélvolas mil veces
De admiracion perplejo,
Sin que alcanzar pudiese
La causa de este efecto.

Pruebo á volar, y al punto
Las alas rebatiendo,
Del suelo me levanto
Cual pájaro lijero.

Y el aire contractando,
De la tierra me elevo,
Presumido y osado
Por tan vasto elemento.

Ufano contemplaba
Entre la tierra y el cielo
Las portentosas obras
Del alto Ser Supremo.

### 119

Las lindes en que tiene
La mar puesta su freno,
El campo de la luna,
Todo de manchas lleno;

Las causas de la lluvia,
Las de un dia sereno,
Las que la ira enfrenan
Del inflamado viento.

Visto tanto en el aire,
Buscaba con anhelo
El centro de la tierra
Para posar mi vuelo.

Recojo los plumajes,
Inclino un poco el pecho,
Y en círculos rondando
Torno á bajar de nuevo;

### 120

Descendiendo con tino
De Matanzas al seno,
De dó la vista fijo
A aquel lugar tremendo.

Donde yertos reposan
Los miserables restos
De aquellos nuestros padres
Que el primer ser nos dieron.

Su vista me horroriza,
Vacilo, me estremezco,
Recordando la causa
De nuestros males fieros.

Allí poso algun tanto,
Mil lágrimas vertiendo
En memoria, aunque vana,
De aquellos años tiernos.

### 121

Que engolfados pasamos
En inocéntes juegos,
Del maternal cariño
Los goces recojiendo.

Yo la sierra veia
Del *Palenque* soberbio,
El suntuoso *Molino*
Con sus vastos terrenos.

Sus puras claras linfas,
Sus jardines amenos,
De donde tantas veces
Salí de flores lleno.

Mas, como no podia
Sufocar en mi pecho
Las tiernas impresiones
Del dulce amor fraterno,

### 122

Ansioso bajo y hallo
Aquel mi caro objeto,
Como robusto etiope
Los trabajos venciendo.

Le miro, me conoce,
Me abraza, yo le beso,
Y ¡oh Dios! entre sus brazos
Sentí crecer mi afecto.

,,Huyamos, pues, le dije,
De este recinto horrendo,
Mas terrible á mi vista
Que la del horco mesmo:

,,Huyamos, caro hermano,
Partamos por el viento;
Por siempre abandonemos
Nuestro enemigo suelo.''

### 123

Entónces cariñoso
En los brazos le estrecho,
Y cual la vez primera,
Las alas rebatiendo,

Aire recojo, y formo
Las columnas de viento
Con que el éter recorren
Los pájaros lijeros.

Levántome orgulloso,
Torno á volar de nuevo,
Mas alegre y ufano
Con mi amoroso peso.

Feliz atravesaba
Poblados y desiertos;
Sobre los anchos mares
Soberbio me recreo.

### 124

Al ver bajo mi vista
Tantos puntos diversos,
Ya libre por el aire
Me sublimo y escelso.

Me tramonto y me juzgo
Gran Señor de los vientos,
Yéndome atrás, dejándo
De América los pueblos;

Tal ya me figuraba
Con sublimado vuelo
Hallar entre las nubes
Algun seguro puesto.

Me afano y sobrepujo
Los encontrados vientos,
Perdiéndome á la vista
Del lince mas atento,

### 125

Y á disfrutar aspiro
Los cánticos del cielo....
Mas ay! en un instante
Todo el espacio veo,

De tan claro y hermoso,
De tan manso y sereno,
Tornarse en noche oscara,
Bramar el noto horrendo.

Rujir el mar abajo,
Tronar arriba el cielo,
Correr los torbellinos
A impulsos de los vientos,

Relámpagos continos
En sus choques vertiendo,
Y en horrorosa guerra
Todos los elementos.

The original printing of Juan Francisco Manzano's poem "Un sueño: A mi segundo hermano" (A Dream: For My Second Brother) in *El Álbum* in 1838. Courtesy of Instituto de Literatura y Lingüística, Yasnay Cuesta.

The fourth stanza introduces the dream sequence derived from Romanticism that fragments the linearity of time and space. In Spanish Romanticism, dreaming is characterized by ascent and descent. In the dream sequence, descent creates a shifting and perpetually open space that defies logic and seldom results in a pleasurable outcome (Rosenberg 21–22). For the Romantics, the dream state, also known as an oneiric space, is unencumbered by logic, existing outside of time and space; it is always open, in constant metamorphosis, and, as such, dreams are spaces where poets and narrators may portray the mysteries of the spirit world. Manzano evoked the atemporality, incongruence, and spontaneity of dreams to achieve two primary objectives: to envisage rescuing his brother from slavery and to portray himself as an African-descended subject rooted in Bakongo-inspired theory about spirits and ancestors.

| | |
|---|---|
| Confuso y agoviado, | Confused and aggrieved, |
| De mil pesares lleno, | burdened by a thousand woes, |
| La soledad buscaba, | I searched for solitude, |
| De los hombres huyendo. | fleeing from man. |
| | |
| Hácia el vecino monte, | Toward the nearby wilderness |
| Que de Quintana el cerro | where Quintana's hill |
| Domina y ameniza | adorns and dominates |
| Los lugares internos, | the inner spaces, |

| Aproximeme á un bosque, | I came to a forest, |
|---|---|
| Albergue donde suelo, | a refuge I frequent |
| Conmigo querellando, | to quarrel with myself |
| Lamentarme en secreto. | and secretly lament. |

| No sé si del cansancio, | Whether from fatigue, |
|---|---|
| O del mismo desvelo, | or lack of sleep, |
| Cerráronse mis ojos | I closed my eyes |
| A un dulce y grato sueño, | For a sweet and pleasant dream (Manzano, |
| | *El Álbum* 116–117) |

My reading privileges the dream sequence as the poem's guiding principle. To decipher the poem's deeper, transcultural meanings, we must examine Catholic doctrines regarding night visions as well as the Kongolese theory of dreams. Nineteenth-century Cuba was a contact zone where Spanish and West Central/West African ideas about spirituality came into dialogue and ongoing dispute with one another under conditions of radical inequality (Dodson 3; Pratt, *Imperial Eyes* 6). By examining Manzano's dreams as a product of intercultural contact, I demonstrate how he introduced African-inspired ideas about ritual by manipulating the dream sequence, which held sacred and secular meanings. Dreams and prophecies have long been a part of European Catholicism, finding their origins in Old Testament accounts like those of the patriarchs Jacob and Joseph (Kagan 38). In sixteenth-century Spain, the Catholic Church and laypersons alike valued dreams, visions, ecstasies, and raptures for their natural and supernatural meanings. These were memorialized in engravings and printed libretti. In religious circles dreams were understood to have two sources; they were of natural origin (from the body) or were supernatural messages that might be deemed divine or diabolical. Since the Protestant Reformation, the Catholic Church feared the spread of heresies and sought to discourage most forms of personal religious expression, fearing they might be unorthodox or even anti-Catholic. The Inquisition prosecuted oneiromancers (dream interpreters), and it impeached individuals whose dreams the Church supposed had been misinterpreted as divine "message dreams" with some bearing on future events (Kagan 10, 38). Although the Holy Office of the Inquisition never established a separate tribunal in Cuba (Palmié, *Wizards* 342), and by 1834 the Spanish Inquisition had been abolished throughout the empire (Payne 74), Catholic priests remained skeptical of the power the laity attributed to dreams and visions.

Father Félix Varela regarded dreams and oneiromancers as a veritable threat to the Church's claims to universal authority. In 1838—the same year Manzano published "Un Sueño"—Varela denounced "todas las apariciones y sueños más ridículos, siempre que sean análogos a sus ideas o promuevan sus intereses" (all the apparitions and most ridiculous dreams that are always comparable to their ideas or promote their interests) (*Cartas* 87). In Varela's formulation, Cuban oneiromancers were mere charlatans that deciphered dreams in ways that promoted their economic and political interests. Varela's condemnation of oneiromancy is apropos for my reading of "Un sueño," because Manzano emerged not only as a dreamer but also as an interpreter of spiritual messages for his brother. But Manzano's dream and his interpretation of that dream require a different set of analytical tools, because the messages he deciphered were analogous to Bakongo-inspired concepts about the nature of dream interpretation.

The late scholar Kia Bunseki Fu-Kiau explains an African theory of dreams from a distinctively Kongolese perspective:

A dream (*ndozi*) is a voiceless communication. It is at the same time a means and a message. This message can be audible, pictorial and scenic. [ . . . ]

The dream can be a reflection of diurnal activities, a repetition of past activities, or a projection of one's own activities and imagination in the future. But most importantly, it can be a warning about a future or imminent event: good or bad news. A dream-interpreter [M'bangudi-a-ndozi],is a person whose sensitivity to and awareness of waves, symbols and their meanings are very high (116, 118).

Manzano portrayed what he dreamt as more than a "repetition of past activities"; his dream was a "pictorial and scenic" message in need of interpretation. The Kongolese theory of dreams is apropos for my reading of "Un Sueño" because within this explanatory framework, Manzano was not an oneiromancer with selfish ambitions, but rather a *M'bangudi-a-ndozi* whose "sensitivity" and "awareness" empowered him to derive meaning from the symbolic world that ancestral spirits had summoned. Manzano translated the forested wilderness, the slave cemetery, magical flight, and even Icarus into a lyrical language that was legible for Florencio and for his broader white readership. In Manzano's poem *el monte* (forested wilderness) is depicted as a refuge from slavery and as sacred space for the African-descended subject that conjures the power of the dead. Manzano described his escape from the plantation euphemistically as "fleeing man." His escape landed him in *el monte*, which became sacred space to enact Bakongo-inspired ritual. The stanzas below bear witness to the initial moments of ritual in poem: Manzano's transfiguration into a winged creature.

| | |
|---|---|
| Quedando así rendido | Having thus surrendered, |
| Entre sus lazos preso; | Bound in its snare; |
| Mas entre poco rato | But after a while, |
| Sobre mi espalda siento | On my back I feel, |

| De muy grandiosas plumas | Made of magnificent feathers, |
| Dos alas, que contemplo | Two wings that I contemplate, |
| Preciosas y pintadas | Precious and painted |
| De mil colores bellos. | A thousand beautiful hues. |

| Revuélvolas mil veces | I move them a thousand times, |
| De admiración perplejo, | Perplexed in admiration, |
| Sin que alcanzar pudiese | Unable to comprehend |
| La causa de este efecto. | The cause of this effect. |
| [ … ] | |

| Visto tanto en el aire, | Having seen so much from the air, |
| Buscaba con anhelo | I eagerly looked |
| El centro de la tierra | For the center of the earth |
| Para posar mi vuelo. | To land from my flight. |

| Recojo los plumajes, | I gather my feathers, |
| Inclino un poco el pecho, | I slightly tilt my chest, |
| Y en círculos rondando | And turning in circles, |
| Torno á bajar de nuevo; | I come down again; |

| Descendiendo con tino | In a well-aimed descent, |
| De Matanzas al seno, | Into the heart of Matanzas, |
| De dó la vista fijo | From where I gaze |
| A aquel lugar tremendo. | On that terrible place, |

| Donde yertos reposan | There lie resting |
| Los miserables restos | The miserable remains |
| De aquellos nuestros padres | Of our parents |
| Que el primer ser nos dieron. | Who gave us our first being (Manzano, *El Álbum* 117–120) |

Manzano's metamorphosis into a bird enables the poetic "I" to transcend temporal and spatial limitations so that flight becomes what Joel James Figarola would call an act of "cultural marronage" (*cimarronaje cultural*), as evident throughout the poem (44–45).[18] By using the phrase "cultural marronage," I contend that the depiction of a maroon character represents an aesthetic novelty, as well as a departure from Spanish Catholicism that advocated redemption without freedom. Manzano's representation of a maroon character in *el monte* is, in an ethnohistoric sense, consistent with Cuban ideas about the forested wilderness as the epitome of sacrality in Bakongo-inspired spirituality.

Lydia Cabrera's informants described *el monte* as the epitome of the sacred, as a physical space that is equivalent to a Christian temple. Due to its significance for my reading, I have quoted her informants extensively.

> Nosotros los negros vamos al Monte como si fuésemos a una iglesia, porque está llena de Santos y de difuntos, a pedirles lo que nos hace falta para nuestra salud y para nuestros negocios. Ahora bien: si en casa ajena se debe ser respetuoso, en la casa de los Santos ¿no se será más respetuoso? (Cabrera, *El monte* 15)

> (We blacks go to the forested Mountain wilderness as if it were a church, because it is filled with Saints and the deceased, to ask for what we need for our health and business dealings. Now then: if one should be respectful in someone else's house, in the house of the Saints shouldn't one be even more respectful?)

In Bakongo-inspired religious thought, the forested wilderness is an African tabernacle because it is a sacred house of worship permeated with divine presence. Unlike the Catholic cathedral, however, African divine spirits and spirits of the departed—commonly referred to in Cuba under a Hispano-Catholic nomenclature as *santos* and *difuntos* (saints and the dead)—inhabit the wilderness. In Bakongo and Yoruba-inspired religions, practitioners show reverence for divine entities that control natural phenomena, for powerful ancestral spirits, and for the recently deceased that occupy space and intervene in the material world (Dodson 51–53). Cabrera's informants imagine the forested wilderness not as a resource for the primitive accumulation of slave merchants, but rather as a sanctuary for all classes of spiritual forces, good and evil, mighty and minuscule. The mountain wilderness became sacred space for African-inspired ritual and a veritable fortress for *palenque* runaway communities, due to its geographic inaccessibility. Africans absconded from sugar plantations in Matanzas and availed themselves of the mountainous and sparsely populated terrain to establish maroon strongholds (Bergad 22, 83). That the Matanzas countryside was a maroon stronghold was certainly not lost on Manzano, as I will discuss shortly.

In the poem Manzano metamorphosed into a bird and sought to land in the center of the earth: "I gather my feathers, / I slightly tilt my chest, / and turning in circles, / I come down again." Manzano's bodily movements warrant analysis, because Cuban *palo monte* priests explain that the *nganga* sits at the center of the cosmogram as a source of strength and stability. Dodson reminds us that in Bakongo-inspired religion, such as *palo monte/palo mayombe*, the *nganga* has three meanings: it is a cauldron filled with sacred material objects, an incorporeal being, or a "powerful devotee of Palo Monte/Palo Mayombe" (89). After his metamorphosis Manzano has become incorporeal, that is, a spirit that transcends time and space. When he lands at the center of the earth, Manzano locates himself firmly in the beyond, and he summons his deceased parents;

thus, he occupies—allegorically at least—the place of equilibrium reserved for the *nganga*. Manzano's entreaty to his deceased parents bespeaks his ethical commitment to "be a father" (Manzano, *Autobiografía* 322) to his siblings. This depiction of Manzano's parents is consistent with the Bakongo-inspired notion of the deceased as *nfumbe* (*nfumbi* in Cuban Spanish) that reside in the kingdom of the dead known in Kikongo as *mpemba*. Manzano's engagement with death in "Un sueño" deviated from the dogma of the 1796 slave catechism, and it clashed with Fray Luis de Granada's sermons on heaven and hell. Necromancy was defined as witchcraft in colonial Spanish America (Bristol, *Christians, Blasphemers* 156), so priests like Félix Varela would have condemned Manzano as "an enemy of divine authority" (*Cartas* 86).

More than two decades after his escape from Matanzas, Manzano had elevated his parents to the stature of *nfumbe* (*mfundi* in the plural), that is, deceased family members that dwell among the ancestors. Simon Bockie writes that only benevolent persons that were committed to community during their lifetimes may enter *mpemba* (84).[19] In Manzano's judgement María del Pilar and Toribio Castro certainly fit that criterion. When Manzano gathers feathers, and is "turning in circles," he improvises upon the Kongolese cosmogram, which, according to Thompson, "signifies ... the circular motion of human souls about the circumference of its intersecting lines" (108). Manzano has taken an ethereal form, and his movement symbolizes the Kongolese existential principle that the human being is a "living-dying-living-being" (Fu-Kiau 35). If Manzano's parents are among the ancestors, then they are endowed with the requisite power to help him unravel the vicissitudes of life.

In flight, Manzano returns to the Matanzas plantation in search of his brother Florencio.

| | |
|---|---|
| Allí poso algún tanto, | There I set down for a while, |
| Mil lágrimas vertiendo | Shedding a thousand tears, |
| En memoria, aunque vana, | Remembering, though in vain, |
| De aquellos años tiernos. | Those tender years |
| | |
| Que engolfados pasamos | That we spent absorbed |
| En inocentes juegos, | In innocent games, |
| Del maternal cariño | Our mother's love |
| Los goces recojiendo. | Joyfully gathering. |
| | |
| Yo la sierra veia | I could see the sierra |
| Del *Palenque* soberbio, | From the lofty *palenque*, |
| El suntuoso *Molino* | The magnificent sugar mill |
| Con sus vastos terrenos. | With its vast estate. |
| [ ... ] | |

| | |
|---|---|
| Mas, como no podia | But since I couldn't |
| Sufocar en mi pecho | Quell in my heart |
| Las tiernas impresiones | The tender impressions |
| Del dulce amor fraterno, | Of sweet brotherly love, |
| | |
| Ansioso bajo y hallo | Anxious, I descend to find |
| Aquel mi caro objeto, | The dear object of my affection |
| Como robusto etiope | As a strong Ethiopian |
| Los trabajos venciendo. | Overcoming his toils. |
| | |
| Le miro, me conoce, | I see him recognize me, |
| Me abraza, yo le beso, | I kiss him, he enfolds me, |
| Y ¡oh Dios! entre sus brazos | And—Oh, God!—in this embrace |
| Sentí crecer mi afecto. | I felt my affection grow. |
| | |
| "Huyamos, pues, le dije, | Let us flee, I told him, |
| De este recinto horrendo, | From this horrible place, |
| Mas terrible á mi vista | More terrible in my view |
| Que la del horco mesmo: | Than Hell itself; |
| | |
| "Huyamos, caro hermano, | Let us flee, dear brother, |
| Partamos por el viento; | Let us leave on the wind |
| Por siempre abandonemos | Let us abandon forever |
| Nuestro enemigo suelo." | Our enemy soil (Manzano, *El Álbum* 120–122) |

Remembering the "innocent games" and their "mother's love" of "those tender years," Manzano cries for the lost innocence, companionship, and familial union of his youth. As he soars over Matanzas, Manzano observes the lofty *palenque* of the African maroons—a community of runaways in which the poet has claimed symbolic membership—and the sugar plantation where he spent many years as a tormented youth. Moved by "The tender impressions / Of sweet brotherly love," Manzano sets out to accomplish the task that he could not achieve in real life: the complete liberation of his brother. Manzano's embrace and kiss of Florencio is highly significant. Hortense Spillers points out, "Touch is probably the single sensual realm that most defines the difference between enslaved and free" [ . . . ] "And touch maybe the first measure of what it means not to be enchained anymore."[20] In "Un sueño" Manzano rescues Florencio while he is yet working on the sugar plantation "as a strong Ethiopian / overcoming his toils." Sylvia Molloy has called the term *Ethiopian* "an ordinary and pretentious euphemism" that López Prieto later used—in *Parnaso cubano* (1881)—to describe Manzano himself (415). In "Un sueño," however, *Ethiopian* has a metaphorical meaning, because the term—commonly used in nineteenth-century literature to designate Africans and those of African descent—enabled Manzano to circumvent the indignity of the word *black* in slave society. Comparable to Manzano's portrayal of his mother in the slave narrative, blackness is devoid of pejorative meanings. And the Bakongo-inspired context lends a cultural dimension to blackness, associating it with spirituality in a manner not seen elsewhere in the poet's works. Blackness becomes subversive for religio-cultural as well as political reasons.

The meaning of marronage shifts in the five stanzas that depict Florencio's rescue. Manzano is a maroon that not only flees the plantation to escape exploitation but also abandons Cuba. Rachel Price has noted that Manzano's use of the word *suelo* accentuated the paradoxical relationship that African descendants had to Cuba. In effect, she observes, Manzano's home is also his "enemy territory" (Price 546). Echoing a classic description of Hell, the poet underscores that Cuba is "enemy soil," a *locus horrendus* where persons of African descent exist to serve the interests of white wealth production. The poem has both cultural and political implications, because even after joining the ranks of free people of color in 1836, Manzano did not achieve true freedom. Abandoning his "enemy soil" is the only way he (and his brother) might be free. But there is an issue that remains unresolved: where will Manzano and Florencio go to find greater peace than the wilderness? Will they go to Africa? The symbolic return to Africa—a commonplace in the Afro-Caribbean oral traditions of Jamaica, Curaçao, and Grenada—(McDaniel 29–30) is implicit in Manzano's ritual and in his choice of the word "abandon." But "Un sueño: A mi segundo hermano" does not answer these queries about Manzano's destiny. Manzano's poems "La visión del poeta compuesta en un ingenio de fabricar azúcar" and "Poesías" enable a further analysis of dreams and visions as an African Cuban portal to the spirit world.

Manzano's "Poesías" (1836)—released the same year as his manumission—read as an aesthetic statement about transculturated poetics. In "Poesías" the classical Greek muse is not a singular source of inspiration because Manzano also invokes dreams and visions as a threshold into the otherworld. Dreams are more than a Romantic trope; they constitute a creative force born of a Bakongo-inspired concept of the cosmos. Manzano reminisced on "el dulce abril de mis perdidos años / do gozo y libertad nunca cupieron" (the sweet April of my vanished years / were joy and liberty could never be). The subsequent verse is a proclamation of Manzano's emancipatory politics: "que es gozo y libertad lo que más amo" (It is joy and liberty that I love most) (Manzano, *Esclavo poeta* 147). The Spanish word *libertad* recurs on three occasions in "Poesías," so the emancipated poet might reiterate what he had contended in an 1834 letter to del Monte "that propensity that by natural principle every man slave has for his rescue" (Manzano, *Obras* 81).

The stanzas below explore the notion that spirits may be the poet's muse.

De la patria del sueño en los encantos
¡cuánta revolución maravillosa
contemplé de aquel mundo imaginario
siempre desconocido, nuevo siempre
para la oscura mente del humano!
¡oh! loca fantasía que pudiste
tomar las reglas del pincel sagrado
y así vestir con materiales formas
un fantástico ser, tuyo es el cuadro:
en tus tintes empapa ahora mi pluma
cuyos bellos colores cotejando
la humana copia ensayaré diciendo
como del genio y la ilusión llevado
a un prado descendí. Creedme, o seres,
que de ilusiones férvidas tocados
revelasteis del hombre los destinos (Manzano, *Esclavo poeta* 147)

(From the motherland of bewitched dreams
how marvelous a revolution
I contemplated that imaginary world
always unknown, always new
for the dark human mind!
oh, maddening fantasy that might
grasp the principles of the sacred brush
and in that way, dress it in material form
a fantastical being, the portrait is yours:
my pen is immersed in your inkwell
whose beautiful colors juxtapose with
the human replica, I will prepare uttering
as if carried by genius and illusion
I descend upon a pasture. Believe me, oh beings,
touched by fervent illusions
that revealed to Man his Destiny)

Manzano's "imaginary world" or "motherland of bewitched dreams" is not the descent into chaos common in Spanish Romanticism that ends in calamity. Rather, his "imaginary world" is a form of wish fulfillment. The dream world is suspended in a constant state of mutability; it remains open, defies temporal logic, and collapses time and space (Rosenberg 21–22). The polysemy of the

Spanish word *encantar* is instrumental in Manzano's construction of meaning, since it may be rendered "to attract," "to delight," "to bewitch," or "to cast a spell." "The motherland of bewitched dreams" enabled the African-descended author to resignify the dreadful connotation that sorcery tales (*cuentos de encantamiento*) had in the slave narrative, so that *encantamiento* might signify creative force. I believe that "sorcery" is an allusion to ritual powers within African Atlantic religions, which, similar to the Yoruba concept of *aché*, denotes collaboration between practitioners and spirit beings to make things happen.

In sixteenth- and seventeenth-century Africa, revelations included dreams, augury, visions, and spirit possession of humans, animals, and inanimate objects (Thornton, *Africa and Africans* 239). In addition to the embodied events of spirit possession and spirit sightings, "New World," *palo monte/palo mayombe* practitioners also receive revelation by way of dreams. For instance, some Bakongo-inspired sacred spaces in Cuba originated in the dream world, where devotees received aesthetic instruction from spirits (Dodson 55, 19). Manzano's use of the dream sequence is consistent with Romantic and Bakongo-inspired conceptions of the oneiric. In "Poesías" the subject is "llevado de mis vagos pensamientos" (carried off by my vague meditations) that transport him to a rooftop adjacent to a wall, where he is left to ponder his fate (Manzano, *Esclavo poeta* 147). Comparable to his other African-descended-themed poetry, magical flight occurs within the dream state, and it is a conduit to revelatory and transformative encounters. But the portrayal of an enraptured body as a site of revelation implies spirit possession.

Manzano was a recent *liberto* (liberated slave); so to be invested with divine creative force in the context of "Poesías" was a formidable act indeed. As Manzano says in the sixth stanza, the human mind is a dark labyrinth in need of divine intercession. Manzano places emphasis on the type of vision that he beheld. I do not read the "loca fantasía" (maddening fantasy) as an instance of black madness—as some persons close to del Monte suspected when Manzano insisted on his freedom (Manzano, *Autobiografía* 123)—but rather as one in which he surrendered his body to the force of spirit. Manzano employs apostrophe to speak directly with the "seres" (beings) that he encountered when carried to a meadow. The liturgical ambiguity of the word "seres" is instructive. When Manzano portrayed the emancipatory power of the saints or his dread of *cosa mala*, he referred to them as "those from other times" and "from the other life" (Manzano, *Autobiografía* 305).[21] Manzano distinguished himself as a mulatto in the autobiography, but here that mulatto persona becomes a host for the multihued metaphors that spirits revealed to him. Manzano's self-representation as a "mulato, y entre negros" (a mulatto, and among blacks) (Manzano, *Autobiografía* 339) did not preclude his participation in African-inspired spirituality. Manzano's vision concludes with the appearance of a meteor that flashes "tres preciosos rayos" (three precious rays of light) (Manzano, *Esclavo poeta*

148). Thompson writes in that Bakongo cosmology, shooting stars have been designated as spirits soaring across the sky (115). Manzano deciphered a prophetic message from the spirits emerging as a gilded inscription in the sky: "*justicia, caridad, beneficencia*" (*justice, charity, beneficence*), the key principles of his emancipatory project (original emphasis; Manzano, *Esclavo poeta* 148).

"La visión del poeta en un ingenio de fabricar azúcar" (The Poet's Vision Composed on a Sugar Plantation) is a lengthy antislavery poem, boasting some fifty-two stanzas that were never published during Manzano's lifetime. Manzano's *visión* of the "torment[s]" that beleaguered him on the plantation, his yearning for liberty, and his veiled references to African-inspired ritual explain why the poem never saw the light of day in Cuba. Moreover, "La visión" is among the antislavery poems that Adriana Lewis Galanes and William Luis unearthed in the 1990s in manuscript collections at the Biblioteca Nacional de Madrid and Yale University respectively. My reading of "La visión del poeta" examines Manzano's recurring themes: the dream sequence, magical flight, spirit revelation, and Bakongo-inspired ritual. In "La visión del poeta," Manzano narrated his tormented life on the plantation with a bit of *magic*. In the poem, visions from the other world astonish him, he takes off in magical flight, and Venus—the Roman goddess of beauty—appears to rescue him from his *locus horrendous*. Manzano introduced the nightingale in "La visión del poeta" not as metaphor for black freedom, but rather as a symbol of emotional camouflage. He wrote: "Y aparenta que canta, pero llora / El terrible dolor que le devora" (And [the nightingale] appears to sing, but it [really] cries / The terrible pain that devours it) (Manzano, *Autobiografía* ). The poem's emphasis on black sentience creates space for an African-descended selfhood that slave society rendered virtually impossible. In lamentation before the Christian God, a disconsolate Manzano is witness to an imminent injury that might befall him: "Me veo a punto ¡Oh Dios! de ser testigo / De un daño que me viene amenazando" (I see myself, Oh God! about to behold / Some harm that menaces me) (Manzano, *Autobiografía* 176). Similar to the nightingale, Manzano chants a miserable hymn that consumes his "pecho sensitivo" (sensitive bosom) (Manzano, *Autobiografía* 176).

Manzano's vulnerability with his readership is reminiscent of his autobiography, and of his poems "La esclava ausente" and "Un sueño." Manzano turns to his ancestors in the fifth stanza to perform a ritual that is resonant with Bakongo-inspired practices.

Unas veces suspiro por la muerte
Mi usurpada fortuna contemplando;
Y con el llanto cruel que el pecho vierte
La paternal ceniza voy bañando,
Otras la fantasía me convierte
En ave por las nubes transitando

Y en mitad del vuelo más propicio
Me siento descender a un precipicio. (Manzano, *Autobiografía* 176–177)

(Sometimes I sigh for death
Contemplating my stolen fate;
And my bosom pours forth a cruel lament
I go bathing myself in [my] father's ashes,
Other fantasies transform me
Into a bird flying through the skies
And in the middle of my prosperous flight
I feel myself descend upon a precipice.)

Manzano's "stolen fate" might have been an allusion to how his mistress dispossessed him of the inheritance his mother had bequeathed him. His autobiography and his letters to del Monte described *fortuna* as an agent of uncertainty in his life. But in "La visión del poeta" *fortuna* clearly referred to a future that had already been usurped. Perhaps what is most striking about this stanza is that Manzano turns so deliberately to his ancestors to resolve his predicament. The most important verse is grammatically simple but semantically dense: "La paternal ceniza  voy bañando" (I go bathing myself in [my] father's ashes) (Manzano, *Autobiografía* 177).  My research has not unearthed anything comparable to this verse either in Cuban  abolitionist fiction or poetry. Manzano's bathing of himself in an ancestor's ashes might be read as his desire to envelop himself in his father's essence, metaphorically speaking. The Spanish word *bañando,* conjugated in the present progressive form is indicative of an ongoing cleansing rite that occurs in a given moment. Manzano alluded to the sacrality of human remains in the autobiography when he characterized the governess's "harsh words were to fall upon the ashes of my poor mother" (Manzano, *Autobiografía* 332). And again, when he portrayed his parents' "miserable remains" (Manzano, *El Álbum,* 120) in "Un sueño." But this obscure verse stands apart from the other representations, because in "La visión del poeta," Manzano does spiritual work with the mortal remains of his deceased father: Toribio de Castro.

Manzano's portrayal of his father's ashes becomes legible if we consider that human remains are vital to  Bakongo-inspired ritual as an animating force. Joel James Figarola wrote, "Al tomar restos humanos en virtud del pacto, se está devolviendo a la vida, aun cuando a una forma especial de vida, al difunto. [ . . . ] Como si el muerto desease pactar antes de, efectivamente, pactar." (By taking human remains in order to make a pact, one is returning life, although another sort of life to the deceased one. [ . . . ] As if the dead person wanted to make a pact before, effectively, making a pact) (268). Figarola says that human skulls and other mortal remains are crucial to the process by which practitioners of *palo monte/palo mayombe*  make sacred pacts with *mfumbi* (spirits of

the dead). Figarola makes a remarkable comparison between Catholic vener-
ation of the  sacred remains of St. James the Apostle—thought to be in the
cathedral in  Santiago de Compostela—and the Kongo-Cuban appropriation
of human remains in ritual (254–255, 268, 284). But Manzano's performance
of a cleansing ritual with the mortal remains of his father in *el monte* clearly
signals Bakongo inspiration.[22] That Manzano sought the transformation of
his "stolen fate" is further reason to interpret this stanza through an African
Cuban cultural lens. We need to further explore the meanings of the Kikongo
word *nfumbe* to understand this point. Todd Ochoa has written extensively
on this:

> *Nfumbe* is a Palo Kikongo word that means "dead one." It is an ambiguous term
> within Palo's language of the dead and means as much "dead person" as "force
> of the dead." It is also the term used to refer to human bones.

> [ ... ]

> Palo's claims to efficacy in fate-transforming works rest to a great degree on
> avowals of singular access to the dead and their powers of revaluation, and for
> this paleras and paleros must accomplish solidifications, however gelatinous, of
> Kalunga [the indiscriminate sea of spirits of the dead], which courses around
> and through their prendas [cauldrons of sacred materials]. Those who approach
> Palo healers for help assume that some version of the dead "resides" within the
> prendas they consult, and by virtue of tending to such obvious versions of the
> dead these healers are able to reshape their fates. (Ochoa 158)

Manzano's father was a *nfumbe* not only because he was a "dead one" but also
because he was "the force of the dead." What Manzano wrote about paternal
ashes implies a belief that his father *resided* within those mortal remains and,
if properly beseeched, might act on his son's behalf. Manzano's poetic persona
held his father's ashes in his hands and proceeded to ritually cleanse himself
with that "versions of dead." In effect, Manzano did spiritual work in order to
enact a sacred pact with his father and to transform his own fate. Manzano's
liturgical posture and his epistemological expectations are akin to those who
approach *palo* healers in search of "fate-transforming work." This verse is
Manzano's *call from the grave*. Consequently, the ritual cleansing is indispensable, Manzano must cleanse himself in order to become a vessel receptive to
ethereal visions. Manzano is transfigured into a bird only after he has purified
himself in his father's ashes.[23]

Magical flight is a trope that enables Manzano's persona to achieve otherwise
impossible feats: escape from bondage, make intimate contact with spirits, and
receive artistic inspiration. Flight is an attempt to escape captivity for the poetic

subject in "La visión del poeta," but the maroon-like bird in "Un sueño" is emblematic of Manzano's post-emancipation sense of duty to liberate his younger brother held in bondage. What I have construed as the representation of Bakongo-inspired ritual is remarkably similar in both poems. Below, I cite at length Manzano's representation of the forested wilderness as sacred space in "La visión del poeta" to illustrate my point. The tenth stanza of "La visión del poeta" returns to the contemplative as a leitmotif intimately correlated with spirit revelation.

> Contemplo aquí los pálidos aspectos
> Del sin ventura suelo donde habito
> Y circúmdanme en torno mil objetos
> Que por doquier aumentan mi conflicto.
> El escabroso monte en esqueleto
> Su adustez y espectáculo inaudito
> Parece estar gimiendo en una urna
> Con la naturaleza taciturna (Manzano, *Autobiografía* 178).

> (Here I contemplate the pallid features
> Of this hopeless land that I inhabit
> And circling about me are a thousand objects
> That multiply my conflict wheresoever.
> The scabrous mountain of skeletons
> Its callous and unmentionable spectacle
> So that is seems to be weeping in an urn
> With Nature silent)

Manzano privileged the sentience and contemplation born of his embodied experience in this stanza of "La visión del poeta." Manzano's confrontation with death—a common trope in Romanticism—devolves into the Romantic grotesque, because in this "hopeless land" the poet must face the disintegration of his world and, possibly, the death of the subject (Rosenberg 104–105, 116). The stanza critiques the slave regime through an incisive description of the ashen, fruitless and sinful landscape where the Christian God—as Manzano exclaimed in "Oda a La Religión"—has abandoned the poet to dwell "where sin is born" (Manzano, *Autobiografía* 143). Despoiled by the *sin* of plantation slavery, the mountainous forested wilderness is bereft of its verdant, lively essence, instead becoming "El escabroso monte en esqueleto" (The scabrous mountain of skeletons). Manzano did not choose the word *palenque* (runaway community) to designate these as the dry bones of fallen maroon warriors, but he did insinuate that skeletal remains, be they indigenous or African, were the site of historical memory of an "espectáculo inaudito" (unmentionable spectacle). The textual silence speaks volumes. The rugged mountain is a funerary space somewhat comparable to the

San Miguel plantation in the autobiography where the poet also witnessed the existential crisis that the Middle Passage had wrought. The difference is that in *el monte* the ancestral remains are most likely those of Africans that erected communities of their own and struggled to maintain autonomy. The "mil objetos" (thousand objects) that encircle the poet suggest Manzano's disorientation with the apparition of maroon spirits. But, as Bakongo cosmology instructs us, spirit contact may also result in the transformation of someone's fate. "La visión del poeta," "Un sueño," and "Poesías," are illustrative of how Manzano mastered the tropes of Spanish Romanticism to compose a transculturated colonial poetry. In all three poems, Manzano employed the Romantic trope of awakening from a dream to insinuate his fear that his dreams might not be fulfilled.

Manzano situated "La visión del poeta," "Un sueño," and "Poesías" in the cultural interstices of colonial Cuba, brilliantly appropriating an abundance of Romantic tropes to reimagine freedom through an African Cuban cultural lens. Manzano disguised Bakongo-Cuban practices in the language of Spanish Romanticism: he evoked the dream state, transfiguration, and magical flight. Dreams enabled Manzano to communicate with his deceased parents, to visit their burial grounds, and to transform himself into a bird that might rescue his brother Florencio. Dreams were the most significant rhetorical device at Manzano's disposal, because they created an oneiric space where multiple religious worlds might coexist. In conclusion, I return to "Un sueño: A mi segundo hermano" to explore Manzano's fear that the political realities of slave society might frustrate his dreams of emancipation and family reunification. Consider that there are three different modes of descent in the poem: descent into the kingdom of the dead, descent onto the plantation to save Florencio, and descent into chaos, which is the poem's Icarus moment.

| | |
|---|---|
| Me tramonto y me juzgo | I traverse [the mountains] and I judge myself |
| Gran señor de los vientos | Great lord of the winds |
| Yéndome atrás, dejando | Leaving behind |
| De América los pueblos; | The nations of America |
| [ . . . ] | [ . . . ] |
| | |
| De salvar, no mi vida— | To save, not my life— |
| Sino la que veo Próximo a padecer, | But rather the one That is nearly lost, |
| Cual Icaro el despeño. | Like Icarus, the precipitous descent. |
| | |
| Entónces ¡oh Díos mío! | Then, Oh my God! |
| Retronando y rujiendo, | Booming and roaring, |
| De tu terrible diestra, | Your terrible Right Hand |
| Con ímpetu violento. | With violent force |

[ ... ]                                        [ ... ]
Me sorprende, y despierto,                     I am surprised, and I awaken,
Buscando entre mis brazos                      Searching in my arms
Lo que llevó mi sueño.                         For the one that my dream took away.
                                               (Manzano, *El Álbum*, 124, 126–127)[24]

Manzano's vision was a dream deferred. His well-aimed descent devolved into chaos when the political winds changed suddenly and, like Icarus, he fell from the sky. Manzano described the abrupt change thus: "De tan claro y hermoso, / De tan manso y sereno, / Tornarse en noche oscura," (From so clear and beautiful / So gentle and serene / The night became dark) ("Un sueño," *El Álbum* 125). Manzano characterized his change of fortunes as "noto horrendo" (horrendous movement) upon the sea. Darkness is the active metaphor to describe an emancipatory vision that had devolved into a nightmare. Like Icarus who flew too close to the sun, Manzano's figurative wings melted into nothingness. And in a final act of brotherly love, Manzano exclaimed, "De salvar, no mi vida—/ Sino que la del que veo / Próximo a padecer, / Cual Icaro el despeño." (To save, not my life / But rather the one that is nearly lost / Like Icarus, the precipitous descent). But Providence was responsible for Manzano's change of fortunes in "Un Sueño."

In the penultimate stanza a divinity reappears, one that is different from the "Alto Ser Supremo" (The High Supreme Being) whose wondrous works Manzano observed. On the contrary, this divinity is furious, and he is merciless: "Retronando y rujiendo, / De tu terrible diestra, / Con ímpetu violento" (Booming and roaring / Your terrible Right Hand / With violent force). The exclamation "Oh my God!" and "Your terrible Right Hand" are clear references to the vengeful Old Testament God, who prevents Manzano from saving his younger brother.[25] Astounded by a violent God, Manzano awakens: "Buscando entre mis brazos / Lo que llevó mi sueño" (Searching in my arms / For the one that my dream took away). If, as I have suggested, we read the poem as a self-referential testimony, we can conclude that three years after Manzano's final letter to del Monte, Florencio's situation remained unresolved. Thunder and lightning from the terrible right hand of the Christian God awakens the slumbering Manzano, and, as if he were a fallen Icarus, the awakening destroys all hope of redeeming Florencio. The Catholic God does not appear as a redemptive figure in the text; rather, he is the patriarch of a society deeply rooted in the exploitation of strong Ethiopian bodies. In fact, the poem is an allegory that manifests a series of events related to Florencio that Manzano cannot write about without first concealing them. The violence of slave society made it impossible for Manzano to exercise agency in the liberation of his lost brother. Manzano's descent into chaos is a deep expression of loss, not the loss of his life or his social status, but rather the irretrievable loss of his younger brother Florencio.

The runaway *slave* turned famous writer was able to rescue his brother figuratively speaking, but he could not in reality save him. Was this poem Manzano's way of explaining that he was unable to launch a successful monetary campaign in the interest of emancipating his brother? In all likelihood, that was true. But because the poem had to pass the censors, Manzano's tongue was tied. The fate of Manzano's brother remains a mystery, because after 1838 Florencio's name disappeared from the historical record.

But a year later, fate seemed to present Manzano with an opportunity that would change his life forever. One afternoon in Havana, Manzano met the infamous revolutionary writer Plácido (Friol 192, 198). Plácido was a young, vibrant, and handsome mulatto poet who was quickly becoming the most famous person of African descent in Cuba. When the two men met circa 1839, Plácido had already become persona non grata in the eyes of the proslavery Spanish government that had incarcerated him on charges that he trafficked in subversive poetry. Manzano and Plácido's friendship evolved into an aesthetic collaboration that had political consequences for both authors, consequences that made them enemies of the state.

## CHAPTER FIVE

# Carnival, the Virgin, and the Saints

## Reading the African Cuban Spirit World in the Poetry of Plácido

### The Geography of Spirit Engagement in Cuban Slave Society

By 1838 Plácido no longer swore allegiance to the Spanish crown; he had reconfigured his political loyalties. Plácido had already made a reputation for himself as a brilliant poet with resolute liberal tendencies when he debuted in 1834, at the Arroyo Apolo festivities in honor of the Spanish prime minister (Bueno, "Cronología," 486). His early work—like "La siempreviva" in praise of the prime minister—commended the liberalism of queen regent María Cristina, who had assumed the regency in 1833 after her husband, King Fernando VII, died. María Cristina governed Spain as proxy for her three-year-old daughter, Isabel (born 1830), and, in honor of her liberalism, Plácido dedicated poetry to the queen and her mother. In 1836 María Cristina enacted a new liberal constitution in Spain. But the crown remained hostile to the demands of its Caribbean and Asian subjects for political representation and democratic reform. The Spanish government barred Cuban, Puerto Rican, and Filipino representatives from attending the Cortes (parliament) between 1834 and 1837. And in 1837 María Cristina introduced "special rules" to govern her remaining Latin American colonies (Aching 48), thus shifting the political landscape. Spanish liberals had initially declared the constitution at Cádiz in 1812 while King Fernando VII was in exile (Fischer 102–103). But María Cristina must have reasoned that freedom of any kind was anathema to the maintenance of white Spanish power in a colony with a burgeoning African-descended population. Moreover, the decisive victory of African-born rebels in the Haitian Revolution (1791–1804) had astonished the Spanish crown, and the royals dreaded that an ascendant class of free blacks might ignite such an insurgency in Cuba. In this political climate, Plácido relocated to Matanzas from 1836 to 1840, where he had lived for several years in his youth. And he began to publish widely in the newspaper *Aurora de Matanzas* (Cué, *Plácido: E poeta* 85). Matanzas boasted a sizable and affluent free black population, with which Plácido became acquainted, and Matanzas became the epicenter of his increasingly radical literary trajectory.

In 1840 Plácido's poetry captured the attention of a European audience when Spanish Romantic Jacinto Salas y Quiroga published his *Viages de D. Jacinto Salas y Quiroga: La Isla de Cuba* in Madrid. Salas y Quiroga marveled at Plácido's daring critique of the queen, remarking that "talvez en la Habana no hubiera impreso, y se puede asegurar que lo mismo, dicho en prosa, hubiera costado caro á su autor" (perhaps in Havana this would not have been published, and we can be sure that the same thing, said in prose, would have cost the author immensely) (182). Salas y Quiroga so admired Plácido's genius that he exclaimed, "Al traves de la incorreción de su lenguaje, hay chispas que deslumbran, y no conozco poeta ninguno americano, incluso Heredia, que pueda acercársele en genio, en inspiracion, en hidalguía, y en dignidad" (Throughout the imperfection of his language, there are astonishing glimmers, and I do not know another [Latin] American poet, not even Heredia, that approaches his genius, inspiration, nobility, and dignity) (173). Salas y Quiroga condemned colonial censorship as an assault on the literary imagination, and he complained of the meager instruction that was available to the lower classes (172–173). He denounced slavery and the clandestine slave trade, but—like white Cuban elites—he also endorsed European immigration to the island (*Viages* 150–152; del Monte 144-145). Salas y Quiroga concluded that "escritores políticos no existen en Cuba" [ . . . ] "La poesía sin libertad, es un dia sin el sol" (political poets do not exist in Cuba [ . . . ] poetry without liberty is a day without the sun) (172). But for him, Plácido represented an exception to the rule, a rare archetype of political courage who had managed to publish fearless assaults on the monarchy in a country that forbade the expression of liberal ideals (181). What Salas y Quiroga referred to as "anomalías inesplicables" (inexplicable anomalies) (181) included the poems "En la proclamación de Isabel II, Sombra de Padilla" (In the Proclamation of Isabel II, The Spirit of Padilla), "La profecía de Cuba a España" (The Prophecy from Cuba to Spain), "La sombra de Pelayo" (The Spirit of Pelayo), and "La muerte de Gesler" (The Death of Gessler), to name but a few.[1]

Plácido and Manzano ushered in the advent of black Cuban writing in the global imagination. Jacinto Salas y Quiroga extolled Plácido's lyrical genius and his audacity in his 1840 travel narrative, and that same year Richard Robert Madden issued an English translation of Manzano's autobiography in London. Madden proceeded to submit Manzano's slave narrative and poetry, along with a lengthy dossier of his own materials, to the World Antislavery Convention in London in 1840, and again in Paris in 1842 (Aching 109; Burton 105). What is more, Plácido and Manzano had become acquainted circa 1839. And as their political significance was in ascendance, they had begun to discuss the realities of slave society, to confer with each other on common literary themes and to exchange unpublished manuscripts. The publication of black Cuban authors in Europe ensured them an international platform to critique slave society and to articulate their aspirations for freedom. But the global stage was a double-edged sword that may have dispersed Plácido's poetry throughout Spain and thus rendered him more susceptible to government surveillance.

Plácido had already begun to pay the political price for his audacity. The authorities arrested Plácido for "La sombra de Padilla" (The Spirit of Padilla) in 1838 (Cué, *Plácido: el poeta* 22). In "La sombra de Padilla," Plácido made an unprecedented claim in the annals of early Cuban literature: he asserted that Cuban subjects of the Spanish crown had a divine right to liberty. And Plácido championed this *right* to liberty in a manner that did not exclude black Cubans. Manzano had done much the same. In an 1834 letter to Domingo del Monte, Manzano spoke of "aquella propension que por prinsipio natural tiene todo hombre esclavo a su rescate" (the predisposition that by natural principle every man slave has for his rescue) (Manzano, *Obras* 81). Manzano's cache of secret letters constituted a freedom narrative where he compelled del Monte to fufill his pledge and purchase his freedom. "La sombra de Padilla" represented an aesthetic shift, because Plácido portrayed an ancestral spirit that voiced revolutionary dissent. Plácido exalted the queen,:"Sabia y escelsa Reina, a quien admira / estasiado de gozo el pueblo hispano" (Wise and sublime queen whom/ the Spanish people admire), but he also commended her majesty, "Oye á un cubano" (Listen to a Cuban) (Valdés, *Poesías completas de Plácido* 391). Plácido exalted the virtues of the sovereign, but he also conjured the spirit of Juan Padilla, a Spaniard that led the *comunero* uprising against absolute monarchy in Toledo in 1520 (Fischer 101). In the vision Padilla called to Plácido, and he identified the presence of another spirit, a wonderful goddess called "LIBERTY" (Valdés, *Poesías completas de Plácido* 392). Padilla anointed Plácido the standard bearer of "LIBERTY" and commanded, "Pues vale mas ser presa de la Parca / Que privado de un déspota monarca" (It is better to be victim of the Grave / Than to be disinherited by a despotic monarch) (Valdés, *Poesías completas de Plácido* 393).[2] In the most incendiary verses of the poem, Padilla exclaimed:

Es el esclavo mónstruo que respira
Crueldad horrenda con la sed de empleo;
Solo de Patria y Libertad al nombre
Defender debe hasta morir el hombre. (Valdés, *Poesías completas de Plácido* 393)

(The slave is a breathing monster.
Horrendous cruelty [for] the thirst of labor:
Only for the name of Country and Freedom.
Should a man defend until he dies.)

Plácido regarded the *slave* as a monstrosity, an aberration of the natural order; the *slave* was prey of the plantocracy that extracted labor from a soulless automaton. Plácido acknowledged the dichotomy between justice and inequality, slavery and freedom. "La sombra de Padilla" is a nationalist poem, but it did not challenge the legitimacy of the queen—as his other poems would— but rather it condemned the economic system that enriched Her Majesty and virtually shattered the human spirit. Juan Padilla admonished Plácido that the love of country and of liberty were the only things a worthy man should die to defend. But even after Plácido was released from prison for writing dissident literature, Matanzas governor Antonio García Oña prevented him from traveling throughout the island without written consent (Cué, *Plácido: El poeta* 88).

Plácido's depiction of Padilla's ghost reads like a common literary trope. But spirit apparitions are a recurrent theme in Plácido's poems and in his fables. Plácido communed with ancestors in his poems, and he described the malicious forces that menace the spirit world. Plácido and Manzano expressed a certain wariness—if not a palpable fear—of malevolent forces within the spirit realm. The poems that best exemplify this particular tenet of Iberian popular piety and African cosmologies are "Fantasmas duendes y brujas" (Ghosts, Spirits, and Witches), "El egoísta" (The Self-Interested Gentleman) and "La figura de un alma" (The Silhouette of a Soul). I analyze these poems for what they reveal about Plácido's religious belief structure, particularly his belief in the inherent dangers of the spirit world.

In this chapter I argue that Plácido's poetry concealed African-inspired ideas about spirit and cosmos in the symbolic language of Catholicism. His spiritual poetry revered ancestors and lauded African-inspired ritual as a means to disrupt the colonial order. African Atlantic ritual emerges as a means to liberation in Plácido's poems about African religious brotherhoods, which I have termed the *cabildo* poems. All of this transculturated colonial literature transcends Catholic notions of black redemption from sin, because it demonstrates how persons of African descent might procure the power necessary to free themselves through ritual practices. Plácido professed the idea of an independent Cuba in "La profecía de Cuba a España" (The Prophecy from Cuba to Spain) and "El juramento" (The Oath). And he broke faith with the Spanish monarchy when he vowed to slaughter despots. Moreover, Plácido conspired with other blacks to abolish slavery and overthrow Spanish rule as a leading figure in the 1844 antislavery movement. Finally, my reading of "La profecía de Cuba a España" and "El juramento" examines how Plácido claimed the prophetic mantle among his interlocutors and commanded political allegiance from his proselytes. Plácido encoded African-inspired ideas about spirit and cosmos in Hispano-Catholic poetry that featured Romantic sentiments comingled with Neoclassical accents.

Plácido published "La figura de un alma" in *Aurora de Matanzas* in the 1840s; it is a fable concerning the apparition of a fearsome spirit that terrified an enslaved community on a plantation. In the poem enslaved Africans discover a nocturnal vision in the likeness of a tiger roaming about the plantation. Subsequently, they refuse to leave their modest dwellings; instead they confer about what they have seen. The slaveholder assembles the enslaved persons to determine the cause of the commotion and presumably to restore the peace on his plantation. Catching sight of the same vision they have seen, he reacts with great trepidation to the shifting image in the dark, invoking the cross: "Magnífica / *Anima mea . . .*! ¡La cruz . . .!" (Magnificent / My soul . . .! The cross!) (Valdés, *Plácido, Gabriel de la Concepción* Morales 421). The invocation of the cross—and, by extension, of the Catholic faith—is an entreaty for divine protection that implies where his religious loyalties lie. In reaction to the owner's trepidation, *una negra ladina*, an enslaved black woman, identifies the roaming silhouette as the spirit of the deceased overseer: "Mas una negra ladina / Contestó:—"Señor, no es eso, / Ese tigre es sin mentira, / El alma del mayoral / Que se murió el otro día" (But a black female slave /Replied:—"Master, that's not it, / This tiger is without a doubt, / The soul of the overseer / That died the other day) (Valdés, *Plácido, Gabriel de la Concepción* 421). The black female character is an astute observer of spiritual phenomena that is capable of *reading* the spiritual geography of the slave plantation in a manner that the white slaveholder cannot.

Plácido wrote "La figura de un alma" in a Christian idiom. The poem describes a wandering soul, an errant and perilous spirit who has neither been rewarded eternal life nor been subjected to infinite damnation. Christian burial entailed an elaborate series of rites: cadavers were carefully cleansed, dressed in finery, perfumed, and surrounded by candles in order to ensure that the soul did not wander for eternity (Hevia 59). The nomadic trajectory of the overseer's soul implies that the Church denied him proper burial, thus setting him adrift to meander aimlessly. Of the three main characters—the enslaved woman, the white male slaveholder, and the wayward spirit—it is the black woman and the estate owner that speak. Their brief exchange, however, does not constitute dialogue, but rather negation. The first instance occurs when the poetic voice says: "But a black female slave / Replied:—"Master, that's not it." After the interjection, the black woman instructs her owner about the identity of the *soul* standing before him, hence revealing herself as a knowing subject. The conjunction *but* signals a departure from the owner's authority, since he is powerless to restore the peace on his own estate. Colonists designed the plantation system to codify white religio-cultural supremacy within Spanish legal discourse so that blacks were subjected to daily prayer, religious instruction, and mass, as well as compulsory baptisms (Knight 125). The black woman's rejection of her owner's assertion is a subtle inversion of the social order, because the *Código negro español* (The Black Slave Code) commanded masters to instruct African and Cuban captives in the rites of Catholicism, not the other way around (Knight 127).

Similarly, Plácido's description of the black woman as a *negra ladina* assigns a sense of historical specificity to the character. *Ladinos* were enslaved persons born abroad that had mastered Spanish, Portuguese, or even French and had been baptized into the Church (Knight 63). Language was a line of demarcation in the socio-racial taxonomy of colonial society. African-born captives that learned to speak Spanish or black Cuban patois were not pejoratively referred to as *bozales*; instead they were considered *ladinos* (Paquette 38).[3] In *Cecilia Valdés*, Cirilo Villaverde perpetuated the stereotype of African intellectual and cultural deficiency manifest by the broken Spanish of newly arrived captives (477–478). But Plácido's nameless female character symbolizes the survival imperative wherein African captives adopted innumerable strategies to comprehend, adapt to, and socially alter a hostile racialized environment. Unlike "El guapo" (The Thug) and "Mi no sé que ha richo" (Me Don't Know what I Said) where the author avails himself of onomatopoeia to replicate black Cuban Spanish, the *negra ladina* demonstrates a command of the Spanish language and an apparent familiarity with Catholicism. Hers is a voice to be reckoned with. Despite her fluency in Spanish, the poem casts doubt on how thoroughly the *negra ladina* has been Catholicized. Plácido's *negra ladina* decodes ethereal presence in a way that is consistent with the historical record that enslaved Cubans bequeathed us. Juan Francisco Manzano and Esteban Montejo's slave testimonies—*La verdadera istoria de mi vida* (1836) and *Biografía de un cimarrón* (1966) respectively—bear witness to the heightened presence of errant spirits on slave plantations whose cadavers had not received proper burial (Barnet, *Cimarrón: Historia* 100, 126).[4]

In Plácido's moral tale, the dead overseer is comparable to the spirits that Manzano and Montejo described, because he also dwelled among what John Mbiti termed "the living dead" (25). Mbiti says that in traditional African religious thought and practice, spirits of the deceased commonly serve as intermediaries between living persons and God. "The living dead" constitute the largest group of intercessors in African religious life, conveying human requests, needs, prayers and sacrifices to God (69–71).

But the dead overseer is a specter of a different ilk; he casts a horrifying silhouette over the enslaved community because he embodied the institutional power of the slaveholder. The overseer is not only an agent of the slaveholding class but also an instrument of the Catholic Church. Esteban Pichardo's 1836 dictionary defines the *mayoral* (overseer) thus: "En toda la isla se aplica esta palabra solamente al hombre blanco asalariado encargado del gobierno y cuidado de las haciendas del campo" (In all of the island, this word applies only to salaried white men in charge of the administration and care of the rural estates) (*Diccionario provincial de voces cubanas* 177). And the 1796 slave catechism explains the religious implications of the overseer's role on the plantation: "He that governs the sugar plantation is the Overseer and the Pope that governs the

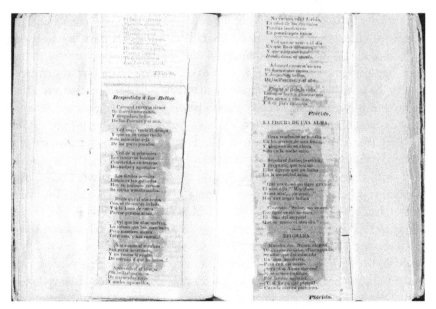

Plácido's fable "La figura de un alma" originally appeared in Aurora de Matanzas, a Matanzas newspaper. Federico Milanés compiled more than one hundred of Plácido's poems to preserve historical memory of the poet. Courtesy of Harvard University.

Church is the Vicar of Jesus Christ. When the Overseer orders you to do something your master commands you [ . . . ] and he that does not fulfill what the Overseer commands does not fulfill his duty" (Barreras 85–86).

In Catholic doctrines, the *mayoral* derived his authority on the plantation from the slaveholder, but that authority was also sanctioned by Jesus Christ. The slave catechism constructed a long line of descent that originated with Christ, who had entrusted the pope with the welfare of the Church. The pope was the Vicar of Christ, that is, the inerrant representative of the Godhead on earth. Papal authority extended to the slave master, who was "the head of this sugar plantation." When read in this light, "La figura de un alma" points out the religious and political power relations on the slave labor camp, because the two forms of authority—religious and racial—were inextricably linked to each other in Cuban slave society. The overseer injured any dark body that stalled, questioned, or dared to defy the racialized religious system he represented. Consequently, the overseer's death is a critique of the plantocracy and of the Catholic theology that undergirded it. As Plácido's black female character quips, the silhouette of this soul—transfigured into a savage beast—is undoubtedly a malevolent spiritual force.

Plácido's account of the overseer not only bestializes a loathsome character but also reflects an African-inspired belief that without proper burial, spirits of the dead may metamorphosize and roam the earth. Lydia Cabrera's informants account for the existence of dreadfully deformed spirits, including animals from the other world. Cabrera based *El monte,* on extensive conversations with religious elders, many who were the direct descendants of enslaved Africans and who in 1954, when the book was first published, had maintained the epistemological integrity of their respective traditions. She wrote:

"En el Monte se encuentran todos los Eshus," entes diabólicos; [ . . . ] la Cosa-Mala, [ . . . ], espíritus ocursos, maléficos, "que tienen malas intenciones"; "toda la gente extraña del otro mundo," fantasmal y horribles de ver. Animales también del otro mundo . . . (*El monte* 13)

("In the forested wilderness, are found all of the *Eshús,*" diabolical entities; [ . . . ] *La Cosa-Mala* (evil things), [ . . . ], dark, maleficent spirits, "that have bad intentions"; "all of the strange people from the Otherworld," phantasmal and horrible to see. Animals, too, from the other world . . . )

Esteban Montejo corroborated Cabrera's ethnography when he explained that the transfiguration of the dead was a common tenet of African-descended oral traditions. Montejo recounted the story of Cayito Álvarez, a Cuban military officer that surrendered to the Spanish. After death, Cayito's spirit roamed the countryside: "Yo me refiero a las luces ésas que salen por la noche en el monte. Y a los jinetes sin cabeza. Dicen muchos que ése es el espíritu de Cayito" (I am referring to illuminations that appear at night in the forested wilderness. And to the headless horsemen. Many say that this is the spirit of Cayito) (Barnet, *Cimarrón: Historia* 190). Montejo implies that Cayito was denied proper burial because he had betrayed the nationalist cause and, as such, was left to wander the countryside. Montejo's testimony and Cabrera's description of how spirits transfigure into monstrosities emerge from African Cuban oral traditions that regarded *muertos* (spirits of the dead) both as prospective allies and as potential adversaries. As Montejo exclaimed, "Si el muerto se acerca a uno, no huir, preguntar: <<¿Qué quiere usted, hermano?" (If a spirit of the dead comes near to you, do not flee, ask: 'What do you want, brother?') (Barnet, *Cimarrón: Historia* 127). Montejo's testimony and Plácido's fables advise that in African Cuban religious life, the dead remain active in the lives of the living.

Plácido revisited the menace of wandering spirits in another fable, "Fantasmas, duendes y brujas" (Ghosts, Spirits and Witches). In "Fantasmas, duendes y brujas" the poetic subject is transfigured into a *ciguapa,* or night owl, who, like *la negra ladina,* advises his countrymen that spirits are nearly ubiquitous and possess great power to do harm (Valdés, *Plácido, Gabriel de la Concepción* 196). Below, I quote the first two stanzas:

En aquellos memorables
Tiempos de Mari-Castaña,
Dicen los viejos que habia
Brujas, duendes y fantasmas.

Los modernos no lo creen;
Miradlo bien, camaradas,
Ahora los hay como entónces,
El caso es que se disfrazan. (Valdés, *Plácido, Gabriel de la Concepción* 196)

(In those memorable
Times of long ago,
The elders say that there were
Witches, spirits and ghosts.

The moderns do not believe it;
Look at this comrades,
They exist today just as they did back then,
Its that they disguise themselves.)[5]

"Fantasmas, duendes y brujas" portrays elders as a repository of spiritual knowl-edge that Plácido's incredulous contemporaries have refused to engage.[6] I read Plácido's emphasis on the need to decipher geographies of spiritual engagement in tandem with the euphemisms he and Manzano were so fond of using in their poetry. Plácido described spirits as "ghosts" and "witches," befitting his hide-and-seek lyrical game. He repeated this technique in his Indianist poems, "A 'El Pan'" (To the Mountain Pan) and "A El Yumurí" (To the Mountain Yumurí). (I examine the Indianist poems later in this chapter). If, as Plácido posited, the human world was impregnated with nonmaterial entities, then spiritual dis-cernment was crucial in colonial Cuba.

Plácido's early nineteenth-century descriptions of errant spirits are compara-ble to Cuban ethnography of the mid-to-late twentieth century about the mean-ing of spirit presence. I examine Reinaldo Arenas's *Before Night Falls* and Miguel Barnet's testimonial about Esteban Montejo to trace a sense of continuity across time and space in Cuban popular religions regarding the spirit world.[7] Reinaldo Arenas described his grandmother's spiritual sensibility in the same language that Plácido had employed more than a century earlier. Arenas was a gay white Cuban writer from Holguín whose grandmother's attitudes about spirit pres-ence, at least to some extent, were remarkably similar to Plácido's mind-set.

My grandmother would tell me stories of apparitions, of men who walked with their heads under their arms, of treasures guarded by the dead tirelessly pacing their place of hiding. [ . . . ] My grandmother knew of some exorcism that prevented the witches from doing too much harm (Arenas 24).

A whole universe died for me when my grandmother died; [ . . . ] I wanted to cry, seeing that face with which a whole era of witches, ghosts, and spirits would disappear, with which all my childhood, the best part of my life, would disappear (Arenas 229).

Arenas's grandmother negotiated an enchanted world chock-full of "witches, ghosts, and spirits" that had to be propitiated much like those Plácido described in his fable of the same name. Arenas's white peasant grandmother practiced popular piety or, perhaps, some form of Spiritism. She predicted the weather by reading the stars, she cured people with medicinal herbs, and she spoke to God as a constant companion (24, 229). I juxtapose popular Catholicism and West African/West Central African beliefs without placing them in interminable conflict with one another. The commonality and overlap are more significant, in this instance, than the differences in ritual practices. Arenas's choice of words is not mere coincidence. Rather, his language suggests that Plácido's "Fantasmas, duendes y brujas" are illustrative of an entanglement of cosmologies part African, part Catholic, but thoroughly Cuban. Cros Sandoval expounds on this: "Popular piety was another major factor that facilitated the survival aspects of African religions in Cuba" (42). The amalgamation of religious beliefs and practices in Plácido's poetry provided space for the persistence of African ideas of spirit and cosmos.

Likewise, Montejo's testimony about African-inspired concepts in postrevolutionary Cuba (after 1959) reiterated the major theses of Plácido's "Fantasmas, duendes y brujas." This passage highlights the startling parallels:

Hoy mismo hay gente que no cree en salidera de muertos, ni nada de eso. Y es que no han visto nada. Los jóvenes que no creen es porque no han visto. Sin embargo, se agotan igual; piensan en otras cosas del tiempo moderno, de los pueblos del mundo, de las guerras y de todo lo demás (Barnet, *Cimarrón* 129).

(Today there are people that do not believe in the visitation of the dead, nothing of the sort. And it's that they haven't seen anything. The young people don't believe in it because they haven't seen it. However, they become overwhelmed all the same; they think about other things of modern times, of the peoples of this world, of the wars and everything else.)

Montejo mused that mid-twentieth-century Cubans had abandoned the African belief in spirit visitation, instead enveloping themselves in the realities of the modern world. Plácido predicted this exercise in disbelief more than a century prior. His proposition was that human beings could not possibly fathom the nature of conflict in the natural world without sustained and reciprocal communication with the spirit realm.

Plácido maintained that angry spirits suffered in their lifetimes and, as a result, became hostile after death.

> Y confesad sin embajes,
> Que en este tiempo hay fantasmas.
> Y muchos peores que aquellas
> De que los viejos nos hablan:
>
> Aquellas la cruz huian,
> Por ser medrosas y mansas;
> Pero éstas son tan terribles,
> Que della la cruz se espanta. (Valdés, *Plácido, Gabriel de la Concepción* 198)[8]
>
> (And so, confess candidly,
> That nowadays there are ghosts,
> And much worse than those
> Of which the elders told us:
>
> Those ghosts fled from the cross,
> Because they were meek and fainthearted;
> But these are so terrifying,
> That they frighten the cross.)

Even the cross recoils at the sight of these spirits. Plácido divested the quintessential symbol of Catholic authority of its power when he implied that the Latin cross might be inadequate to exorcise "estos duendes de *ley brava*" (spirits that abided by a law of cruelty) (Valdés, *Plácido, Gabriel de la Concepción* 197). If the Church is unable to perform an exorcism, then Plácido's black and mulatto (and white) interlocutors must go elsewhere to find a remedy for their metaphysical crises. Plácido erected an edifice of sacred authority among his interlocutors in "Fantasmas, duendes y brujas" and "La Figura de un alma" by offering them an alternative path to the spirit world. Plácido's fables demonstrated an unorthodox way of knowing and beseeching *muertos*, virgins, and saints that transcended the confines of Catholic dogma.

"Fantasmas, duendes y brujas" and "La figura de un alma" depict the dead as living entities subsequent to their demise. "El egoísta," published in the 1840s in *La Aurora de Matanzas*, describes a confrontation at a Cuban cemetery between a socialite and a gravedigger. In the poem, the gravedigger rebukes the wealthy man for trampling the remains of his grandfather in order to pick up a measly sum for his grandson. The following seven stanzas draw attention to important nuances in the text:

Contemplando un poderoso
Las fosas de un cementerio,
Vió una moneda mohosa
Y levántola del suelo.

"Ven á mi bolsillo (dijo)
Dichosa mitad de medio,
Que son cadena y corona
Serás hija de mi nieto."

–"Señor, no pises ahí,
(Esclamó el sepulturero)
Mira que abajo reposan
Las cenizas de tu abuelo."

Mas él sin curar de nada,
Prosiguió pisando el puesto,
Por ver si hallaba cuartillas
Para adornar á sus nietos.

Nada hay para el egoista
Sagrado en el universo:
En los templos donde á Dios
Quema el sacerdote incienso:

En los lugares que inspiran
Un santo recojimiento,
Cuando la peste y el hambre
Diezman y aterran al pueblo.

Él, esteriormente imita
Los relijiosos acentos,
Finje un alma compasiva
A los dolores agenos.[9]

(A powerful man that contemplated
The graves of a cemetery,
Saw a moldy old coin
And lifted it off the ground.

"Come to my pocket (he said)
Lucky half *medio*,
Those are *cadena* and *corona*[10]
You will be the daughter of my grandson."

"Sir, don't trample over there,
(The gravedigger exclaimed)
Look, beneath your feet lie
The ashes of your grandfather."

But without changing a thing,
He went on trampling the gravesite,
To see if he might find a silver coin[11]
To adorn his grandchildren.

For the self-centered man, there is nothing
Sacred in the entire universe:
In the temples where God is found
The priest burns incense:

In the places that inspire
A blessed purification,[12]
When hunger and the plague
Decimate and terrify the people.

On the surface, he mimics
The religious accents,
He feigns a compassionate soul
Towards the grief of others.)

As with most fables, the poem's premise is quite simple: the selfish aristocrat takes pride in material things, unaware that death will disinherit him. Plácido did not identify either character in racial terms; instead, he relied on the cultural assumptions of the reader to codify the gentleman as white and the gravedigger as black. Villaverde's Romantic color-writing novel *Cecilia Valdés* also portrayed the gravedigger as a black man. Villaverde wrote that in nineteenth-century Cuba, black gravediggers wearing the appropriate uniform escorted cadavers to the cemetery for proper burial (538). Both anonymous characters are representative of particular socioeconomic and religious positionalities. Plácido is accusatory: the gentleman is a "Hipócrita miserable" (miserable hypocrite) who feigns compassion for the destitute by impersonating Catholic religious rhetoric. His is a false piety because "Y su Dios, es el DINERO" (MONEY is his God). The egoist represents the white slaveholding elite that scavenged for wealth, trampled bodies, and thrashed about for loose change in a country of penniless souls.

The religious hypocrisy of white Catholic society is the object of Plácido's critique. But given his considerable ties with the Church, he was wary of assailing the institution; so he lambasted a parishioner for whom nothing was sacred, not even ancestral remains. Quite simply, the egoist is not a devout Catholic. But there is also a sense that the white Creole hypocrisy of this character is informed by an abiding sense of impurity, as irreligious as it is immoral. Yet again, the black Cuban subject, not the Catholic Church, is a repository of spiritual knowledge. The gravedigger's admonition, "Look, beneath your feet lie / The ashes of your grandfather," indicated that this was a Christian cemetery.[13] Catholic funerary ritual was a solemn, yet theatrical performance flanked with smoldering candles, the celebration of mass, and clerical prayers for the salvation of the departed. The cleansing of the corpse preserved the body for eternal life, and in a symbolic (and perhaps literal) sense, the deceased remained within the living religious community (Hevia 19–20, 59). Still, the white aristocrat did not hold death to be sacred.

Plácido juxtaposed a normative religious rite, the burning of incense in the Christian temple, with a marginalized ritual practice, the *santo recojimiento* (a blessed purification) of the graveyard. The comparison of religious practices is a recurring technique in Plácido's transculturated poetry. The text achieves a chiasmus of sorts: both rites perform spiritual cleansing, but they emerge from different liturgical traditions, reflect disparate religious epistemologies, and remedy different ills. Cuban ethnographer José Millet defines *recogimiento* as a ritual cleansing in Cuban Spiritism that purifies space from the injurious power of evil spiritual forces:

> Rito espiritista que tiene la finalidad de retirar de un recinto—casa particular o plantel—determinadas malas corrientes o efectos negativos dejados en él por espíritus de perturbación o por muertos enviados por otras personas para causar daños (Millet 37).

> (A spiritist rite whose objective is to remove from a given place—a home or a group of people—certain bad currents or negative intentions left behind by perturbed spirits or spirits of the dead that other people have sent to do harm.)

*Espiritismo* is not a religion of African inspiration, but adherents do work with the spirit realm in a manner that is closely aligned with Afro-Caribbean beliefs. Regarding the proliferation of Spiritism, Cabrera noted, "Lo cual no supone debilitamiento de la fe en los Orishas ni abandono de los cultos de raíz africana: el espiritismo marcha con ellos de la mano, estrechamente unidos, a pesar

de sus pretensiones de espiritualidad . . ." (This does not suppose the debilita-
tion of faith in the *orishas* or the rejection of cults with African roots: Spiritism
marches hand in hand with those traditions, intimately united, despite its pre-
tensions to spirituality . . . ) (30). Although the white Catholic feigns religious
devotion, the gravedigger is the custodian of sacred memory that consecrates
the cemetery in order to appeal to otherworldly powers.

The black gravedigger's sensibilities are comparable to the spiritual discern-
ment of the enslaved black woman in "La figura de un alma" and the acumen of
the poetic voice in "Fantasmas, duendes y brujas." Without exception, Plácido's
black characters are clairvoyant, because they perceive destructive spirit forces
within slave society: persons that were denied proper burial and the overseer's
spirit. Dodson expounds on Cabrera's contention that Spiritism "marches hand
in hand with those [African-inspired] traditions" (30). Dodson wrote:

> Practices of this family of Espiritismo are characteristically filled with transcul-
> turated and reconstructed components of the island's Africa-based religions,
> Palo Monte/Palo Mayombe, Vodú, Regla de Ocha/Lucumí, as well as with prac-
> tices from Cuban folk Catholicism. Cruzado appears in many forms because it
> was born in the islands' multicultural and multireligious environment. Of this
> tendency to multifaceted expression, Don Fernando Ortiz once wrote, "When
> the Cuban African men practice a religion, whichever this may be, they tend to
> add: 'according to my way.'" He was acknowledging the reality that practitioners
> adapted religious traditions to the particularities of their Cuban-African life-
> styles and cosmic orientation. Cruzado is just such a constructed sacred tradi-
> tion that represents the "Cuban way." (Dodson 127)

Dodson explains that Cuban Spiritism is replete with transculturated and
reconstructed "components" of several African-inspired traditions, including
the Bakongo-inspired *palo monte/palo mayombe*. So, when Plácido summoned
Spiritist rituals, he was acknowledging the "multireligious environment" that
he had been socialized into. Plácido's environment encompassed Spanish
Catholicism as well as myriad beliefs of West African and West Central African
inspiration. Generally, scholars date the diffusion of Spiritism in Cuba to the
1860s, when such doctrines reached the island from Europe and the United
States (Román 221). But "El Egoísta" boasts an ethnohistoric distinction in early
Cuban literature as the first known representation of *espiritismo* in Cuban
poetry. Plácido demonstrated a belief in the perpetual presence of the dead
in these three poems, and he advised the need to propitiate them so that one's
destiny would not be adverse. But indigenous spirits of the dead appeared in
Plácido's repertoire as symbols of nationalist resistance to the iniquities of
Spanish slave society.

## The Revenge of Hatuey in Plácido's Indigenist Poetry

Plácido's indigenist poetry was a rhetorical vehicle for Cuban proto-nationalism. Plácido's portrayal of the precolonial Ciboneys of western Cuba and the Taínos of Hispaniola transformed *indios* (Indians) from mere victims of Spanish genocide into veritable symbols of resistance to empire. "A 'El Pan'" (To the Mountain Pan) and "A El Yumurí" (To the Yumurí Valley) are poems abounding with metaphors and euphemisms that depict indigenous Caribbeans as ancestral spirits inhabiting the forests and the mountains of Guajaibón in Pinar del Río and in the Yumurí Valley in Matanzas. Critics have attributed early Cuban indigenism to Plácido and his literary tutor, Ignacio Valdés Machuca. Cuban scholar Samuel Feijóo writes that Valdés Machuca and Plácido provided the basis for the Indianist school of Cuban poetry ("Plácido 368").[14] Plácido's interest in indigenist poetry may be the consequence of his early literary influences in Havana. In 1832—two years prior to his first publication—Plácido met white liberal writers Ignacio Valdés Machuca, Ramón Vélez Herrera, and Francisco Iturrondo (Cué, *Plácido: El poeta* 21, 155). In the early 1830s, Machuca also introduced Manzano to Domingo del Monte, the leading Cuban humanist, who later became Manzano's literary tutor (Cué, *Plácido: El poeta* 155; Friol 195–196). Indigenist poetry was a form of dissident literature among young white Cuban Romantics in search of anticolonial symbols that might evade government censorship (Paquette 258). But Plácido adopted Ciboney and Taíno characters as much more than symbols of anticolonial resistance; he rendered them ancestors of a pre-Hispanic Cuban nation to be *reborn*.

In "A 'El Pan,'" Plácido resignified the Catholic altar from a space for officiating Holy Communion into a sacred space inhabited by the ancestors of indigenous societies that the Spanish had destroyed. Below are four stanzas from the poem:

Atalaya del golfo mejicano,
Que erguido brillas, gigantesco altar,
Donde te colocó de Dios la mano
Sobre el nivel del espumoso mar.

Soberbio Pan, de cañas coronado,
[ . . . ]

Salve, monte feráz, viva memoria
De un tiempo inmemorial que feneció,
Vago recuerdo de ignorada historia
Que entre místicas sombras se ocultó.

Los vivientes que algun dia
Triscaban en tu espesura,
Hoy salen como las hadas
Al resplandor de la Luna.
[ ... ]

Así las bellas fantasmas
En la noche te saludan,
Hasta que el alba en oriente
La vuelta del Sol anuncia;

Entónces rápidas vuelan,
En la inmensidad se ocultan,
Y solo se oyen sus ecos
Que repiten <<¡Cuba . . .! Cuba!>> (Valdés, *Plácido, Gabriel de la Concepción*
    264–265)

(Watchtower of the Gulf of Mexico
Standing erect you shine, colossal altar
Where God placed his hand
Above the level of the frothy sea

Haughty Mountain Pan, crowned with reeds
[ ... ]

Hail, fecund mountain, living memory
From time immemorial that departed,
Vague remembrance of history forgotten
That hid between mystical shadows.

The living beings that one day
Frolicked in your dense forests,
Today they come out like fairies
To the brilliance of the Moon.
[ ... ]

In that way, the beautiful ghosts
Greet you at night,
Until the dawn in the East
The turn of the Sun announces;

Then quickly they fly away
Obscuring themselves in the immensity

And only their echo is heard
Repeating <<Cuba . . .! Cuba!>>)

Plácido does not recover a lost history in "A 'El Pan'" but rather an "ignorada historia" ([a] history ignored) that discourses of Spanish cultural supremacy had silenced. The poem beckons an indigenous ancestral presence embedded not in the written record, but rather in the mountain wilderness that preserves primordial memory. Plácido's "mystical shadows," "fairies," and "beautiful ghosts" refer to the spirits of indigenous Cuban forebears that still occupy the forested mountains of Pinar del Río that they once physically inhabited. Again, Plácido chose the Spanish word *sombra*, which means "shadow" and "spirit," as he had in "La sombra de Padilla" and "La sombra de Pelayo." Incorporeality does not mean the loss of presence, because "time immemorial that departed" is indicative of an anachronistic temporality ungoverned by European notions of historical time.

The residual presence of an indigenous past was legible within Plácido's geographies of spirit engagement on the Cuban countryside. In Plácido's indigenist poetry, the hillside and mountains could be read as *locus amoenus*, a trope from Spanish Romanticism. Although certainly plausible, such a reading is unlikely because of the symbolic meaning of the mountain in these poems. In "A 'El Pan,'" the speaker likens the mountain to an altar, thus attributing a sense of spirituality to an otherwise ordinary rhetorical device. The poetic voice exalts El Pan, a massif in the Guaniguanico mountain range in Pinar del Río, as a vast altar touched by the hand of God and ever so gently crowned with reeds. Plácido's choice of the forested mountain as cultural symbol infuses local color into the text and situates *el monte* in a transculturated Cuban religious framework with historical specificity. *El monte* was a recurring trope in "A El Yumurí," but Plácido depicted the Yumurí Valley as the sacred burial grounds of the Taíno *cacique* Hatuey.

The aboriginal landscape reappeared in "A El Yumurí," an ode dedicated to Valdés Machuca that summoned the memory of Hatuey, an indigenous *cacique* whom the Spanish burned alive for his vehement resistance to conquest.[15] The following are the two stanzas in question:

Así los séres, que Jehová creara
Como revelacion de su existir,
Derriban la virtud que les ampara,
Y anhelando gozar van á morir.

Quien sabe si en tu fondo cenagoso
Algun tesoro oculto se hallará,
O en subterráneo oscuro misterioso,
De Hatuey entero el esqueleto está (Valdés, *Plácido, Gabriel de la Concepción* 269).

(In that way, the beings that Jehovah created
As a revelation of his existence,
Squander the virtue that accompanies them
And longing to take pleasure, they will die.

Who knows if in the swampy muck and mire
Some hidden treasure might be found,
Or in the dark, mysterious subterrain,
Hatuey's intact skeleton might lie.)

The dense forested Valley of Yumurí does not relinquish the memory of ancestral resistance to Spanish conquest. Plácido excavated the sacred remains of
Hatuey as an emblem of anticolonial sentiment. The stanza is evocative of the
*longue durée* that predates Antonio Nebrija's 1492 Spanish grammar that rei-
fied the imperial project in three ways. Nebrija's grammar made the writing
of vainglorious accounts of *conquistadores* possible; it provided the linguistic
foundation for a racist juridical framework; and it made the publication of religious literature accessible to a broad readership. But Plácido was referring to an
unwritten text, the land as hallowed ground, which was an alternative means
to inscribe the past. The poet's query was unchanged; he probed the landscape
as a palimpsest encoded with an obscure narrative where, "Estará escrita una
historia" (A history shall be written) (Valdés, *Plácido, Gabriel de la Concepción*
271). Plácido decreed that the *ignorada historia* of "A 'El Pan'" shall be rendered
visible in written discourse. "A 'El Pan'" is the commemoration of Taíno and
Ciboney "historia[s]" that enabled Plácido to assert a right to the land that preceded the conquest that Diego Velázquez had commandeered in 1511 (Pérez 26)
    Hatuey was an insurgent Taíno *cacique* that arrived in Cuba from western
Hispaniola (modern-day Haiti), where he established a stronghold in the Punta
de Maisí. Hatuey and his forces had begun their war against the Spanish in
Haiti, yet withdrew to regroup in Cuba. Departing from Baracoa to confront
Diego Velázquez, Hatuey led his people into battle against the Spanish invasion
but was quickly defeated and taken prisoner by the Spanish, who condemned
him to death. A Franciscan priest read the death sentence to the cacique, who
is said to have listened "with resignation" (Pettway, "Páginas salvadas" 206, 208–
209; S. Johnson 72). Plácido celebrated Hatuey as an unconquerable symbol of
resistance to foreign domination. Hatuey remained defiant till the end, despite
being taken captive and sentenced to being burned at the stake. Hatuey refused
conversion to Catholicism, particularly when his captors informed him that
the Spanish would be in Heaven (S. Johnson 72–73). Plácido's representation of
the intact skeleton was a reimagining of Hatuey's assassination. In his rendering, the flames did not consume Hatuey's corpse. Although Spaniards burned
Hatuey at the stake, the fire did not consume the *cacique's* skeleton, which

symbolizes the indestructibility of the indigenous ancestral spirit. Plácido combined the tenacity of ancestors with divine condemnation of Christian hypocrisy. The word *Jehovah* foregrounds Old Testament accounts of divine judgment so that redemption is infeasible for white Catholics. Plácido critiqued the Spanish genocide of Ciboney, Taíno, and Arawak societies. Spaniards enslaved indigenous peoples, and as a result these communities suffered decimation at the hands of European communicable diseases (Pérez 18–20, 28–30).[16] The sixteenth-century Spanish invasion of Cuba precipitated an ecological disaster of biblical proportions for Arawak, Ciboney, and Taíno societies. Spaniards redistributed vast parcels of cultivated indigenous land among themselves and, in so doing, acquired the available sources of sustenance. They dedicated large parcels of land to cattle raising and coerced indigenous survivors of genocide into involuntary servitude known as *encomiendas* and *repartimientos*. Not only did Spanish colonists displace indigenous families, but the colonial authorities relocated them to different settlements sited near Spanish towns in order to facilitate the exploitation of an indigenous labor force and the political process of Catholic religious conversion. Indigenous persons became the principal labor force in the early colonial period. They mined quarries and panned streams for gold; they planted crops, tended cattle, and became house servants. The Spanish impact on indigenous Cuban societies was sudden, catastrophic, and utterly irreversible (Pérez 28–29).

But Hatuey also possessed a symbolic meaning for Cuban conspirators of African descent that organized the 1844 movement. Some insurgents sought to rename Cuba for the Haitian *cacique* that had so valiantly sacrificed his life in tenacious defiance of the Spanish invasion (Paquette 256). Cuban conspirators sought to establish the same type of political identification with Hatuey that Africans had established with Haiti upon the triumph of the Haitian Revolution in 1804. Africans liberated themselves from French slavery and renamed Saint Domingue according to the aboriginal name for the land. Black insurgents called themselves *indigène*, though nearly half of the rebels had been born in Africa. Haitian indigenism contended that the formerly enslaved, not the slaveholders, had a rightful claim to the land they had toiled (Fischer 242). If one reads "A El Yumurí" and "A 'El Pan'" in concert with an ode Plácido dedicated to Andrés de la Flor, a Cuban-born officer commissioned in the Mexican military, it becomes clear that Hatuey was also a metaphor for anticolonial warfare. Here are two stanzas from "Al general mejicano (hijo de Cuba) Don Andrés de la Flor" (1839).

No cual brindis de siervo
temeroso
Que al libre como tú, no fuera
honroso,

Inciensos recibir de un bardo
esclavo.
[ … ]

Pero mi corazón es por esencia
Muy más libre que el águila en el
cielo
¡Adiós! Gloria de Cuba y
heredero
Del aliento de Hatuey … salud
amigo; (Cué, *Plácido: El poeta* 290)

(Not comparable to an offering from a servant
frightened
That free like yourself, would not be
honorable,
Receive this incense from a slave poet.
[ … ]

But my heart is in essence
Much freer than the eagle in the
heavens
Farewell! Glory to Cuba and to
the heir
Of the breath of Hatuey … greetings
friend)

Andrés de la Flor was implicated in the Black Eagle Conspiracy, along with José María Heredia, José Teurbe Tolón, Mariano Tarrero, and Manuel Rodríguez (Horrego Estuch, *Plácido: el poeta* 107). Plácido portrayed himself as *un bardo esclavo* (a slave poet) that did not enjoy the freedom that Andrés de la Flor had achieved in Mexico. This was one of few examples ("The Man and the Canary" is another) in which Plácido referred to himself as a slave poet, a moniker commonly used to refer to his contemporary Juan Francisco Manzano. Plácido entrusted the poem to the general as a memento of the Cuban homeland, but even as it evoked memory of an inchoate nation, it prophesied a freedom yet to come. Plácido only feigned being *un bardo esclavo*, since his heart was freer than the eagle itself. This reference to *el águila* could be interpreted as a veiled allusion to the general's involvement in the Black Eagle Conspiracy. But the aforementioned verse is not clear in this respect. Conceivably, the eagle—a commanding bird of prey—functions as a symbol of unencumbered freedom.

Plácido's images of El Pan and the Yumurí valley rescued the indigenous from the margins of Cuban religious history and foregrounded their *right* to land that the Spanish had usurped. The altar was a sanctuary for ancestral spirits whose primordial presence was axiomatic in African-inspired traditions that venerate such ancestors as part of an inclusive conception of the spirit world. Indigenous and African persons shared knowledge of spirits, they believed in the interconnection of ancestors and the land, and they performed ancestral reverence. Moreover, the Spanish conquest imposed comparable, albeit different, sociopolitical statuses on both groups (Dodson 85, 102). Sonya Maria Johnson points out that Taínos privileged the use of skeletal remains in rituals to beseech ancestors, and such rituals were entirely consistent with the Bakongo-inspired belief structure, where mortal remains are objects that enable humans to commune with the powers of the spirit world ("Bones Cry Out" 91). In my estimation, Plácido's indigenist poetry evoked the memory of Taíno cacique Hatuey and described his intact skeleton to pay homage to a cultural history of religious transculturation that had yet to be written in the first half of the nineteenth century. "A 'El Pan'" is a contestation of the conquest and proselytizing of indigenous and African persons whose symbolic juxtaposition constitutes resistance to Spanish domination. Plácido's transgressive representation of the altar countersignifies Christian notions of piety, evokes the ancestral memory suffused throughout the forests, and creates space for indigenous selfhood. Comparable to the self-dissembling nature of the poem, "the fairies," "beautiful ghosts," and physical remnants of Hatuey are hidden from sight, though the nationalist resonance of their cry <<¡Cuba . . . ! Cuba!>> does not go unheeded (Valdés, *Plácido, Gabriel de la Concepción* 265). Plácido's indigenous characters ascribe a sense of nationalism to the word *Cuba*; their utterance is a battle cry that countersignifies the imperial notions of the slave colony as island paradise. This is what I am describing as a transculturated colonial text because the inscription of a Taíno or Arawak subject encoded not only a new literary aesthetic but also a political project that reclaimed the island from the domination of proslavery interests. For Plácido, the Spanish conquest was a catastrophe that devastated pristine landscapes and institutionalized racialized slave labor. The colonial era desecrated ancestral domains, and it invited the spiritual forces of malevolent overseers and their African victims to haunt the land.

### Swearing Oaths and Prophesying Ruin: Plácido as a Prophet of the African Diaspora

After 1840 Plácido traveled frequently between Matanzas, Villa Clara, Cienfuegos, and Havana where he disseminated seditious ideas via poetry and mounted an insurgent network in secretive meetings. Plácido became acquainted with influential members of free black society outside of his Matanzas community, and he sought their material support for the impending rebellion. But most notably Plácido availed himself of his notoriety to recruit would-be black and mulatto rebels and administer loyalty oaths to his proselytes. Juan Nepomuceno Valdivia—a wealthy merchant—was among Plácido's most intimate contacts in Villa Clara. Nepomuceno met so frequently with the poet and other mulattoes that the governor of Villa Clara suspected them of conspiratorial activities and surveilled Plácido's every move. Governor Aniceto Valverde later arrested Plácido, and though an influential friend intervened to have him released, Plácido could not escape the moniker of public enemy number one (Cué, *Plácido: El poeta* 86–87). In addition to *La Aurora de Matanzas*, Plácido also collaborated in *El Eco de Villa Clara*. There he published "El juramento" (The Oath), an incendiary sonnet that swore, "Ser enemigo eterno del tirano, / Manchar si me es posible mis vestidos, / Con su execrable sangre por mi mano" (To be the eternal enemy of the tyrant / If it is possible, to tarnish my vestments, / With his detestable blood, by my hand) (Cué, *Plácido: El poeta* 88).[17] Seldom had Plácido rebuked the queen, or so openly advocated for retribution in his poetry. "El juramento" was a declaration of war. The publication of "El juramento" in 1840, and "La profecía de Cuba a España" (Prophecy from Cuba to Spain) shortly prior, marked a watershed moment in his brief literary career. Plácido had devised a *poetics of conspiracy* to subvert Spanish Catholic claims to universal authority and, more importantly, to disseminate antislavery ideas in African-descended communities. It is this poetics of conspiracy that interests us here, because Plácido believed in the intrinsic power of language, the power to change the immediate outcome of events and to present himself as a prophet against empire.

Plácido's rhetorical arsenal was defined by an abiding belief in prophecy. Plácido practiced an insurgent spirituality consisting of three axes: the power of prophecy to portend black liberation, the African *cabildo* as an organizing principle, and the loyalty oath as a speech act that consecrates the dark body for revolution. In this vein he composed "La profecía de Cuba a España," "El juramento," ¡Habaneros Libertad!," "La Virgen de Rosario," and "El diablito." First, Plácido fused biblical imagery and neoclassical symbolism in "La profecía de Cuba a España" to prophesy that Cubans—represented as an African lion— would rise up against Spain and restore "la libertad divina" (divine liberty) to their homeland (Valdés, *Plácido, Gabriel de la Concepción* 655). Secondly, he situated himself symbolically within the *cabildo* and seemed to imply that religious brotherhoods should be the organizing principle for the impending antislavery insurgency. This was particularly radical, because *cabildos* preferred African priests to govern their affairs, not light-skinned mulattoes. Mulattoes held membership in *cofradías* that were under the auspices of the Catholic Church (Landers 145). But within Plácido's conspiratorial gatherings, his *cabildo,* so to speak, the poet admonished blacks and mulattoes to recruit what an elderly witness described as "hombres de pecho" (valiant men) (Finch, *Rethinking*

134). Several witnesses confessed that Plácido had administered them oaths to conceal the plot and to swear absolute allegiance to give up their lives before revealing anything to their white enemies (Pettway, "The Altar, Oath, Body" 1; Finch *Rethinking*, 135–136). To this end, loyalty oaths were a pervasive means to effectively organize antislavery revolts, maintain secrecy, and ensure unity among insurgents.[18] The 1844 movement that Plácido helped to organize struck terror in the hearts of colonial authorities because it enjoyed widespread appeal among blacks, enlisted both the enslaved and free populations, and was composed of multiple nuclei that crisscrossed the urban/rural divide (Pettway, "The Altar, the Oath" 9). Plácido's poetry was especially powerful because Bakongo and Yoruba-inspired ideas about spirituality were the subtext of otherwise conventional poetry. But this African-inspired religious ethos may have escaped the notice of the military tribunal that convicted Plácido. There is no mention of it in the trial records that I have perused. In what remains of this chapter, I argue that African cosmology animated some of the seditious literature that Plácido extemporized, recited, and even published. Plácido's belief in African-inspired ideas of spirit and cosmos emboldened him to abandon the Catholic narrative of redemptive suffering and to reimagine the possibilities for black freedom.

Plácido claimed the prophetic mantle of the Hebraic tradition in "La Profecía de Cuba a España: En los días de Doña Isabel de Borbón" (The Prophecy from Cuba to Spain: In the Days of Doña Isabella of Bourbon). Prophets were messengers of God, indigent men on the margins of immoral societies that seldom heeded their cries for repentance. Plácido depicted Cuba as diametrically opposed to the Spanish Empire. In the poem, Plácido transformed himself from the queen's vassal into a free citizen of African descent within an emerging Cuban nation. Plácido swore an oath of vengeance against tyrants before "el Dios de la gran Naturaleza" (the great God of Nature) (Valdés, *Plácido, Gabriel de la Concepción* 654). And he masqueraded the identity of this "God of Nature" by naming him for the supreme god of the Romans, Jove. The neoclassical reference to a long-forgotten pagan god was more than a facade; it was a transcultural moment in the text where Plácido signaled his allegiance to a non-Catholic notion of the Supreme Being. But Plácido was a Cuban prophet. The prophetic poet bespoke love for Cuba in the first two stanzas of the poem: "Loor á la virtud; al mundo pasmo. / Canoros cisnes de pátria mia! / ¿Dó están los ecos que al lejano polo / Llevaba el raudo Eolo" (Praise to virtue; to the world astounded / Sweet swans of my Fatherland! / Where are the echoes of the distant pole that carried the winds of Aeolus) (Valdés, *Plácido, Gabriel de la Concepción* 654). The speaker in the poem sang the praises of "my fatherland" as a nationalist gesture in defiance of the queen's authority in the slave colony. And he summoned his "plácida lira" (placid lyre) by name so that he might compose verses to Her Majesty (Valdés, *Plácido, Gabriel de la Concepción* 654). Plácido reclaimed Neoclassical imagery, and he employed apostrophe to invoke spiritual power over animate and inanimate objects. It is the power of the spoken word over seemingly inanimate objects that Plácido relied on in his blueprint for insurgency.

"La profecía de Cuba a España" abounds in neoclassical images that represent the global conflict between European empires and their Caribbean colonies. There are four metaphors that represent Cuba in this poem: Cuba is Carthage, the African city-state that defied Rome; Cuba is a majestic Caribbean woman crowned with lemon blossoms; Cuba is Osiris; and Cuba is an African lion, "león vestido de cordura" (a lion clad with reason). Plácido exclaimed an eternal hatred for Spanish tyranny in the third stanza.

> Calle el que tema: yo no temo, y canto.

> Como en las aras del supremo Jove
> Juró Asdrubal rencor á los Romanos
> Y les mostró de Marte la fiereza,
> Yó ante el Dios de la gran Naturaleza,
> Odio eterno hé jurado á los tiranos. (Valdés, *Plácido, Gabriel de la Concepción* 654)

> (Be still he who is afraid: I do not fear, and I sing.

> As in honor of the Supreme Jupiter
> Hasdrubal swore resentment for the Romans
> And showed them Mars's ferocity
> Before the God of Nature,
> I have sworn an oath of eternal hatred for tyrants.)

Carthage was the refined African city-state that challenged Roman hegemony in the Mediterranean world and pledged to exact revenge on the empire. Plácido provoked the Spanish Empire circa 1839 by making Carthage the metaphor for Cuba, and Rome the symbol of Spanish Empire. Carthage corresponds to modern Tunisia; the Phoenicians, who hailed from modern-day Lebanon, founded Carthage in 814 BCE. Carthage was a sovereign political entity that negotiated treaties with neighboring states by the sixth century BCE. (Cowherd 23). The Romans defeated the Carthaginians that the African General Hamilcar Barca commanded. And Rome took possession of Sicily in the first Punic War, 264–241 BCE. Displeased by his defeat at the hands of the Romans, Hamilcar set out to restore Carthaginian prestige by conquering southern Spain. After Hamilcar died nine years later, his son-in-law Hasdrubal replaced him (Cowherd 24). Plácido cited Hasdrubal's animosity for the Romans to provide his readers with a historical exemplar of African resistance to European power. Thus, Plácido—like Hasdrubal of African antiquity—swore "odio eterno . . . a los tiranos" (eternal hatred ... for [European] tyrants) (Valdés, *Plácido, Gabriel de la Concepción* 654) that had enslaved black people. Plácido's oath was a sacred vow before the God of Nature, swearing an abiding abhorrence for despotism. (Mars is the Roman god of war) The choice of words is not inconsequential. The Spanish verbal phrase "hé jurado" has three possible translations: "I have sworn," "I have taken a vow," or "I have made an oath." All three renderings carry similar connotations, but in the immediate context of this poem, I have chosen to render the verse: "I have sworn an oath," since it communicates the combative disposition of the speaker. And when the author did use the poetic "I," he expressed antagonism toward the monarchy or swore an oath of antipathy.

Cuba emerges from the waters of the Atlantic in the fourth stanza, crowned with palm leaves, orange blossoms (*azahares*), and prophecy on her lips. She is a majestic Caribbean woman rising at dawn to condemn her captors. Cuba's gaze is no longer a peripheral glance; rather, it is an audacious glare signifying the advent of an emergent national voice.

Mostró Cuba la frente
Coronada de palmas y azahares,

Y los ojos tornando
A la doliente y desgraciada Iberia,
Alzó la voz, hablando
Al nuevo Atila del rebelde bando:
[ ... ]

¡Qué ...! ¿presumes reinar ...? ¿Cuál será el trueno
Que aterre y venza del saber los hijos?
[ ... ]

Tiembla y huye, infeliz: la edad presente
No sostiene traidores coronados,
Y si tu horda vandálica insolente
Lograr pudiera su perverso encono
Fueras siempre un esclavo sobre un trono,
Mas nunca un rey. Tu furibunda saña
No ejercerás jamás, fiera alimaña,
Que humillarse el poder á un cruel vestiglo (Valdés, *Plácido, Gabriel de la Concepción* 655)

(Cuba exposed her brow
Crowned with palm leaves, and orange and lemon blossoms,
Toward aggrieved, disgraced Iberia,

She raised her voice, speaking
To the new Attila of the rebellious lot:

. . .

What! Do you presume to reign . . .? Where is your thunder
That terrifies and vanquishes the knowledge of the children?

. . .

Tremble and flee, unfortunate soul: the present age
Does not tolerate enthroned traitors,
And if your Vandalic insolent horde
Could achieve your perverse viciousness
You would always be a slave on a throne,
But never a king. Your furious wrath
You will never implement, furious scoundrel,
Humbling the power of a cruel monster.)

Cuba emerges as a paradoxical feminine figure, because she is remarkably beautiful and fiercely combative. Cuba is personified as a self-possessed mother to all that reside in her borders. Cuba prophesies to Spain spewing invective and condemnation. She boasts a crown of flowers and palm leaves that render her an imposing, even majestic, figure. The poem does not racialize Cuba, but her crown of *azahares* does situate her geographically within Moorish Spain among the Andalusian orange groves.[19] *Azahares* is a Spanish word with an Arabic etymology that refers to white blossoms on orange, lemon, and citron trees. The choice of words is not without rhetorical effect, because *azahares* is a metaphor for a medieval African or Arab woman with brown or dark mahogany skin.[20] Plácido portrayed Cuba as a brown-skinned woman boasting a crown of flowers on the shores of the Caribbean Sea.

Because Cuba is either an African or a mulatto woman, her discursive power might also be associated with that of an African divine spirit like Ochún or her sister Yemayá. The poem certainly does not name her thus. And Plácido does not equate the female character in "La profecía de Cuba a España" with a path to the Virgin Mary or a Catholic saint that Africans had transculturated with an *orisha*. Nevertheless, lemon blossoms link Plácido's Cuba to Ochún because, as Candice Goucher writes, "yellow or amber-colored foods such as honey, lemon, palm oil, and peppers represented Oshun, the goddess of love and wealth" (142).[21] Cuba stands at the seashore, dressed in royal finery like Yemayá, the divine sovereign of the sea in Yoruba cosmology. And her feminine beauty is emblematic of Ochún, the sensual and seductive spirt of sweet waters (Murphy; Castellanos 39–40). If Cuba stands at the edge of the island glaring at her Spanish captors, then she likely situates herself in Baracoa, where the river meets the sea. Plácido's Cuba is *hija de las dos aguas* (daughter of both waters); she is sweet and salty, beautiful yet vengeful. Cuba personified traverses cultural, religious, and aesthetic boundaries. With regard to Yemayá and Ochún, Otero reminds us, "The relationship between these two entities highlights an openness to religious interaction in the history of the African Diaspora" (86–87).

David Brown points out that Yemayá is "the sea, the archetypal mother of the world," and "a warrior" (371). Cuba, too, is a warrior-mother who prophesies the death of despotism, "Y el Despotismo vil muerde la tierra, / Y rabia, y tiembla, y brama, y desaparece." (And vile Despotism bites the dust / And seething, trembling, and bellowing, it disappears) (Valdés, *Plácido, Gabriel de la Concepción* 656). The Manichean divisions, slave/free, black/white, and colonizer/colonized are inverted so that Cuba turns her eyes to Iberia to denounce the sovereign as a slave. Cuba, rather than Spain, comprehends the true nature of freedom and justly struggles to achieve it. Plácido's impression that Isabel II was unfit to sit on the throne is also reflected in the historical conditions of her coronation. Isabel's father, King Fernando VII, rescinded the Ley Sálica, which had forbidden women to rule since 1713. In so doing, Fernando VII thwarted his brother Don Carlos María Isidro from becoming king, and he ensured that his daughter would rule (Comellas 23, 27). Ironically, Spanish liberals promoted parliamentary government, male suffrage, the constitutional separation of powers, and the abolition of the Inquisition. While liberals waged civil war to institute and maintain reforms in the metropole, liberalism was an illusion in Spain's remaining overseas colonies (Fischer 102–103). Plácido's misogynistic undertone— "Fueras siempre un esclavo sobre un trono / Mas nunca un rey" (You would always be a slave on a throne, / But never a king)—was a way to deconstruct Isabel's legitimacy. If Fernando VII had not rescinded the Ley Sálica, a woman could have never returned to the Spanish throne.

In "La profecía de Cuba a España," Plácido decreed that revolution would come at the hands of an African lion armed with *la Justicia* (Justice). The poet spoke of an impending black insurgency in the prophetic voice.

No lo tolera la moderna España
Ni la consiente la opinión del siglo.
¡Huye y tiembla, infeliz! que si fiado
Vés al leon vestido de cordura,
Contener su fiereza sólo es dado
A la regia piedad, y á la hermosura:
Mas ¡ay de tí! si eriza la melena
Y el cuerpo estriba en la potente garra,
Y colérico salta, y ruge, y truena.
Y se lanza en los campos de Navarra.
Al bélico rugido resonante

Verás disperso el fanatismo ciego,
Y al renacer la libertad divina,
Al grito heróico de Padilla y Riego
Alzarse un Bravo, aparecer un Mina.>>
[ ... ]

    El nombre del progreso en áurea nube
Por la Justicia y el honor llevado,

. . .

Vencen sus hijos la sangrienta guerra,
Y el Despotismo vil muerde la tierra,
Y rabia, y tiembla, y brama, y desaparece. (Valdés, *Plácido, Gabriel de la*
    *Concepción* 655–656)

(Modern Spain will not tolerate it
 Neither will the opinion of the century consent.
Tremble and flee, unfortunate soul! If perhaps
You see a lion clad with reason,
 It is a given that he restrains his ferocity
For regal piety, and for beauty:
But woe to you if his mane sticks up
And your body lies within his powerful claws
And he leaps furiously, and roars, and rumbles.
And he launches in the fields of Navarra.
To the bellicose roar resounding
You will see blind fanaticism scatter,
And as divine liberty is reborn,
To the heroic cry of Padilla and Riego
A Bravo rising up, a Mina appearing.[22]

    The name of progress in a gilded cloud
Carried by Justice and honor, . . .
The bloodstained war conquers your sons,
And vile despotism bites the dust
And rages, and trembles, and bellows, and disappears.)

Plácido prophesied that Cuban lions would rise up leaping, roaring, and thun-
dering against the queen until *la libertad divina* (divine liberty) was reborn.
Plácido maintained a symbolic relationship to Africa as the cradle of his racial/
cultural identity, so it is reasonable that the African lion and Carthage were his
chosen metaphors for insurgent Cuba. The African lion epitomized a warrior
spirit that Plácido believed insurgent blacks and mulattoes would embody in

the near future. Cubans of African descent would remove the proverbial mask and take up arms against Spanish colonialism and slavery. But there was more to the symbolic world that Plácido constructed. Plácido's prophecy foreshadowed a direct armed confrontation between Cuba and Spain, the colonized and the colonizer, black and white, much in the same way that Cuban José Antonio Aponte (1812) and African American Nat Turner (1831) had done before him.

In 1831 Nat Turner revolted against slavery with a small army of sixty enslaved and free black men in Southampton County, Virginia. Turner's disciples held him to be "The Prophet," and together they executed some fifty-five white southerners (Gray 2). Makungu Akinyela says that Nat Turner practiced a form of Protestant Christianity that was deeply influenced by an African-centered cosmology of resistance/resilience, which is embedded within his testimony. Nat Turner absorbed biblical images and stories, and as his visions demonstrate, he particularly valued the apocalyptic and messianic symbolism. Turner appropriated the Hebrew prophetic tradition of deliverance as an allegory for African American liberation from racial slavery in the antebellum south. Nat Turner made use of the scriptures to grant authority to his desires for black freedom (Akinyela 269–270).

Nat Turner claimed that God had given him esoteric knowledge, knowledge of the elements and the revolution of the planets, and that since his youth he had been predestined for a special vocation among his people. These signs and omens were outward manifestations of Turner's power, and they endowed him with sacred authority among enslaved Africans. Nat Turner's prophecies conjured the image of a Serpent, the biblical symbol for Satan, which God commanded him to fight. In perhaps his most significant and vivid vision, Turner witnessed white spirits and black spirits engaged in spiritual warfare beneath a darkened sun (Gray 10–11). Nat Turner confessed the details of his visions and his understanding regarding the nature of evil, subsequent to his arrest.

> And about this time I had a vision—and I saw white spirits and black spirits engaged in battle, and the sun was darkened—the thunder rolled in the Heavens, and blood flowed and streams—and I heard a voice saying, "Such is your luck, such you are called to see, and let it come rough or smooth, you must surely bear it."

[...]

> And on the 12th of May, 1828, I heard a loud noise in the heavens, and the Spirit instantly appeared to me and said the Serpent was loosened, and Christ had laid down the yoke he had borne for the sins of men, and that I should take it on and fight against the Serpent, for the time was fast approaching when the first should be last and the last should be first (Gray 10, 11).

I am interested in Turner's image of "white spirits and black spirits engaged in battle" (Gray 10) because it is reminiscent of the apocalyptic imagery Aponte evoked in his *libro de pinturas* (book of drawings). Aponte's *libro de pinturas* depicted a battle between Abyssinian (Ethiopian) and Portuguese armies. Aponte's interrogators regarded this as an arresting image, because "the picture included two black men on horseback who carried the severed and bloody heads of what appeared to be two white (not Moorish) men" (Ferrer, *Freedom's Mirror* 313). The depictions of "race war" (Ferrer, *Freedom's Mirror* 313)—language that I borrow from Aponte's interrogators and that the military tribunal alluded to in 1844—seems apropos for the visions that Nat Turner and José Antonio Aponte conjured. Aponte's and Turner's allegories differed from Plácido's African metaphors and Neoclassical symbols. But all three prophets of African descent shared the core belief that black liberation would be achieved by defeating a nefarious white army. While Aponte and Turner envisioned black and white combatants ensnarled in spiritual warfare, Plácido imagined an African lion roaring and leaping into battle against Spain. Nat Turner prophesied that the United States would be engulfed in a war against slavery; and to his mind, he obeyed what God commanded him to do: destroy the Serpent. Wasn't Nat Turner's prophecy fulfilled when the United States plunged into civil war in 1861? And José Antonio Aponte's 1812 insurgency lingered in national memory decades after his execution. Aponte's name became a byword among white Cubans that cried, "Más malo que Aponte" (Worse than Aponte), to describe a perverse or wicked person (Villaverde 90). So, in all likelihood, Plácido received word of Aponte's 1812 rebellion.[23] Plácido fashioned himself in the diasporic tradition of José Antonio Aponte (and Nat Turner), for whom prophecy was a precursor to a war against slavery and the myth of white supremacy that justified it.[24]

Plácido's prophecy endowed him with sacred authority within black and mulatto communities, an authority that he harnessed to devise loyalty oaths and administer them to his co-conspirators. Loyalty oaths were a pervasive means to effectively organize antislavery revolts, maintain secrecy, and ensure unity among insurrectionists (Pettway, "The Altar, the Oath" 9). Such oaths were not uncommon in Caribbean colonial history. In Jamaica in 1760, and Saint Domingue (later Haiti) in 1791, enslaved Africans embraced the loyalty oath as a covenant between coreligionists in a righteous struggle against slavery. Tacky's Rebellion in Jamaica in 1760 had endangered British control for the first time since the maroon wars of the 1730s (V. Brown 37). Vincent Brown describes how African cosmology informed the oaths that Tacky's rebels swore.

Tacky, an enslaved African from the Gold Coast led the most extensive and well-coordinated slave revolt in the eighteenth-century British Caribbean, with obeah men as his closest counsellors. Tacky and his co-conspirators called upon the shamen to use their charms to protect them from bullets and to administer binding loyalty oaths. Significantly, the oaths were made up of a concoction of blood, rum and *grave dirt*. The rebellion ultimately failed, but its aftermath showed direct competition between different forms of sacred authority in stark relief. (37–38)

Obeah practices had multiple African origins, including Igbo and Kongolese antecedents (V. Brown 36); perhaps the Kongolese influence explains the significance of grave dirt in the oaths that Tacky administered. Brown demonstrates that the oath was performative; it was a hallowed speech act and a prescribed ritual activity thought to make adherents invulnerable to attack. In Cuba, José Antonio Aponte relied on a protocol of clandestine oaths to transmit information among diverse nuclei of insurgent activity. Aponte's protocol of secret oaths was so effective that even after his movement had inspired uprisings throughout Cuba in 1812, the Spanish government remained unaware of the larger conspiracy (I. Miller 82).

The judgment against Plácido and other leaders of the 1844 movement is a self-legitimating, racialized narrative designed to preserve Cuba as an ever-faithful possession within the Spanish Catholic imaginary. The administering of loyalty oaths was integral to the government's portrayal of Plácido as a subversive and, when read closely, provides clues about the spiritual ethos that informed his emancipatory project. This passage from the trial record describes the political function of loyalty oaths:

> Desde entónces vemos cooperar en el proceso estas razas unidas para llevar á cabo su inicuo proyecto: se ensancha el círculo de la junta creando otra secundarias de la clase de morenos en la casa de Márcos Ruiz y Manuel Quiñones; vemos así mismo probado por declaraciones suficientes la concurrencia de algunos pardos á ella, miembros éstos de la principal anteriormente instalada, que Plácido en ella y Pimienta en otros puntos recibian horrendos juramentos al individuo que se iniciaba, bien fuese negro ó pardo, sobre el esterminio de todo blanco, y el de guardar el mayor sigilo, negando en el caso de ser sorprendidos.[25]

(From that point on we saw the cooperation of the two races united in the process to carry out their iniquitous project: they broadened the circle of the rebel junta creating second-tier agents from the class of free blacks in the home of Marcos Ruiz and Manuel Quiñones; this is proven by ample testimony [regarding] the participation of some mixed-race persons on the rebel junta, members of the [original] chief junta that was previously established, with Plácido and Pimienta sitting on it [and] at other points in time they administered horrendous oaths to the individuals that were initiated, whether they were black or of mixed race; regarding the extermination of all whites, and to guard the greatest caution denying the plot in case they are discovered . . . )

The Spanish government construed the loyalty oath as a seditious speech act that had united free blacks and mulattoes who had conspired to massacre the white population. The notion of racial unity between lighter- and darker-skinned African descendants troubled colonial authorities because it implied the collapse of a racial hierarchy designed to nullify African-descended political power. As demonstrated in a preceding chapter, Plácido's satirical poetry posited a broad notion of African-descended community by negating the seductive power of whiteness and positioning mulatto racial origins in Africa. What the government called "the cooperation of the two races" was a chief tenet of Plácido's political project. In the government account, the poet is grouped among the leaders of the initial conspiratorial junta who proselytized free blacks and mulattoes and compelled them to swear oaths of white extermination, revealing nothing to their enemies lest they be assassinated. The oath is an avowal of political and racial allegiance in the judgment against Plácido; it creates space for free blacks and mulattoes to conspire against the socio-cultural order, devising an "iniquitous project" at the home of Marcos Ruiz and Manuel Quiñones.

Scholars have not much researched the loyalty oath as a component of the counterhegemonic thinking that informed the 1844 movement. To my knowledge, no literary scholars in either Cuba or the United States have seriously engaged the topic. Even so, I am familiar with historians that have touched upon the matter: Aisha Finch, Jane Landers, and Robert Paquette. Jane Landers offers an abridged discussion of the loyalty oath, mentioning Plácido's 1840 poem entitled "El juramento" (The Oath), but she does not analyze its religio-political significance to the 1844 movement (204, 227). Finch's extraordinary book *Rethinking Slave Rebellion in Cuba: La Escalera and the Insurgencies of 1841–1844* represents a watershed moment in Cuban historiography. Finch proves that enslaved and free conspirators issued "grave oaths of loyalty and silence" to initiate other persons into the movement ("Insurgency at the Crossroads" 425, 429). She acknowledges the sacred character of such oaths and, more importantly, corroborates that on several occasions Plácido administered such oaths to prospective rebels (*Rethinking* 135–136).

The literary record corroborates what the government claimed: Plácido administered loyalty oaths to black and mulatto conspirators. Colonial authorities cited "El juramento" (The Oath) among the poems named in the indictment (Horrego Estuch, *Plácido: el poeta* 56) because it read as a prophetic call to insurrection and advocated for an insurrection against tyranny. The loyalty oath was central to Plácido's religious poetry. The oaths not only broke faith with the monarchy but also implied that Plácido's co-conspirators may have believed his prophecy would be fulfilled. Giorgio Agamben's *The Sacrament of Language* is critical to my reading of Plácido, because he examines the political history of the oath. Agamben situates the oath in the intersection between religion and politics (Prodi qtd. in Agamben 1), so that the utterance performs both a sacred and secular task. The oath represents a pact, a sociopolitical agreement between diverse interlocutors within a given polity. Political crises arise when the sworn oath has been disregarded or even dishonored by one or all of the actors in question. Agamben also explores how Christian monotheism establishes a precise correlation between words and reality. Ergo, the words of God are oaths since he alone swears truly (Philo qtd. in Agamben 21). Agamben's philosophical archaeology of the oath allows for a religio-political reading in which Plácido's transculturated text is perceived as a blueprint that might foment the political conditions necessary for revolution.

I have cited Plácido's sonnet in its entirety to draw a contrast with the government's story and, in doing so, to contemplate the discursive relationship between the loyalty oath and the altar upon which ritual is performed.

A la sombra de un árbol empinado
Que está de un ancho valle a la salida,
Hay una fuente que a beber convida
De su líquido puro y argentado

Allí fui yo por mi deber llamado
Y haciendo altar la tierra endurecida,
Ante el sagrado código de la vida,
Extendidas mis manos he jurado:

Ser enemigo eterno del tirano,
Manchar, si me es posible, mis vestidos
Con su execrable sangre, por mi mano.
Derramarla con golpes repetidos;
Y morir a las manos de un verdugo,
Si es necesario, por romper el yugo. (Plácido qtd. in Cué, *Plácido: El Poeta* 87–88)

(In the shadow of a towering tree
That stands at the end of an ample valley
There is a fount that bids you
Drink its pure and silvery water

There I went by my duty called
And making an altar of the hardened earth,
Before the sacred code of life,
My hands extended, I have sworn an oath.

To be the eternal enemy of the tyrant,
If it is possible, to tarnish my vestments,

With his detestable blood, by my hand.
Shedding it with repeated blows
And dying at the hands of an executioner,
If need be, to break the yoke.)

Yet again, Plácido countersignifies religious tropes steeped in Spanish Catholic history: the altar, the divine calling, and the oath of fidelity. In the first two stanzas, the African-descended persona is called to perform a solemn duty in a shaded area boasting a fount of pure water. He proceeds to make an altar of the hardened earth. The divine calling in "El juramento" situates Plácido within the normative discourse on religion, since it is customary in Catholic liturgy to swear vows to God and the saints and to receive oaths. But Plácido inverted the function of the oath so that the spoken word was a sacred speech act prophesying destruction to come and obliging the poet to discharge his duty. The nature metaphors—the tree and hardened earth—were not coincidental, because, as my analysis of the indigenist poetry points out, Cuba was the ancestral fatherland, the lost *nación* in possession of a history ignored that Plácido promised to restore.

Plácido constructed a transculturated ritual object of his own where blacks and mulattoes pledged allegiance across the racial/ethnic divide in defiance of racial hierarchy. Plácido dreamt of a new religio-political order where Africans and their descendants professed oaths that would refuse subservience to Spain, subvert Catholic authority, and, most importantly, consecrate the dark body for revolution. The altar must be further theorized in the Cuban religious context because of its liturgical function in Plácido's poetry. José Millet expounds on this matter; he describes the altar as "santuario, sagrario, mesa, o gradas, donde son colocados objetos de diversa índole con función ritual" (a sanctuary, a ciborium, or multitiered platform, where objects of diverse ritual function find space) (7). Ritual performance is the essential role of the altar, but in contrast to Catholic liturgy, the African Cuban altar is what Dodson calls "sacred space" (62), which is used to make sacrifices to African divine spirits and ancestors (Millet 7). Whereas Millet's definition is taxonomical, Dodson's notion encompasses the epistemological dimensions of such space, defining them as "constructed assemblages of shared awareness that articulate a three-dimensional symbolic expression of the body of knowledge" (62).

Plácido did not describe the physical contours of the altar, but he was explicit about its function: the altar was sacred space to profess loyalty oaths "before the God of Nature" (Valdés, *Plácido, Gabriel de la Concepción* 654). By evoking the "the God of Nature," instead of Jesus Christ, Plácido gestured toward a Bakongo-inspired idea of the divine where the forested wilderness—not the Catholic conception of heaven—is the epitome of the sacred (Cabrera, *El monte* 15). What is more, Plácido's altar of "hardened earth" is reminiscent of Bakongo-Cuban and (even Abakuá) conceptions of the natural world, which may have been inspiration for this poem. Lydia Cabrera's informants explained, "'La ceiba es el altar de los ganguleros', que bajo ella 'montan', construyen, animan sus ngangas y prendas. Estas, se depositan bajo las ceibas, para que se incorporen la virtud de su sombra y se fortalezcan." (The ceiba tree is an altar to *palo monte* practitioners that mount, construct [and] animate their *ngangas* and *prendas* beneath it. They deposit them beneath the ceiba trees so they will absorb the virtue of its shadow and strengthen them) (*El monte* 166).[26] In Plácido's poem the tree is not an altar per se, and the *nganga* does not visibly perform any role in the ritual. The *nganga* embodies three diferent but related meanings: it is a cauldron filled with sacred material objects, an ethereal being, or a formidable devotee of *palo monte/palo mayombe* (Dodson 89; Figarola 311). But the sacred silhouette of the "towering tree" creates space for insurgents to swear oaths of retribution against slave society. Plácido's poem draws inspiration from the Bakongo-inspired ritual insofar as both discursive practices acknowledge the sacredness of the shadow in ritual performances.

Abakuá is an all-male Cuban initiation society with origins in the Old Calabar region of Nigeria and Cameroon. Africans founded the first lodge outside Havana in Regla in 1836 (I. Miller 13–14, 41). In the Abakuá tradition, Cabrera writes, "Abasonga "juró ante el altar—Abasí . . .—al lado de la palma" (Abasonga swore an oath before the altar—Abasí [God] . . . beside the palm tree) (*El monte* 287). In *El monte*, Abasonga is the name of an African king from the Cross River region that witnessed the consecracation of the first *bongó* drum. Abasonga swore an oath to Abasí [God] before an altar after witnessing the blessing of the drum (*El monte* 286–287). Ivor Miller explains that Ábásí is a commonly accepted name for the Supreme Being in Abakuá tradition and throughout the Cross River region (I. Miller 114). The Abakuá ritual also bears a certain resemblance to "El juramento," because comparable to Plácido's poetic subject, the Abakuá adept swears an oath to the Supreme Being beside a sacred tree. Plácido did not name "the towering tree" in his sonnet; rather, as was characteristic of his transculturated poetics, he anticipated the reader would either interpret the aforesaid tree as the ceiba common in Bakongo-inspired rituals, or as the palm tree in the Abakuá religious imaginary. Thus, "El juramento" mirrors an entanglement of African cosmologies and Catholic symbols indicative of Plácido's pluriversal engagement with Cuban religious multiplicity.

"El juramento" does not name the array of objects arranged on the ground, but the poem certainly subverted the hegemonic concept of an altar in Catholicism: a consecrated surface within the cathedral walls safeguarding the sacrament. *Cuba* was Plácido's altar, his native soil imbued with the presence of the Haitian cacique Hatuey that cried out for retribution. Plácido devised an oath to unite blacks and mulattoes as a racially constituted polity. Nevertheless, if Plácido was to forge consensus amongst disparate groups of African descendants, he would have to sever the convenant between the monarch and her

Cuban subjects. Plácido deligitimized oaths not only between the queen and her vassals in "El juramento" but also in "La profecía de Cuba a España." Despite the dedication to Queen Isabella II (1833–1868), "La profecía de Cuba a España" is not an ode. Rather, it is a poem brimming with symbolic violence, where Plácido rebukes Her Majesty as one of several "traidores coronados" (crowned traitors) and as "un esclavo sobre un trono / Mas nunca un rey" (a slave upon the throne but never a king) (Valdés, *Plácido, Gabriel de la Concepción* 655).

Plácido theorized that racial slavery was a problem of political as well as metaphysical dimensions. By claiming the prophetic mantle of the Old Testament, Plácido appropriated the symbolic language of moral authority at the center of Spanish Catholicism in a way that was amenable to his black and white readerships. In "La profecía de Cuba a España" and "El juramento," Plácido seized the symbolic instruments of Catholicism; he usurped their social legitimacy and turned prophecy and the oath of fidelity into instruments that might achieve black Cuban freedom. Plácido prophesied about the Cuban war against Spanish colonialism and slavery long before the 1868 Grito de Yara, which launched the Ten Years War. Moreover, Spanish revolutionaries dethroned Queen Isabel II that very same year in the Glorious Revolution (Burdiel 191). This chapter concludes with an analysis of Plácido's representation of the African *cabildo* as cultural space that enabled blacks to produce antislavery discourse and mount an insurgency. Plácido's blueprint for revolution might remain illegible if we fail to contemplate "el sagrado código de la vida" (the sacred code of life), that obscure notion of retributive justice in "El juramento." Though many scholars have acknowledged the political character of this sonnet, no one has analyzed *the sacred code of life*, until now. It is my contention that Plácido's sacred code of life will reveal the religious character of his revolutionary project of emancipation.

### Rehearsing Revolution: Carnival and Black Brotherhood in Plácido's Poetry

The *cabildo* takes center stage in Plácido's poetry depicting African-inspired spirituality. Plácido represented *cabildos* as sacred space where blacks conceived, consolidated, and performed a cultural identity defined, in part, by their own notions of religiosity. "A la Virgen del Rosario" (To the Virgin of the Rosary), "Mi no sé que ha richo" (Me Don't Know What I've Said), and "El Diablito" (The Little Devil) provide three different portrayals of the *cabildo* in early nineteenth-century Cuba. "A la Virgen del Rosario" is a Petrarchan sonnet in honor of Our Lady of the Rosary that demonstrates the *cabildos'* ostensible affiliation with the Catholic Church. But that sense of respectability vanishes in "Mi no sé que ha richo," the onomatopoeic fable depicting life within the *cabildo*. The poem portrays chants in African languages, drumming, and the making of vulgar, even bestial, sounds. Similarly, in "El diablito" Plácido transformed the gaiety of song, dance, and drumming into a staging ground for an insurgency against Spanish colonialism. I have found no mention of Plácido's *cabildo* poems among nineteenth-century observers. Conceivably, these poems—like much of Plácido's writing—were deemed far too inelegant, unadorned, or clumsy to be taken seriously. But Sibylle Fischer has correctly observed that Plácido's poetry neither submits to the rigor mandated by aesthetic law nor deposes it (90–91). I demonstrate that Plácido's *cabildo* poems were not a frivolous foray into *costumbrismo* (color writing); rather, they were a staging ground for the conspiratorial activities for which the colonial state executed him.

Africans in Cuba founded *cabildos* patterned on Spanish *cofradías* (Catholic confraternities) beginning in the sixteenth century (del Carmen Barcia 58; Finch, *Rethinking* 160).[27] In colonial Cuba *cabildos* were mutual aid societies organized by ethnicity; they planned dances, participated in religious processions, and collected monies to purchase members' freedom. *Cabildos* elected a king, a queen, and an array of presiding officers that performed different functions (Finch, *Rethinking* 160). Though Catholicism was the legitimate religion throughout the empire, colonial officials did not coerce Havana *cabildos* to submit to Church supervision until 1755, when Bishop Morell de Santa Cruz intervened to transform them into "Templos de Dios" (temples of God) (del Carmen Barcia 68–69). Cuban historian María del Carmen Barcia unearthed records testifying to 109 different African *cabildos* in Havana alone (57). African brotherhoods in Havana, Matanzas, and elsewhere in Cuba claimed multitudinous ethnic identities, and—as in other parts of the African Diaspora in Latin America—they adopted ethnonyms such as *carabalí*, *congo*, or *lucumí* that signaled the name of their putative regions of origin.[28] For example, the *carabalí* name referred to persons from southeast Nigeria, among whom the Igbo, Efik, and Ekoi ethnicities were most prominent (del Carmen Barcia 57, 157). *Lucumí* referred to Yoruba-speaking Africans of multiple ethic origins, and in the nineteenth century *lucumí* became nearly synonymous with captives from the former Oyo Empire (del Carmen Barcia 157). The *congo* ethnonym applied to West Central Africans from modern Angola, the Democratic Republic of the Congo, and even Mozambique (del Carmen Barcia 157). Each *cabildo* boasted a patron saint, such as Our Lady of the Rosary, Saint Barbara, or Saint Anthony, this was part of Bishop Morell de Santa Cruz's visible legacy (del Carmen Barcia 162–163). Plácido's poem celebrated one of the most prominent liturgical traditions among colonial Afro-Latin Americans: reverence for Our Lady of the Rosary (del Carmen Barcia 73).

Plácido published "A la Virgen de Rosario" in *La Aurora de Matanzas* in 1836. The publication revealed Plácido's new emphasis on Matanzas, where he lived until 1840, and where he developed extensive political networks (Cué, *Plácido: El poeta* 85). Plácido's poetic voice exhorts his brothers to join with him in extolling the Virgin of the Rosary. Naturally, this description of the Virgin Mary as a divine figure of maternal protection exemplifies *marianismo* (the cult of the Virgin Mary) as a path to complete knowledge about the mysteries of salvation through Jesus Christ. But Plácido's sonnet does not represent the Mother of God as the protector of white Catholics, but rather enshrines her as the rightful guardian of her African-descended children. I quote the sonnet in its entirety to make my point.

Load, cofrades, con sonoro canto
A la fúlgida estrella matutina,
Mística rosa, cándida ambarina,
Risa del cielo, del Averno espanto.

Un sol contemplareis bajo su manto
De vivísima lumbre peregrina,
Y un globo inmenso de virtud *divina*
En cada *cuenta* del rosario santo.

Su proteccion es signo de *alegria*:
Ella os afianza en vida la victoria,
Y cuando llegue de la muerte el dia,

Leyendo el Rey de Reyes vuestra historia,
Por el excelso amparo de María
Os abrirá las puertas de la Gloria. (original emphasis; Valdés, *Plácido, Gabriel de la Concepción* 10)

(Laud, my brethren, with a resounding chant
To the bright Morningstar,
Mystical rose, innocent amber color
Laughter of Heaven, Terror of Hell

You will contemplate the sun beneath her garments
Of the most vibrant pilgrim fire
And a globe of *divine* virtue
In each *bead* of her holy rosary

Her protection is a sign of *jubilation*:
She assures you victory in life,
And when the day of death arrives

As the King of Kings reads your past,
By the eminent refuge of Mary
She will open the doors of Glory to you)

Apparently, the *cofrades*—a Spanish term for members of a *cofradía* or *cabildo*—
heed the teaching of the bishop, who decided to "administrarles el sacramento
de la confirmación, y rezar el Santísimo Rosario [ . . . ] delante de una imagen de Nuestra Señora" (administer to them the sacrament of confirmation,
and pray the Holy Rosary [ . . . ] before an image of Our Lady) (del Carmen
Barcia 66–67). The bishop conferred liturgical prominence on the Virgin Mary
and assigned the rosary as the appropriate devotional device for Africans unfamiliar with slave catechism. The African-descended speaker is also a member
of the religious brotherhood, and he seems to embrace priestly advice by cel-
ebrating the Virgin's divine custodianship: "Her protection is a sign of *jubilation*: / She assures you victory in life, / And when the day of death arrives /
[ . . . ] She will open the doors of Glory to you" (Valdés, *Plácido, Gabriel de la
Concepción* 10). Plácido portrays the Virgin Mary as a heavenly mother who
watches over her faithful children on earth and assures their place in eternity
after death. Furthermore, the Virgin is revered for her numerous virtues: "You
will contemplate a sun beneath her garments / Of the most vibrant pilgrim
fire / And a globe of immense *divine* virtue / In each *bead* of the holy rosary"
(Valdés, *Plácido, Gabriel de la Concepción* 10). Mother Mary is a beneficent figure beneath whose garment shines a brilliant pilgrim sun so that in each bead
of the rosary, divine virtue is found. The rosary has a protracted significance in
the history of Catholic devotional prayer.

The medieval Catholic Church offered the rosary to illiterate parishioners as
an object of devotion, reverence, and loyalty; a palpable sign of divine presence.
It is a string of beads to be held in one's hands, caressed, and manipulated; it is a
tangible object of personal devotion. Devotees count the prescribed prayers with
the rosary beads. By some estimates, Europeans have recited the rosary since the
seventh century, but not until the twelfth century did it become a litany (Labarga
153). Catholic scholars debate the origins of the rosary, but there is no doubt
that Spanish armies and missionaries used the cross and the rosary as symbols
of "la verdadera fe" (the true Faith) in sixteenth-century evangelization efforts
(154–155, 158). Dominican priests transplanted *cofradías* devoted to the Our Lady
of the Rosary to Spanish America in the 1500s; and their devotional work was
fruitful (159–160). Africans in Renaissance Spain and colonial Spanish America
were not immune from the Virgin of the Rosary's influence. Sixteenth-century
Cádiz is a case in point, because it boasted a "cofradía . . . 'de los morenos'" in
devotion to Our Lady of the Rosary. The practice flourished so that she became
the city's patron saint (160). When the Dominican order founded their convent
in Lima in 1554, they instructed that black religious brotherhoods throughout
the viceroyalty be placed under the auspices of the Virgin of the Rosary. In 1580
in Quito, Ecuador, religious orders established two different *cofradías* devoted to
the Virgin of the Rosary, one for enslaved Africans and another for indigenous
converts (161). By the time Plácido published his sonnet in 1836, the rosary had

A 1784 image of the Virgin of the Rosary at the Convent of Santa Cruz in Granada, Spain. The caption reads: "The Most Holy Mary is venerated in the Royal Convent of Santa Cruz of the City of Granada."

become a quotidian Catholic prayer across the globe (169), and it enjoyed a particular resonance in Salvador da Bahia, where most black Brazilian confraternities were under her protection (del Carmen Barcia 161).

But Plácido deconstructed the respectable image of *cabildo* members chanting the Virgin's virtues when he depicted the inner workings of African *cabildos* in the fable "Mi no sé que ha richo." "Mi no sé que ha richo" (Me Don't Know What I Said) depicts the *cabildo* in local color as a carefully ordered social space where Africans, referred to with the contemporary descriptor *etíope* (Ethiopian), gather to sing, dance, and play instruments of their own design. As the stanzas below prove, neither Catholic symbols nor liturgical devices have any place in this poem.

En la bulliciosa
Tarde de un domingo,
Cuando los etiopes
Con fláutas y pitos,
Y atambores bailan
Y cantan reunidos:
Un capataz viejo,
Por sabio tenido,
(Siguiendo la moda
Que tanto ha cundido
De fingirse doctos
Hasta los borricos.)

—<<¡Chilencho, parente!>>
En alta voz dijo.

[ . . . ]

Su discurso hizo.

Mujió como toro,
Silbó como grillo,
Cantó como gallo,
Brincó como chivo. (Valdés, *Plácido, Gabriel de la Concepción* 405–406)

(On a noisy
Sunday afternoon
When the Ethiopians
With flutes and whistles
And drums break into dance

And sing in unison:
An old *cabildo* leader,
Taken for a wise man
(In the fashion that has spread
Of feigning erudition
Even asinine persons)

—<<Chilencho, partner!>>
Said he in a loud voice.

[ ... ]

He pronounced his discourse.

He lowed like a bull,
Whistled about like a cricket,
Crowed like a rooster,
Jumped up and down like a goat.)

Presumably, the poem is a derisive depiction of the *cabildo*, because the speaker characterizes the elder's speech as the inarticulate grunts of an animal. When asked by the membership what he has said, the *cabildo* leader replies, "Mi no sé que ha richo" onomatopoeic Cuban Spanish for "Me don't know what I said" (Valdés, *Plácido, Gabriel de la Concepción* 406). Onomatopoeia signals that the *cabildo* leader—also known as a *capataz*—spoke *bozal*, not standard Spanish. But the racialized portrayal of an African character that communicates with animal grunts, rather than in Spanish, is actually directed at Plácido's white contemporaries.[29] The last two stanzas indicate as much: "¡Cuántos escritores / De soberbia henchidos, / Publican discursos, / Al mar parecidos / En que no conocen / Ni fin ni principio! / Y si les preguntan / Su fiel contenido, / Dirán como el negro: / 'Yo no sé que he dicho'" (How many writers / Overblown with arrogance, / Publish articles, / Which like the ocean / They know / Neither beginning nor end! / And if you were to ask them / Their true content / Like the black man they would say: / 'I don't know what I've said') (Valdés, *Plácido, Gabriel de la Concepción* 406). The fable appeared to mock Africans, but Plácido's true objects of derision were white writers who published nonsense rather than true knowledge. The fable compared them to "el negro," whom slave society equated with intellectual deficiency and moral subpersonhood.

But there is more to this fable than a critique of apocryphal white erudition. Plácido's portrayal of song, dance, and chanting within the *cabildo* is a historically accurate representation of African-inspired practices that preserved ancestral memory among Africans. Sunday performances occurred within the private space of the *cabildo*, and only members were privy to their meaning. Del Carmen Barcia writes "La cultura de los africanos se transmitía de forma oral, [ . . . ] un elemento vital en esa narración era la mímica a través de la cual imitaban los movimientos y los voces de los animales" (African culture was transmitted orally, [ . . . ] one vital element of these narratives was the mimicry of animal movements and voices) (176). "Mi no sé que ha richo" unearths African oral traditions within the *cabildo* and bears witness to Plácido's status as a cultural insider. This fable alludes to African-inspired religious performativity—especially the consciousness-altering power of African drumming—that "A la Virgen del Rosario" so carefully conceals. But "A la Virgen del Rosario" also hid how Plácido negotiated his cultural politics with the Matanzas priesthood. The *sonoro canto* (resounding chants) of "A la Virgen del Rosario" devolved into what white onlookers considered the *cantos salvajes* (savage chants) (Ortiz, *Los Cabildos* 36–37) of the *cabildos'* Day of Kings procession.

Plácido's representation of the Matanzas *cabildo* is consistent with a broader narrative strategy that conferred symbolic importance upon the region, which housed a burgeoning free black and mulatto elite. Matanzas, of course, is where Father Manuel Francisco García served as parish priest and as the poet's benefactor. "A la Virgen de Rosario" is a striking representation of how Matanzas *cabildos* negotiated with two interlocutors at once: the African-descended community and the Catholic priesthood. With regard to the *cabildos'* relationship with the Matanzas authorities, del Carmen Barcia reveals there was greater leniency in the provinces than in Havana, where processions were confined to certain festival days (74). African *cabildos* in Matanzas maintained a centuries-long tradition of transculturated religious devotion to their patroness, the Virgin of the Rosary, with one stipulation: the governor of Matanzas required the parish priest to give his consent (del Carmen Barcia 73–74). Plácido was engaged in a complex game of political intrigue: he could join in *cabildo* celebrations without relinquishing his respectable Catholic image. In fact, Plácido's statement to the military commission corroborates his involvement in *cabildo* festivities in Matanzas. Plácido wrote: "En este estado de cosas llegaron las máscaras del año de cuarenta y uno, y deseoso de verlas en MATANZAS, olvidé a DELMONTE Y SUS DEMENCIAS, hasta Abril o Mayo de cuarenta y dos . . ." (In this state of affairs the Masquerades of [eighteen] forty-one arrived, and wanting to see them in MATANZAS, I forgot DELMONTE AND HIS MADNESS, until April or May of [eighteen] forty-two . . . ) (Cué, *Plácido: El poeta* 299). Plácido wrote this account to the military tribunal to distance himself from del Monte, whom the government also suspected of conspiracy in 1844. In so doing, he acknowledged that the carnival masquerades that *cabildos* organized were part and parcel of his religio-cultural experience. Plácido divulged the hidden transcript of the African *cabildo*, a religious transcript that he was intimately familiar with and sought to mobilize for political reasons.

Plácido's fable "Mi no sé que ha richo" originally appeared in *La Aurora de Matanzas*, a Matanzas newspaper. Courtesy of Harvard University.

The Virgin of the Rosary as the patron saint of an African *cabildo* is a thematic departure from Plácido's poems about the Passion of the Christ, because it presents a path to the divine that has been gendered female. According to the speaker, devotion to Mother Mary, not Jesus Christ, will open the doors of glory. The divine feminine as a path to God is significant to my reading, because "A la Virgen de Rosario" and "El diablito" epitomize a tenet of Catholicism and Yoruba-inspired spirituality: the power of spiritual intermediaries to convey messages to God and act on behalf of the faithful (Sandoval 39). Certain words in "A la Virgen de Rosario" invite the reader to ponder the double entendre beneath the aesthetic surface: *cofrades*, *victoria*, *ambarina*, and the Virgen del Rosario herself. The poem promises the *cofrades*—which, in the Matanzas context, are black brethren—victory in life and death. The idea that Our Lady of the Rosary will "open the doors of Glory to you" (Valdés, *Plácido, Gabriel de la Concepción* 10) is a reference to the redemption from sin, which permits Catholics to enter into heaven on Judgment Day. As the 1796 slave catechism points out, "the Virgin looks upon us with a good visage, and speaks to God on our behalf. She is our patroness, she asks God to forgive our sins" (Barreras 141). But there is another type of *victoria* that the poem alludes to; the patroness offers her African children victory during their arduous lives. The poem alludes to another meaning of *victoria* that is inconsistent with the catechist teaching about the Virgin but reminiscent of the Yoruba *orisha* Dadá, with whom Africans transculturated the Virgin of the Rosary. The African brotherhood does not pursue victory over sin;

rather, the brethren battle to triumph over slavery that binds some of its members. I read this poem in praise of the Virgin Mary through an African Cuban cultural lens as an ode to the *orisha* known as Dadá.

Plácido channeled the reader's gaze in disparate but equally plausible directions. The poetic persona disrupts Cuban racial politics, because *pardos* and *morenos* (free mulattoes and free blacks) typically preferred membership in religious brotherhoods sanctioned by the Catholic Church known as *cofradías*, not in *cabildos* that boasted an African-born membership of enslaved and free men and women (del Carmen Barcia 50).[30] Similarly, Plácido portrayed the Virgin Mary with an "amber color" (Valdés, *Plácido, Gabriel de la Concepción* 10), that is, the yellowish to brownish color of fossil resin; in this poem the Virgin is a brown-skinned patroness. This is consistent with sacred representations throughout colonial Spanish America, where the Virgin Mary was depicted as a *mestiza* or even a black woman (Brewer-García 111, 122). In the context of this poem (and in his satires), Plácido disavows light-skinned privilege, for he is a mulatto member of an African cabildo that transculturated the image of the Virgin of the Rosary with Yoruba-inspired understandings of the divine spirit Dadá.

African-inspired spirituality is not premised on the Catholic concept of religious conversion where the soul is redeemed from damnation; rather, African traditions initiate persons into complex familial systems composed of human as well as spiritual constituents (Dodson 51, 73–74). In Yoruba cosmology Dadá is the divine protector of children and the royal sister of the warrior spirit, Changó.[31] Plácido portrayed Africans in the Matanzas *cabildo* as the children of Changó's royal sister, Dadá. In Yoruba-inspired religion, Dadá is bejeweled, with a cowrie-encrusted crown and plaited African hair, illustrative of her great wealth and spiritual stature (D. Brown, *Santería* 189-191, 194). Yoruba-inspired oral tradition describes this divine female spirit in nature metaphors: she lives by the sacred ceiba tree and is the proprietor of vegetables (Cros Sandoval 301). In their respective traditions, the Virgin of the Rosary and Dadá are recognized for their female attributes; they are maternal figures that watch over and protect their children. We may read Dadá as the comforting matriarch that bestows economic prosperity upon the brotherhood. While this is certainly a plausible reading, I think the notion of "victory" embeds an insurgent subtext into an otherwise typical Cuban sonnet, because Changó is a chief warrior spirit in the Yoruba pantheon.

The Virgin of the Rosary is subterfuge for Dadá, whose children are not accustomed to peace, but rather warfare. The silences and double meaning destabilize the elite rationale for writing a Petrarchan sonnet, which white literati endorsed as the pinnacle of lyrical expression. "A la Virgen de Rosario" mirrors transculturative processes at work in Cuban religion in the early nineteenth century; this is a transculturated poem because African-inspired ritual, not Catholic doctrine, brings order to the space. The representation of Our Lady of the Rosary does not constitute cultural mimicry, because the Virgin Mary as Dadá changes the purpose for the gathering, and she creates space for alternative epistemological propositions. Plácido's dismissal of what Homi Bhabha has termed "colonial mimicry" (86), is evidenced in his representation of the *cabildo* not only as a progenitor of cultural practice but also as a righteous avenger of retributive justice.

"El diablito" is a fable wherein the *cabildo* emerges as the focal point of insurgent activity in Plácido's blueprint for revolution. The poem depicts the Day of Kings festivities from divergent points of view: to white onlookers, carnival is drunken revelry, but for blacks, it is cultural marronage and embodies hidden meanings. In the vein of "Fantasmas, duendes y brujas," "La figura de un alma," and "El egoísta," this poem inverts the center/periphery dichotomy because the speaker is a culturally adept observer of El Día de Reyes (Epiphany) procession. The masquerader performs as a member of his *cabildo*, hence linking festival performance with African-inspired spirituality, which, in this particular case, is not coded in ostensibly Catholic rituals and symbols. As Brown has also noted, carnival was "a potentially dangerous moment," a liminal space for the inscription of political messages (D. Brown, *Santería* 39). What is more, African *cabildos* in Matanzas were the organizational nuclei of the 1844 plantation uprisings known as La Conspiración de la Escalera (Brown 38), where blacks and mulattoes sought to abolish slavery, depose the colonial regime, and institute a government of African descendants on the island (Paquette 256, 263–264). I maintain that Plácido resignified the masquerader so that the *little devil*—a much-maligned character—prophesies retributions to befall slave society. But, as in his other fables, Plácido introduced the Africanesque masquerader through two different cultural lenses: one black and African, and the other white and Catholic.

> Érase una claraboya
> Donde estaban embutidos
> Con primoso cuidado
> Varios transparentes vidrios,
>
> Simétricamente puestos,
> Y de colores distintos:
> Verdes, rojos, negros, blancos,
> Cenicientos y amarillos.
>
> Desde allí varios curiosos,
> Cada cual por su cuadrillo,
> Miraba los transeuntes
> Que asomaban al camino;

Pero como cada uno
Tuviese los ojos fijos,
Y por prismas diferentes
Eran los objetos vistos;

Ninguno, por todos era
Mirado en igual sentido,
Y así, la desigualdad
Era el verdadero tipo (Valdés, *Plácido, Gabriel de la Concepción* 370)

(There was a window in the ceiling
Where different pieces of transparent glass
Were inserted
And symmetrically placed,
With exquisite care,[32]

And of distinctive colors:
Green, red, black, white
Gray and yellow.

Various onlookers,
Each from his own angle,
Gazed at the passerbys
That emerged onto the road;

But as each one
With their eyes fixed,
And through different prisms
Viewed the objects

Not one
Was observed the same by all,
And so, inequality
Was the true type.)

The word *claraboya* in the first stanza, which translates to "skylight" or "window in the ceiling," sets the stage for a discussion about disparate religious perspectives regarding Day of Kings processions. The *claraboya* does not function as a classically colorless window, because it has been fashioned "of distinctive colors" (Valdés, *Plácido, Gabriel de la Concepción* 370). Plácido used the multi-hued stained-glass window as a symbol of the Christian cathedral and as a way to introduce the prism as a rhetorical device. In the fourth and fifth stanzas,

Plácido wrote: "But as each one / With their eyes fixed, / And through different prisms / Viewed the objects / Not one / was observed the same by all, / And so inequality / Was the true type" (Valdés, *Plácido, Gabriel de la Concepción* 370). *Desigualdad* or "inequality," is a play on words about the myriad ways readers might interpret the symbolism, music, dramaturgy, and dance of the carnival event. But this *inequality* also speaks to the racial disparities within slave society that informed disparate ways of viewing African-inspired spiritual traditions. In contradistinction to the *negra ladina* from the fable "La figura de un alma" who correctly interprets spiritual phenomena, carnival spectators in "El diablito" distort and obfuscate the festival masquerader as a maleficent entity known as the Devil within the Judeo-Christian worldview. Fernando Ortiz provides insight into this misnaming; he explains that white Catholics thought that "the motley disguises, leaps and cabrioles [and] horns" of African masquerades simulated representations of the devil from the Corpus Christi procession in Cuba (Ortiz qtd. in Brown 48). This is certainly true, but the onlooker's misrecognition had other dimensions.

As far back as the fourth century, some Catholic theologians assigned blackness a negative aesthetic value and associated blackness with evil, with a "lower hemisphere" (Branche, *Colonialism and Race* 43). The notion that phenotypical blackness was a metaphysical sign of evil did not dissipate in Renaissance Europe; on the contrary, it flourished in Spanish poetry and theater, reaching new levels of artistry and rhetorical sophistication (Branche, *Colonialism and Race* 67). The Spanish conceived of the Devil as a black man, and they disguised themselves as blacks to represent Satan (Fra-Molinero, "Los negros como figura" 11). The rhetorical relationship between blackness and evil continued to thrive in Spanish Catholic theology in the "New World." Jesuit priest Alonso de Sandoval—known for proselytizing Africans in seventeenth-century Cartagena de las Indias—claimed that he was saving them from the power of the Devil (Olsen, *Slavery* 19). The 1796 Cuban slave catechism, examined previously, characterized the Devil as one of "nuestros enemigos" (our enemies); and the other foes were "gente mala y nuestro propio cuerpo" (evil people and our own bodies) (Barreras 149). Catechists taught that the Devil was the *slave's* nemesis and that the slave master was a legitimate representative of papal authority (Barreras 85–86). Africans disagreed. The Devil, as such, did not exist in African cosmologies. In Yoruba cosmology, evil emanates from several cosmic forces, amounting to what Kola Abimbola has termed a "poly-demonic conception of evil" (Abimbola qtd. in Ogungbemi 81–82). Contemporary white Cuban descriptions of Africanesque masquerades provide historical evidence of their theological confusion.

Ramón Meza described January 6 processions meticulously through a prism that differed significantly from Plácido's (Ortiz, *Los cabildos y la fiesta* 26–27):

Desde los primeros albores del día, oíase por todas partes el monótono ritmo
de aquellos grandes tambores, [ . . . ] Los criados abandonaban las casas muy de
la mañana; y de las fincas cercanas a la población acudían las dotaciones: [ . . . ]

En el centro del corro bailaban dos o tres parejas, haciendo las más extravagan-
tes contorsiones, dando saltos, volteos y pasos, a compás del agitado ritmo de
los tambores. La agitación y la alegría rayaban en frenesí.

[ . . . ]

A las doce del día la diversión llegaba a su apogeo. En las calles de Mercaderes,
Obispo y O'Reilly era una procesión no interrumpida de diablitos. [ . . . ] los
marineros de todas las naciones que bajaban en grupo para presenciar medio
azorados aquella exótica fiesta (26, 27).

(From early dawn, you could hear the monotonous rhythm of those large
drums all over the place, [ . . . ] The slaves abandoned their homes very early in
the morning; and the groups of black slaves left the plantations to come: [ . . . ]

In the middle of the chorus two or three couples danced, making the most
extravagant contortions, leaping, and doing turns and steps to the beat of the
frantic rhythm of the drums. Agitation and joy broke out in frenzy.

At midday, the diversion came to a peak. On Mercaderes, Obispo and O'Reilly
Streets there was an uninterrupted procession of little devils. [ . . . ] sailors from
every nation came down the street in one group to see that exotic revelry)

Meza situates the festival in exotic space as a frenetic and entertaining African
diversion on Cuban soil involving elaborate costume, drums, dancing, and acro-
batic movements. The dominant gaze discards the possibility that the festival performance might represent sacred ritual to members of the *cabildos* involved.[33]
In this portrayal, African-inspired masqueraders are wildly superstitious individuals akin to Father Félix Varela's notion that the *supersticioso* is beneath reason and worthy of Christian contempt (*Cartas* 86). But Meza's interpretation
is white noise, indiscriminately speaking of "diablitos" and distracting from
African-inspired epistemological claims so that the masker is rendered unintel-
ligible. There is no reference to the particulars of costume, dance, or percussion
performance. As Pratt says, the colonized Other is depicted as a homogenized
"*they*" suspended in a timeless present tense with no future and no reputable
past (63, 64). On this point, Walker explains that El Día de Reyes masqueraders were arbitrarily referred to as "diablitos," and, for this reason, he complicates

nineteenth-century writings about January 6 festivals that allude to *little devils*, given that they may refer to any number of African Cuban masqueraders (49–50).

In the white Cuban imaginary, El Día de Reyes festival was a spirited, dance-obsessed, and drunken debauchery, much like Bishop Morell de Santa Cruz had described African-inspired processions less than a century earlier. As Plácido's poem suggests this popular perception neglected the core meanings that the *cabildo* membership constructed around the performance. El Día de Reyes was not a creative anomaly but one of many diasporic performative traditions. African-descended public performance traditions thrived throughout the Americas during the slave period; hailing from New England to New Orleans, appearing in the Anglophone Caribbean as Jonkunnu, in Venezuela as Devil Dance and in Brazil as Maracatu (Walker 3–4). To demonstrate the inherent double meaning of carnival, Walker cites a formerly enslaved North Carolina minister who said African descendants "used to have to employ our dark symbols and obscure figures to cover up our real meaning" (17). The African-American Protestant minister's commentary on "dark symbols" demonstrates that that carnival performed an African-inspired epistemological orientation that was hidden from public view. Unfamiliar observers often rendered such performances entertaining spectacles and nineteenth-century Cuban descriptions were no exception.

Plácido deconstructed the hegemonic notion of the masquerade. He decentered the public gaze in order to elucidate the performer's epistemological claims and, most importantly, to underscore the cultural agency of African *cabildos* on El Día de Reyes.

> Mas como hay en todas cosas
> Accidentes imprevistos,
> Sucedió ser aquel dia
> *El seis de Enero*, (está dicho).

> Y un inesperado objeto,
> A ponerles la ley vino:
> Era un *diablito* bailando
> Al frente de su cabildo.

> Como á la vez cien colores
> Brillaban en su vestido,
> Mirado en todos los cuadros
> Era el personaje mismo.

> Uno de los observantes
> Más que todos reflexivo:

—-"¡Ved ahí lo que es el mundo! . . ."
(A sus compañeros dijo).

Siempre es el mismo sujeto
El que hace á todos partidos;
Él baila todos los años
Y es siempre el mismo *diablito*. (original emphasis; Valdés, *Plácido, Gabriel de
    la Concepción* 371)

(Nevertheless, there are always
Unforeseen events,
And that day it happened to be
The sixth of January, (or so it's said).

An unforeseen object,
Came to impose the law upon them:
It was a little devil dancing
In front of his *cabildo*.

All at once one hundred colors
On his outfit shone,
Seen in the checkered pattern
It was the character himself.

One of the onlookers
More contemplative than the others:
—"Look at what the world has become!"
(He said to his companions).

It's always the same subject
He who is always present;
He dances every year
And it's always the same *little devil*.)

I believe *el diablito* may have been the ideal symbol of antislavery insurgency,
because it gave voice to an political project that merged racial egalitarianism with
knowledge of African-inspired ritual. Carnival represents more than the inversion of social structures; it joins play with ritual, mockery with solemnity, and
within its liminal space there is a powerful realm of spiritual possibility. The last
five stanzas specify when the celebration takes place, directly link the masquerader's performance to the *cabildo*, and explain the function of the performance.
Although the public misconstrues the dance, the masker parades before his

*cabildo* on January 6 to fulfill a specific function: "A ponerles la ley vino" (He has come to impose the law upon them) (Valdés, *Plácido, Gabriel de la Concepción* 371). Plácido's transculturated text toys with the subject/object dichotomy so that the "inesperado objeto" (unforeseen object) imposes the law of retribution. On the surface the linguistic construction is contradictory, because the object of public scorn acts on behalf of the African *cabildo* as a subject that unleashes retribution from the otherworld on an unsuspecting Cuban public.[34]

Plácido's masquerader is an African-descended male subject, mischievous yet serious, provocative but condemnatory. Carnivalesque laughter is rooted in a fear and anxiety of the unknown: "Burlábanse á la vez todos / del caminante sencillo; / (Porque entre muchos es fácil / Burlar á un solo individuo)" (At the same time everyone mocked / The lone traveler / (Because it is easy for many to laugh at an individual) (Valdés, *Plácido, Gabriel de la Concepción* 370, 371). The masquerader mocks unsuspecting bystanders that derisively chuckle caught unawares that he has come to impose the law upon them. The masquerader's authority to invert the social order is not derived from the colonial regime but exists in spite of it. In fact, his source of power is otherworldly, because it originates with the African ancestors that the colony exploited to build its economic power. Again, Walker explains that African-descended populations in Havana would have conceived of festival maskers as a means of reconnection with Africa. Masquerades in West African and West-Central African societies were seen as the embodiment of ancestral spirits who visit the temporal world to offer advice and counsel to the living. Among these is the Egungun of Yoruba-speaking ethnicities and the Efik and Ejagham leopard dancers from the Cross River region of Nigeria and Cameroon. Yoruba-speaking ethnicities from southwest Nigeria and those from the Old Calabar Cross River region left an indelible mark on nineteenth-century African Cuban spirituality. Daniel Walker suggests that not every carnival masker can be traced to his specific African origin (50). But, I believe that Africans and their descendants comprehended the dancing masquerades in Cuba as a reunion with the continent of their forebears. Somewhat akin to Manzano's metamorphosed winged creature, the dance of Plácido's carnival masquerade looks back and gestures, disrupting colonial temporality in order to suture the fragmented voices of the African ancestral subject.

Whereas some contemporary sources described African-inspired masquerades arbitrarily as "little devils" (Walker 49–50), African *cabildos* differentiated their performances from one another by adopting distinct sartorial profiles. David Brown explains the *cabildos'* boundary-marking practices in some detail:

> The Lucumíes, Congos, Ararás, Mandingas, and Carabalíes were immediately dinstingushable by their clothing and markings. For example, the Ararás were known for their remarkable facial cicatrizations and necklaces of shells and animal teeth; the Mandingas stood out for their sartorial luxury: wide silk pants,

Victor Landaluze's painting of the African Cuban masquerade most closely resembles the Abakuá society, an all-male initiation society.

short jackets, and turbans, all bordered with *marabout* (feather boa). *Ñáñigos* (Carabalí-derived Abakuá groups) were known for their peculiar plumed wooden emblems (madero emplumado). Most remarkable were the hooded *íremes*, who stalked, kneeled, and crawled in the angular feline movements of the Abakuá society's "leopard spirits." (Brown, *Santería* 49–50)

Plácido's carnivalesque subject does not display scarification or necklaces of animal teeth, nor is he bejeweled in silk pants and turbans. Bearing these distinctive ethnic descriptions in mind, Plácido's masquerade is most reminiscent of the Abakuá *íreme*, because both subjects boast a multihued custome with a checkered pattern. Plácido portrayed a carnival subject that, "Como a la vez cien colores / Brillaban en su vestido, / Mirado en todos cuadros" (Valdés, *Plácido, Gabriel de la Concepción* 371) (All at once one hundred colors / On his outfit shone, / Seen in the checkered pattern." The verse "Mirado en todos cuadros" is an artful pun, because the Spanish word *cuadros* can be rendered "portraits," as in the depiction of images, or "checkered pattern" as in "a cuadros." Both plausible translations demonstrate how the nuances within "El Diablito" shape meaning in divergent ways for different interlocutors. It is worth noting that the checkered pattern of Plácido's festival masquerade is reminiscent of Abakuá's affinity for leopard symbolism.

David Brown explains that masqueraders of the Old-Calabar Abakuá society were known as *íremes*. As Abakuá adept Jesús Nasakó explains, the *íreme* masqueraders were "spirit 'messengers'" and "manifested, materialized, represented spirit" (*Light Inside* 115). These material envoys of the otherworld embodied ancestral spirits and "mythological characters" (Brown, *Light Inside* 116–117). *Íreme*, the leader of *cabildo* processions, conducted and executed purifications to send away evil influences that inhabited the physical world (Brown, *Light Inside* 155). *Íreme* exercised a multi-faceted role: "*íreme* is a transformational figure between domains: the human, the natural, and the otherworldly" (120). Costume was integral to *íreme* performance and was active in the process of meaning making. The masquerader's costume was typically colorful, highly textured, and made of various materials to resemble the leopard, which is emblematic of the virility and deftness in Abakuá masculinity, a black fraternal society whose epistemological foundations are grounded in the Old Calabar Cross River region covering modern Nigeria and Cameroon (*Light Inside* 119).

But Matanzas, not Havana, was the cultural and intellectual epicenter of Plácido's political activities. And the Abakuá male-initiation society did not appear in Matanzas until the 1860s, and then only with the support of Havana lodges (I. Miller 99, 101). Nevertheless, we cannot rule out an Abakuá inspiration for Plácido's masquerade. The African Cuban ethnic group known as *carabalí*—whose cultural foundations lie in the Cross River region—had already established their first *cabildo* in Matanzas by 1816 (I. Miller 99–100). And, the first Abakuá lodges were founded outside Havana in 1836; the poet traveled frequently between Havana and Matanzas. Moreover, the first Abakuá *íremes* also emerged in 1836 (D. Brown, *Santería* 50), so their advent on the African Cuban cultural scene was contemporaneous with Plácido's writing of this poem. By the 1850s the *carabalí* had become the largest reported African community in the city of Matanzas and had established nine *cabildos*. Ivor Miller writes that the Cabildo Carabalí Bríkamo Niño Jesús contributed to the founding of the first Abakuá lodge in Matanzas in 1862 (Miller 99–100). Thus, religio-cultural paradigms from the Cross River region were already present to some degree in Matanzas prior to 1862. So, it is not unreasonable to conclude that Plácido's carnivalesque subject in "El diablito" emulated the Abakuá *íreme* of Old-Calabar origins.

Plácido's masked *cabildo* dancer is consistent with the West-African masquerade traditions. And Plácido's masquerade is thematically consistent with his indigenist poetry; as "materialized, represented spirit," *íreme* is active within this larger notion of a geography of spirit engagement where he is charged with the purification—the cleansing, if you will—of the contaminated landscape of Cuban slave society. The *íreme* character is an embodied African ances-tor spirit that channels "el aliento de Hatuey" (the breath of Hatuey), which Plácido evoked in a poem honoring white Cuban insurgent General Andrés de la Flor. Plácido manifested the unmitigated power of the utterance "the breath of Hatuey" (Cué, *Plácido:Eel poeta* 290) in the poems "El diablito" and "A El Yumurí," because he had sworn fealty to Hatuey, revered his sacred remains, and invoked a political pact based on Haitian antislavery ideology.

The symbolic pattern in Plácido's religious verse bears a striking resemblance to his conspiratorial activities, and it provides heretofore unknown insight into the religious context in which he forged the conspiracy. Scholars have well doc-umented Plácido's participation in the conspiracy, but until now they had disre-garded the African-inspired religious character of his revolutionary blueprint. Accounts written by Plácido's contemporaries expose the quasi-religious char-acter of his conspiratorial activity. Manuel Federico D'Aure attested to Plácido's frequent visits to the homes of the African-descended elite in Matanzas in the 1840s. D'Aure was a Cuban of Haitian (and presumably French) descent whose family took up residence in Pueblo Nuevo, a free black neighborhood in Matanzas in 1839; he made Plácido's acquaintance that same year, around age twelve. I have consulted D'Aure's letter at Harvard University and would like to draw attention to what it advises about Plácido's spiritual practices. Below, I cite two passages of the letter.

Vicitaba Placido mi casa cuando á ella venian á parar sus amigos Luis Gigaut de la Habana, Ramón Ponce, que despúes me enseñó mi oficio de albañileria, [ . . . ]

Recuerdo que plácido siempre venia á la casa despedise cuando se iba á la Habana á ver a su madre en los dias de su santo y su cumpleaño, [ . . . ]

Siempre que iba desde Matánzas á Pueblo Nuevo, visitaba nuestra casa y en los dias de su Santo Siempre le dedicaba un Soneto, á mi madre que todo que lo leia selebraban. [35]

(Plácido would visit my house when his friends stopped by; Luis Gigaut from Havana, Ramón Ponce who later trained me in my trade of bricklaying [ . . . ]
I remember Plácido would always come to my house to say goodbye when he went to Havana to see his mother on her saint's feast day and on her birthday [ . . . ]

When he came to Pueblo Nuevo in Matanzas, he always visited our home and on his saint's feast days he always dedicated a sonnet to my mother so that everyone that heard it would celebrate)

D'Aure's letter is short on details regarding the nature of Plácido's relationship to individuals that the Spanish government suspected of conspiratorial activity. Because D'Aure was an adolescent in 1839, he did not form part of Plácido's inner sanctum, nor was he privy to his political strategies. Despite the letter's many silences, it does corroborate my analysis: Matanzas was the focal point of Plácido's personal religious devotion, and perhaps more significantly, there was a religious character to the African-descended social network he maintained.

D'Aure become acquainted with Plácido in 1839 and witnessed him partake in *fiestas de santos* (saints' feast days) at the family home. Although Plácido returned to Havana to celebrate his mother's birthday and her saint's day, he expressed reverence for his *santo* in Manuel D'Aure's home in Matanzas. Again, the choice of location was not fortuitous. Such celebrations in honor of the saints were reminiscent of the *cabildo*, because mulattoes performed in private space, free of the dominant gaze. Plácido's tendency to resignify ostensibly Catholic rituals should be brought to bear to perform a counterhegemonic reading of private encounters among African descendants. Esteban Montejo's testimonial narrative sheds light upon the African-inspired conception of the *fiestas de santos*.

Montejo's account is apropos to my analysis of euphemism and subterfuge in Plácido's writing because he describes nineteenth-century celebrations of the saints from an African-descended Cuban perspective.

> Ellos decían san Juan, pero era *Oggún*. Oggún es el dios de la guerra. En esos años era el más conocido en la zona. [ . . . ]

> A las fiestas de santo había que ir con mucha seriedad. Si uno no creía mucho, tenía que disimular. A los negros no les gustaban los intrusos. Nunca les han gustado. Por eso yo iba de lo más tranquilo, oía el tambor; eso sí, miraba a los negros y después comía (Barnet, *Biografía* 83).

> (They said San Juan, but it was Oggún. Oggún is the god of war. In those years he was best known in the area. [ . . . ]

> You had to be very respectful when you went to the saint's fiesta. If you didn't believe, you had to hide it. Blacks don't like intruders. They have never liked them. That's why I went real quiet. I listened to the drums. I watched the blacks and I ate something) (Barnet, *Biography* 76).[36]

Montejo's autoethnographic account corroborates the transculturation of Yoruba divine spirits with Catholic saints, and it portrays African drumming and feasting as liturgical practices. Montejo reiterates that practitioners excluded intruders; similarly, Plácido's cohort of coreligionsists did the same. Lydia Cabrera's account is comparable to Montejo's portrayal. Cabrera explained that on saints' feasts days where "En las fiestas lucumís, en los toques de tambor en acción de gracias con que se honra y se divierte a los orishas" (in the Lucumí festivities, during the drumming parties to give thanks, they honor and amuse the orishas) in a manner that "la posesión es sugerida por los tambores y la maracas, los cantos y los bailes" (possession is induced by drums, and maracas, chants and dances) (El monte 33). D'Aure provides no account of Plácido's ritual activities, thus creating a silence within the cultural archive. But Haitian-born conspirator Luis Gigaut frequented D'Aure's home to visit Plácido, so we might infer that their esoteric gatherings held political and spiritual significance. Plácido's devotion to the saints cannot be disregarded because he practiced *his* saint's day rituals behind closed doors in communion with other African descendants that shared a similar antislavery worldview. Moreover, Plácido confessed to the military commission that his relationships with free *pardo* and black communities in Matanzas involved his attendance at saints' feast day festivities on three separate occasions (Cué, Plácido: El poeta 197, 199–200). Likewise, my analyses bear out that while Manzano's devotion to the saints enabled his escape from the plantation, Plácido's devotion was an instrument of conspiracy and collusion.

Regarding cultural space, Walker points out that "African-descended populations redefined space in a manner that countered the debilitating effects of the slave regime's space-centered social control initiatives" (19). In "El diablito," Epiphany is transformed into a commemoration of African-inspired spirituality, the Christ child is decentered (in fact, Jesus Christ is not mentioned at all), and the dancing masquerader becomes the focal point of public observance. Therefore, the poem deconstructs the official purpose of the celebration, transculturating carnival to meet the objectives of the African-descended subject. Although the festival masquerader is a lone traveler, his dance is not an act of individual volition, since it represents "spirit messengers"—either of the dead or of ancestors long gone—and emanates from a collectivized social space. The subtext of Plácido's religious poetry suggests that the sacred code of life is linked to the conduct of prospective insurgents. I submit that *the sacred code of life* was a political code of conduct informed by the esoteric knowledge of the *cabildo*, encoded in subtexts, and performed in a quotidian manner. Plácido's *ireme* character professes this sacred code and vows to exact revenge against the Spanish colony. The gyrating dance movements, mocking gestures, and condemnatory stance epitomize the collective will of indigenous and African ancestors. In "El diablito" pageantry depicts an absolute inversion of the social order, since Africans invoke retributive justice and impose the law on the very society that has enslaved them.

The depiction of the festival masquerader as an agent of retributive justice mirrors the allegations brought against Plácido in the 1844 proceedings. Alleged co-conspirators Lorenzo Caballero, Pascual Hernández, and Generí Chávez testified that the poet attended a Día de Reyes celebration in the Matanzas home of Santiago Álvarez. According to their testimony, Plácido met with other persons of African descent to devise an island-wide conspiracy against the whites, after sharing a meal with his host (Cué, "Plácido y la conspiración" 177). Congregating on a religious holiday to conspire against the plantation slave economy demonstrates that Plácido and other conspirators deconstructed and resignified Christian festivals so that such holy days served the sacred purposes of an antislavery worldview. Moreover, at the Cuban National Archive, I uncovered a little-known government report about the 1844 movement that maintains that El Día de Reyes held tremendous symbolic importance for black and mulatto conspirators, who had designated said day to commemorate their triumph over Spain at the Morro Fortress in Havana.[37]

The accusations I have discussed here—regarding the poems "La profecía de Cuba a España," "El juramento," and "El diablito"—call into question the religious identity of Gabriel de la Concepción Valdés. Plácido's religious-themed poems and Catholic self-portrait in the deathbed letter to his wife, María Gila Morales, are far from conclusive, because—like most free people of color in the early 1800s—he had more than sufficient reason to claim allegiance to the Catholic Church. As I demonstrated previously, Plácido wrote some of his Catholic poems while in prison, perhaps to dissuade his accusers of his association with subversive elements within Cuban society. Admitting that he was knowledgeable about African-inspired spirituality would have imperiled any number of important social ties he had with the white elite and possibly done away with the publication of his poetry altogether. Naturally, this need to safeguard his reputation was exacerbated after his arrest in 1844.

In "Un improvisador cubano: El poeta Plácido y el juicio de Menéndez y Pelayo," Manuel Sanguily further problematizes Plácido's religious identity.

Y en la <<Plegaria>> ¿es acaso natural que invocando a Dios, le llamara: <<Rey de los Reyes, Dios *de mis abuelos?*>>

¿Parece por ventura procedente que Plácido recordara como uno y el mismo al Dios de sus abuelos maternos, que era el Dios de los cristianos, y al Dios de sus abuelos paternos, que debió ser un *fetiche*? (original emphasis; Sanguily 172)

(And in la <<Plegaria>> is it perhaps natural that when invoking God, he would call him: <<King of Kings, God *of my grandparents?*>>

Does it perhaps seem natural that Plácido would remember as one and the same the God of his maternal grandparents, the Christian God, and the God of his paternal grandparents, which must have been a *fetish*?)

Sanguily questioned Plácido's authorship of the well-known and much studied "Plegaria a Dios," which is thought to be one of the final poems the poet wrote before his execution. Sanguily supported his argument by reminding his readership that Plácido's cultural and religious identity was drawn from two diametrically opposed sources: Spanish Catholicism and African-inspired spirituality. This is an accurate statement. However, Sanguily was mistaken to think that Plácido would not refer to the Christian God as *el Rey de los Reyes*, since he did so in two 1843 poems, "A la Resurrección" and "A la muerte de Cristo."

Plácido traversed a colonial world defined by religious multiplicity but legally confined to Catholic liturgical norms and governed by the aesthetic idiom of Spanish literature. He was baptized as an infant and married in the Church, and he relished the privileges that his close relationship to clergymen permitted. But Plácido's antislavery philosophy rejected the Catholic concept of redemption. Unlike other poets of either African or European descent, Plácido portrayed African-inspired spirituality in poems that problematize the discourse on religion, advise an alternative path to the spiritual realm, and, on occasion, subvert the political authority of the colony. This is no small matter, since his thematic choices provided colonial authorities with reason to suspect his involvement in anticolonial activities that eventually led to his execution in 1844. Plácido used Catholicism, Romanticism, and Neoclassicism as a symbolic language for the representation of an African-inspired conception of the spirit world where the land was the sacred domain of the ancestors that had been defiled by racial slavery and thus cried out for redemption. In Plácido's project of emancipation, the destruction of monarchy was indispensable, for it heralded the spiritual rebirth of the Cuban nation and established a social order based on racial egalitarianism. An African-inspired conception of the spirit world was the focal point of Plácido's struggle for liberation, thus signaling a transformative moment in Cuban cultural history.

## CHAPTER SIX

# Black Cuban Literati in the Age of Revolution

Gabriel de la Concepción Valdés

and Juan Francisco Manzano

¿Por qué pues ha de ser solo Plácido
el apóstol de la discordia?
—PLÁCIDO

### Deconstructing the Colonial Narrative in the Cuban Archive of 1844

The Spanish government depicted the antislavery movement as a violent story of intrigue and chaos. The official narrative characterized the uprisings as "la conspiracion proyectada por la gente de color . . . para el esterminio de la parte de la poblacion blanca de esta Isla", that is, "the conspiracy devised by the people of color . . . to exterminate . . . the white population of this Island."[1] By construing the antislavery movement as a project of racial extermination, the government portrayed white Cubans as the plausible victims of ethnic cleansing and simultaneously silenced African-descended aspirations for abolition and racial egalitarianism. This rhetorical omission established the discursive strategy of the text: repossess the island as a bastion of white Hispanic values under siege by the impending destruction of African barbarism.[2] But if whites were to be deemed innocent in a society where they had enslaved Africans since the sixteenth century, the government needed a metaphor to symbolize their purity. Spanish authorities resolved this dilemma by anointing the white woman as symbol of the ever-faithful isle.[3] In the official narrative, Cuba emerged as a white Spanish woman, fertile yet chaste, noble, and innocent. Blackness threatened to defile Cuba as it had defiled Haiti some forty years prior. The specter of the Haitian Revolution (1791–1804) loomed large in the government account of the events of 1844, as the psychosexual undertones in the subsequent passage reveal. Below, I cite a passage from the judgment against the town of Bainoa, where the military commission alleged that free blacks and mulattoes had joined with enslaved Africans on rural plantations to murder the "peaceful inhabitants."

> Se afectaba una tranquilidad aparente en la raza de color tanto libre como esclava; pero no habia uno solo que no hubiera prenetrado la ponzoñosa intriga de los crueles asesinos de aquellos pacíficos moradores. En todas las fincas habian arreglado y combinado su bárbaro y destructor plan; estaban elejidos los principales caudillos para el dia en que debia rasgarse el sangriento velo de la anaraquìa y el asesinato: no hay una sola declarcion que no revele el inhumano objeto de la jente de color, cuya tendencia era la de acabar con todos los hombres blancos, dejando entregado el débil sécso á los horrores que eran consiguientes.[4]

> (There was an apparent tranquility among the people of color both freemen and slaves; but there wasn't one of them that hadn't penetrated venomous plot to cruelly murder those peaceful inhabitants. On all the farms they had gotten together and collaborated on their barbarous and destructive plan; the chief *caudillos* had been designated for the day in which they would tear back the bloody veil of anarchy and assassination: there isn't one testimony that didn't reveal the inhuman intentions of the people of color, whose proclivity was to do away with all white men, subjecting the weaker sex to impending horrors.)

The judgment against Bainoa portrayed enslaved and free African descendants as a violent monolith, lying in wait to massacre the "pacíficos moradores" (peaceful inhabitants). The phrase "pacíficos moradores" was a claim to white innocence that effaced the physical horrors and psychological torments of racial slavery. Not only was whiteness the absence of contamination (Branche, *Colonialism and Race* 87), but it is also presupposed the civilizing influence of Spanish Catholicism. The white Catholic community emerged in the document as the antithesis of savagery. But there was no defense of the slaveholder per se; rather, the text insinuated that blacks and mulattoes had placed the colonial racial hierarchy under siege. Still, there was a gendered subtext to the government's claims that insurgents had devised a plan to murder all white inhabitants: the annihilation of all white men would give black men sexual license to inflict unspeakable horrors upon white female bodies. Thus, the Spanish word *morador* refers to white male inhabitants; it does not signify white women in any way. Anarchy and assassination are coupled with the defilement of the white female so that white readers of the *sentencia* (the judgment)—a largely male audience to be sure—would be filled with an abiding sense of dread and revulsion. By construing people of color as a monolith—rather than as discrete racial groups beset with antagonisms amongst themselves—the narrative played a game of hide-and-seek with Cuban racial discourse. The notion that blacks and mulattoes belonged to different races disappeared within the text, only to reassert itself again (Nwankwo 35–36). The colonial state argued that free mixed-race people (*pardos, mulatos*), free blacks (*morenos libres*), and enslaved blacks (*negros*) had concocted a plot that implicated activity on all the plantations in western Cuba (Nwankwo 35–36). But the colonial authorities needed to pinpoint the intellectual agents of this conspiracy; so, they assigned blame to the British government, to white Cuban reformers, and, most significantly, to free mulattoes.[5]

The Spanish government condemned free persons of color (*libertos*) as the intellectual architects of a genocidal plot against whites. In their version of events, free mulattoes had seduced otherwise passive black slaves on rural plantations throughout western Cuba, as another psychosexual passage from the judgment against Bainoa reveals.

> En las fincas, en los caminos y hasta en los mismos bohíos, penetraban los libertos, esparciendo por todas partes sus maléficas ideas: no se ocupaban de otra cosa hacia algun tiempo; la semilla habia penetrado en todas direcciones, y solo faltaba la señal para dar principio al horrendo sacrificio.[6]

> (The freedmen penetrated the farms, the country roads and even the *bohíos* [slave huts] themselves, disseminating their maleficent ideas: they haven't concerned themselves with anything else for some time now; the seed had penetrated in all directions, and they only needed a sign to set in motion the horrifying sacrifice.)

The *sentencia* was crafted in the religio-moral idiom of Catholicism; such a narrative depicted white Catholics as blameless children of God and regarded Africans as errant souls that had violated a divinely sanctioned social order. Thus, the rape allegory was the most powerful image the colonial state could furnish, even more powerful than the threat of massacre. Penetration was the chosen metaphor to characterize the freedman's power and influence over rural plantation populations. Penetration alludes to the sexual act and implies a sort of symbolic violence and impropriety, an uninvited infiltration, so to speak, since the urban and rural areas of colonial society—representing free and enslaved persons respectively—were thought to be disparate sociocultural spheres. In this way, freedmen emerged as the dominant actors in the government's *sentencia,* as individuals that had violated the most intimate spaces of plantation life to indoctrinate would-be rebels. But the *libertos'* greatest crime was not the fantasy of forcing themselves on white women; rather, it was the penetration of the African mind with revolutionary ideas. Not only did the interlopers force their way into plantation dwellings, but they also dispersed the seed of their maleficent ideas in every direction imaginable, making revolution

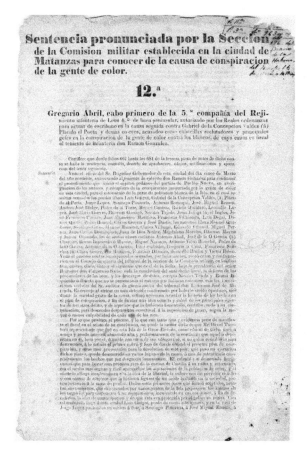

The Spanish government condemned Plácido and his African-descended conspirators to death for "the conspiracy devised by the people of color . . . to exterminate . . . the white population of this Island." Courtesy of Oficina del Historiador de la Ciudad de la Habana, Eusebio Leal.

difficult to contain. The colonial government portrayed Plácido and Manzano as mulattoes who had pierced into black consciousness with dangerous ideas of mayhem and revolution.

In 1844 Spanish authorities detained Gabriel de la Concepción Valdés and Juan Francisco Manzano for conspiring against the colonial state in a horrific scheme to exterminate the white population. Government officials not only questioned Plácido and Manzano's shadowy meetings, clandestine communiqués, and travel plans but also probed them about subversive literature. Interrogators inquired about a "pohetica alusiva a planes contrarios a la tranquilidad y seguridad de esta Isla" (poetics alluding to plans contrary to the tranquility and security of the Island) (Friol 207). Spanish interrogators launched a concerted effort to define Plácido and Manzano's *poetics of conspiracy*, as I shall call it. By "poetics of conspiracy" I am referring to the instrumentality of spoken-word poetry to disseminate seditious ideas, incite passions, and convey a spiritual paradigm for revolutionary exploits. Colonial officials plied Plácido and Manzano with questions that suggest a preoccupation with the transcendent power of poetry to alter consciousness. The Spanish government's suspicions about seditious literature mirror the abolitionist atmosphere of the 1830s. In 1833 the British abolished slavery in its Caribbean colonies, and in 1835 Great Britain compelled Spain to consent to another antislave trade treaty (Paquette 92, 132). Perhaps of even greater significance, slave rebellions throughout Cuba had become frequent roughly ten years prior to the arrests of Manzano and Plácido in 1844 (Midlo Hall 56). The colonial government employed all manner of surveillance, interrogation, and torture to discern the origins of "the conspiracy of the people of color" and, perhaps more significantly, to determine the intellectual character of the 1844 antislavery movement.

The military tribunal convicted Plácido of being the president and mastermind of "del horrendo crímen de la conspiración contra la raza blanca" (of the horrendous crime of conspiracy against the white race). The tribunal concluded that Plácido had circulated revolutionary concepts by way of his poetry and that he had carried messages from town to town (Cué, *Plácido: El Poeta* 102; Horrego Estuch, *Plácido: el poeta* 56), even visiting slave plantations.[7] But the "horrendos juramentos" (horrendous oaths) that Plácido administrated most appalled the colonial regime, because the ritual of oath taking successfully recruited insurgents and broke faith with the queen of Spain.[8] On June 28, 1844, colonial authorities executed Plácido on charges of treason, having him shot in the back.[9] Manzano would survive the ghastly ordeal, but the authorities charged him with aiding and abetting a conspiracy to abolish slavery and depose the regime. The captain general detained Manzano because his vocation as a poet provided him an edifice of authority within black communities, and his formidable network of friends—who had also fallen under suspicion—made him a suspect (Manzano, *Esclavo poeta* 12–13). Colonial authorities acquitted Manzano of the charges levied against him, and they released him from their custody. But the military tribunal kept Manzano (and Pedro Bonard) under surveillance for the term of a year ("vigilándoseles por el término de un año").[10] A month later, Manzano was arrested again, subjected to further questioning, and imprisoned until November 1845 (Friol 64–66). And although the military tribunal never convicted Manzano of a crime, the trauma he experienced may have silenced his pen forever.

For more than a century, historians have privileged Plácido's role in the 1844 antislavery movement while neglecting, or denying altogether, the relationship Manzano had to that same conspiracy. Manzano's status as an enslaved person prompted one scholar to read him as a domesticated *mulato*, a tragic, feeble, and injured personality incapable of meaningful resistance (DeCosta-Willis, "Self and Society" 9, 11). For instance, William Luis absolved Manzano of any involvement in the 1844 insurgency by claiming that Plácido had falsely accused him of "los delitos de la sublevación contra el regimen colonial" (the crimes of insurrection against the colonial regime) ("Introducción" 60). But this chapter probes a series of documents that suggest otherwise and challenge what Luis and other scholars have maintained regarding the antislavery movement. I perform a close read-ing of primary documents: the judgment against chief conspirators, Plácido's statement to the military tribunal, letters of the accused, and, perhaps most sig-nificantly, the joint interrogation of Manzano and Plácido. I explore a series of questions that have yet to be examined: What did Manzano know about the 1844 antislavery movement? And when did he know it? What role might Manzano have played in the conspiracy? And finally, what type of narrative emerges in the documents regarding Plácido's and Manzano's camaraderie and collaboration? How did Plácido's role in the 1844 movement differ from Manzano's?

Government accounts of black uprising created silences and obscured insurgents' motives to underscore the legitimacy of state power. The intersec-tional historicist methods of Marisa Fuentes and Aisha Finch have informed my reading practices. Fuentes views the archive as a repository of colonial dis-courses that filters the past through white voices both male and female. And she subverts the selective histories of the archive by reading the scarred body of African women as text (15–16). Similarly, Aisha Finch argues that in 1844 the Spanish colonial state relied on the language, bodies, activities and even epistemologies embedded within Cuban slave testimony to compose a narra-tive of "selective truths" (11). For the purposes of this chapter, it is important to point out that a notary public transcribed the joint interrogation of Plácido and Manzano from the oral register to written narrative. Consequently, their dialogue appears as a third-person summation of their statements. The text presents some other problems: the syntax is obtuse and unwieldly, and inter-rogators ask leading questions that invite Manzano and Plácido to incriminate themselves. Moreover, Manzano and Plácido dissembled to avoid torture and execution, which further complicates an already difficult hermeneutical task. To make the trial record legible, I have adopted an interdisciplinary historicist method that draws upon religious ethnography, literary theory, and intersec-tionality. I examine the military commission's racialized account by reading between the lines, observing silences, and speaking where the text does not. In effect, I read the archive from the periphery privileging the language, actions, and epistemology of African descendants.

### The Subversive Covenants of Manzano and Plácido:
### A Rereading of the 1844 Antislavery Movement

Manzano introduced himself to Plácido in Havana at a cockfight circa 1839; it was a fortuitous exchange that would forever change their lives. Plácido and Manzano became close friends; they often dined, imbibed brandy, and con-versed about poetry at length (Friol 192, 198). Though Manzano was a cause célèbre in his own right, Plácido was the most prominent, influential, and visible Cuban writer in 1839. Plácido's celebrity and the broad appeal of his poetry did not escape Manzano's notice (Friol 198). But the nature of Plácido and Manzano's relationship changed radically when the government detained them for anticolonial activities. Colonial officials questioned the nature of their acquaintance, inquired about the poetry they had written, and sought to determine the character of their interactions with Domingo del Monte. Del Monte had also been accused of conspiracy, though he was living in self-imposed exile in Paris (Del Monte y Aponte, "Dos poetas" 84–85). The authorities initially mistook Juan Francisco Manzano for someone identified as Manuel Manzano. But in a statement to the governor of Matanzas, Capitan General Leopoldo O'Donnell suggested that Juan Francisco might also imperil the regime's power, given the renown he enjoyed as a poet among Cubans of African descent (Azougarh, ed. 12–13). O'Donnell wrote:

Sr. Gobernador de Matanzas

[ ... ]

han sido presos y puestos incomunicados a disposición de V.E. los pardos Gonzalo y Francisco Manzano, para lo que pueda importar y por si hubiera alguna involuntaria equivocación; y con más razón cuando estos gozan en el público de muy mala nota con particularidad el $2^o$ que es poeta, compositor de comedias y otros discursos, motivo porque entre los de su color pasa por hombre de gran saber y es considerado en sus reuniones extraordinariamente ... (Manzano, *Esclavo poeta* 12–13).

(Governor of Matanzas

[ ... ]

they have been arrested and are being held incommunicado to the disposition of Your Excellency the mulattoes Gonzalo and Francisco Manzano, for what it matters. And if there was some inadvertent error, and with more reason [because] both of these men enjoy public notoriety. Particularly, the second one is a poet, a composer of theatrical pieces and other discourses, for this reason he passes as a man of great knowledge among those of his color and in their meetings, he is considered extraordinary ... )

The brief passage is telling. Not only did the Spanish military government know who Juan Francisco Manzano was, but also—as with his accomplice Plácido—they had kept him under surveillance ever since he acquired his freedom in

1836. As far as the captain general was concerned, Manzano posed a threat to state power because blacks and mulattoes regarded him as a "man of great knowledge." And since Manzano could publish nothing in Cuba without government sanction, the authorities were familiar with everything he had issued on the island. The captain general's letter reconstructs, albeit partially, the mise-en-scène where Manzano recited, improvised, and performed his most radical poetry within African Cuban community. Manzano had written several letters to del Monte while still enslaved, imploring him to fulfill his promise to purchase his freedom in exchange for writing a slave narrative (Manzano, *Autobiografía* 120, 127). After his emancipation, Manzano aided the abolitionist cause by publishing his autobiography in Europe (Manzano, *Autobiografía* 122), and his lyrical work had been translated into English and French. Manzano effectively became an exemplar to other Cubans of African descent. Manzano might have spoken to other blacks about how he had vanquished slavery through repeated appeals to the *orishas*, a type of oppression that Plácido never suffered in his own flesh. Manzano might have recalled his heroic escape from Matanzas to Havana under the cover of night and inspired his audiences with stories about how he had taught himself to read and write. Though we have no transcript of Manzano's private conversations, the captain general's extensive knowledge of his literary work suggests that Manzano exercised considerable political authority within communities of African descent.[11] Manzano's political authority was grounded in his standing as a *liberto* (liberated man) and his production of "otros discursos" (other discourses) (Manzano, *Esclavo poeta* 12–13) that challenged the proslavery narrative.

Plácido and Manzano forged divergent rhetorical strategies in an eleventh-hour appeal to exonerate themselves. Manzano adopted a three-pronged approach to refute charges of racial conspiracy. He portrayed Domingo del Monte as a disinterested humanitarian with whom he maintained narrow ties, he depicted his own emancipation from slavery as an act of largesse, and he depoliticized his literary commitments. But, perhaps most notably, Manzano characterized his ties to Plácido as benign amusement and revelry. I have indicated when the interrogator questioned Plácido or Manzano, and I have specified when either writer provided an answer by using capital letters. My interventions make an otherwise obtuse third-person summation of Plácido's and Manzano's testimonies legible.

In the passage below, Manzano replies to interrogators' questions about the abolitionist poetry he was allegedly commissioned to write.

Recuerde cuál, y diga si entre sus composiciones pohéticas ha hecho alguna dirigida al Gobierno Inglés, por la protección que este dispensaba para llevar a cabo la libertad de los esclavos de esta Isla, y en caso de afirmativa, diga quién le hizo el encargo de esta composición, qué título le dio, a qué personas la entregó

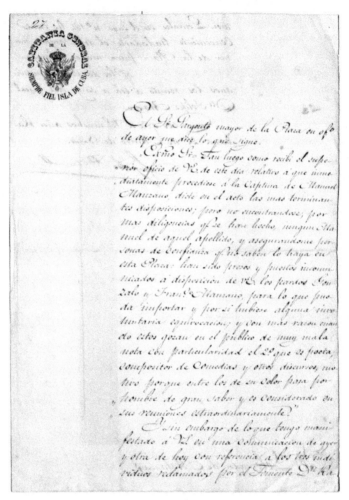

The image above is the first page of a government letter justifying the imprisonment of Juan Francisco Manzano on the basis that he was a well-regarded and influential author of African descent. Courtesy of Harvard University.

y que estipendio recibió por este trabajo, dijo: Biene en conocimiento de haber sido hablado e imbitado, por un pardo residente en la Habana, llamado Luis Jigó, para que le hiciese varias composiciones sobre el particular que contiene esta pregunta, haciéndole varias ofertas, pero que el declarante nunca satisfizo el deseo de Jigó (Friol 196).

(QUESTION c: Recall which one [poem] and whether or not among the lyrical compositions that he [Manzano] had completed if any had been addressed to the British government, for the protection that aforesaid government would provide to carry out the liberty of the slaves of this island, and if it is true, say who commissioned this poem, the title they gave it, to whom it was delivered and the compensation that he [Manzano] received for this work, [ANSWER] he said: it comes to mind that he had spoken to and was invited by a free resident of mixed race in Havana, known as Luis Gigaut, requesting that he make various compositions about the topic that the interrogator's question referred to, that [Gigaut] made him several offers, but the witness never satisfied his wishes.)

The authorities plied Manzano with questions about poems he had purport-edly been commissioned to write in praise of British abolitionism. Great Britain appeared as an agent provocateur, a puppet-master sowing seeds of sedition among disgruntled mulattoes and promising the crime of black freedom. The colonial authorities held that this elusive body of poetry lauded Great Britain for "the protection that the aforesaid government would provide to carry out the liberty of the slaves" (Friol 196). The trial record depicted the British govern-ment as a phantom with tentacles throughout the Caribbean and promises of black liberty on its lips. The government plied Manzano with additional ques-tions. They inquired about the poem's title, who had commissioned it, and the stipend Manzano was to receive for writing it. Manzano acknowledged the exis-tence of a subversive literary project. But he claimed that it was not del Monte who had commissioned the work, but rather Luis Gigaut (or Jigó as it appears in the record), an elusive Havana resident who had conceived the plot. Manzano testified that Luis Gigaut—presumably of Haitian descent—had "made him sev-eral offers" to aid and abet the antislavery movement by writing poetry. But Manzano had spurned Gigaut's advances and he insisted that "[he] never satis-fied his wishes" (Friol 196).

The government inquest about Manzano's politics took another turn when the interrogator asked about his private conversations with Plácido regarding poetry.

Recuerde que conversaciones haya tenido con dicho Placido, referente a pohe-sias, y si asi mismo no le ha espresado haber hecho alguna por la cual hubiese recibido el estipendio de una onza de oro, dijo: Que siempre se han encontrado en la calle se han convidado mutuamente a tomar brandi, que han hablado de sus composiciones nombrando cada cual las que había hecho, pero que nunca le espresó haber recibido una onza de oro por una de sus composiciones, por-que nunca ha sucedido esto . . . (Friol 198).

(QUESTION d: If he remembers the conversation that he had with the afore-said Plácido, in reference to poetry, and if he had expressed having written one for which he received an ounce of gold as a stipend, [ANSWER] he said: That when they ran into each other on the street they always invited each other out to drink brandy, that they had spoken about, naming the [specific] titles of the poems they had written, but that he [Manzano] had never spoken [with

Plácido] about having received an ounce of gold for one of his poems, because that never happened.)

Manzano characterized his friendship with Plácido as little more than drunken revelry. And he insinuated that they seldom conferred about literature, typically conversing about little more than the names of their poems. Manzano's denials that he had been compensated for writing abolitionist poetry would be plausible only if he could convince authorities that Plácido was his drinking buddy. By depicting Plácido as a socialite, Manzano condemned himself and his friend to a perpetual state of boyhood, thus confirming colonial stereotypes about black masculinity.

In one of the more dramatic scenes from the trial record, colonial officials brought Plácido and Manzano into the same room to conduct a joint interrogation. They invited Plácido to confirm, negate, or otherwise shape Manzano's testimony. The passage below begins with Plácido answering a question about the nature of his relationship to Manzano.

> Conoce al que tiene presente, que es Juan Francisco Manzano el mismo a quien se contrae en la parte de su ampliacion confesoria que se ha leido, y el propio que le espresó habia hecho la pohesia en cuestion por encargo del Sr. D. Domingo Delmonte, recordando que tambien le manifestó había percibido por ello una buena gratificacion, que esta composicion no se la enseñó, [ . . . ] que es falso lo que espresa sobre no haber hablado ni entregado pohesias suyas al que absuelve pues ha tenido en su poder unos cuatro o cinco años composiciones inecditas de Manzano que este le ha entregado, y que por último todos cuanto ha espresado es cierto y como tal se lo sostiene. Oido lo cual por Manzano repuso se sostenia en lo que habia dicho, añadiendo que su confianza con Valdes, estaba muy distante de llegar a tal grado, pues aun cuando es cierto media amistad, y que con esta se han pagado mutuamente convidadas de brandi, y que en una ocasion fue a su casa, y le imbitó a una comida en su casa, cuya imbitacion recuerda en este momento se le hizo también a Luis Jigó . . . (Friol 202).

ANSWER: He [Plácido] knows the individual present, Juan Francisco Manzano the same individual who provided the ample testimony that has been read aloud, and the same individual [Manzano] that expressed to him [Plácido] that he had composed the poem in question commissioned by Mr. Domingo del Monte, recalling that he had [Manzano] also expressed that he had received considerable compensation, [and] that he didn't show him this poem, [ . . . ] but it is untrue what he [Manzano] says about them not exchanging their poems with one another [because] the one that absolves himself [Plácido] has had in his possession for 4 or 5 years Manzano's unpublished poems that he [Manzano] had given him, and finally that everything he [Plácido] has expressed is true exactly as he maintains it.

ANSWER: Upon hearing this Manzano countered, he insisted on what he had said [previously], adding that his confidence in Valdés was far too inadequate to come to that point, because although they certainly had a friendship, and for that reason they had both cheered each other by inviting each other to drink brandy, and that on one occasion he [Manzano] went to his [Plácido's] house, and he invited him to share a meal in his [Plácido's] house, an invitation he now remembers was also extended to Luis Gigaut . . .

As Plácido faced Manzano, his life hung in the balance, and anxieties ran high. Plácido insisted that his camaraderie with Manzano was much more than drunken merriment despite what his friend had claimed. He maintained that Manzano had not only written poetry in praise of British abolitionism but that he had also expressed "una buena gratificacion" (good gratification) for having done so. Plácido's version of events rendered Domingo del Monte, not Luis Gigaut, the agent provocateur that compensated Manzano for writing abolitionist poetry. Plácido shifted the locus of control away from free African-descendants and toward white aristocrats like del Monte, who, according to him, had conspired against the Spanish crown. But neither was Manzano blameless. Plácido's assertion that Manzano had experienced a "buena gratificacion" depicted Manzano's sense of pleasure at being involved in the 1844 antislavery movement. Plácido described Manzano as an aesthetic collaborator, and he established a critical link between aesthetics and politics that Manzano would not easily refute.

Desperate to unravel suspicions that he had abetted the 1844 racial conspiracy, Manzano claimed that he had resided in del Monte's Havana household a mere twenty days, during which he served as his cook (Friol 189, 201). Likewise, he insisted "segundo, porque no tan solo no le ha manifestado haber hecho la composicion en loor del Gobierno Ingles por su humanidad en la libertad de la esclavitud" (secondly, because he [Manzano] did not write any poem in praise of the British government for its humanitarianism in the abolition of slavery) (Friol 201). Manzano absolved himself of his previous political commitments. And he further distanced himself from Plácido, saying, "q^e. nunca le ha hablado sobre composiciones poheticas, ni le ha entregado nunca obra suya de esta especie" (that he [Manzano] had never spoken to him [Plácido] about lyrical compositions and that he had never presented any such literary work to him) (Friol 201). But the notion that Manzano knew Plácido for nearly five years but never collaborated artistically with him is highly implausible and was in all likelihood untrue.

Plácido and Manzano made claims and counterclaims throughout the course of the investigation. They debated whether or not del Monte had commissioned

Manzano to write abolitionist poetry or if the plot to disseminate such work was the brainchild of a Haitian man known as Luis Gigaut. Below, Manzano characterized his long-standing relationship to del Monte as the result of his gratitude for the role the aristocrat had played in purchasing his freedom.

> Que en este tiempo nació nuestra soberana la Reyna Dᵃ Isabel segunda, en cuya época los poetas habaneros cantaron a tan fausto acontecimiento, entre cuyo número se encontraba el declarante, resultando a consecuencia de esta canción, el que Sor. Domingo Delmonte y D. José de la Luz le dicen la libertad, como así consta la carta que como tal libre se le estendio y conserba en su poder su esposa María del Rosario de Rojas. . . (Friol 195)

> [ . . . ]

> y que aun cuando este Sŏr le mostraba confianza y cariño nunca podria ser esto suficiente ni para encargarle una pohesia en Materia tan espuesta, ni para espresarle sus ideas con respecto al plan que ha dejado traslucir en su dicho Valdes, el cual puede estar penetrado de el, pues como ha declarado tubo sus secciones tres o cuatro ocasiones con el Sr. Delmonte en su gabinete, a pesar que crea a este Sŏr incapaz de semejantes planes (Friol 201).

> (ANSWER: At that time, our sovereign Queen Doña Isabel II was born, and the poets of Havana intoned such a magnificent occasion, and the declarant [Manzano] was counted among that number, as a result of that poem, Mr. Domingo del Monte and Don José de la Luz [y Caballero] gave him his liberty, just as the letter they gave [me] testifies, which my wife, María del Rosario de Rojas has in power.

> [ . . . ]

> (ANSWER: And even though this gentleman [Domingo del Monte] showed him trust and affection this would never be enough to commission him [Manzano] [to write] a poem on such dangerous matters, neither to divulge his ideas with respect to the plan that Valdés has revealed in his statement. He [Plácido] must have pierced into the plan, since, as he testified, on three or four occasions he was with Mr. del Monte in his bureau, although he [Manzano] regards the gentleman [del Monte] to be incapable of [hatching] such plans)

Manzano's unyielding defense of del Monte was intended to protect his benefactor. It was public knowledge that he had maintained very close ties to that faction of white reformist literati; hence, his defense of del Monte was also an effort to exonerate himself. Manzano did not accuse Plácido of being a conspirator during the interrogation, but he came close to doing so. Rather, Manzano intimated that his friend had considerable knowledge of the plot, saying, "He must have pierced into the plan" somehow (Friol 201). Manzano portrayed himself as an artist and a loyal subject of the Spanish crown, but he also implied that he was far too unenlightened for "political matters" (Friol 202). In his words, del Monte would have never commissioned a former *slave*— who knew nothing of politics and was a lesser poet—to compose a political poem (Friol 196, 201–202).

One of the most revealing things about Manzano's testimony is the way he misled the military commission about the story of his emancipation. Manzano said nothing of his ritual devotion to St. Anthony, also known as Elegguá in Yoruba spirituality (Lucero Mundo in Bakongo practices), which had secured his escape from Matanzas to Havana circa 1817. Manzano explained in his autobiography, "I still believe they [the saints] afforded me the occasion and watched over me the night of my escape from Matanzas to Havana, as we shall see. Taking the almanac, all the saints of that month were prayed to daily by me."[12] Under duress, Manzano reasserted the public face of his identify; he identified as a Roman Apostolic Catholic (Friol 194) and made no references whatsoever to African-inspired spirituality. Likewise, he suppressed the slave narrative he had written at the behest of del Monte and that Richard Madden had championed in abolitionist circles in Europe. Manzano portrayed his manumission as an act of noblesse oblige, asserting that his gracious benefactors had freed him in exchange for an ode honoring the birth of Queen Isabel II (Friol 195). In fact, Manzano did dedicate a poem to the queen of Spain. But he published that poem in a newspaper in 1831, many years prior to his emancipation in 1836 (Friol 99–104). Manzano's rewriting of the past enabled him to absolve del Monte of culpability, deny the subversive nature (and the very existence) of his autobiography, and proclaim himself a Catholic subject beholden to the crown.

Plácido had become public enemy number one with thirty-two accusations on his head. He never evaded surveillance. His brief career was marked by three prior arrests, grounded in the government's lingering suspicions that he had conspired against whites (Cué, *Plácido: El Poeta* 86, 89). Plácido never accused Manzano of sedition; but his testimony placed Manzano within earshot of conspiratorial planning. In Plácido's version of events, Manzano not only existed within the spatial geographies of conspiracy but had also actively collaborated with insurgent leaders. And though he had imbibed spirits and discussed women with Plácido, Manzano maintained there was inadequate trust between them to have exchanged unpublished work (Friol 202, 205).

Manzano's denials, silences, and untruths disguised the political subtext of his literature in an effort to refute testimony that situated him among the architects of the movement. Though the whereabouts of the mysterious poetry remained unknown, Manzano and Plácido largely concurred about the purposes for which it was commissioned. The poem (or poems) was to pursue a trajectory similar to Manzano's memoirs: it was to be written, delivered to the British consul, dispatched to London, and published as abolitionist propaganda (Friol 190, 204).[13] But Plácido and Manzano differed with regard to the project's brainchild. Plácido insisted that del Monte had commissioned the work. But Manzano averred that del Monte was incapable of such a scheme and that Luis Gigaut had charged him to write a series of subversive poems (Friol 201, 204). According to Manzano, the poems would be published in Europe and circulated on the island. Manzano testified that "que estubiese seguro, cogeria el premio dentro de muy breve tiempo, pues el yugo de la esclavitud se sacudiria muy breve" (he [Gigaut] was certain, that it would be rewarded in very little time, so that the yoke of slavery would be shaken off) (Friol 204). Luis Gigaut emerged as a mysterious foreign element, a sophisticated seducer in search of proselytes and prospective victims. The historical record paints a more nuanced yet incomplete portrait of Gigaut. Luis Gigaut received an exquisite education in Switzerland, traveled extensively in the circum-Caribbean region, and was regarded as an ally of the people of color (Paquette 246–247).

The judgment against Plácido and other chief conspirators expounds on the role that foreign agents Luis Gigaut and David Turnbull played in providing political impetus for the inception of the 1844 movement to abolish slavery and dethrone the Spanish colonial government.

> Con tal embajada llega á esta ciudad Luis Guigot, pardo de cierta inteligencia, y en la casa de Jorge Lopez patentiza su mision á éste, á Santiago Pimienta, á José Miguel Roman, á Antonio Bernoqui, á Pedro de la Torre y á Gabriel de la Concepcion Valdes: en dos sesiones que tuvieron quedan estos individuos adheridos á las ideas del ex-cónsul Turnbull, y riegan la semilla de la revelion haciendo prosélitos, Plácido el Poeta. [14]

> (Through that embassy Luis Gigaut arrived in the city, a free mulatto of certain intelligence, and in the home of Jorge López he made evident his mission to him, to Santiago Pimienta, to José Miguel Román, to Antonio Bernoqui, to Pedro de la Torre and to Gabriel de la Concepción Valdés: in two different meetings that they held, these individuals agreed with the ideas of the former [British] consul Turnbull, and they watered the seeds of rebellion making proselytes, (of) Plácido the Poet . . . )

The judgment against the leaders of the conspiracy described Luis Gigaut as an intelligent British agent who had seduced Plácido, Santiago Pimienta, Antonio Bernoqui (the militia leader Jorge López), and other prominent free mulattoes with British ideas of liberty. The home of Jorge López was the scene of the purported crime of ideological seduction. Moreover, the trial record stated that Gigaut had served as a translator in Veracruz, Mexico, and perhaps most importantly, had traveled to Cuba from Haiti by way of New Orleans to pursue separatist politics that would achieve slave emancipation (Paquette 241, 252). That Luis Gigaut was the only person Manzano accused of conspiracy bespeaks his desperation to uphold his innocence, even if that meant impugning prominent free blacks.[15] But he was not alone; most of Plácido's accusers were also fellow African-descended conspirators that wrestled to save themselves.

Manzano celebrated his literary collaborations with white Creole writers. He acknowledged Cuban Indianist writer Ignacio Valdés Machuca, who had orchestrated the publication of his first compilation and introduced him in the 1830s to Domingo del Monte. Del Monte's invisible hand had "limar los defectos de ortografia que notaba en ellos" (polished the orthographical defects that he noted) (Friol 195–196).[16] But the 1840 publication of *Poems by a Slave in the Island of Cuba, Recently Liberated*—along with the antislavery poem "Un sueño" (A Dream) released in Cuba in 1838 and two years later in translation—is more than ample evidence of political collaboration. (We do not know if the government was aware that Madden had published Manzano's slave narrative in London.) I have argued that Manzano's notion of emancipation, his allusions to Afro-Caribbean spirituality, and his particular aims were incongruent with white Creole liberalism that yearned for self-governance and the inviolability of property rights. Even so, his collaborative work with Cuban whites and Irish abolitionist Richard R. Madden (Burton 103, 107) represented an alliance that was not simply editorial but also political.

Plácido's testimony not only negates Manzano's claim to naïveté but, in my view, also reveals that they were politically aligned in a broader project to achieve African-descended liberation. Manzano's description of his friendship with Plácido as mere gaiety does not withstand scrutiny. Even though they quarreled about who the culprit was, both men corroborated that Manzano had sustained a friendship with Plácido. They agreed that Manzano had attended underground meetings at Plácido's house where Luis Gigaut was also present and was more than conversant about the plan to write and distribute abolitionist poetry in Cuba and abroad. The notion that Manzano formed part of a subversive body of African-descended men but remained ignorant of their politics is doubtful. In fact, it is Manzano's attendance at the gatherings and his fluency in the details of the plot that lends credence to Plácido's assertion about their previous alliance.

Plácido's final statement in his confrontation with Manzano suggests a friendship undergirded by mutual trust.

Valdes le repuso y argulló que su confianza y amistad es suficiente para haberle hecho tal manifestacion, que lo confiese así, pues bien sabe que la hay, q$^e$ su dicho es muy cierto, y en cuanto a lo que espresa de ser D. Domingo Delmonte

Poeta, aunque es cierto, tambien lo es que los Poetas se convidan para hacer sus composiciones sobre un mismo asunto, por las diferentes ideas que a cada cual se le ocurren y que por último diga es cierto hizo tal composicion, pues es la verdad, Manzano le repuso sosteniendo lo que habia dicho, y no adelantándose otra cosa en esta confrontación, sosteniendo cada cual lo que habia dicho se dio por concluido el acto, que por hallarlo conforme despues de haberseles leido, lo ratificaron, firmando con dicho Sõr y presente Escribano (Ramón Gonzalez).

Juan Fran^co Manzano, Gabriel de la C. Valdes (Friol 202–203)

[ANSWER:] Valdés responded and contended that their trust and friendship is sufficient in order to have expressed such things, and that he confesses it so, because he knows well that there is such trust, that what he has said is true, regarding what he says about Don Domingo del Monte the poet, although that is true, it is also true that poets meet together in order to write their compositions about a common theme, because of the different ideas that occurs to each of them and finally he [Plácido] says it is true but he [Manzano] wrote that poem, that is the truth,

[ANSWER:] Manzano countered standing by what he had already said, and not adding anything else in this confrontation, each individual stood by what he had said in the interrogation. [With that statement] the matter concluded after having read it, they ratified it signing it with the aforesaid Mr. (Ramón González) and the notary public present.

Juan Francisco Manzano, Gabriel de la C. Valdés

Plácido's far more plausible story depicted their exchange of ideas, underscored that they had written on common themes, and even implied what Manzano most feared: that their poetry shared common political objectives (Friol 202–203). Naturally, Plácido did not assert that they had conspired against the colonial state. But he repudiated Manzano's denials when he confessed, "pues ha tenido en su poder unos cuatro o cinco años composiciones inecditas de Manzano que este le ha entregado" (he has had in his possession for four or five years unpublished poems that Manzano had given to him) (Friol 202). Plácido twice alleged that Manzano had in fact authored a poem in praise of British abolitionism at del Monte's behest (Friol 202–203).

Manzano had a complicated history of aesthetic collaborations with white authors and in all likelihood had discussed political ideas and shared his unpublished work with Plácido. The exchange of obscure poems—whose titles neither Plácido nor Manzano disclosed to the authorities—was indicative of a desire to devise a political discourse in opposition to slave society. In a country where the immense majority of blacks and whites were illiterate (Saco 74–75), Plácido and Manzano could—and apparently did—disseminate subversive ideas through spoken-word poetry. This meant that they could divulge David Turnbull's plan "al dar a toda persona de color los derechos que la naturaleza les concede" (granting to all persons of color the rights that Nature bestows on them) (Friol 196). The captain general himself remarked to the governor of Matanzas that among persons of African descent, Manzano "is regarded as a man of great knowledge" because of the poetry, dramatic pieces and "otros discursos" (other discourses) that he had composed (Manzano, *Esclavo poeta* 13). David Turnbull's ideas about black freedom were not new to Manzano. As early as 1823, Manzano had articulated the principle of natural rights in his unpublished poem "La esclava ausente." And in his correspondence with del Monte he had remarked upon "aquella propension que por un prinsipio natural tiene todo hombre esclavo a su rescate" (the propensity that by natural principle every man slave has for his rescue) (Manzano, *Obras* 81). Unpublished poetry evaded the scrutiny of colonial censorship. Francisco Calcagno—a white abolitionist—admitted that Cubans had circulated Plácido's poems "El juramento" and "¡Habaneros Libertad!" by word of mouth and in written form among a broad swath of the public (22). Moreover, according to Jesús Orta Ruiz, Cuban independence fighters sang "¡Habaneros Libertad!" in the trenches as they struggled for Cuban independence from Spain (1868-1898) (58). The Spanish government acknowledged that Plácido and Manzano had subverted the symbolic order in their literature, thus fomenting revolutionary change in a society made wealthy by black exploitation.

That Manzano and Plácido seemed to implicate each other (without accusing the other of treason) suggests that Manzano became skeptical of the ideas espoused by Plácido and Gigaut and, at some point, broke faith with conspiratorial leaders. Though he never accused Plácido of a racially motivated plot, Manzano often implied that his counterpart knew more of such matters than he did (Friol 201). Manzano's insistence that Plácido had organized a series of travels throughout the island and even abroad was, perhaps (Friol 205), the most damning testimony he offered. However, Manzano did not submit any specifics regarding Plácido's alleged plans to travel outside Cuba (Friol 206). This may have been a deliberate attempt to spare Plácido's life. We do not know that for certain. But this particular silence is significant, because Manzano knew of Plácido's imprisonment in Trinidad, Cuba, one year prior and presumably could have identified the anticipated destinations. When asked if Luis Gigaut and Plácido had exchanged letters about the conspiracy, Manzano feigned ignorance, but he did admit that Plácido had dispatched Gigaut to collect a letter from Matanzas, the contents of which he knew nothing (Friol 206). Because of his standing among the free people of color, Manzano could not plausibly divorce himself from Plácido and Gigaut.

But he professed ignorance of critical details, and he insinuated black culpability so he might circumvent the antiwhite epithet that had made Plácido public enemy number one.

## The Eleventh-Hour Appeal of *Plácido El Poeta*

Plácido's statement to the president of the military commission was a protracted defense of his innocence and an affirmation of his racial politics. Plácido's eleventh-hour appeal was an apologia about race, nation, and identity that he purportedly wrote himself.[17] He denied involvement in the conspiracy, even though his words disclosed considerable knowledge of the plot. His extensive knowledge of the plot was also evident in his joint interrogation with Manzano. Rather than deny the existence of an anticolonial conspiracy, Plácido depicted himself as "una VICTIMA DESIGNADA" (an APPOINTED VICTIM), besieged by whites and people of color alike in an effort to protect powerful white subversives (Cué, *Plácido: El Poeta* 304). Plácido attempted to exonerate Cubans of African descent by insisting that whites had authored the conspiracy themselves, which was propped up by British ideas of liberty (Cué, *Plácido: El Poeta* 105, 297). In the final section of this chapter, I explore what Valentin Mudimbe has termed "the epistemological locus" (16) of religious practice. And, though Plácido and Manzano engaged African ideas of spirit and cosmos, Manzano's politics of slave emancipation did not constitute a revolutionary project for Cuban independence.

Plácido sought to deflect a mounting chorus of accusations. He insisted that he was a benign creature of the arts, a loyalist who had fallen victim to the machinations of white abolitionists. His approach relied on the plausible denial of political agency. But given his sociocultural roots in African-descended communities in Havana, Matanzas, Trinidad, and Cienfuegos (among other places), Plácido could not exonerate himself without first vindicating his fellow black and mulatto co-conspirators. His account constitutes an inversion of the racial hierarchy: whiteness is deemed subversive so that *blackness* might be above reproach. Plácido never admitted guilt; rather, he insisted that he was a bystander, a lowborn poet incapable of inciting rebellion.

> Ynútiles serán Señor á mi entender cuántos afanes emplee el Gobierno para hallar la causa motriz de estos acontecimientos en las clases de pardos y morenos, ellos no son á lo más otra cosa que unos INSTRUMENTOS CIEGOS de maquinaciones MAS PROFUNDAS Y ANTIGUAS manejadas por manos mucho más PODEROSAS Y HABILES que las de estas AUTOMATAS, y los hechos que paso á esponer probarán que mi aserción no carece de fundamento. (original emphasis; Cué, "Plácido y la conspiración" 193).

Plácido's prison cell at Hospital Civil de Santa Isabel de Matanzas, where he was incarcerated prior to his execution in 1844.

(It will be useless, Sir, in my opinion, whatever energy the government may employ in order to find the prime mover of these events in the classes of free mulattoes and free blacks. They are nothing more than some BLIND INSTRUMENTS of OLDER AND MORE PROFOUND MACHINATIONS managed by hands much more POWERFUL AND CAPABLE than those of these AUTOMATONS. And the facts that I explicate will prove that my assertion is not unfounded.)[18]

Plácido's rhetorical strategy counters the subversive nuance in much of his poetry, the alleged purpose of his many travels throughout the island, his impressive network of powerful white and African-descended acquaintances—some of whom also fell under suspicion—and a litany of past imprisonments. Plácido professed membership in *las clases de pardos y morenos* throughout the text. Although several African descendants—some of whom are cited by name in this statement—had accused Plácido of leading the conspiracy, the poet never once implicated them. Not only did Plácido repudiate his involvement in the plot, but he also denied having the intellectual wherewithal to effect change in a system of white racial domination.[19]

Akin to Manzano's 1834 arrangement with del Monte, Plácido entered into a quid pro quo with the military commission. Pedro Salazar would intercede on his behalf with the captain general if he exposed everything he knew about the conspiracy (Cué, *Plácido: El Poeta* 297). Plácido silenced the prophetic voice of "El juramento," "La profecía de Cuba a España," "¡Habaneros Libertad!," and "El diablito." He claimed to be a loyal vassal "resuelto a cumplir con los deberes que me imponen la naturaleza, la humanidad y mi patria" (resolved to fulfill the duties that nature, humanity and my country oblige me) (Cué, *Plácido: El Poeta* 304). Plácido's loyalist rhetoric is reminiscent of poems he, Manzano, and white Creoles composed in praise of the liberal democratic impulses of the queen regent María Cristina and her daughter Queen Isabel II. By presenting himself as a loyal vassal and a patriot, Plácido again gestured toward different audiences; he defended free and enslaved blacks and mulattoes alike, even while feigning praise for the very regime that subjugated them. Plácido's claim to virtue made him a Romantic bard who—although more knowledgeable of *asuntos políticos* (political matters) than Manzano—was also a would-be government informant who nearly confessed del Monte's treasonous schemes in order to be useful to "the fatherland" (Cué, *Plácido: El Poeta* 299). There is a complex double entendre at play here, because like Manzano, Plácido's *patria* is not del Monte's. Since his first arrest in 1838 for writing "La sombra de Padilla," Plácido knew that military authorities considered his poetry subversive and were wary of his ever-increasing notoriety among the lower social orders. But if Plácido was to be deemed innocent, the counternarrative had to assign blame elsewhere.

Plácido's statement reads as an indictment of whiteness that identified three prime movers of conspiracy: Cuban abolitionists, pro-independence agitators, and agents of the British government (Cué, *Plácido: El Poeta* 309–310). In Plácido's portrait of conspiracy, white Creole abolitionists conspired to enlist free blacks and mulattoes in their struggle against Spain with ideas of liberty, slave emancipation, and promises of British munitions and tactical support. And, among these conspirators, Domingo del Monte was the chief architect (Cué, *Plácido: El Poeta* 298, 300–301, 312). Plácido testified that del Monte convened with him in private and even appeared in black and mulatto neighborhoods to converse about South American general Antonio José de Sucre, who in 1821 "este fue el primero que aconsejó que la independencia de la Isla de Cuba debía hacerse al revés de las de los otros países de América" (was the first that advised that the independence of the Island of Cuba should come through other countries of [Latin] America) (Cué, *Plácido: El Poeta* 298). Del Monte's foray into extramural neighborhoods represented an incursion into African Cuban sociocultural space that the military commission would not ignore, because the inner, not outer, district was the administrative, economic, ecclesiastical, and military center of the capital (Deschamps Chapeaux 5). The seduction of subversive ideas—psychosexual rhetoric that the government also employed in the judgment against black and mulatto conspirators—designated the wall as a symbolic divide that white Cubans had traversed to enlist blacks and mulattoes in their cause. Plácido sought to dissuade del Monte of "un plan de sangre en que él mismo perecería" (a bloody plan in which he himself [Del Monte] would perish). And he insisted, "YO NO HABIA NACIDO para guerrero SINO PARA POETA" (I HAD NOT BEEN BORN a warrior BUT A POET). But del Monte rejoined that even women had fought like heroines for Latin American independence (Cué, *Plácido: El Poeta* 299). Del Monte policed the boundaries of masculinity to insinuate that Plácido's cowardice was dishonorable and unbefitting a man of color. Furthermore, Plácido claimed that del Monte had even proposed to send him abroad "desde donde escribiría a favor de LA IGUALDAD excitando a los de mi clase, y que el se encargaría de hacer CIRCULAR mis obras en secreto, lo cual les daría mayor importancia" (where he would write in favor of EQUALITY rousing up those of my class, and that he [del Monte] would take charge to CIRCULATE my works in secret, thus granting them greater consequence) (Cué, *Plácido: El Poeta* 299).

I do not believe Plácido's accusations are without historical merit. Manzano and Plácido did not quarrel about their ties to del Monte, nor did they deny the existence of a project to disseminate subversive poetry. Only the nature of their collaboration with the wealthy reformer was in dispute. Del Monte had collaborated extensively with Manzano, white Cuban writers, and British agents like R. R. Madden to abolish the African slave trade to Cuba. The implication is that he may have also pursued Plácido to make him into a political agent on the island and perhaps abroad, while maintaining plausible deniability. Plácido had similar exchanges with Spaniard Miguel de Silva, who introduced him to prominent white intellectual Francisco de la Luz y Caballero. Miguel de Silva admonished Plácido not to neglect poetry "para ir infundiendo ideas favorables a la abolición de la esclavitud, que era un principio de humanidad adoptado por todos los hombres de *probidad* y talento del mundo culto" ([that would] arouse ideas favorable to the abolition of slavery, which was a principle of humanity adopted by all men of *decency* and talent of the enlightened world) (emphasis original, Cué, *Plácido: El Poeta* 300).[20] The testimony also named Spanish Romantic Jacinto Salas y Quiroga, who traveled to Cuba circa 1839, and Francisco Chacón y Calvo as members of that subversive ilk (Cué, *Plácido: El Poeta* 299, 301). Plácido claimed that abolitionist Benigno Gener had issued him a copy of Salas y Quiroga's travel narrative so that he would distribute it among free African descendants. Though he admitted he had shared the book with someone named Antonio Escoto, he did not address its content; rather, he described it as "nocivas a la tranquilidad del país" (harmful to the tranquility of the country) (Cué, *Plácido: El Poeta* 307).[21] But Jacinto Salas y Quiroga was more charitable in his judgment of the poet. In *Viages* (1840), Salas y Quiroga boasted that no Latin American poet, not even José Maria Heredia, was comparable to the "genio, inspiracion, hidalguía y dignidad" (genius, inspiration, nobility and dignity) of Plácido (173). Salas y Quiroga was astounded by the political bravado of "La profecía de Cuba a España," "La sombra de Pelayo," and the use of the word *liberty* in a poem dedicated to the queen regent. He mused that such literature could only have been published in Matanzas (173-175, 181-182). Salas y Quiroga's soaring praise for Plácido's liberal posturing lends credence to the poet's assertion that white abolitionists sought to make him an agent of conspiracy among *pardos* and *morenos*.

The military authorities issued arrest warrants for Domingo del Monte and José de la Luz y Caballero, but both men evaded apprehension because they were living abroad. (Del Monte departed Cuba in 1842 before the conspiracy had been uncovered.) And Benigno Gener fled to England to evade arrest. But famous reformer Félix Tanco y Bosmeniel had no such luck; the authorities suspended him from his job as postal administrator in Matanzas and arrested and detained him (Paquette 224). As far as we know, the military authorities knew nothing of *Petrona y Rosalía*, his unpublished antislavery novel. However, Plácido did insist that Tanco y Bosmeniel also knew Luis Gigaut (Cué, *Plácido: El Poeta* 306–307), something he admitted. For this and other reasons, the captain general suspected Tanco y Bosmeniel of spreading dangerous ideas (Paquette 224, 247). Gertrudis Gómez de Avellaneda's novels *Sab* and *Dos mujeres* were forbidden by the censors for their "subversive" and "immoral doctrines," but the author was spared arrest because she too was living abroad (Paquette 223–224). Although the authorities brought pressure to bear on Domingo del Monte's slaveholding relatives, the Alfonso and Aldama families, in 1846, the Spanish government acquitted del Monte of conspiracy in absentia (Paquette 262–263).

Plácido's denial of agency and his contention that persons of African descent were merely "BLIND INSTRUMENTS" (Cué, *Plácido: El Poeta* 193) in a high-stakes political game enabled him to deconstruct the official narrative of blackness as genocidal psychosis. Plácido could not plausibly deny that free blacks and mulattoes had knowledge of the plot. His confreres had already testified against him, and the walls were closing in around him. Plácido maintained that people of color were incompetent and incapable of being the architects of an elaborate political scheme. He laid blame for the 1844 movement at the feet of white aristocrats that had been advocating for the abolition of the slave trade to Cuba. Plácido's story to the military commission had its own logic. If free African descendants were mere pawns in masterful hands, then certainly they could not have concocted an intricate plot to eradicate the white population.

Furthermore, Plácido bemoaned the imminent catastrophe to befall Cuba, writing, "determiné pues partir FUERA de la isla por no ser espectador y acaso víctima de la CATÁSTROFE que juzgaba inevitable" (I determined to

DEPART from the island as not to be a spectator and perhaps a victim of the CATASTROPHE that I judged inevitable) (Cué, *Plácido: El Poeta* 300). Plácido discarded his invective against Queen Isabel II from the poem, "La profecía de Cuba a España." The poem roared, "You would always be a slave on a throne / But never a king" (Valdés, *Plácido, Gabriel de la Concepción* 655). He acknowledged, solemnly, that his destiny was in Her Majesty's hands (Cué, *Plácido: El Poeta* 313). In order to negate the impression of African-descended agency, Plácido insisted that freeborn blacks and mulattoes didn't possess collective knowledge of the plot. Rather, he contended: "Por esto parecerá a primera vista que se ha conservado entre ellos el secreto de un plan de conspiración; pero en realidad no es otra cosa que una porción de SECRETOS AISLADOS" (Because of this it may appear at first sight that they have preserved a secret plan of conspiracy among themselves; but in reality, it's nothing but a bunch of ISOLATED SECRETS) (Cué, *Plácido: El Poeta* 304). In this way Plácido not only sought to avoid condemnation but also challenged the emerging narrative of a united black collective sworn to destroy the white population and possess the land for themselves. The existence of esoteric knowledge in black and mulatto hands— something akin to what the Spanish called witchcraft—implied that conspiracy had not only a military component but a metaphysical one as well.

The perception of African-descended disunity was crucial to Plácido's counternarrative, because it enabled him to obfuscate the symbolic parallel between African cosmology—manifest in some of his poetry—and the epistemological locus of *black* conspiracy. I believe Plácido's denial of his locus of control was a sophisticated means to conceal knowledge and thus keep faith with the revolutionary cause. He argued that though the sudden appearance of General Francisco de Senmanat had been consequential to the 1843 black uprising in Havana, free blacks and mulattoes had not coordinated his arrival to the capital.[22] Plácido contended that that white conspirators exploited African descendants as pawns in their political game and had prearranged Senmanat's arrival. Ergo, Plácido's rancorous critique:

> ¡Cuántas copas de Champaña se habrán apurado al presente en loor de las víctimas que se inmolarán para EXASPERAR estas clases, que ni pueden unirse entre sí por la natural ANTIPATÍA que se profesan, ni ligarse a ninguna maquinación oculta por la imposibilidad que hay de CONSERVARSE UN SECRETO entre ellos (Cué, *Plácido: El Poeta* 302).

> (How many glasses of champagne would they imbibe in this moment in praise of the victims sacrificed to EXASPERATE these classes, that can't even unite among themselves owing to the natural ANTIPATHY that they profess for one another, nor bind themselves to hidden machinations because of their inability to PRESERVE A SECRET amongst themselves.)

This portrait of racial antagonism among *pardos y morenos* (free mulattoes and free blacks) was reminiscent of Plácido's critique of pigmentocracy in his satirical poems "Que se lo cuente a su abuela" and "Si a todos Arcino dices." Plácido alluded to colonial stereotypes of the feeble racialized Other to protect his coconspirators and preserve their secrets. And he portrayed the current state of affairs wherein thirty-two people had accused him of rebel recruitment and leadership of the conspiracy.[23] But the testimony of black and mulatto co-conspirators destroyed the image Plácido had carefully crafted of people of color as mere pawns in the hands of the master. Plácido's co-conspirators ascribed to him an explicit sense of agency and an African-descended worldview informed by revolutionary ideas.

### "I Was Not Born a Warrior but a Poet": Plácido's Final Rhetorical Stand

I read the testimony against Plácido in dialogue with his statement to the military commission and his poetry, in search of rhetorical equivalences. It is the epistemological locus of Plácido's seditious activities that interests me here, because the distinctly African Atlantic ethos of those actions reveals the nature of his revolutionary activity. The military tribunal understood Plácido's loyalty oaths as seditious discourse that severed ties to the Spanish crown, ensured unity among the two races [read: blacks and mulattoes], and pledged the destruction of the white race.[24] As he had already testified, Plácido acknowledged having attended the gathering at Jorge López's residence, but he feigned ignorance about what had taken place among those gathered. Plácido wrote: "En la comida de –casa de JORGE LÓPEZ en que se dice que hubo un JURAMENTO, bien pudo ser, [ . . . ] pero dije entonces y repito ahora que NO OÍ TAL JURAMENTO, a mí se me propuso un brindis sin decirme a qué y yo no lo quise aceptar." (They say there was an OATH at dinner in the home of JORGE LÓPEZ, there may have been [ . . . ] but I said then and I repeat now that I DIDN'T HEAR ANY SUCH OATH, they made a toast without telling me what it was for and I didn't consent) (Cué, *Plácido: El Poeta* 309–310). Plácido denied that he had either administered oaths or received them from another party to disguise the existence of an African-descended polity that would defy white hegemony. But the testimony against him suggests otherwise.

According to diverse accounts, Plácido not only witnessed the swearing of oaths but also administered them (Finch 34). José de la O. García testified that Plácido compelled every man present to swear an oath at the home of Marcos Ruiz in December 1843. García testified that the men pledged to recruit more insurgents and to annihilate their masters and all white enemies when the revolutionary moment arrived. The coachman testified that "he received the oath from Plácido the poet, who called the attendees one by one, and asking them to make the sign of the cross with their right hand, they swore [to do as described above]; this being concluded, they withdrew, Plácido charging them to gather together as little as possible so as not to become suspicious" (Finch, *Rethinking* 135–136). In a different locale, a free black carpenter testified that insurgents obliged him "to make the Sign of the cross, and by the sun that gives us light, kissing the earth two times and promising to die or vanquish, [swear that he would] die before revealing the secret. . . ." (Finch *Rethinking* 136). Another prisoner, Secundino Arango, testified that in 1840 Plácido had initiated him into the conspiracy to exterminate the white population, but owing to their mutual trust, the poet did not require him to swear an oath (Cué, "Plácido y la Conspiración " 178).[25] Under interrogation, other persons of African descent accused the poet of conspiracy, or of close ties with the British consul, or of having initiated them into the seditious movement (Cué, "Plácido y la Conspiración" 178). Aisha Finch characterizes the 1844 movement in masculinist terms as a "deeply militaristic" plan in which Plácido performed a pivotal role. The sacred oath preceded the performance of ritual in Plácido's narrative strategy and within his sphere of conspiratorial activity. As the testimony bears out, Plácido's transgressive speech act subverted Catholic doctrine so that the sign of the cross—a liturgical device in honor of the Holy Trinity—initiated African descendants into the revolutionary cause. Making the sign of the cross and kissing the earth is evocative of the sonnet "El juramento," where the poetic "I" made an altar of the hardened earth, swore a vengeful oath, and executed the tyrant. Plácido tarnished his vestments with the blood of Spanish royalty in the poem. The dissemination of Plácido's incendiary poem "El juramento"—by word-of-mouth and in written form (Calcagno 22)—enabled the poet and his co-conspirators to stage revolution that could be achieved only through the racial unity of blacks and mulattoes.

Black and mulatto testimonies paint a portrait of Plácido that is consistent with his *cabildo* poems in a number of ways: they emphasize the creation of cultural space and the avowal of African spiritual knowledge as a prerequisite for sacred brotherhood. Plácido's coreligionists-turned-accusers described secret meetings where Plácido administered loyalty oaths to would-be insurgents to die before revealing anything to their white enemies. José María Mondejar, an elderly black gentleman, testified that in 1843 Plácido had privately sought to recruit him to the conspiracy already afoot (Finch, *Rethinking* 133). In Mondejar's account Plácido described a militaristic plan where "blacks" would rise up against their Spanish oppressors and take possession of the land for themselves. When Mondejar expressed doubts about the plan, Plácido declared that blacks would govern themselves as in Haiti, where "when any white person went [to Haiti], they had to follow their orders" (Finch, *Rethinking* 134). As Plácido asserted in the statement to the military commission, Mondejar also maintained that the British would provide firearms and munitions in support of the black insurgency (Finch, *Rethinking* 134).[26] Plácido admonished his co-conspirators "to take heart and not to be a coward," and Mondejar "resolved to prepare the blacks [for the insurrection]" (Finch *Rethinking* 134). Apparently taking a nod from Plácido, Mondejar disseminated reports that the Haitian monarchy would also provide assistance to Cuban insurgents (Finch *Rethinking* 138). But Mondejar's testimony is important for other reasons. José María Mondejar possessed knowledge of African-inspired rituals and spiritual practices, and he sold talismans to enslaved people on rural plantations (Finch, *Rethinking* 133) that were necessary in the organization of the antislavery movement. Mondejar claimed to have met secretly with Plácido on five separate occasions and insisted that one such meeting had taken place in the *cabildos*. When questioned about Plácido's possible ties to Jamaica—an apparently uncorroborated claim—his one-time co-conspirator asserted, "Perhaps, because Gabriel is the Devil."[27] Even if the betrayal of Plácido by thirty-two blacks and mulattoes was evidence of government pressure, perhaps under torture and of the detainees' concerted efforts to escape execution, we must still contend with the discursive parallels between the testimony against the poet, his written statement to the military commission, and his poems.

Mondejar's testimony about a secretive meeting with Plácido in the *cabildos* is a direct reference to African religious confraternities. Likewise, Plácido's presence at a series of conspiratorial gatherings from 1840 to 1843 meant that the black and mulatto private sphere afforded similar accoutrements as the African *cabildo*, since insurgents transmitted esoteric knowledge, conspired against their oppressors, and formed a sacred fraternity to break the Spanish yoke on the island of Cuba. Not only did black and mulatto testimony portray Plácido as a revolutionary who conspired to annihilate the white population, but black and mulatto testimony also proves that conspirators recanted their oaths and reneged on their promise to partake in an emerging African-descended political structure. For obvious reasons, Plácido's statement to the military commission says nothing of *cabildos*, but his liturgical emphasis on the saints' feast days, and especially on El Día de Reyes in Matanzas, lends credence to Mondejar's claim that he had met with Plácido in a *cabildo*. Furthermore, Cuban historian Manuel Martínez Escobar argues that Plácido held membership in secret societies.

> Plácido era un agente activo de las sociedades secretas que alentaron la rebelión de los esclavos, dispuestos a secundarla al producirse sus éxitos iniciales. Era un propagandista revolucionario que se jugaba diariamente la vida en pos de un ideal, y no una víctima inocente de la persecución colonial, como por algunos se le pinta, restando prestigios a su memoria y regateándole la gratitud de sus compatriotas. Remedios era uno de los mayores focos de la conspiración (56).

> (Plácido was an active agent of the secret societies that incited the slave rebellion, [and] were positioned to support the rebellion after it produced its initial

success. He was a revolutionary propagandist that risked his life daily for an ideal, and not an innocent victim of colonial persecution, as some have portrayed him, diminishing the prestige of his memory and disputing the gratitude of his countrymen. Remedios was one of the main nuclei of the conspiracy.)

Martínez makes one of the most forceful statements in Cuban historiography regarding Plácido's culpability, and also claiming that the African *cabildo* was the locus of his conspiratorial activities. Regrettably, Martínez provides no support for his claims and does not cite his sources. But Martínez's unsubstantiated claims should not be dismissed. Some fragments of the trial record attesting to Plácido's association with *cabildos* coincide with his poetry about the same topic. Plácido's poem "A la Virgen del Rosario" celebrated the patroness of black militias throughout Latin America. The poem was couched in a subtle militancy, because Plácido pledged that the Virgin of the Rosary, otherwise known as the Yoruba *orisha* Dadá, would guarantee victory to her followers and ensure them safe passage to the otherworld. And "El Diablito" transformed Christian carnival into a blueprint for rebellion. Plácido described the African masquerade as ancestral spirit in physical form that had come "to impose the law upon them" (Valdés, *Plácido, Gabriel de la Concepción* 371). The poems were in conversation with each other, and they implied that Africans would exact revenge against Cuban society in the name of their enslaved ancestors.

Plácido's apologia was in fact a self-incriminating narrative. Not only did it situate him within conspiratorial discourse—which the author ascribed to the agitation of white subversives—but also, perhaps more seriously, his statement corroborated that the juntas emerged within a religious context. In his statement to the military commission, Plácido described three scenarios wherein *pardos* and some whites celebrated saints' day festivities (Cué, "Plácido y la conspiración" 197, 199–200) in a racially mixed atmosphere that patrician José Antonio Saco feared would become "una democracia perfecta" (a perfect democracy) (Saco, 41). For Plácido, the rhetorical emphasis on white involvement buttressed his much reiterated claim that whites had seduced politically naive blacks and mulattoes: chief among them was Santiago Pimienta, whom he characterized as "el mas idiota" (the greatest idiot) (Cué, *Plácido: El Poeta* 312).[28] Esteban Montejo explains that the *fiestas de santos* were transculturated rituals wherein black practitioners played the drums and fed the *orishas* that were camouflaged as Catholic saints to conceal their true character from the Spanish (83). In Montejo's account Spaniards appear as the uninitiated spectators of a polyvalent ritual event whose deeper meanings are hidden from them. But a careful reading of Plácido's testimony reveals the decidedly profane nature of the *fiesta de santos* that white Cuban aristocrats attended. Plácido's description of one such *fiesta de santos* in the home of Dionisio Rodríguez, a *pardo*, will suffice to illustrate this point. Plácido wrote, "Otras reuniones de esta naturaleza, donde concurren estos hombres con el fin de saciar sus desenfrenadas pasiones, y después de hacer alarde de una falsa filantropía para prostituirles las esposas y seducirles las hijas" (Other gatherings of this sort, where these men meet with the purpose of satistfying their unbridled passions. And, after making a show of their false philanthropy [they] prostitute the wives and seduce the daughters) (Cué, *Plácido: El poeta* 303). Plácido rebuked white male aristocrats in the strongest possible terms for feigning humanitarianism in order to prostitute African–descended women and dishonor their families. Plácido held African Cuban ritual as sacred—which the poems, "A la Virgen de Rosario" and "El diablito" bear out. White artitsocrats had not only dishonored African-descended women but had also defiled the ritual event. Plácido was not alone in his critique. In 1832 José Antonio Saco also inveighed against the vulgarity of *fiestas de santos*, writing that such religious celebrations had devolved into "pretexto, para que hombres y mujeres corran a bandadas de barrio en barrio, [...] en pos del juego y del escándalo" ([a] pretext for men and women to run around in hordes from neighborhood to neighborhood, [...] in search of gambling and scandal) (Saco 55). The hypocrisy and irreligiosity of the white aristocratic class distressed Plácido, who like Juan Francisco Manzano had placed liturgical emphasis on rituals that invoked a transculturated notion of the saints.

Historians concur that the British consul and white Cubans circulated ideas of freedom among free blacks and mulattoes, something that Plácido also attested to (Paquette 245; Cué, *Plácido: El Poeta* 297, 304). But the white freedom project was reform, not revolution. It defined liberty in terms of property rights and elite participation in colonial governance. Indubitably, del Monte attempted to abolish the slave trade to Cuba in order to ensure the phenotypical whiteness of the island and hasten the creation of a white Catholic polity. In the aggregate, the testimonies of Santiago Pimienta, Miguel Naranjo, José de la O. García, José María Mondejar, and Secundino Arango, among others, constitute a distinctly African Cuban spiritual ethos where retributive justice, not political reform, was the sworn objective. Mondejar's incendiary claim that Plácido envisioned the Haitian Revolution as a conceptual blueprint for the 1844 movement is substantiated by my research at Harvard University. Don Blas de la Onus, a mulatto insurgent, alleged that Plácido was the chief conspirator and had given orders in Havana, Trinidad, Villa Clara, and all throughout the interior for insurgents "degoll[ar] á todos los blancos" (to cut the throats of all the whites). Don Blas claimed that Plácido was to become the president of a new Cuban republic of African descendants. Don Blas also confessed that Plácido had sent an emissary to the Haitian government, which already boasted a network of anonymous agents on Cuban soil.[29] African-inspired ritual at the Bois-Caïman ceremony in 1791, set into motion the spiritual ethos for the Haitian Revolution, and loyalty oaths were acts of initiation that consecrated blacks for the only successful revolution in world history that enslaved persons ever achieved. In 1843–1844,

Haiti was embroiled in hostilities to defend its claims on the Spanish half of the island.[30] So, it is doubtful that the Haitian government was prepared to shore up the black insurgency in Cuba (Paquette 252). But there can be no doubt that Plácido modeled his emancipatory project on Haitian antislavery as the sum of his conspiratorial activities suggests.

Cuban historiography has been unable to corroborate that Plácido was the president of the rebel junta, as the government alleged, but he certainly played more than an ancillary role in the affair. The symbolic parallel between the testimony of co-conspirators, his statement to the authorities, and his literature bear out that Plácido was more than a courier and a propagandist (Paquette 259; Cué 102). Plácido was among the chief architects of an anticolonial faction conceived through the transculturated lens of an African Atlantic spirituality. Plácido maintained ties with British consul David Turnbull and his agent, Luis Gigaut, and he certainly was knowledgeable of their seditious project. In 1841 Gigaut resided at Plácido's home while conducting conspiratorial activities in Matanzas (Castellanos 127). Persuaded by Gigaut, Plácido assembled men, administered loyalty oaths, and carried messages via seditious poetry during his extensive travels. Although Plácido exclaimed, "jamás me haya mezclado con los esclavos, ni resultado la menor alteración en ellas" (I have never mingled with the slaves, or caused the slightest perturbation among them), he did admit to visiting slave plantations (Cué, "Plácido y la conspiración" 200). Plácido collapsed the symbolic and the real; he conceived the spiritual ethos of revolution through an African Cuban religious paradigm whose emphasis on ancestral presence and ritual temporalities enabled interlocutors to rehearse revolutionary activity. Plácido was an architect of discourse whose poetry administered sacred oaths, enacted retributive justice against the white slaveholder, and dethroned the tyranny of the Spanish queen. His emancipatory project constituted the recovery of a Cuban "nacion" (Valdés, *Poesías de Plácido* 194), a pre-Hispanic fatherland that according to some conspirators was to be named for Hatuey in the footsteps of Haitian revolutionaries (Paquette 256–257). Plácido's confraternity did not negate Africa as the origin; rather, he premised brotherhood on African-inspired spirituality and grounded it in an inclusive notion of racial community.

Plácido took his last rhetorical stand. He reiterated that whites and their agents had effectively deceived the *pardos* into acquiescence, but in a rhetorical shift he also implicated certain people of color. The final pages of the hastily written statement mentioned three parties involved in the 1844 movement: Jorge Bernoqui, Santiago Pimienta, and José Erice. Plácido claimed that Bernoqui and Pimienta had fallen victim to the delusions of Luis Gigaut and became convinced that perhaps slave insurrections would pressure the whites (read: the Spanish government) to "DISPENSAR A LOS PARDOS LAS MEJORAS QUE PRETENDÍAN" (BESTOW UPON THE FREE MULATTOES THE

PROGRESS THEY SOUGHT) (Cué, *Plácido: El Poeta* 311).[31] In the same breath, however, he insisted that Pimienta lacked the mental wherewithal to intelligently conspire against whites. But Plácido still insisted that although Pimienta and Bernoqui were not guiltless, they were political pawns in the hands of the powerful British government. However, Plácido did not extend the desire to rescue Pimienta from execution to José Erice, his wife's brother-in-law. Erice was a free militiaman who had confessed involvement in the antislavery movement and later committed suicide. Plácido claimed, "PARECE QUE ERICE y sus compañeros habían trazado UN PLAN DE SANGRE DIGNO DE ELLOS, Y QUIZA INDICADO por el CÓNSUL INGLES, MUY DIFERENTE DEL DE LOS PARDOS" (APPARENTLY ERICE and his accomplices had devised a BLOODY PLAN WORTHY OF THEM, AND PERHAPS DESIGNATED by the ENGLISH CONSUL, VERY DIFFERENT THAN [the plan] OF THE FREE MULATTOES) (Cué, *Plácido: El Poeta* 311). In a racialized gesture, Plácido ascribed the moniker of genocide to José Erice, saying that free blacks had concocted a barbarous plan—without the consent of the *pardos* (free mulattoes)— to "MATAR A TODO EL QUE NO TUVIESE PELLEJO NEGRO" (TO KILL EVERYONE WITHOUT BLACK SKIN) (Cué, *Plácido: El Poeta* 312). Plácido appealed to light-skinned privilege, disassociated himself from blackness, and implied that he too might fall victim to a gruesome plot devised by people intent on destroying the tranquility of the island. But Plácido's condemnation of Erice also implied that free mulattoes had concocted an anticolonial plot of their own, a plot in which Plácido was implicated. This signified a rupture in the narrative of racial unity and a disavowal of loyalty oaths that prompted the collapse of Plácido's sacred brotherhood in terms both figurative and real.

Robert Paquette offers a comprehensive portrait of the black/mulatto coalition. Paquette believes that the government narrative identified the racial fissures that divided persons of African descent (251). By design, Hispanophone Caribbean pigmentocracy established whiteness as the aesthetic ideal, invested it with socioeconomic power and actively promoted antagonisms among *pardos* and *morenos*. Even so, Paquette says that at one point a *pardo-moreno* alliance did exist, but it lost force because some *pardos* abandoned the collaborative project. Comparable to the José Antonio Aponte conspiracy of 1812, free persons of color believed that their cause would be impossible unless it were buttressed by enslaved Africans and their descendants in the Havana-Matanzas-Cárdenas black belt of western Cuba. The black/mulatto conspiratorial committee discussed massive plantation uprisings that would distract soldiers in the municipalities and consume their resources. But the political outcome of a multiracial revolution was never certain. Paquette is doubtful that such a union of disaffected groups—whites, *pardos*, and *morenos*—would have agreed about how to address socio-racial hierarchies or the nature of postrevolutionary state formation (251).

## Conclusion

The coalition that Plácido forged among blacks and mulattoes splintered, and ultimately collapsed. But the government narrative about the events of 1844 substantiates that the Cuban color hierarchy did not fundamentally transform the white/nonwhite racial dichotomy. The arrests, detentions, torture, executions, and expatriations that justified the appellative *el año del cuero* (The Year of the Whip) disproportionately fell to people of African descent. Africans and African descendants suffered the overwhelming brunt of colonial retribution. More people died from starvation, cruel beatings, and other torturous forms of punishment than were executed. This had a devastating effect on the overall size of free and enslaved populations. Between 1841 and 1846, the number of enslaved persons sharply declined, from 436,495 to 326,759, while the free populace lost nearly four thousand people (Midlo Hall 59–60). In colonial Cuba, dark bodies were inexorably equated with blackness, as the interrogation of Manzano and Plácido, Manzano's prison letter to a friend, and Plácido's statement to the military commission attest. Manzano may have saved himself from deportation by implying that Plácido and Luis Gigaut were in cahoots, but he could not liberate his body from the *blackness* that the military tribunal had ascribed to him.

Manzano's letter to del Monte's mother-in-law, Doña Rosa Alfonso de Aldama (Cué, *Plácido: El Poeta* 309), is one of the least-examined texts ever produced during the course of these events. The document detailed the torture and psychological abuse Manzano endured while sequestered. Between 1844 and 1845, colonial authorities imprisoned Manzano and prosecuted him on two separate occasions; they questioned him and tortured him. In June 1844 Manzano was acquitted of the charges brought against him at roughly the same time that Plácido was executed in Matanzas.[32] However, a month following his acquittal, Manzano's fortunes changed when the authorities detained him for further questioning. The prosecution subjected Manzano to maltreatment and held him until November 1845 (Friol 64–66). Manzano's letter from prison to Doña Rosa dated October 5, 1844, reads like a personal triumph over adversity crafted in the language of Catholicism.

> Entré en el consejo, se me consedio la palabra para poner, quitar o desir en mi defenza y aun con bastante conternado con aquel espectaculo tan nuebo para mi, y de hombres que me lloraban, pues ninguno crelló que escapase, ¡tal era la condición de la cita que me iso Matoso, de deber dar cuenta del plan de conspiración por aber estado acomodado ocho meses con el señor Dn. Domingo tanto en la Habana como en Matanzas y otras que segun me dicen está impresa la causa y . . . Entonces no parece sino que el espiritu santo descendio sobre mi cabeza para inspirarme las boses con que pude combencer al consejo de mi inosencia. (Manzano, *Obras* 92)

(I went before the military tribunal, they gave me permission to testify, refute or speak in my defense. And although devastated by such a spectacle so new to me, and with men that wept for me, because no one believed that I would escape [with my life]. Such were the circumstances of the testimony that Matoso [Plácido] gave about me, that I should give account of the conspiratorial plan having resided eight months with Mr. Don Domingo not only in Havana but also in Matanzas and other things published in the case [against me] . . . Then, it seemed as if the Holy Spirit descended upon my head to inspire me with the words with which I was able to convince the court-martial of my innocence.[33]

Colonial authorities arrested Manzano yet again to corroborate Plácido's claims that they had aligned themselves politically, and to further inquire about Manzano's relationship with Domingo del Monte. That authorities detained Manzano after Plácido's execution, suggests that there were lingering suspicions about his role in the antislavery movement. Manzano described his acquittal to Doña Rosa triumphantly comparing the scenario to ancient Rome, "este consejo fue como en Roma" (this tribunal was like in Roman times) when a man unjustly accused was vindicated for all to see (Manzano, *Obras* 92). Manzano emerged as a Cuban Spartacus "fui puesto en plena livertad, con gozo aplauso y admiración de la mayor parte de sus abitantes" (I was fully liberated, to jubilant applause and the admiration of most of the inhabitants) (Manzano, *Obras* 92). In Manzano's rendering of the trial, his innocence is never in doubt to his supporters; loyal men weep for him, and they rejoice when he is released from custody. Rome was the Neoclassical metaphor in Manzano's letter that rendered him a *civilized* mulatto and created distance, at least rhetorically, between him and Plácido.

Manzano characterized Plácido's testimony about him thus: "se le ocur-rio a Gabriel Matoso o Placido el poeta, manchar mi reputación con una sita tan descabellada, que solo sirbió para prover los estrabios de su mal guiada imaginación" (It occurred to Gabriel Matoso or Plácido the Poet, to defile my reputation with a hare-brained meeting [with authorities], that only served to prove the deviance of his rambling imagination) (Manzano, *Obras* 91). This is the most significant rhetorical gesture within the text, because in this letter Manzano betrayed a dead man. Manzano conflated Plácido's poetic genius with madness. Manzano maintained that Plácido had not only written bad poetry with his "rambling imagination" but had also invented sensational accounts of conspiracy with no basis in truth. Nonetheless, Manzano admitted to "having resided eight months with Mr. Don Domingo not only in Havana but also in Matanzas" (Manzano, *Obras* 92), something he had denied previously under interrogation. This further corroborates that Manzano shielded del Monte—who had been involved in the conspiracy—in order to save himself and his network of powerful white allies.

Manzano discarded every allusion to African-inspired spirituality and proclaimed himself an orthodox Catholic. In Manzano's letter to Doña Rosa, the Holy Spirit descended upon him as if upon John the Baptist. Hence, his words to the military tribunal were sacred, persuasive, and, above all, efficacious. Manzano not only survived the trials and tribulations that devastated the lives of the free black artisan class; he also emerged as a virtuous poet, at least on paper. But Manzano's triumphant narrative of his release from prison was marred by the reality of state-sanctioned violence against black bodies. Colonial soldiers tortured Manzano, leaving him to despair for his life.

> . . . así de carsel en carsel de sepos en sepos de bartolina en bartolina, de calabozo en calabozo, de cordillera en cordillera, viendo agorarse mis fuerzas, cuanto de oprovios por ese camino a pie desde Matanzas a la Habana, cuanto de burlas dicterio necesidades sin comer mas que un solo dia una comida en Jaruco, por espasio de seis dias de camino, [...] cuanto de sopapos en mi cara pues yo no sé que recomendasiones traia yo para los capitanes de partido. viendo el que mas se ha singularisado conmigo en seberidad, el de Aguacate, este despues de casi descolluntarme un brazo en el amarrado me metio tan fuerte sopapo de atras para adelante que me vio ir adar contra un horcon con la frente, dandome memorias para los que me esperaban en la eternidad: ( . . . ) (Manzano, *Obras* 94)

> (and so, from jail to jail, from pillory to pillory, from dungeon to dungeon, from mountain to mountain, seeing my strength wither away, such contempt on this road from Matanzas to Havana by foot, such mockery, such taunts, my bodily functions, without eating except for one meal in Jaruco, on the road over a period of six days, [...] so many slaps in the face. I don't know what recommendations I [had to] offer the captains seeing that the one who was the most severe with me was Aguacate, this after almost pulling my arm out of its socket. He backhanded me so hard that my forehead crashed into a wooden post, leaving me with memories of those waiting for me in eternity.

Manzano's account is conspicuously reminiscent of the frequent floggings, confinement, and public shame that he suffered on El Molino sugar plantation. The soldier that escorted Manzano from Matanzas to Havana replaced the overseer and the mistress as the lawful agent of violence. The dark body was once again detained, placed on public display to be scorned, deprived of daily nourishment, and beaten senselessly. Manzano explained to Doña Rosa that one of the guards nearly dislocated his arm from its socket. What is more, the prisoner endured all of this while being forced to take a six-day journey from Matanzas to Havana on foot. Manzano despaired of life, saying that the excruciating torment convinced him that death was imminent, but, as Friol suggested, "el morir sin muerte" ([this was] death without dying) (66). Even as an individual who was legally free, Manzano could be dispossessed of his own body. He beseeched Doña Rosa: "suplico vmd: no se imponga nadien de esto; una palabrita podrá comprometerme mas de lo que estoi" (I ask Your Grace, not to share these details with anyone; one little word could compromise me more than I already have been) (Manzano, *Obras* 96).[34] Manzano's body had been rendered an object of amusement and contempt even after emancipation from slavery. Plácido, however, suffered a worse fate.

One critic argued that Plácido's mulatto body was a site of convergence and resistance to whiteness. José Buscaglia-Salgado writes that Plácido's *mulataje* made him unknowable to white Creole society (xiv, 234). But I have shown that the colonial state certainly did not ascribe to him any such ambiguity. Literary criticism has largely misread Plácido's racial allegiances, either dismissing his claims to African ancestry based on skin color privilege or by neglecting the African Cuban social and conspiratorial networks he maintained. A government report I examined in the Cuban National Archive, which is virtually unknown to scholars of the 1844 antislavery movement, paints a radically different picture of the poet.

> este individuo sin embargo de tener un color bastante claro y de haber nacido de una muger blanca, jamas [palabra inelegible] pertenecer á esta clase y aun se le oyó decir algunas veces que preferia ser el primero de la clase de color[35]

> (this individual although of a rather light [skin] color and having been born of a white woman, never [illegible word] to belong to that class and was even over-heard saying on some occasions that he'd rather be the first among the people of color)

For all of the subterfuge and religious double entendre in his poetry, Plácido was clear about his racial politics. Plácido represented a veritable threat to white supremacy because he contested the mulatto desire for whiteness, he engaged the emancipatory promise of his African religious heritage, and he coalesced a sacred brotherhood whose inner sanctum broke faith with the Spanish crown to erect a new political order. The almost white status that Pedro Barreda and José Antonio Fernández de Castro consign Plácido is not a pervasive factor in his lyrical representations of race, nor does it signify the political character of his insurgent activities against what in one poem he termed the "engañosa raza" (the deceitful race) (Valdés, *Plácido, poeta, y mártir* 154). Plácido vehemently critiqued colonial Cuba as a space designed by white men to fulfill their erotic fantasy of absolute power (Cué, *Plácido: El Poeta* 303). And, in the final analysis, he believed that poetry, above all else, had been his perdition.

Plácido was aware that his life remained in the hands of the very queen he had cursed, so he reminded the military commission that he had never failed to bestow praise on "la *Excelsa* Nieta de San Fernando y a su Augusta Madre" (the Sublime Granddaughter of Saint Fernando and her August Mother) (Cué, *Plácido: El Poeta* 313).[36] But it was not Plácido's use of poetry to applaud the powerful that the queen sought to silence, but rather his genius for subverting the symbols upon which her authority relied.

> mis relaciones con *Jorge Bernoqui* y Pimienta Y LA FATAL ESTIMACIÓN QUE ME HAN DADO MIS VERSOS, les ha hecho CREER FIRMEMENTE a unos que yo era DIRECTOR, y otros, que estando cierto, en que no es así le conviene decir que lo creen. (original emphasis, Cué, *Plácido: El poeta* 311)

> (my relationship with *Jorge Bernoqui* and Pimienta AND THE FATAL ESTEEM THAT THEY HAVE GRANTED MY VERSES, has made some of them FIRMLY BELIEVE that I was the RINGLEADER, and others, being certain that isn't the case, find it convenient to say that it is.)

There is something instructive about the narrative tension in this passage when the apologia virtually devolves into a confession. Plácido inadvertently admitted to a poetics of conspiracy that had enabled him to sow seditious ideas, rouse emotion, and impart a spiritual paradigm for revolutionary exploits.

# EPILOGUE

On June 20, 1844, Spanish authorities executed Plácido in Matanzas before a firing squad. The military tribunal ordered that Plácido be shot in the back as the chief architect, recruiter, and instigator of "the conspiracy devised by the people of color in this city, for the extermination of the white population of the island."[1] But after months of torture and sensory deprivation, Plácido stood erect. Plácido's composure bespoke his resoluteness, and his final words rang out like a poet's last cry, "Adiós mundo." How Plácido died became the stuff of legends, rendering several popular versions that historians have questioned. But the testimony from US consul in Matanzas, T. M. Rodney, bears witness to the solemnity of Plácido's death. Rodney recalled, "Plácido [ . . . ] sustained himself like a man and died true game, the first fire he received three balls but [it] did not kill him and he sang out tira (fire) (adios mundo) goodbye world" (Paquette 260–261). But Plácido was not alone. The government executed the notorious Plácido el Poeta alongside an illustrious catalogue of co-conspirators that reads as a Who's Who of free black Cuban society: Jorge López, a painter and a lieutenant of a black battalion; Santiago Pimienta, a Matanzas plantation owner; Andrés Dodge, a prominent dentist; and Manuel Quiñones. The execution notice, published in Matanzas on June 28, 1844, left no doubt concerning their culpability:

> At six o'clock in the morning today the [following] prisoners received the death penalty, having been shot, [ . . . ] persuaded of the horrendous crime of conspiracy against the white race, for promoting rebellions among the blacks on certain plantations with the pernicious objective of dissolving the rightful submission that has always governed all plantations. These miserable instruments of the most depraved machinations of immoral men, of men deserving the curse of the living and the opprobrium of coming generations, have paid at the gallows for their weakness in collaborating with the plans of other men.[2]

Plácido and his iniquitous band of men had fallen prey to the "depraved machinations" of the British government and their secret agent Luis Gigaut. The government identified the 1844 movement as the brainchild of British abolitionism.

Even so, the colonial state could not deny that Cubans of African descent had organized an antislavery crusade that enjoyed exceptional support among blacks, effectively conscripted both enslaved and free persons and was composed of many centers of seditious activitity that traversed the urban/rural divide. The Spanish government feared Plácido more than any other Cuban because he had invented a blueprint for revolution that might dissolve "the rightful submission" of blacks to whites. The authorities executed Plácido to silence that silvery tongue that had condemned the Queen of Spain, even going as far in one poem as to call her, "a *slave* on the throne but never a king" (italics mine, Valdés, *Plácido, Gabriel de la Concepción* 655).

But the fact that Manzano escaped the ignominious fate that befell the other black conspirators of the 1844 antislavery movement did not escape notice. The prosecutor didn't seem to know what to do about Manzano. He arrested and detained Manzano and questioned him in isolation and then conjointly with his erstwhile collaborator Plácido. But Manzano's highly symbolic poetry and his penchant for double entendre did not come close to the acerbic tenor of Plácido's revolutionary poems. So the authorities acquitted Manzano. Even though they released him, the military tribunal sentenced Manzano to a year of careful surveillance. Yet the government launched a new case against Manzano a month later, and this time he was imprisoned until November 1845. Plácido suffered the ultimate act of silencing: death. When Captain General Leopoldo O'Donnell executed Plácido, he dutifully obeyed the queen's directives "not to spare any means to cut off the branching out that Plácido the Poet's [deeds] has indicated."[3]

What was brilliant about the 1844 antislavery movement was its attempt to bridge the urban/rural divide and to cohere the cultural distance between enslaved Africans and free African descendants. That sociocultural distance was such that it constituted a chasm between free black Cubans—particularly the mixed-race elite—and enslaved Africans. Manzano and Plácido's collaboration was imperative, because it enabled the free black junta to seek broad consensus among an African-descended constituency, ofttimes through the invisible cultural labor of spoken-word poetry and lyrical recitals. Plácido and Manzano exercised the discursive power of popular poetry in Cuba where the overwhelming majority of blacks and whites were illiterate and the public entertained itself at cockfights, improvisations, and minstrel shows. Despite all its power to censor the printed word, repress abolitionist ideas, and even incarcerate prominent writers, the Spanish government could never surveil what was spoken within African *cabildos*. Neither could authorities account for political chatter at private dinner parties in African-descended neighborhoods. Nor could they curtail the manifold ways that blacks appropriated Catholic rites for their purposes at festivities designated to honor the one *true* religion. Essentially, this meant the authorities could not control African Cuban political discourse,

ALCANCE A LA AURORA DE MATANZAS.

VIERNES 28 DE JUNIO DE 1844.

EJECUCION DE JUSTICIA.

A las seis de la mañana de hoy han sufrido la pena de muerte, pasados por las armas, los reos Gabriel de la Concepcion Valdes, conocido por Plácido Jorge Lopez, Santiago Pimienta, José Miguel Roman, Andrés Dodge, Pedro Torres, Manuel Quiñones, Antonio Abad, José de la O, álias Chiquito, Bruno y Miguel, convencidos del horrendo crímen de conspiracion contra la raza blanca, promoviendo rebeliones en las dotaciones de algunas fincas, con el pernicioso objeto de disolver la debida sumision que en todas ellas ha reinado siempre. Estos miserables, instrumentos de las mas depravadas maquinaciones de hombres inmorales, de hombres que merecen la maldicion de los vivos y el oprobio de las jeneraciones venideras, han pagado en el patíbulo su debilidad en secundar los planes de aquellos. La vindicta pública ha quedado satisfecha, y el imperio de las leyes ha demostrado este dia que jamás quedará impune el delito, y que do quiera que asome el jérmen del mal será sofocado y castigados severamente los culpables. Los pueblos de esta preciosa Antilla, á vista del castigo que ha sido impuesto á los principales instigadores del crimen, deben estar seguros de que la tranquilidad del pais jamas será turbada, pues sus enemigos son hartos mezquinos y miserables para poder contrarestar las sabias medidas que en esta ocasion han sabido desplegar nuestras beneméritas Autoridades. Seguidos los trámites de la causa con la debida celeridad, el consejo de guerra de la Seccion de la Comision Militar ejecutiva en esta ciudad, les impuso la merecida pena, que aprobada por el Escmo. Sr. Capitan jeneral con la consulta del Sr. Auditor de guerra, ha sido llevada á efecto este dia, purgando su delito tantos miserables que en su obcecacion creyeron ver realizadas sus perversas maquinaciones.

Algunos periódicos estranjeros mal informados ó con siniestras intenciones, se han complacido en alarmar á las naciones comerciales haciéndoles entender el estado crítico en que supenían se encontraba nuestra Isla de resultas de estos acontecimientos, y así es la poca que felizmente ha gonado siempre esta, lejos de tendicion, merced á su ilustrado Gefe crée, fuese capaz á turbarla la despreciable intentona de cuatro miserables dignos de compasion. Nosotros no apesar de esto se han visto corroboradas, pudiéndose decir que nunca ha habido mas sabor de embarcaciones; el comercio y las transacciones mercantiles no han sido paralizadas, y la confianza ha reinado en todas sus operaciones. Con esto lejos su adeuano escrito á las prensas estranjeras. La Isla de Cuba, donde sus habitantes blancos son ilustrados y leales, donde reina la union y existe una fuerza numerosa de todas armas, con Autoridades y Jefes á la cabeza que han sabido derramar su sangre en los campos de batalla, nada tiene que temer de las asechanzas de los malvados que conspiran contra su bienestar.

The official announcement of Plácido's execution by the Spanish government. The announcement appeared on June 28, 1844, in the Matanzas newspaper *La Aurora de Matanzas.* Courtesy of Oficina del Historiador de la Ciudad de la Habana, Eusebio Leal.

because it often emerged in oral exchanges on Havana and Matanzas street corners, behind closed doors and in slave barracks on plantations. And when black political discourse did emerge in printed form, Plácido and Manzano had often disguised African-inspired spiritual ideas to the extent that government censors were unable to detect them, much less ascertain their political meaning.

Insurgents not only relied on the spoken word to disseminate antislavery ideas but also administered loyalty oaths so that the rebels might break faith with the Spanish crown and become coreligionists in an antislavery crusade. I have shown that the loyalty oath was more than a commitment to insurgency; it was also a sacred speech act that the military tribunal considered "the political method" by which Africans and their descendants preserved their secrets from their Spanish and white Cuban enemies. Such a *political method* enlisted would-be rebels into the movement, ensuring their loyalty to the abolitionist cause and to an ambitious project that placed the Spanish government in the crosshairs.[4] Blacks and mulattoes administered loyalty oaths in urban areas and throughout the Cuban countryside in various nuclei of insurgent activity and organization.

Africans and their Cuban descendants did not have the same relationship to the Catholic Church. But archival records suggest that both groups acknowledged the sacred authority of loyalty oaths, cherished the power within the speech act, and swore oaths with the same solemnity and sense of duty (Pettway, "The Altar, the Oath" 21, 24). Plácido devised the loyalty oath as an organizing principle to unify disparate groups of free and enslaved blacks into a critical mass that might confront the Spanish Empire.

As I have already shown, the historical record proves that loyalty oaths were central to the organization of the insurgency. Numerous other conspirators testified that they had sworn oaths of allegiance to the movement, including free black men: Dámaso Ramos, Antonio Márquez, Mariano Pérez, Gavino Montes de Oca, Gregorio la Ceí, Jacobo Fernández, and Secundino Arango (Finch 258). A free black carpenter testified that insurgents had obliged him "to make the sign of the cross, and by the sun that gives us light, kissing the earth two times and promising to die or vanquish, before revealing the secret. . . ." (Finch 136). In this regard, Plácido was central to the organization of the insurgency, and his lyrical work—where he swore an oath to slay tyrants—constituted part of a spiritual blueprint for African-descended revolution on the island. Plácido ordained sacred oaths to cement religio-political connections between disparate social sectors and, ultimately, to enable the otherwise fractured movement to cohere. Black Cuban rebels countersignified the *signum crucis*—a Catholic symbolic practice honoring the Holy Trinity—and they commissioned it as part of an initiation into insurgency. But the sign of the cross was not desacralized in their ritual practices. Rebels engaged Catholic symbolic practices in a way that was reminiscent of the sacred oaths that Plácido conjured up in the poems "El juramento" (The Oath) and "La profecía de Cuba a España" (Prophecy from Cuba to Spain). Making the sign of the Cross and kissing the earth is evocative of the sonnet "El juramento" where the poet made an altar of the hardened earth, swore an oath of retribution, and blemished his garments with the queen's blood.

Plácido's satires "Si a todos Arcino dices" (If Arcino Says to Everyone), "¡Oh . . .! no juegue, que me moja" (Don't Play Around You'll Get Me Wet), and "Que lo cuente a su abuela" (Let Him Tell That to His Grandmother), among others, were a political intervention into broader intracultural conversations amongst blacks and mulattoes. The 1844 movement could not conceivably flourish, nor could it ultimately triumph over white supremacy, if blacks and mulattoes did not manage to put aside colorism and forge an enduring cultural harmony. Some of Plácido's final statements in the trial record strongly suggest that the 1844 antislavery movement failed, at least in part, because African descendants of differing hues and social standing did not discard their differences. Colonial authorities dreaded the prospect of racial unity among lighter- and darker-skinned African descendants, because it portended the collapse of a pigmentocratic hierarchy devised to nullify African-descended political power. Plácido's satirical poetry posited a broad notion of African-descended community, because in cultural and racial terms it situated the mulatto's origins in Africa. In fact, what the government called "the cooperation of the two races" was a chief tenet of Plácido's political project.[5]

Manzano professed a mulatto racial identity in order to escape blackness, the nadir of slave society. And there is no evidence to suggest that he ever abandoned that position. But Plácido's mockery of mulattoes suggests that Manzano's preferred racial designation was not uncharacteristic of colonial African descendants. Africans identified in terms of ethnicity before the Atlantic slave trade, and the development of a black racial identity was a gradual process that ensued over multiple generations. Africans often identified with their own cultural, geographic, and ethnic criteria, such as *congo* or *lucumí* (Childs 118). But I have shown that Manzano's racial persona did not erode his entrenched religious and cultural identities. Manzano's consistent engagement with African cosmology qualifies some of his poetry and his autobiography as what I have termed *transculturated colonial literature* where he did not seek redemption from the Christian God but rather strove to acquire the power necessary to emancipate himself and liberate his siblings. Manzano mastered Spanish aesthetic forms so that he might manipulate their meaning and advocate in the interest of African-descended freedom. Ironically, his greatest political intervention did not take place in Cuba, but rather in Europe when Madden published an English translation of his autobiography in London in 1840. Madden then proceeded to present his findings on the horrors of Cuban slavery at the World Anti-Slavery Convention in London in 1840, and again in Paris in 1842. Though Madden deprived Manzano of credit for his own writings by removing his surname from the publication, Manzano's slave narrative and his antislavery poetry were among the most formidable rhetorical instruments that the Irish abolitionist had at his disposal. Manzano's autobiography contributed to Madden's effort to undermine the myth that Cuban slavery was more humane than elsewhere (Aching 109; Burton 105).

Plácido's and Manzano's poetry (and to a lesser extent their prose) bridged the sociocultural divide between free blacks and enslaved Africans by evoking the power of African cosmology through coded references to Catholic saints and paths to the Virgin Mary that had been transculturated with Yoruba and Bakongo divine spirits. When Manzano evoked Saint Anthony as the saint that had liberated him from the planation, Africans would have understood Saint Anthony as the spirit of the crossroads: Elegguá or Lucero Mundo, depending on the names their particular traditions (either Yoruba or Bakongo-inspired) had assigned him. And when Plácido signaled to his *cabildo* brethren that "She [the Virgin of the Rosary] assures you victory in life" (Valdés, *Plácido, Gabriel de la Concepción* 10), men and women in African religious confraternities would have interpreted that as a praise song for Dadá, sister of the Changó warrior spirit. Plácido's reference to the Virgin of the Rosary as a spirit able to grant victory to her most loyal disciples not only evoked the patron saint of the Matanzas *cabildo* but also conjured the cultural memory of the protector of Afro-Latin American militiamen that had chosen the Virgin of Rosary as the guardian of their brotherhoods throughout the Diaspora. The Angolan *cabildo* in Recife, Brazil, selected Our Lady of the Rosary as their patron saint, and, as Africans had done in Matanzas, they celebrated their *orisha* on Catholic feast days (Childs 101). That Dadá was the sister of the Changó warrior spirit confirms the religious militancy that blacks in Matanzas and throughout Latin America associated with this Yoruba divine spirit. By invoking the Virgin of the Rosary as Dadá, Plácido reiterated what had, since his 1838 poem, "The Spirit of Padilla" already become a militant trope in his writing. These poems represented the "branching out" of Plácido's cultural influence that the queen of Spain sought to extinguish forever.[6]

Manzano moved on the periphery of the insurgency movement. He was knowledgeable of the plans that the rebel junta had hatched, he attended at least one meeting with Luis Gigaut, and he provided ideological support for the antislavery cause through his poetry and prose. Manzano's political work was comparable to that of other black and mulatto conspirators. But certain mysteries remain regarding the complete nature of his involvement. For instance, we do not know if Manzano ever swore the oath that Plácido administered to others, or if he abjured it. The evidence suggests that Manzano formed part of the 1844 antislavery movement. But perhaps he reneged because of his long-standing loyalty to white Creoles like Domingo del Monte. We do not know for sure. Manzano ultimately confessed under interrogation that Plácido was his friend, though he denied that their camaraderie was politically motivated. It was. Manzano exchanged unpublished poems with Plácido, and they chose common themes to write on. But the details of Plácido and Manzano's conversations about aesthetics are probably unknowable. No archival evidence has surfaced to corroborate that the poets colluded to write about African-inspired spirituality in their literature. But as I have demonstrated in this book, an African Cuban spiritual worldview certainly undergirded some of their work not only as a cultural identifier, but also as a means of theorizing African-descended freedom from colonialism and slavery. One of the problems that arise for cultural historians is that we do not know how many of Manzano's and Plácido's unpublished poems—available only in manuscript form—were in circulation in the years leading up to that fatal moment when the government discovered the 1844 movement.

By the time Manzano introduced himself to Plácido circa 1839, both poets were already espousing the doctrine of African-descended liberation in their work. And the authorities had imprisoned Plácido the previous year for his poem "The Spirit of Padilla." In the poem, an ancestral spirit from sixteenth-century Spain introduces Plácido to the spirit of LIBERTY, for whom he must slay the tyrant. Manzano made common cause with Plácido's project of African-descended liberation, and he also embraced literature as a way of doing politics within white literary circles and on street corners within his own communities. Manzano ascended to a place of political prominence within communities of African descent, a fact that did not escape the notice of Cuba's military government. During the 1844 proceedings, Captain General Leopoldo O'Donnell acknowledged that African descendants regarded Manzano as "a man of great knowledge" (Manzano, *Esclavo poeta* 12–13). Manzano had been free for only three years in 1839, and he remembered vividly the pivotal role that his poem "My Thirty Years" and his autobiography had played in securing his freedom. Plácido visited plantations and spoke with African captives to infiltrate carceral landscapes with his message of liberty. Their spoken and written poetry, chock-full of double entendre and symbolism, was designed to alter black Cuban political consciousness. Both poets harnessed the power of African divine spirits and of ancestral spirits in a protracted war against slavery. Manzano even invoked the image of waging warfare against slavery in the poem "Thirty Years" when he wrote: "But nothing is for me like [this] arduous war / That in fruitless yearning I have endured / If I measure, Oh God! What is to come" (Manzano, "Mis treinta años" 97–98). Although Manzano reneged on the 1844 movement—like many other black conspirators—his subversive poetry and autobiography situated him within a radical political terrain.

Plácido and Manzano pursued power in a society premised on the domination and "thingification" of black women, men, and children: a society that depended on the perpetual theft of black physical and intellectual labor. Plácido's and Manzano's transculturation of early Cuban literature submitted an archetype for black sovereignty unmoored from the principles of messianic redemption. Theirs was a radical notion of liberty that did not espouse Christianity as a rationale for black freedom.[7] This fact alone sets Manzano and Plácido apart from their Caribbean, African American, and black British counterparts such as Mary Prince, David Walker, William Wells Brown, Frederick Douglass, and Olaudah Equiano, who all professed the myth of Christianity's civilizing mission.

In the second half of the nineteenth century and at start of the twentieth, black writers in Cuba and the United States cherished Plácido and Manzano within an emerging African diasporic literary tradition. But either the poets were not remembered for their radical politics of black freedom, or critics construed them through a Christian paradigm that denied the complexity and the power that African-inspired religious knowledge had afforded them.

As a testament to Plácido's enduring fame, Arturo Schomburg published a commemorative piece in 1909 at the centenary of his birth, entitled, "Placido: A

Cuban Martyr."[8] What might be described as a posthumous encounter between the black studies scholar from Puerto Rico and an African Cuban revolutionary poet has been largely relegated to the dustbin of literary history.

Though Schomburg's essay constitutes but a minor part of an impressive body of work, the decision to write about Plácido—and to a lesser extent Manzano—bespoke a desire for canon formation unbound by national tradition. Schomburg's essay on Plácido was part of a broader project of literary archeology that he articulated in "The Negro Digs Up His Past" (1925). Schomburg not only exhumed the memory of Plácido but also expunged antiwhite conspiracy from Plácido's record. Schomburg ascribed to Plácido and Manzano the sobriety, rectitude, and dignity of black masculine respectability. For Schomburg, Plácido was both a martyr and an innocent man; he was a lyrical genius whose aptitude far exceeded that of his white contemporaries Heredia and Milanés. But Schomburg reduced Manzano to little more than Plácido's contemporary. Schomburg reiterated the most common motifs about Manzano: he was born into slavery, emancipated by benevolent Havanese gentlemen, and attained the same artistic stature as Plácido (4). Manzano was important to Schomburg because his presence implied that Plácido was not a sui generis mulatto writer, but rather a member of a larger black literary enclave. Moreover, Schomburg admired Plácido so much that he christened one of his sons "Plácido Carlos" (Des Verney 35).

Schomburg's proverbial visit to the cemetery to exhume, if you will, the ancestral bones of Plácido and Manzano was a way to construct a diasporic past that was not only black but also Latino. Manzano and Plácido and Schomburg share several points of convergence: they adopted writing as a technology of freedom, they endorsed the power of the secret, they thrived within black confraternity, and they pursued emancipatory projects. But in order to *make* the Negro future, Schomburg depicted Plácido and Manzano as impeccable exemplars of the Negro past.

Nearly half a century before Schomburg's essay, Plácido and Manzano had become a cause célèbre in African American abolitionist circles. William Wells Brown, Martin Delany, and even James Weldon Johnson positioned Manzano and Plácido at the epicenter of an emerging diasporic tradition.[9] Brown and Delany were the first among black American writers to embrace their Afro-Latin American counterparts either as historical figures in the case of the former, or as fictionalized characters in Delany's novel *Blake* (1861). In *The Black Man, His Antecedents, His Genius and His Achievements* (1863), Brown celebrated Plácido alongside Denmark Vesey and Haitian revolutionary Toussaint Louverture. Apparently knowing little of Plácido, Brown superimposed Manzano's narrative on Plácido's biography. He identified Plácido as a *slave* and claimed that Plácido's fictive condition as a bondsman justified the antislavery insurgency he had devised (89). Brown anticipated the Cuban cry for independence,

# Placido

## A CUBAN MARTYR

**By A. A. Schomberg**
New York, N. Y.

Black Puerto Rican bibliophile, Arturo Schomburg, published
this article in 1909, to celebrate the centenary of Plácido's birth.

known in Spanish as the *Grito de Yara* (1868), five years prior to its inception. But in Brown's version, the white planter Carlos Manuel de Céspedes would not ignite the struggle; rather, enslaved Cubans would chant the songs of their poet-martyr; their cry would be "Placido and Liberty" (90).[10] Martin Delany's novel *Blake; or, The Huts of America* depicted a pan-American iteration of the Haitian Revolution. Delany addressed the dismay of white elites that the Haitian Revolution might incite insurrection throughout the Western Hemisphere (Nwankwo 55). Delany constructed the Plácido character as a mulatto who transverses national, class, and skin color hierarchies to articulate a pan-African notion of blackness (Nwankwo 57). There are important parallels between the fictive and historical Plácido: the belief that literature is inherently political and that the religion of the oppressed might liberate them. In *Blake*, Plácido recites a poem invoking the Christian God to break the chains of "Africa's sons and daughters" so that "Ethiopia's sons" might rejoice (Nwankwo 259–260).

African American criticism enlisted Manzano and Plácido as Latin American brethren in a diasporic athenaeum, but critics closer to home had little use for Plácido and typically regarded Manzano as a sorrowful Negro, a piteous soul whose "chained lyric" intoned the tragedy of his subjugation.[11] Domingo del Monte published "Dos poetas negros" from the safety of Paris in

1845. Del Monte engaged a racial paradox: he situated Plácido above Manzano within pigmentocratic hierarchy even while pronouncing both poets black. Del Monte said nothing of Plácido's execution as the ringleader of a movement to dethrone the government, abolish slavery, and institute an African-descended republic. Del Monte derided Plácido as a sycophant; he denied the poet the immense symbolic power the military tribunal had ascribed to him. Moreover, del Monte equated Manzano's suffering with the nobility of his own aesthetic theory ("Dos poetas" 84–85). Del Monte was not the only nineteenth-century critic to dishonor Plácido on the basis of aesthetic impurity. White Puerto Rican intellectual Eugenio María de Hostos decried Plácido's poetry as "vain literary beauties" that extoled the queen while Cuba and Puerto Rico cursed her. But the dismissal of Plácido's verse as inelegant once again obfuscated his refusal to subsume the black emancipatory project under the banner of national independence (Fischer 97, 105).

Critics have looked askance at African-inspired religious representations in Plácido and Manzano and, as such, have ignored texts that lend themselves to such an interpretation. Though these writers' African ancestry was rarely in dispute, scholars did not conceive blackness and *latinidad* as an amalgamated whole, but rather as mutually exclusive constructs ensnared in ideological and aesthetic conflict. For many scholars in Cuba and North America, black colonial depictions of Africanity, in any form, was simply inconceivable. But this book has demonstrated that African Cuban spirituality made a different type of black freedom imaginable for Cuban writers, a concept of freedom unfettered by the redemptive narrative of colonial Catholicism.

Schomburg's acquittal of Plácido not only cleansed him of the iniquity of antiwhite sedition for which he was executed but also seemed to reflect the moniker granted him by the black Cuban press: "[PLÁCIDO] THE IDOL OF BLACK CUBANS" (Sanguily, "Otra vez Plácido" 187). The moniker was most certainly befitting, because by 1909—when Schomburg published the article— Plácido (and to a lesser degree Manzano) had been esteemed for more than fifty years in an emerging black Cuban press.[12]

Plácido and Manzano were not the first Cubans of African descent to produce literature. That honor belongs to Manuel del Socorro Rodríguez for his writings commemorating Spanish royalty in 1788, and to Juana Pastor for *décimas* and a sonnet she composed in 1815 (Arrom 386). But Manzano and Plácido were the indisputable architects of a black Cuban discursive tradition that theorized emancipation through the lens of African Atlantic religion.[13] Antonio Medina y Céspedes—the great black Cuban educator—was Manzano's intimate acquaintance, and a central figure in the establishment of the black press.[14] Antonio Medina founded the first black Cuban newspaper, El Faro, in Havana in 1842, two years prior to Plácido's and Manzano's imprisonment on charges of antiwhite conspiracy (*El periodismo*, Deschamps Chapeaux 50).

Medina produced the literary magazine *El Rocío* in 1856, where he paid homage to Manzano and Plácido by reissuing their poetry. Medina's commemoration is ample proof that Manzano and Plácido were more than dead poets to be reminisced; they were pioneers within an emerging literary tradition, and an inspiration to black Cuban literati in a post-1844 political moment (*El periodismo*, Deschamps Chapeaux 103). Medina defied colonial authorities that forbade the queen's subjects to recite Plácido's poetry, consecrate his memory, or even utter his name (Paquette 265).[15] Black Cubans continued to commemorate Plácido as a poet-martyr well into the late nineteenth century. In 1889, under free press laws, Cubans of African descent established the Matanzas newspaper *Plácido*, and another in Santa Clara that they christened, *Homenaje a Plácido.* In 1892 Manuel T. Aday debuted another publication in Palmira, Oriente, also named for the poet (*El periodismo*, Deschamps Chapeaux 73, 93).

Manzano and Plácido's literature was emblematic of one of the fundamental tropes of Cuban culture: the use of language (written, spoken, and gestural) to assert and refute meaning at the same time. Plácido and Manzano transformed Cuban literature through the representation of African cosmologies, but they achieved this transformation without modifying the basic structure of the text.

By way of conclusion, Manzano's and Plácido's writings represented an anomaly in the birth of Cuban letters, because they portrayed African ideas of spirit and cosmos, which transformed and ultimately transculturated the meaning of religious and aesthetic tropes. While Manzano conceived freedom as the spiritual and corporeal redemption of the captive body, Plácido's emancipatory project constructed blacks and mulattoes as a single racial polity who swore sacred loyalty oaths to achieve unity. Nevertheless, Plácido's and Manzano's disparate concepts of emancipation were, in part, illustrative of their social origins. In Plácido's narrative the destruction of monarchy was imperative, for it heralded the spiritual rebirth of the Cuban nation and established a social order based on racial egalitarianism. Conversely, Manzano imagined the spiritual and material reclamation of the enslaved body as the core of a liberatory project whose emphasis lay with the abolition of racial slavery. Plácido's and Manzano's political collaboration imploded. But despite their disparate racial projects, an African-inspired conception of spirituality was the focal point of Manzano's and Plácido's struggle for black liberation.

# NOTES

## Prefatory Note on Racial Terminology

1. See Juan Francisco Manzano's *Juan Francisco Manzano's Autobiografía del esclavo y otros escritos*, edited by William Luis (296).

2. See Daisy Cué Fernández's article "Plácido y la Conspiración de la Escalera" in *Revista Santiago* (145–206) and her book *Plácido: El poeta conspirador*.

## Chapter One

1. *El Laberinto, Periódico Universal* conflated Plácido's life with his contemporary Manzano. The newspaper claimed that Plácido was a former slave whose freedom wealthy liberals had purchased. In fact, Plácido was a free mulatto and his accomplice Manzano had been manumitted when wealthy landowners bought his freedom in exchange for his autobiography in 1836. Biblioteca Nacional de Madrid. See *Hemeroteca Digital, El Laberinto*, Biblioteca Nacional de Madrid, August 16, 1844, pp. 13–14, hemerotecadigital.bne.es/issue.vm?id=0003698297&search =&lang=es. Accessed 4 July 2019.

2. See Lisa Surwillo's *Monsters by Trade: Slave Traffickers in Modern Spanish Literature and Culture*.

3. *Sentencia pronunciada por la Seccion de la Comision militar establecida en la ciudad de Matanzas para conocer de la causa de conspiración de la gente de color*. This document belongs to the "Plácido Collection" in the Oficina del Historiador de la Ciudad de la Habana: legajo 648, expediente 16.

4. In the 1830s, almost ten years prior to Plácido's execution as the alleged leader of La Escalera conspiracy, there were uprisings on sugar and coffee estates in Jaruco, Matanzas, Macurijes, and near Havana. In 1837 there was a revolt in Manzanillo and others in 1840 in Cienfuegos and Trinidad. The next year enslaved workers who were constructing the Palace of Aldama in Havana rebelled and were executed. Please see Gwendolyn Midlo Hall's *Social Control in Slave Plantation Societies: A Comparison of St. Domingue and Cuba* (56).

5. Eugene Genovese is quoted in Ada Ferrer's *Freedom Mirror: Cuba and Haiti in the Age of Revolution* (11).

6. Dorotea in *Francisco* and Petrona in *Petrona y Rosalía* are two sides of the same coin, because both protagonists are victims of rape by their iniquitous white male enslavers. In the mold of female Romantic characters, neither Petrona nor Dorotea is equipped with the fortitude to defy male advances, and unlike their white female counterparts, they are without the supposed protections of patriarchy. Rosalía's invocation of the Virgin Mary is a frantic plea for mercy, for she is horrified by her mistress's lack of empathy, and by Doña Concepción's repeated, albeit unsuccessful, attempts to abort the fetus her son fathered. The novel's denouement devolves into an unvarnished condemnation of Don Antonio and his son Don Fernando articulated through

the lens of Christian religio-moral discourse. As Claudette Williams explains, Tanco y Bosmeniel deconstructs the presumption of white moral superiority through a portrayal of the Cuban slave regime's sexual brutality of black and mulatto women ("The Devil in the Details" 138, 140). But, akin to Dorotea's predicament in the novel *Francisco*, Catholicism does not challenge the racialized slave system but rather facilitates the maintenance of power.

7. Plácido was the pseudonym of Diego Gabriel de la Concepción Valdés, also known as Matoso or *Plácido el poeta* (Plácido the Poet). I use his birth name and the pseudonym Plácido interchangeably throughout the book.

8. In his 1886 anthology, Sebastián Alfredo de Morales attributed some 669 poems to Plácido, including 200 that had never been published or had been issued only in newspapers with scant circulation. Moroccan scholar Abdeslam Azougarh counted some seventy-one poems in Manzano's collected lyrical work.

9. José Amores was a sacristan in Caraballo, Cuba, that exercised the duties of a Catholic priest. See my article in Jerome Branche's *Black Writing, Culture and the State*.

10. In *Up from Slavery*, Booker T. Washington wrote that enslaved African Americans relied on double-voiced Christian rhetoric that celebrated freedom in the afterlife while actually referring to emancipation from slavery in this life (10).

11. In 1842—two years prior to Plácido's and Manzano's imprisonment on charges of antiwhite conspiracy—Antonio Medina founded *El Faro* in Havana, the first black Cuban newspaper. Please see *El Negro en el periodismo cubano en el siglo XIX* by Pedro Deschamps Chapeaux (50).

12. José Antonio Aponte alluded to the biblical prophecy about Ethiopia in Psalms 68:31, just as the Barbadian mason Prince Hall and African American intellectual David Walker had done. See Ada Ferrer's *Freedom's Mirror: Cuba and Haiti in the Age of Revolution* and St. Clair Drake's *The Redemption of Africa and Black Religion*.

13. Under interrogations Manzano explained that Ignacio Valdés Machuca introduced him to Domingo del Monte after he had already published two collections of poetry (Friol 195–196, 212).

14. Domingo del Monte directed educational affairs for the Havana Economic Society (la Sociedad Económica de Amigos del País) and collaborated in early Cuban newspapers.

15. Mahommah Gardo Baquaqua was a central African man from Zoogoo that was taken captive and shipped to Brazil. Baquaqua's narrative is the only known narrative about the life of a former Brazilian slave. See *The Biography of Mahommah Gardo Baquaqua*.

16. Throughout the book, I use "enslaved person" to emphasize that the legal status of captive Africans and their descendants did not adequately describe the fullness of their collective or individual identities. However, when necessary, I use the term "slave" in reference to colonial jurisprudence.

17. We do not know when Manzano wrote "The Poet's Vision." But William Luis discovered that the poem constituted part of another dossier of Manzano's work located at Yale University that was in the possession of white Cuban abolitionist Nicolás Azcárate ("Azcárate's Antislavery Notebook" 334–335, 339). In Virgil's *Aeneid*, Venus performs seemingly incompatible roles: she is an erotic diety and a maternal figure. See Edward Gutting's article "Venus' Maternity and Divinity in the Aeneid" (61). I am grateful to my colleague Kevin Tsai at the University of South Alabama for engaging with me in enlightening conversations about Venus's role in Roman mythology.

18. See Nwankwo's *Black Cosmopolitanism* for more on Plácido's biography (96–97), and Eugenio María de Hostos, *Obra literaria selecta* (213).

19. Plácido published an article of literary criticism in the *Diario de la Habana*, January 26 (27), 1834. The newspaper is part of rare collections in Instituto de Literatura y Lingüística in Havana.

20. The Anglo-Spanish Treaty of 1817 set up the Mixed Court of Justice to prosecute slave trading after Great Britain outlawed it (Luis, *Literary Bondage* 35).

21. The Vatican issued five additional papal bulls between 1443 and 1481 regarding African slavery: *Dudum cud ad nos* (1436); *Rex Regum* (1443); *Divino amore communiti* (1452); *Romanus Pontifex* (1455); *Inter caetera* (1456); *Aeterni Regis* (1481). See Luis N. Rivera Pagán (28).

22. Pope Alexander VI was born Rodrigo Borja in Xativa, Spain, in 1431, and died in Rome in 1503. He was known as the Borgia Pope.

23. In 1513 Pedrarías Dávila wrote the *Requerimiento*, in preparation for Spanish incursions into the Latin American mainland. The *Requerimiento* was written to acquire consent of indigenous people to convert them to Catholicism (Rivera Pagán 34–35).

24. See Vincent Brown on the uses of obeah in Jamaica (35–36). Sonya Maria Johnson—a cultural anthropologist and scholar of Bakongo-inspired religion in Cuba—makes use of the term "African cultural archive."

25. The Yoruba did not constitute a singular African culture; rather, Yoruba was the lingua franca of several precolonial Nigerian ethnic groups and kingdoms: Ife and Oyo, among others. Yoruba-speaking Africans shared a common religious mythic origin as descendants of Oduduwa, and they accepted the city of Ile Ife as a sacred site. Yoruba-speaking Africans were cosmopolitan, highly organized people that were involved in long distance trade (Reis 81–82).

26. Andrew Apter borrows Wyatt MacGaffey's definition from *Religion and Society in Central Africa: The Bakongo of Lower Zaire.*

27. See Melville Herskovits's *The Myth of the Negro Past* (292–299).

28. See the late Cuban scholar James Joel Figarola, *La brujería cubana: El palo monte* for more about the differences between Kongolese and Yoruba cosmologies (25).

29. See the appendix to the *Archaeology of Knowledge* by Michel Foucault (216).

30. Bishop Juan José Díaz de Espada was born in Arroyabe, Spain, in 1756 and died in Havana, Cuba, in 1832. Cuban historian Eduardo Torres Cuevas presents the abolitionist writings of Bishop Espada as a philosophical precursor to Father Félix Varela's famous 1823 essay "Memoria que demuestra la necesidad de extinguir la esclavitud de los negros en la Isla de Cuba" condemning human bondage (Torres Cuevas 69).

31. See Ileana Rodríguez on Domingo del Monte's "liberalismo reformista" (reformist liberalism) (37–39).

32. See William Luis's *Literary Bondage* (39).

33. See Walter Mignolo, "On Pluriversality," www.waltermignolo.com/on-pluriversality/.

34. See Félix Varela's two volumes of *Cartas a Elpidio sobre la impiedad, la superstición, el fanatismo en sus relaciones con la sociedad*, 1836, and 1838 respectively.

35. See the "Plácido Collection" in the Oficina del Historiador de la Ciudad de la Habana: legajo 648, expediente 15. Also see Daisy Cué Fernández, "Muerte y resurrección del poeta Plácido."

36. See Robert Paquette on the historicity of the Ladder Conspiracy of the 1840s (263–264).

37. See Domingo del Monte, "Dos poetas negros," and Cintio Vitier, "Dos poetas cubanos, Plácido y Manzano."

38. See Jerome Branche's *Colonialism and Race in Luso-Hispanic Literature*, for a discussion of the tendency to diminish the role of black agency in the study of slave emancipation (117–118, 125).

## Chapter Two

1. I refer to Manzano's life story variously as "the autobiography," the "slave narrative," and "*la historia de mi vida*" or "*istoria de mi vida*," in accordance with the language the poet himself

used to describe his work. See "La intelectualiad negra en Cuba en el siglo XIX: El caso de Manzano," by Sonia Labrador-Rodríguez (13).

2. Anselmo Suárez y Romero gave the second part of Manzano's autobiography to Ramón de Palma, who lost or otherwise disappeared part 2 of the manuscript ("Introducción" Luis 45).

3. Three years following Guirao's article, José Luciano Franco published a transcription of Manzano's slave narrative, which was the first time it appeared in the original Spanish. See Azougarh (16).

4. *The Imitation of Christ* (1471) has been widely attributed to Thomas à Kempis, but some debate remains regarding its authorship. See Kenneth Strand's "The Brethren of the Common Life: A Review Article of R. R. Post's *The Modern Devotion*."

5. Gerard Groote (1340–1384) is considered to have been the founder of *devotio moderna*. See Kenneth Strand's "The Brethren of the Common Life: A Review Article of R.R. Post's *The Modern Devotion*."

6. This definition comes from the *Merriam-Webster's Dictionary* online: www.merriam -webster.com/dictionary/mortification.

7. See the Trans-Atlantic Slave Trade Database: www.slavevoyages.org/. Also, see Linda Heywood, "Slavery and Its Transformation in the Kingdom of Kongo: 1491–1800," for an explanation of how sixteenth-century Kongolese royalty—that had typically sold foreign-born captives—began increasingly to enslave rivals in the 1600s and 1700s as internal strife worsened and civil war raged (3, 22).

8. Phillis Wheatley was born circa 1753 in West Africa, somewhere between present-day Gambia and Ghana. As a young African girl, she was taken captive in 1761 aboard the slave vessel *Phillis* and later purchased by Bostonians John and Susanna Wheatley. See *Poems on Various Subjects, Religious and Moral*.

9. See Pichardo's *Diccionario provincial de voces cubanas* (1836) (177).

10. This is my translation of a passage in Miguel Barnet's book.

11. He knew only the name his master assigned him, since, as was custom, his owners named him for Don Juan Manzano, giving him the first name and surname.

12. See the 1875 edition of Esteban Pichardo's *Diccionario provincial casi razonado de vozes y frases* (70).

13. The sugar production process had several steps that needed to be carried out in quick succession: the cutting of large and heavy sugar cane stalks, hauling those stalks to be ground, the immediate grinding of the cane, the boiling and evaporation of cane juice (*guarapo*), and finally the crystallization of the sugar. The entire sugar production process had to completed within a few hours (Midlo Hall 16–17).

14. *Chino* was the racial classification for the offspring of a black person and a mulatto in colonial Cuba (70). Manzano's use of the diminutive *chinito* to describe how others saw him on the plantation also suggests that his mother was considered black and his father a mulatto. See Childs. In Ivan Schulman's edition, Evelyn Picon Garfield translates "el mulatico de la Mar." as "María's little mulatto" (115). There does not seem to be any basis, however, for this rendering in the text. In the context of this passage, it appears that *de la Mar.* is an abbreviation for the *Marquesa*, which suggests that, in this instance; Madden's 1840 translation is the more accurate of the two (Manzano, *The Life and Poems* 100). As such, I have adopted his phrasing for my above-cited translation.

15. See Michel Foucault's definition of panopticism in *Discipline and Punish* (201).

16. In *Cimarrón: Historia de un esclavo*, Miguel Barnet states that slave masters refused to refer to the offspring of enslaved women as children but instead called them *criollitos*, using the diminutive for *criollo*. Barnet explains that this word was intended to be offensive and to dehumanize children born to enslaved persons (10).

17. I have adopted Susan Willis's translation of the passage beginning with the paragraph "It had hardly begun to grow light . . ." from her book chapter "Crushed Geraniums: Juan Francisco Manzano and the Language of Slavery" in the anthology *The Slave's Narrative: Texts and Contexts* (210).

18. Robert Richmond Ellis writes that like much of Manzano's autobiography, the passages are out of sequence so that the administrator that raped Manzano was Don Saturnino Carrías, not Don Lucas Rodríguez of Santo Domingo (428).

19. *Morena* (dark-skinned woman) was a euphemism in the Hispanophone Caribbean referring to an African-descended woman of a mahogany hue. As Claudette Williams points out in *Charcoal and Cinnamon: The Politics of Color in Spanish Caribbean Literature*, *trigueña*, denoting a wheat-colored woman, and *morena* stand in place of the epithets *negra* and *prieta*, which indicate African phenotypes (19).

20. See Father Richard Bennett's lecture "Catholic Mysticism and the Emerging Church Reexamined." *YouTube*, uploaded by Dave Flang, 31 Dec 2009, www.youtube.com/watch?v =OfI9H1ZajLs.

21. Mircea Eliade explains that in non-Abrahamic faiths the High God abandons humanity after the creation of the world. The High God became a *deus otiosus*, because he removed himself from that which he brought into existence. See Charles Long's *Significations* (56–57).

22. The 1789 *Código Negro Español* was a summary of slave law based in part on the *Siete Partidas*, a thirteenth-century medieval legal code for Catholic Spain. *Código Negro Español* differed from previous summaries of the law, introducing ameliorative measures to protect enslaved persons and to penalize abusive masters.

23. This is my transcription and English translation of "A Jesús en la cruz." Manzano's poem "A Jesús en la cruz," and "La muerte de Jesus" by Ramón Vélez and "A la muerte de Jesus" by F. Orgaz, are in the rare newspaper collection in the Instituto de Literatura y Lingüística in Havana, Cuba.

24. My transcription of "A Jesús en la cruz" from the rare newspaper collection in Instituto de Literatura y Lingüística in Havana, Cuba, reveals a different orthography than Abdeslam Azougarh's transcription. In *Suite para Juan Francisco Manzano*, Roberto Friol's transcription of the last word in the first verse of the final stanza renders "nudo" (knot) not "mudo" (mute) (134).

25. José Jacinto Milanés—who authored the Matanzas newspaper *La Madrugada* and was well acquainted with Plácido—published "En la muerte de nuestro Señor Jesucristo" in 1850, a sonnet that replicates the same theme as other poetry about the Passion of the Christ (Castellanos 19).

## Chapter Three

1. See "The Magic of Homeric Verses" by Derek Collins (211–236.) Also see "Pindar" by R. C. Jebb (144–183.)

2. Please see *Acerca de Plácido* by Salvador Bueno to consult Manuel Sanguily's articles on Plácido (Sanguily, "Un improvisador cubano [El poeta Plácido y el juicio de Menéndez y Pelayo]," and "Otra vez Plácido y Menéndez y Pelayo [Reparos a censuras apasionadas]," 160–175, 176–190).

3. *La Igualdad* was a black Cuban newspaper dating from 1892 to 1894 directed by Juan Gualberto Gómez. See *Cuba Contemporánea* (Guiral Moreno 70).

4. José de la Luz y Caballero was a white Cuban patrician also implicated in the Ladder Conspiracy (Horrego Estuch 223). Unlike Plácido, Luz y Caballero was absolved of all charges brought against him.

5. *Sentencia pronunciada por la Seccion de la Comision militar establecida en la ciudad de Matanzas para conocer de la causa de conspiración de la gente de color.* This document belongs

to the "Plácido Collection" in the Oficina del Historiador de la Ciudad de la Habana: legajo 648, expediente 16.

6. *Ejecución de Justicia*. This document is within the "Plácido Collection" in the Oficina del Historiador de la Ciudad de la Habana.

7. For a primary document on *fiestas de santos* (saints' feast days), see the Manuel D'Aure letter at the José Augusto Escoto Cuban History and Literature Collection (MS Span 52) at the Houghton Library at Harvard University.

8. See Daisy Cué Fernández, *Plácido: El poeta conspirador*; Ifeoma Nwankwo, *Black Cosmopolitanism*; and Vera Kutzinski's *Sugar Secrets: Race and the Erotics of Cuban Nationalism* for an analysis of Plácido's love poetry.

9. See Sebastián Alfredo Morales's brief biographical writing in the José Augusto Escoto Collection at Houghton Library. Ms Span 52 (552–560) Houghton Library Harvard University.

10. See literary critic Richard Jackson's pioneering study *The Black Image in Latin American Literature* (1976) for a discussion of black as object in abolitionist literature.

11. José Augusto Escoto Cuban History and Literature Collection (MS Span 52), Houghton Library, Harvard University.

12. According to Daisy Cue Fernández, who has studied the history of drawings made of Plácido, the Dubrocq portrait, published in Manuel García Garófalo Mesa's book *Plácido, poeta y mártir*, although still imprecise, appears to be the most accurate (Cué, *Plácido: El poeta* 29, 44–45).

13. See Daisy Cué's *Plácido: El poeta conspirador* for more on nineteenth-century descriptions of Plácido.

14. All translations are mine unless otherwise noted.

15. The 1903 Buenos Aires edition of Plácido's complete works, also published in Mexico and Havana, reproduce the Morales portrait of Plácido in statuesque Greco-Roman form.

16. Most of the punctuation marks originate with the Daisy Cué Fernández's transcription of the original cited in Domingo Figarola Caneda's book *Plácido (poeta cubano) contribución histórico literaria*, but I have added the conjunction *but* in my translation for clarity purposes.

17. See the book *Acerca de Plácido* (1985) edited by Salvador Bueno and *Plácido: Bicentenario del poeta* (2009) compiled and edited by Carmenate Urbano.

18. I have adopted one verse from Vera Kutzinski's English translation of Plácido's poem, "Let Him Tell That to His Grandmother." The verse in question is "Than the rind of bacon" ("Unseasonal Flowers" 155). I am responsible for the English translation of all remaining verses of the poem.

19. See Jerome Branche's *Colonialism and Race in Luso-Hispanic Literature* for more on post-Darwinian theories of social hygiene (15).

20. I have modified the order of the final two verses of the second stanza of "If Arcino Says to Everyone" to provide a more natural-sounding translation.

21. I have rendered the second appearance of this refrain differently, adding the word *hair* to the final verse in order to accentuate its double meaning.

22. My research at Harvard University confirms the arrest and detention of Pilar Poveda in four different government letters from 1845, nearly a year following Plácido's execution. See José Augusto Escoto Cuban History and Literature Collection (MS Span 52) at the Houghton Library, Harvard University.

23. See Baltasar Fra-Molinero's *La imagen de los negros en el teatro del Siglo del Oro* (1995).

24. Margaret Olsen is responsible for the translation of this citation from Alonso de Sandoval's *De instauranda* (1627).

25. *Ejecución de Justicia*. See the "Plácido Collection" in the Oficina del Historiador de la Ciudad de la Habana.

26. Plácido wrote several poems in honor of the parochial church of Matanzas and its parish priest, Father Manuel Francisco García: "Muerte del Redentor" (Death of the Redeemer) and "Nacimiento de Cristo" (The Birth of Christ), "A la colocación de la primera piedra en la nave de la iglesia parroquial de Matanzas" (In the Positioning of the First Stone of the Nave of the Parish Church of Matanzas), "A la bendición de la nave construida en la Iglesia parroquial de Matanzas" (In the Blessing of the Nave Constructed in the Parish Church of Matanzas"), and "Al Sr. Dr. D. Manuel Francisco García, con motivo de la bendición de la segunda torre erijida en esta iglesia parroquial" (To Mr. Dr. Manuel Francisco García, the Blessing of the Second Tower Erected to the Parochial Church).

27. The city of Matanzas was founded in the late seventeenth century. See Charles Warren Currier (135).

28. Plácido likened Father Manuel Francisco García to Moses's brother Aaron in the poem "A la bendición de la nave construida en la Iglesia parroquial de Matanzas" (In the Blessing of the Nave Constructed in the Parish Church of Matanzas"). See Morales's 1886 edition of Plácido's work (612–615).

29. Scholars attribute *The Imitation of Christ* (1471) to Thomas à Kempis, though some debate remains regarding its authorship. See Kenneth Strand's "The Brethren of the Common Life: A Review Article of R. R. Post's *The Modern Devotion.*"

30. Among the most conventional of Plácido's religious-themed poems are "Muerte de Jesucristo," (Death of Jesus Christ), "A la resurrección de Jesús" (To the Resurrection of Jesus), "Muerte del Redentor" (Death of the Redeemer), "A la resurrección" (To the Resurrection), "A la muerte de Cristo" (To the Death of Christ), and "Nacimiento de Cristo" (The Birth of Christ).

31. "Adiós a mi lira" (Farewell to My Lyre), "Adiós a mi madre" (Farewell to my Mother), and "Plegaria a Dios" (Plea to God) are the poems that Plácido is believed to have composed during his final incarceration at the Santa Isabel Hospital in Matanzas in 1844. See Sebastián Alfredo de Morales's 1886 edition of Plácido's poetry (664–668).

32. A letter dated July 9, 1844, addressed to the president of the military commission attests to the clandestine circulation of Plácido's poetry and letters. José Augusto Escoto Cuban History and Literature Collection (MS Span 52) in the Houghton Library at Harvard University.

33. García Garófalo Mesa says that Plácido composed this poem during Holy Week while imprisoned in Trinidad in 1843 (150).

34. Spanish government documentation as regards Cuba carried a colonial seal that read "La siempre fiel isla de Cuba" (The ever-faithful isle). (MS Span 52) in the Houghton Library at Harvard University.

35. "Informe manuscrito dividido en cinco capítulos donde trata de conspiraciones y sublevaciones de negros esclavos con fecha al parecer de 1843. Prisión del pardo Gabriel de la Concepción Valdés, conocido bajo el seudónimo Plácido." Fondo Donativos y Remisiones, legajo 544, expediente 14, Archivo Nacional de Cuba.

36. There is some disagreement about the time and place of the publication of "Mi prisión." According to Alfredo de Morales, "Mi prisión" was written early in 1844, but other critics disagree, instead claiming that Plácido composed it in Trinidad. See the Morales and Mesa editions.

37. Though the 1887 edition was the fifth time *Poetas de color* was published, the Plácido chapter may have been written in 1879. Calcagno writes that thirty-five years had passed since the poet's execution in 1844 (24).

38. Williams Wells Brown and Martin Delany were the first among black American writers to embrace Manzano and Plácido either as historical figures in Brown's *The Black Man, His Antecedents, His Genius and His Achievements* (1863), or as fictionalized characters in Delany's novel *Blake* (1861).

39. *Sentencia pronunciada por la Seccion de la Comision militar establecida en la ciudad de Matanzas para conocer de la causa de conspiración de la gente de color* held in Oficina del Historiador de la Ciudad de la Habana, courtesy of Eusebio Leal.

## Chapter Four

1. I used two sentences from Evelyn Picon Garfield's English translation of Manzano's autobiography appearing in Ivan Schulman's *Autobiography of a Slave by Juan Francisco Manzano* (121).

2. Manzano married twice in the Catholic Church. Manzano's first wife was Marcelina de Campos, a free black woman, who widowed him. Later, Manzano married María del Rosario Díaz, a free mulatto woman (*parda*) in 1835. He referred to his second wife in his letters to Domingo del Monte and in his poetry as Delia (Friol 162–163).

3. My transcription from the autograph manuscript housed at the Biblioteca Nacional José Martí.

4. I think the author's reference to godparents in this passage does not refer to his white baptismal godmother, María de la Luz de Zayas, but is most likely a nod to blacks that served as *padrinos*.

5. In this instance I have used Evelyn Picón Garfield's English translation of a modernized Spanish version of Manzano's slave narrative. See Ivan Schulman's bilingual edition of Juan Francisco Manzano's slave narrative: *Autobiografía de un esclavo/Autobiography of a Slave* (1996).

6. The above-cited is my transcription of the original manuscript found in the Biblioteca Nacional José Martí in Havana, Cuba.

7. Carmen Luz Cosme-Puntiel is one of the few scholars in Hispanic Cultural Studies that have examined Manzano's literature through the lens of African cosmology. Cosme-Puntiel examines Manzano's mastery of writing as the personification of Elegguá in her doctoral dissertation, "En honor a Elegguá: Máscaras y trampas trazando los caminos de Juan Francisco Manzano" (2014). Also see her journal article "La grafía manzaniana: El lenguaje escrito mediante la metáfora y la prosopopeya." See David Sebastian Cross's dissertation, "The Role of the Trickster Figure and Four Afro-Caribbean Meta-Tropes in the Realization of Agency by Three Slave Protagonists" (2013).

8. This is my transcription of the manuscript found in la Biblioteca Nacional José Martí in Havana, Cuba.

9. This is my transcription of the manuscript found in the Biblioteca Nacional José Martí in Havana, Cuba.

10. See *Merriam-Webster's Online Dictionary*: www.merriam-webster.com/dictionary /fanaticism.

11. See Sebastián Alfredo de Morales's explanation that it was a crime to utter the word *libertad* (liberty, freedom). See the José Augusto Escoto Collection in Houghton Library at Harvard University.

12. The novena is a nine-day act of devotion that includes prayers, religious readings, and litanies consecrated to God, the Virgin Mary, and the saints.

13. See Cuban scholars Rómulo Lachatañeré and Natalia Bolívar Aróstegui for more on the transcultuation of Elegguá with Catholic saints.

14. See Daniel Walker's *No More, No More: Slavery and Cultural Resistance in Havana and New Orleans.* Walker writes that wooden artifacts representing Elegguá, dating from the mid- to late nineteenth century, have been located (52–53).

15. See José Luciano Franco, *La presencia negra en el nuevo mundo,* and Laird Bergad, *Cuban Rural Society in the Nineteenth Century: The Social and Economic History of Monoculture in Matanzas.*

16. Professor Pablo García Loaeza of West Virginia University translated "A Dream: For My Second Brother" from the original Spanish into English. I have revised the Spanish-to-English translation of the poem to enhance readability.

17. Throughout this book I have cited from a digital copy of the original manuscript of the poem included in *El Álbum*, vol. VII, 1838, ed. Ramón de Palma, Imprenta de la R. Oliva, housed at the Instituto de Literatura y Lingüística, Institute of Literature and Linguistics.

18. In *La brujería cubana: El palo monte*, Joel James Figarola writes that "cultural marooning" (*cimarronaje cultural*) refers to enslaved individuals who, during the colonial period, placed the bones of their deceased in *ngangas* to fulfill promises made when they were living.

19. In contradistinction to Catholic and Protestant Christianity, the Kongolese have not traditionally defined benevolence in terms of an individual commitment to God. See Simon Bockie, *Death and the Invisible Powers: The World of Kongo Belief*.

20. See Hortense Spillers's lecture "Shades of Intimacy: What the Eighteenth Century Teaches Us."

21. In contemporary Cuban hip-hop, *seres* (beings) is the equivalent of "spirits of the departed" or "*muertos*." See Hermanazos, "Se van los seres," *Paz y amor*. 2010.

22. Todd Ochoa reminds us: "However, Ocha/Santo sovereigns do not contain nfumbe, so the influence of west African notions of divinity on Cuban-Kongo prendas-ngangas-enquisos must be restricted to those of metaphoric affinity" (159).

23. See Jason Young's *Rituals of Resistance: African Atlantic Religion in Kongo and the Low Country in the Era of Slavery* on Bakongo-inspired practices of the Gullah of South Carolina (170). Also see Lydia Cabrera's *El monte* (269–270). Todd Ochoa defines *Kalunga* as an indistinguishable sea of spirits of the dead encompassing all that have existed or might possibly come into being (34). See his *Society of the Dead*.

24. I translated these four stanzas from "A Dream" into English. But I used three lines from Dr. García's translation: "Booming and roaring / Your terrible Right Hand / With violent might." I changed the expression "violent might" to "violent force."

25. See Psalms 17:7, 60:5, and 21:8 for more on the right hand of God in Judeo-Christian belief.

## Chapter Five

1. Plácido embraced William Tell and Don Pelayo as nationalist symbols of resistance against tyranny in his poems "La muerte de Gesler" (The Death of Gessler) and "La sombra de Pelayo" (The Spirit of Pelayo). According to Swiss legend, Albrecht Gessler was a fourteenth-century tyrant whose government gave rise to Swiss nationalist William Tell. Gessler ordered the arrest of Tell. But William Tell, a gifted archer, managed to escape and killed Gessler with one shot (Dundes 327). Don Pelayo is celebrated as a Spanish national hero who defeated the African Moors in the eighth century and supposedly initiated the so-called Reconquest of Iberia (Montenegro and del Castillo, "En torno a la conflictiva fecha" 8, 15).

2. See the posthumous edition of Plácido's poetry published in Paris in 1856.

3. In peninsular Spanish the word *bozal* means "muzzle," a degrading epithet used in slave societies to denote the silencing and physical subjection of captive Africans.

4. See Manzano's autobiography in the Biblioteca Nacional José Martí.

5. For more on the history of the phrase, "tiempos de Mari Castaña" see: http://www .revistaelabasto.com.ar/97_zimmerman_Del_tiempo_de_Maricastania.htm.

6. See *Refranes de negros viejos* by Lydia Cabrera for more on the black and white elders she described as *los viejos* (1–6).

7. It is unknown when Plácido wrote/published "Fantasmas, duendes y brujas."

8. "Sin embajes" is either an orthographical error or a variant of the Spanish expression "sin ambages," meaning to speak straightforwardly.

9. "El egoísta" is an arcane poem within Plácido's collected works that was published in *La Aurora de Matanzas*, presumably in the 1840s. The copy that I am citing hails from the Federico Milanés Collection, part of the José Augusto Escoto Archive at Harvard University. Ms Span 52 (445 a). I have modified the use of quotation marks in "El egoísta," which in the original sometimes appear backward.

10. Coins from the colonial era.

11. *Cuartilla* was a Mexican silver coin.

12. *Recogimiento* is a spiritist rite that cleanses a home from certain negative forces or from the negativity generated by evil spirits or by spirits of the dead that someone has sent with the intent to cause harm (Millet 37).

13. Ms Span 52 (552–560), Houghton Library Harvard University.

14. See Daisy Cué, *Plácido: El poeta* for more on José Fornaris and El Cucalambé, who followed in the footsteps of indigenism's originators: Plácido and Ignacio Valdés Machuca (174–175).

15. See Robert Paquette's *Sugar Is Made with Blood* for more on Hatuey's symbolic importance for the conspirators of 1844 (256–257).

16. See *The 1812 Aponte Rebellion in Cuba* by Matt Childs for more on the limited survival of Cuban indigenous into the eighteenth century (56).

17. Daisy Cué engages the debate about where Plácido published "El juramento" (The Oath) in *Plácido: El poeta conspirador* (87).

18. José Augusto Escoto Cuban History and Literature Collection (MS Span 52) Houghton Library, Harvard University.

19. "Moor" is derived from the Latin word *Mauri*, which literally means "black" or "dark in complexion." The Romans referred to northwest Africa as Mauretania (Pimienta-Bey, "Moorish Spain," 184–185). Jerome Branche explains that the Almoravids that invaded Spain in 1108 were phenotypically black Africans. Spanish King Alfonso X described them thus: "el mas fremoso dellos era negro como la olla" (the most handsome of them was black as a pot) (70–71). See Branche, *Colonialism and Race*.

20. Plácido's Romantic love poetry is replete with examples of tropical nature as a metaphor for the beauty of Afro-Caribbean women; see "La flor de café" (The Coffee Blossom) and "La flor de la caña" (The Sugarcane Blossom). See Ifeoma Kiddoe Nwankwo's *Black Cosmopolitanism* (101–102). Also see Vera Kutzinski's article "Unseasonal Flowers" (157).

21. See Lydia Cabrera, *El monte*, for more on the use of *azahares* in rituals involving Ochún (304).

22. Rafael de Riego Núñez was a Spanish military general who, in 1820, proclaimed a return to the liberal Constitution of Cádiz in Cabezas de San Juan. General Riego's proclamation and subsequent insurrection prevented Spain from amassing an army to defeat Latin Americans waging independence wars (Buldain Jaca, "Causas de pronunciamiento" 7; "Insurrección de Rafael del Riego," www.ecured.cu/Insurrecci%C3%B3n_de_Rafael_del_Riego). Francisco Xavier Mina was a pro-independence Spanish rebel who resisted French occupation. When King Fernando VII returned to the Spanish throne and renounced the liberal Constitution of Cádiz, Mina critiqued the king and was forced to flee Europe (Harris Gaylord Warren, "Mina, Francisco Xavier" www.tshaonline.org/handbook/online/articles/fmi46).

23. See Cirilio Villaverde's novel *Cecilia Valdés o La Loma de Ángel* (1882).

24. See Frantz Fanon's essay "On Violence" from *The Wretched of the Earth* (1963) for his discussion of colonialism and violence.

25. *Sentencia pronunciada por la Seccion de la Comision militar establecida en la ciudad de Matanzas para conocer de la causa de conspiración de la gente de color.* See the "Plácido Collection" in the Oficina del Historiador de la Ciudad de la Habana: legajo 648, expediente 16.

26. In the Bakongo-inspired religious traditions, *prenda* is a synonym for *nganga*. A *prenda* in contemporary Spanish is an article of clothing. See Joel James Figarola's *La brujería cubana:*

*El palo monte* for more on *prendas* and the *ngangulero*, which James Figarola spells differently than Cabrera. Todd Ochoa defines *ngangulera* (*ngangulero*) as "'a person who works a nganga'" (274). See Ochoa's *Society of the Dead*.

27. See *Los ilustres apellidos: Negros en la Habana colonial* by María del Carmen Barcia for more on the earliest African *cabildo* in Cuba organized in Santiago in 1535 (58).

28. See Stephan Palmié for more on the construction of New World ethnic identity, in "Ethnogenetic Processes and Cultural Transfer in Afro-American Slave Populations." (347).

29. See David Brown's *Santería Enthroned* for more on the *capataz* as the ruler of a kingdom (*reinado*) (34–35).

30. Historian María del Carmen Barcia says that although it was unlawful for *cabildos* to accept enslaved persons as members, such prohibitions did not prevent the enslaved from joining (50).

31. In *Los negros brujos*, Fernando Ortiz writes that the Yoruba *orisha* Dadá is the protector of newborn children (43).

32. I have changed the order of the verses in my English translation to achieve a clearer meaning of the stanza.

33. For more descriptions of El Día de Reyes, see *Los cabildos y la fiesta afrocubanos* (36–37).

34. The king and queen of the African *cabildo* marched through the streets of Old Havana to the palace of the captain general, where they pledged loyalty to the Spanish government. See Ivor Miller.

35. Ms Span 52 (552–560), Houghton Library, Harvard University.

36. I have cited from the English translation of *Biography of a Runaway Slave* by Miguel Barnet.

37. "Informe manuscrito dividido en cinco capítulos donde trata de conspiraciones y sublevaciones de negros esclavos con fecha al parecer de 1843. Prisión del pardo Gabriel de la Concepción Valdés, conocido bajo el seudónimo Plácido." Fondo Donativos y Remisiones, legajo 544, expediente 14, Archivo Nacional de Cuba.

## Chapter Six

1. *Sentencia pronunciada por la Seccion de la Comision militar establecida en la ciudad de Matanzas para conocer de la causa de conspiración de la gente de color.* See the "Plácido Collection" in the Oficina del Historiador de la Ciudad de la Habana: legajo 648, expediente 16.

2. I am referring to the judgment against the town of Bainoa, Cuba and surrounding towns. The judgment is found in the José Augusto Escoto Cuban History and Literature Collection (MS Span 52), Houghton Library, Harvard University.

3. José Augusto Escoto Cuban History and Literature Collection (MS Span 52), Houghton Library, Harvard University.

4. See the judgment against the town of Bainoa. José Augusto Escoto Cuban History and Literature Collection (MS Span 52), Houghton Library, Harvard University.

5. The *Sentencia* against the town of Bainoa describes the pervasive character of the 1844 antislavery movement. José Augusto Escoto Cuban History and Literature Collection (MS Span 52), Houghton Library, Harvard University. Carlota Lucumí and Fermina Lucumí stood at the helm of the antislavery insurgency that erupted on the Triunvirato plantation in November 1843 (Finch 88, 147–48, 260).

6. José Augusto Escoto Cuban History and Literature Collection (MS Span 52), Houghton Library, Harvard University.

7. See the *Ejecución de Justicia. Alcance a la Aurora de Matanzas* in the "Plácido Collection" in the Oficina del Historiador de la Ciudad de la Habana, legajo 648, for the names of the nine others executed.

8. *Sentencia pronunciada por la Seccion de la Comision militar establecida en la ciudad de Matanzas para conocer de la causa de conspiración de la gente de color.* See the "Plácido Collection" in the Oficina del Historiador de la Ciudad de la Habana: legajo 648, expediente 16.

9. *Ejecución de Justicia. Alcance a la Aurora de Matanzas.* See the "Plácido Collection" in the Oficina del Historiador de la Ciudad de la Habana: legajo 648.

10. *Sentencia pronunciada por la Seccion de la Comision militar establecida en la ciudad de Matanzas para conocer de la causa de conspiración de la gente de color.* See the "Plácido Collection" in the Oficina del Historiador de la Ciudad de la Habana: legajo 648.

11. In addition to the poem "Un sueño: A mi segundo hermano" (1836), Manzano published a play in 1842 with North African Muslim characters, entitled *Zafira* (Sapphire) (1842), that featured an antislavery subtext. See Olsen's article "Manzano's *Zafira* and the Performance of Cuban Nationhood" (135–158).

12. My transcription of the original manuscript of Manzano's autobiography in the Vidal Morales y Morales Collection at the Biblioteca Nacional José Martí in Havana, Cuba.

13. This does not mean that either writer confessed that Manzano's autobiography had been published in England; they did not. However, in 1840, Madden published it in London.

14. See the *sentencia* in "Colección Plácido" in the Oficina del Historiador de la Ciudad de la Habana, courtesy of Eusebio Leal.

15. Further research remains to be done to determine the full extent of Manzano's knowledge of conspiracy.

16. Roberto Friol proves that Domingo del Monte was not responsible for the early publication of Manzano's 1821 collection, *Cantos a Lesbia.* See *Suite para Juan Francisco Manzano* (212). Given that Manzano became acquainted with Ignacio Valdés Machuca first, I believe that in all likelihood Valdés Machuca brought his first publication, *Cantos a Lesbia*, to press.

17. See historian Robert Paquette's thoughts on the role of torture in exacting testimony in *Sugar Is Made with Blood* (261).

18. I have cited Robert Paquette's translation from the original Spanish in *Sugar Is Made with Blood* (261). Only the last sentence of the passage, which does not appear in Paquette, is my own translation.

19. In 1899 Manuel Sanguily obtained Plácido's statement to the military commission from Vidal Morales y Morales, a prominent intellectual who preserved Manzano's work. In personal interviews, Daisy Cué claimed that the aforesaid statement is a faithful reproduction of Sanguily's copy of the original testimony (*Plácido: El Poeta* 314). Sanguily implemented uppercase letters to place emphasis on certain phrases within the document (Cué, "Plácido y la conspiración" 206). I have not seen the original testimony of Plácido but have consulted Daisy Cué's copy on multiple occasions.

20. Luz y Caballero and de Silva apparently offered Plácido protection in exchange for his cooperation. See Cué, *Plácido: El Poeta* (301).

21. Plácido implied that Santiago Pimienta also had a copy of Jacinto Salas y Quiroga's *Viages,* and that Pimienta had circulated that copy among free blacks (Cué, *Plácido: El Poeta* 307).

22. For more on Francisco de Sentmanat, a white Cuban adventurer who had participated in the Black Eagle Conspiracy, see *Sugar Is Made with Blood* (258).

23. Polonia Gangá was the enslaved woman who betrayed the conspiracy organized by her peers. See *Sugar Is Made with Blood* (214).

24. *Sentencia pronunciada por la Seccion de la Comision militar establecida en la ciudad de Matanzas para conocer de la causa de conspiración de la gente de color.* See "Plácido Collection" in the Oficina del Historiador de la Ciudad de la Habana, legajo 648, expediente 16.

25. The testimony of Secundino Arango is an outlier with respect to the statements of other black and mulatto conspirators. Arango ascribed a psychosexual dimension to the conspiracy

that would later appear in the official judgment. Along with the eradication of the white male population, black women would also be eliminated so that black and mulatto men could take possession of white women and start a miscegenated race on the island. See Cué, "Plácido y la conspiración" (178).

26. Claudio Brindis testified that Luis Gilper, a carpenter, had initiated him into the conspiracy and that British agents planned to equip Plácido with firearms in Matanzas. See Cué, "Plácido y la conspiración" (177–178).

27. Cuban National Archive, legajo 39, Military Commission, folio 196–201, number 1. I am indebted to historian Aisha Finch for generously sharing this archival source with me.

28. Santiago Pimienta was the *hijo natural* (illegitimate son) of a Catholic priest, Father Nicolás González de Chávez. Pimienta was a *pardo* slaveholder who owned La Paciencia, an estate in Matanzas province. See *Sugar Is Made with Blood* (255).

29. See the letter that prosecutor Antonio Sosa wrote dated March 23, 1844. José Augusto Escoto Cuban History and Literature Collection (MS Span 52), Houghton Library, Harvard University.

30. On the collapse of the government of Haitian president Jean Pierre Boyer, see Paquette.

31. Jorge Bernoqui testified that Plácido introduced him to Luis Gigaut in late 1841 or in 1842. According to Bernoqui, Gigaut admitted that he was an agent of David Turnbull and was seeking to recruit fellow *pardos* in the struggle for slave emancipation. Though his testimony was taken before Plácido wrote the statement to the military commission, Bernoqui painted a similar portrait of racial strife between blacks and *pardos* as did Plácido. He insisted that light-skinned mixed-race persons never intended on allying with blacks, whose ferocity made them enemies of all who were not black. See Paquette (253–254).

32. *Ejecución de Justicia*. See the "Plácido Collection" in the Oficina del Historiador de la Ciudad de la Habana. 33. Plácido's father was Diego Ferrer Matoso, a free quadroon barber. Matoso was one of Plácido's nicknames.

34. The family of María de la Luz y Zayas, Manzano's baptismal godmother and former mistress, defended him in court. Her son-in-law, Don Wenceslao de Villa Urrutia—husband of Doña María de los Dolores Montalvo y Zayas—successfully defended Manzano against the government's charges (Friol 211). On June 3, 1844, Manzano's defense attorney imputed Plácido of conspiracy, calling him "the chief spokesman of the uprising." See Friol (209).

35. *Informe manuscrito dividido en cinco capítulos donde trata de conspiraciones y sublevaciones de negros esclavos*. Donativos y Remisiones, legajo 544, expediente 14. The Cuban National Archive.

36. Plácido mistakenly referred to Queen Isabel II as King Fernando VII's granddaughter, though in reality she was his daughter.

## Epilogue

1. *Sentencia pronunciada por la Seccion de la Comision militar establecida en la ciudad de Matanzas para conocer de la causa de la conspiracion de la gente de color*. See the "Plácido Collection" in the Oficina del Historiador de la Ciudad de la Habana: legajo 648, expediente 16.

2. *Ejecución de justicia*. See the "Plácido Collection" in the Oficina del Historiador de la Ciudad de la Habana, courtesy of Eusebio Leal.

3. Cuban National Archive. Real orden, legajo 14, expediente 259.

4. José Augusto Escoto Cuban History and Literature Collection (MS Span 52). Houghton Library, Harvard University.

5. *Sentencia pronunciada por la Seccion de la Comision militar establecida en la ciudad de Matanzas para conocer de la causa de conspiración de la gente de color*. This document belongs

to the "Plácido Collection" in the Oficina del Historiador de la Ciudad de la Habana: legajo 648, expediente 16.

6. Cuban National Archive. Real orden, legajo 14, expediente 259.

7. Daniel Atkinson employed the term "black liberty and sovereignty" in "Feets Don't Fail Me Now." In a personal conversation, Atkinson explained black sovereignty thus: "I can easily say that it is akin to a lot of other notions, but a very easy parallel is to Audre Lorde's "Caring for myself is not self-indulgence, it is self-preservation, and that is an act of political warfare." Meaning Afro-American cultural sovereignty is the same as any other American's notion, only, we as a people have to navigate a path laid by explicit and implicit White supremacy. Therefore, Afro-American sovereignty is the revolutionary act of an Afro-American actively exploring, expressing and controlling one's own contribution to the Afro-American narrative and vernacular culture, free of caveat."

8. Arturo Schomburg published "Placido: A Cuban Martyr" in a Norfolk, Virginia newspaper called the *New Century* in 1909 (Des Verney Sinnette 31).

9. See James Weldon Johnson's 1921 preface to the *Book of American Negro Poetry*. Like Schomburg in the preceding decade, Johnson deemed Plácido, "the greatest of all the Cuban poets" and boasted that the fervor of his genius surpassed that of José María Heredia (McKay, Gates Jr. eds. 899–900). See Miriam DeCosta Willis's essay on Carter G. Woodson's opinion of Plácido (45).

10. See Ada Ferrer, *Insurgent Cuba*, about the Cuban wars for independence.

11. See Domingo del Monte, "Dos poetas negros," in *Ensayos críticos de Domingo del Monte*. Del Monte did not identify Plácido as the son of a quadroon barber and a Spanish dancer, but rather as the offspring of a white man and a mulatto woman (84).

12. See Deschamps Chapeaux, *El negro en el periodismo cubano del siglo XIX*.

13. Manuel del Socorro Rodríguez was the first-known Cuban poet of African descent, publishing "Elogio de Carlos III" in 1788. See Arrom and Portuondo (Arrom 386; Portuondo 13;). Juana Pastor released two lyrical collections, *Décimas* and *Soneto* in 1815, six years prior to Manzano's *Poesías líricas*. See Trelles (33).

14. Antonio Medina y Céspedes was born in Havana in 1829. See Calcagno and Trelles (Calcagno 91–92; Trelles 34).

15. On February 23, 1844, Queen Isabel II issued a decree instructing the authorities to determine the origin and instigators of the rebellion on Matanzas sugar plantations. See the Cuban National Archive, legajo 132, expediente 150.

# WORKS CITED

Aching, Gerard. *Freedom from Liberation: Slavery, Sentiment and Literature in Cuba.* Bloomington: Indiana University Press, 2015.

Adorno, Rolena. *Writing and Resistance in Colonial Perú.* 2nd ed. Austin: University of Texas Press, 2000.

Agamben, Giorgio. *The Sacrament of Language: An Archaeology of the Oath.* Stanford, California: Stanford University Press, 2010.

Akinyela, Makungu M. "Battling the Serpent: Nat Turner, Africanized Christianity and a Black Ethos." *Journal of Black Studies,* vol. 33, no. 3, 2003, pp. 255–280. *JSTOR,* www.jstor.org/stable /3180833. Accessed 27 November 201.

Andrews, George Reid. *Afro-Latin America, 1800–2000.* New York: Oxford University Press, 2004.

Andrews, George Reid. "Spanish American Independence: A Structural Analysis." *Latin American Perspectives,* vol. 12, no. 1, 1985, pp. 105–132.

Anzaldúa, Gloria. *Borderlands: La Frontera.* 2nd ed., San Francisco: Aunt Lute Books, 1999.

Apter, Andrew. *Black Critics and Kings: The Hermeneutics of Power in Yoruba Society.* Chicago: University of Chicago Press, 1992.

Arenas, Reinaldo. *Before Night Falls.* Translated by Dolores M. Koch. New York: Penguin Books, 1994.

Arredondo, Alberto. *El negro en Cuba.* Havana: Editorial "Alfa," 1939.

Arrizón, Alicia. *Queering Mestizaje.* Ann Arbor: University of Michigan Press, 2006.

Arrom, José Juan. "La poesía afrocubana." 1942. *Revista Iberoamericana,* revistaiberoamericana .ptt.edu, file:///Users/matthewjospehpettway/Downloads/1078–4350–1-PB.pdf. Accessed 13 Aug 2018.

Arroyo Martínez, Jossiana. *Travestismos culturales: Literatura y etnografía en Cuba y Brasil.* Pittsburgh: Iberoamericana, 2003.

Arroyo Martínez, Jossiana. *Writing Secrecy in Caribbean Masonry.* New York: Palgrave Macmillan, 2013.

Atkinson, Daniel. "Feets Don't Fail Me Now: Navigating an Unpaved, Rocky Road to, through, and from the Last Plantation." *Civic Labors: Scholar Activism and Working-Class Studies,* edited by Dennis Deslippe, Eric Fure Slocum, and John W. McKerley. Urbana: University of Illinois Press, 2016, pp. 54–65.

Atkinson, Daniel. "Re: Black Sovereignty." Received by Matthew Pettway, June 27, 2018.

Augier, Ángel, ed. *José María Heredia: Obra poética.* Havana: Editorial Letras Cubanas, 2003.

Awolalu, J. Ọmọṣade. "Sin and Its Removal in Traditional African Religion." *Journal of the American Academy of Religion,* vol. 44, no. 2, 1976, pp. 275–287. *JSTOR,* http://www.jstor.org /stable/1462340. Accessed 2 June 2016.

Azougarh, Abdeslam. "Destino y obra de Juan Francisco Manzano." *Juan Francisco Manzano: Esclavo poeta en la Isla de Cuba,* by Azougarh, pp. 9–14. Ediciones Episteme, 2000.

Bakewell, Liza. "Frida Kahlo: A Contemporary Feminist Reading." *Frontiers: A Journal of Women Studies*, vol. 13, no. 3, 1996, pp. 165–189.

Barnet, Miguel. *Biografía de un cimarrón*. Buenos Aires: Ediciones del Sol, 1987.

Barnet, Miguel. *Biography of a Runaway Slave*. Translaed by W. Nick Hill. New York: Pantheon Books, 1994.

Barnet, Miguel. *Cimarrón: Historia de un esclavo*. 2nd ed. Madrid: Siruela, 2000.

Barreda, Pedro. *The Black Protagonist in the Cuban Novel*. Amherst: University of Massachusetts Press, 1979.

Barreras, Juan García. *Explicación de la doctrina cristiana acomodada a los negros bozales*. Havana, 1818.

Basso Ortiz, Alessandra. *Los gangás en Cuba: La comunidad de Matanzas*. Havana: Fundación Fernando Ortiz, 2005.

Bennett, Richard. "Catholic Mysticism and the Emerging Church Reexamined." *YouTube*, uploaded by David Flang, 31 Dec. 2009. www.youtube.com/watch?v=OfI9H1ZajLs.

Bergad, Laird W. *Cuban Rural Society in the Nineteenth Century: The Social and Economic History of Monoculture in Matanzas*. Princeton: Princeton University Press, 1990

Bhabha, Homi K. *The Location of Culture*. London: Routledge, 1994.

The Bible. New International Version. Zondervan, 2011.

Biblioteca Nacional de España: Hemoroteca Digital. *El Laberinto Periódico Universal*. http://hemerotecadigital.bne.es/issue.vm?id=0003698297&search=&lang=es. Accessed 18 September 2018.

Bockie, Simon. *Death and the Invisible Powers: The World of Kongo Belief*. Bloomington: Indiana University Press, 1993.

Bolívar, Natalia Aróstegui. *Los orishas en Cuba*. Havana: Ediciones Unión, 1990.

Branche, Jerome. *Colonialism and Race in Luso-Hispanic Literature*. University of Missouri Press, 2006.

Branche, Jerome. "'Mulato entre negros' (y blancos): Writing Race, the Anti-slavery Question and Juan Francisco Manzano's Autobiografía." *Bulletin of Latin American Research*, vol. 20, no.1, 2001, pp. 63–87.

Brewer-García, Larissa. "Imagined Transformations: Color, Beauty and Black Christian Conversion in Seventeenth-Century Spanish America." *Envisioning Others: Race, Color and the Visual in Iberia and Latin America*, edited by Pamela Patton, pp. 111–141. Leiden, The Netherlands, Koninklije Brill, 2016.

Bristol, Joan Cameron. *Christians, Blasphemers, and Witches: Afro-Mexican Ritual Practice in the Seventeenth Century*. Albuquerque: University of New Mexico Press, 2007.

Bristol, Joan Cameron. "The Church, Africans, and Slave Religion in Latin America." *Cambridge History of Religions*, edited by Virginia Garrard-Burnett, Paul Freston, and Stephen C. Dove, pp. 198–206. New York: Cambridge University Press, 2016.

Brown, David H. *The Light Inside: Abakuá Society Arts and Cuban Cultural History*. Washington, DC: Smithsonian Books, 2003.

Brown, David H. *Santería Enthroned: Art, Ritual and Innovation in an Afro-Cuban Religion*. Chicago: University of Chicago Press, 2003.

Brown, Vincent. "Spiritual Terror and Sacred Authority within Jamaican Slave Society." *Slavery and Abolition*, vol. 24, no. 1, 2003, pp. 24–53.

Brown, William Wells. *The Black Man, His Antecedents, His Genius and His Achievements*. Boston: James Redpath, 1863.

Bueno, Salvador. *Historia de la literatura cubana*. 3rd ed. Havana: Editorial Nacional de Cuba, 1963.

Bueno, Salvador. "Cronología." *Acerca de Plácido*. Havana: Editorial Letras Cubanas, 1985.

Bueno, Salvador. "El polémico caso del infortunado Plácido." *Acerca de Plácido*. Havana: Editorial Letras Cubanas, 1985.

Buldain Jaca, Blanca E. "Causas de pronunciamiento de 1820 y su éxito." *Régimen político y preparación de Cortes en 1820*. Congreso de los Diputados, Serie IV: Monografías, no. 13, pp. 22–33. Madrid, 1988. http://clio.rediris.es/pdf/uned.pdf. Accessed 20 Sept. 2018.

Burdiel, Isabel, "Isabel II: Un perfil inacabado." *Ayer*, no. 29, 1998, pp. 187–216.

Burton, Gera. *Ambivalence and the Postcolonial Subject: The Strategic Alliance of Juan Francisco Manzano and Richard Robert Madden*. New York: Peter Lang, 2004.

Buscaglia-Salgado, José F. *Undoing Empire: Race and Nation in the Mulatto Caribbean*. Minneapolis: University of Minnesota Press, 2003.

Butler, Judith. "Your Behavior Creates Your Gender." *YouTube*. Uploaded by Big Think, 6 June 2011. www.youtube.com/watch?v=Bo7°2LYATDc.

Cabrera, Lydia. *El monte: Igbo finda, ewe orisha vititi nfinda*. Miami: Ediciones Universal, 2006.

Cabrera, Lydia. *Refranes de negros viejos*. Miami: Ediciones CR, 1970.

Calcagno, Francisco. *Poetas de color*. 1868. 5th ed. Havana, 1887.

Casals, Jorge. *Plácido como poeta cubano*. Havana: Publicaciones del Ministerio de Educación, 1944.

Castellanos, Jorge. *Plácido, poeta social y político*. Miami: Ediciones Universal, 1984.

Childs, Matt D. *The 1812 Aponte Rebellion in Cuba and the Struggle against Atlantic Slavery*. Chapel Hill: University of North Carolina Press, 2006.

Collins, Derek. "The Magic of Homeric Verses." *Classical Philology*, vol. 103, no. 3, 2008, pp. 211–236. *JSTOR*, www.jstor.org/stable/10.1086/596515. Accessed 27 Sept. 2018.

Comellas, José Luis. *Isabel II: Una reina y un reinado*. Barcelona: Editorial Ariel, 1990.

Cosme-Puntiel, Carmen Luz. *En honor a Elegguá: Máscaras y trampas trazando los caminos de Juan Francisco Manzano*. 2014. University of Massachusetts. PhD dissertation.

Cosme-Puntiel, Carmen Luz. "La grafía manzaniana: El lenguaje escrito mediante la metáfora y la prosopopeya." *CS*, no. 12, 2013, pp. 377–412.

Cowherd, Carrie. "Roman and Carthaginian Spain: The Black Presence." *Afro-Hispanic Review*, vol. 2, no. 2, 1983, pp. 23–25. *JSTOR*, www.jstor.org/stable/23053734?seq=1#page_scan_tab_contents. Accessed 17 Feb. 2016.

Cross, David Sebastian. *The Role of the Trickster Figure and Four Afro-Caribbean Meta-Tropes in the Realization of Agency by Three Slave Protagonists*. 2013. University of South Carolina, PhD dissertation.

Cros Sandoval, Mercedes. *Worldview, the Orichas, and Santería: Africa to Cuba and Beyond*. Gainesville: University Press of Florida, 2006.

Cruz, Mary. "Plácido y el tema negro." *Bohemia*, 1970, pp. 80–81.

Cué Fernández, Daisy. *De antaño*. Santiago de Cuba: Ediciones Santiago, 2011.

Cué Fernández, Daisy. *Plácido: El poeta conspirador*. Santiago de Cuba: Editorial Oriente, 2007.

Cué Fernández, Daisy. "Plácido y la Conspiración de La Escalera." *Revista Santiago*, 1981, pp. 145–206.

Currier, Charles Warren. "The Church of Cuba: An Outline from the Earliest Period to the Capture of Havana by the English (1492–1762)." *Catholic Historical Review: For the History of the Church in the United States*, vol. 1, 1916, pp. 128–138. *JSTOR*, www.jstor.org/stable/25011310. Accessed 27 Sept. 2018.

Dalleo, Raphael. *Caribbean Literature and the Public Sphere: From the Plantation to the Postcolonial*. Charlottesville: University of Virginia Press, 2011.

Davis, David Brion. *The Problem of Slavery in Western Culture*. New York: Oxford University Press, 1988.

DeCosta-Willis, Miriam. *Blacks in Hispanic Literature: Critical Essays*. National University Publication. Kennikat Press 1977.

DeCosta-Willis, Miriam. "Self and Society in the Afro-Cuban Slave Narrative." *Latin American Literary Review*, vol. 16, no. 32, 1988, pp. 6–15.

Delany, Martin. *Blake; or, The Huts of America*. Edited by Floyd J. Miller. Boston: Beacon Press, 1970.

Del Carmen Barcia, María. *Los Ilustres apellidos: Negros en la Habana colonial*. Havana: Ediciones Boloña, 2009.

Del Monte y Aponte, Domingo. "Dos poetas negros." *Ensayos críticos de Domingo del Monte*, edited by Salvador Bueno, pp. 84–85. Havana: Editorial Pablo de la Torriente, 2000,

Del Monte y Aponte, Domingo. *Escritos de Domingo del Monte*. Edited by José A. Fernández de Castro. Havana: Cultura, 1929.

Deschamps Chapeaux, Pedro. *Los cimarrones urbanos*. Havana: Editorial de Ciencias Sociales, 1983.

Deschamps Chapeaux, Pedro. *El negro en el periodismo cubano en el siglo XIX*. Havana: Ediciones R, 1963.

Des Verney Sinnette, Elinor. *Arthur Alfonso Schomburg: Black Bibliophile & Collector*. Detroit: Wayne State University Press, 1989.

Dodson, Jualynne. *Sacred Spaces and Religious Traditions in Oriente Cuba*. Albuquerque: University of New Mexico Press, 2008.

Douglass, Frederick. *Narrative of the Life of Frederick Douglass: An American Slave*. New York: Barnes and Noble, 2003.

Drake, Jamil. "The Idea of Black Religion." In author's possession, 2018.

Drake, St. Clair. *The Redemption of Africa and Black Religion*. Chicago: Third World Press, 1977.

Dubois, Laurent. *Avenger of the New World: The Story of the Haitian Revolution*. 1st ed. Cambridge: Belknap Press of Harvard University Press, 2004.

Dundes, Allan. "The 1991 Archer Taylor Memorial Lecture, The Apple-Shot: Interpreting the Legend of William Tell." *Western Folklore*, vol. 50, no. 4, 1991, p. 327.

Elena Díaz, María. *The Virgin, the King and the Royal Slaves of El Cobre: Negotiating Freedom in Colonial Cuba, 1670–1780*. Stanford: Stanford University Press, 2000.

Eliade, Mircea. *The Sacred and the Profane: The Nature of Religion*. Orlando: Harcourt, 987.

Ellis, Robert Richmond. "Reading through the Veil of Juan Francisco Manzano: From Homoerotic Violence to the Dream of a Homoracial Bond." *PMLA*, vol. 113, no. 3, 1998, pp. 422–435.

Erskine, Noel Leo. *Decolonizing Theology: A Caribbean Perspective*. Maryknoll, New York: Orbis Books, 1981.

Esténger, Rafael, ed. *La vagancia en Cuba*. Havana: Talleres Tipográficos de Editorial LEX, 1946.

Fabelo, Simeón Teodoro Díaz. *Cincuenta y un patakíes afro-americanos*. Caracas: Monte Ávila Editores, 1983.

Falola, Toyin. "Èṣù: The God without Boundaries." *Èṣù: Yoruba God, Power, and the Imaginative Frontiers*, edited by Toyin Falola, pp. 3–37. Durham: Carolina Academic Press, 2013.

Fanon, Frantz. *Black Skins, White Skins*. New York: Grove Press, 1967.

Fanon, Frantz. *The Wretched of the Earth*. New York: Grove Press, 2004.

Feijóo, Samuel. *El negro en la literatura folklórica cubana*. Havana: Editorial Letras Cubanas, 1987.

Feijóo, Samuel. "Plácido: Flores e indio azteca" *Sobre los movimientos por una poesía cubana hasta 1856*, pp. 36–42. Havana: Universidad Central de Las Villas, Dirección de Publicaciones, 1961.

Feijóo, Samuel. "Plácido: Inicio prematuro de la escuela siboneísta." *Sobre los movimientos por una poesía cubana hasta 1856*, pp. 42–45. Havana: Universidad Central de Las Villas, Dirección de Publicaciones, 1961.

Fernández de Castro. *Órbita de José Antonio Fernández de Castro*. Edited by Salvador Bueno. Havana: Ediciones Unión, 1966.

Ferrer, Ada. *Freedom's Mirror: Cuba and Haiti in the Age of Revolution.* New York: Cambridge University Press, 2014.

Ferrer, Ada. *Insurgent Cuba: Race, Nation, and Revolution, 1868–1898.* Chapel Hill: University of North Carolina Press, 1999.

Figarola, Joel James. *La brujería afrocubana: El palo monte aproximación al pensamiento abstracto de la cubanía.* Santiago de Cuba: Editorial Oriente, 2006.

Finch, Aisha K. *Insurgency at the Crossroads Cuban Slaves and the Conspiracy of La Escalera, 1841–1844.* Dissertation, New York University, 2007, Proquest.

Finch, Aisha K. *Rethinking Slave Rebellion in Cuba: La Escalera and the Insurgencies of 1841–1844.* Chapel Hill: University of North Carolina Press, 2015.

Finch, Aisha K. "Scandalous Scarcities: Black Slave Women, Plantation Domesticity, and Travel Writing in Nineteenth-Century Cuba." *Journal of Historical Sociology,* vol. 23, no. 1, 2010, pp. 101–143.

Fischer, Sibylle. *Modernity Disavowed: Haiti and the Cultures of Slavery in the Age of Revolution.* Durha: Duke University Press, 2004.

Flynn, Maureen. "The Spiritual Uses of Pain in Spanish Mysticism" *Journal of the American Academy of Religion,* vol. 64, no. 2, 1996, pp. 257–278.

Foucault, Michel. *The Archaeology of Knowledge and Discourse on Language.* Translated by Alan Sheridan. New York: Pantheon Books, 1972.

Foucault, Michel. *Discipline and Punish: The Birth of the Prison.* Translated by Alan Sheridan. New York: Vintage Books, 1977.

Fraginals, Manuel Moreno. "Africa in Cuba: A Quantitative Analysis of the African Population of Cuba." *Comparative Perspectives on Slavery in New World Societies,* vol. 292, no. 1, 1977, pp. 187–201.

Fraginals, Manuel Moreno. *El ingenio: Complejo económico y social cubano del azúcar.* Barcelona: Editorial Crítica, 2001.

Fra-Molinero, Baltasar. *La imagen de los negros en el teatro del Siglo del Oro.* Madrid: Siglo Veintiuno Editores, 1995.

Fra-Molinero, Baltasar. "Los negros como figura de negación y diferencia en el teatro barroco." *Hipogrifo,* 2014, pp. 9–11.

Franco, José Luciano. *La presencia negra en el nuevo mundo.* Havana: Casa de las Américas, 1968.

Frey, Sylvia. "Remembered Pasts: African Atlantic Religions." *The Routledge History of Slavery,* edited by Gad Heuman and Trevor Burnard, pp. 153–169. London: Routledge, 2011.

Friol, Roberto. *Suite para Juan Francisco Manzano.* Havana: Editorial Arte y Literatura, 1977.

Fuentes, Aisnara Perera Díaz, and María de los Ángeles Meriño. *Esclavitud, familia y parroquia en Cuba: Otra mirada desde la microhistoria.* 1st ed. Santiago de Cuba: Editorial Oriente, 2006.

Fuentes, Marisa J. *Dispossessed Lives: Enslaved Women, Violence, and the Archive.* Philadelphia: University of Pennsylvania Press, 2016.

Fu-Kiau, Kia Bunseki. *African Cosmology of the Bantu-Kongo: Tying the Spiritual Knot, Principles of Life & Living.* 2nd ed., Athelia Henrietta Press, 2001.

Galanes, Adriana Lewis, ed. *Poesías de J. F. Manzano, esclavo en la isla de Cuba.* Madrid: Editorial Betania, 1991.

García, Enildo. *Cuba: Plácido, poeta mulato de la emancipación.* New York: Senda Nueva de Ediciones, 1986.

Gaylord Warren, Harris. "Mina, Francisco Xavier." www.tshaonline.org/handbook/online/articles/fmi46. Accessed 4 Sept. 2018.

Goldgel, Victor. "Unwilling Impostors, Willing Victims: Passing in Two Nineteenth-Century Cuban Novels." *Fake Identity? The Imposter Narrative in North American Culture*, edited by Caroline Rosenthal and Stephanie Schäfer, pp. 126–142. Frankfurt: Campus Verlag, 2014.

González Páges, Julio César. *Macho, varón, masculino: Estudios de masculinidades en Cuba.* Havana: Editorial de la Mujer, 2010.

Goucher, Candice. *Congotay! Congotay! A Global History of Caribbean Foods.* New York: Routledge, Taylor & Francis, 2014.

Granada, Fray Luis. *Obras de V.P.M. Fray Luis de Granada con un prólogo y la vida del autor,* edited by José Joaquín de Mora. Madrid: Imprenta y Estereotipía de M. Rivadeneyra 1850.

Gray, Thomas R. *The Confessions of Nat Turner, the Leader of the Late Insurrection in Southhampton, Virginia.* Southhampton: Lucas and Deaver, print, 1831.

Guanche, Jesús. *Africanía y etnicidad en Cuba (Los componentes étnicos africanos y sus múltiples denominaciones).* Havana: Ediciones Ciencias Sociales, 2009.

Guerreiro, Henri. "El San Antonio de Padua de Mateo Alemán: Tradición hagiográfica y proceso ideológico de reescritura. En torno al tema de pobres y poderosos." *Criticón Centro Cervantes Virtual,* no. 77, 1999, pp. 5–52. www.cvc.cervantes.es/literatura/criticon/PDF/077/077_006.pdf. Accessed 7 Aug. 2018.

Guiral Moreno, Mario. *Cuba contemporánea: Su origen, su existencia y su significación.* Havana: Molina y Compañía, 1940.

Guirao, Román. "Poetas negros y mestizos de la época esclavista." *Bohemia,* 1934, pp. 40–41, 123–124.

Gutting, Edward. "Venus' Maternity and Divinity in the *Aeneid*." *Materiali e discussioni per l'analisi dei testi classici,* no. 61, 2009, pp. 41–55.

Hall, Gwendolyn Midlo. *Social Control in Slave Plantation Societies: A Comparison of St. Domingue and Cuba.* Baltimore: Johns Hopkins Press, 1971.

Hartman, Saidiya. *Scenes of Subjection: Terror, Slavery, and Self-Making in Nineteenth-Century America.* New York: Oxford University Press, 1997.

Helg, Aline. *Our Rightful Share: The Afro-Cuban Struggle for Equality, 1886–1912.* Chapel Hill: University of North Carolina Press, 1995.

Herskovits, Melville J. *Myth of the Negro Past.* Boston: Beacon Press, 1990.

Hermanazos. "Se van los seres." *YouTube,* uploaded by Altafonte Music Distribution S.L., 6 March 2016. www.youtube.com/watch?v=-s5ooADJDAM.

Hevia Lanier, Oilda. *Prácticas religiosas de los negros en la colonia.* Havana: Editora Historia, 2010.

Heywood, Linda. "Slavery and Its Transformation in the Kingdom of Kongo: 1491–1800." *Journal of African History,* vol. 50, 2009, pp. 1–22. JSTOR, www.jstor.org/stable/40206695. Accessed 1 Jan. 2019 201.

Horrego Estuch, Leopoldo. *Juan Gualberto Gómez, un gran inconforme.* Havana: Editorial de Ciencias Sociales, 2004.

Horrego Estuch, Leopoldo. *Plácido: El poeta infortunado.* Havana: Talleres Tipográficos de Editorial Lex. Amargura, 1960.

Hostos, Eugenio María de. *Obra literaria selecta.* Edited by Julio César. Caracas: Biblioteca Ayacucho, 1988.

Howard-Pitney, David. "The Jeremiads of Frederick Douglass, Booker T. Washington and W.E.B. Dubois and Changing Patterns of Black Messianic Rhetoric, 1841–1920." *Journal of American Ethnic History,* vol. 6, no. 1, 1986, pp. 47–61. JSTOR, http://www.jstor.org/stable/27500485. Accessed 29 May 2014 201.

Huerga, Álvaro. "IV Centenario: Dos pistas de reflexión: Fray Luis de Granada, Guía de hombres." *El Ciervo,* vol. 37, no. 449/450, 1988, pp. 25–27.

Ibáñez García, Miguel Ángel. "La misa de San Gregorio: Acalaraciones sobre un tema iconográfico. Un enjemplo en Pisón de Castrejón (Palencia)." *Norba: Revista del Arte*, 1991, pp. 7–17.

"Insurrección de Rafael del Riego." *EcuRed: Conocimiento con todos y para todos*. www.ecured.cu/Insurrecci%C3%B3n_de_Rafael_del_Riego. Accessed 4 Sept. 2018.

Jackson, Richard. *The Black Image in Latin America*. Albuquerque: University of New Mexico Press, 1976.

Jebb, R. C. "Pindar." *Journal of Hellenic Studies*, vol. 3, 1882, pp. 144–183.

Jiménez, Luis A. "Nineteenth Century Autobiography in the Afro-Americas: Frederick Douglass and Juan Francisco Manzano." *Afro-Hispanic Review*, vol. 14, no. 2, 1995, pp. 47–52.

Johnson, James Weldon. "From the Book of American Negro Poetry, Preface." *The Norton Anthology of African-American Literature*, 2nd ed., edited by Nellie McKay and Henry Louis Gates Jr., pp. 883–905. New York: W. W. Norton, 2004.

Johnson, Sonya Maria. "Bones Cry Out: Palo Monte/Palo Mayombe in Santiago de Cuba." Dissertation, East Lansing, Michigan State University, 2012.

Kagan, Richard. *Lucrecia's Dreams; Politics and Prophecy in Sixteenth Century Spain*. Berkeley: University of California Press, 1990.

Knight, Franklin W. *Slave Society in Cuba during the Nineteenth Century*. 1st ed. Madison: University of Wisconsin Press, 1970.

Kutzinski, Vera. *Sugar's Secrets: Race and Erotics of Cuban Nationalism*. Charlottesville: University Press of Virginia, 1993.

Kutzinski, Vera. "Unseasonal Flowers: Nature and History in Plácido and Jean Toomer." *Yale Journal of Criticism*, vol. 3, no. 2, 1990, pp. 153–179.

Labarga, Fermín. "Historia del culto y devoción en torno al Santo Rosario." *Scripta Theológica*, vol. 35, 2003, pp. 153–154, 159–161, 169.

Labrador-Rodríguez, Sonia. "La intelectualidad negra en Cuba en el siglo XIX: El caso de Manzano." *Revista Iberoamericana*, vol. 62, no. 174, 1996, pp. 13–25.

Lachatañeré, Rómulo. *El sistema religioso de los afrocubanos*. Havana: Editorial de Ciencias Sociales, 2001.

Landers, Jane G. *Atlantic Creoles in the Age of Revolutions*. Cambridge: Harvard University Press, 2010.

Lane, Jill. *Blackface Cuba, 1840–1895*. Philadelphia: University of Pennsylvania Press, 2005.

Levine, Lawrence W. *Black Culture and Black Consciousness: Afro-American Folk Thought from Slavery to Freedom*. New York: Oxford University Press, 1978.

Long, Charles H. *Significations: Signs, Symbols, and Images in the Interpretation of Religions*. Philadelphia, Fortress Press, 1986.

López Mejía, Adelaida. "Race and Character in 'Cien años de soledad.'" *Theory in Action*, vol. 6, no. 1, 2013, doi:10.3798/tia.1937–0237.13002. Accessed Jan. 2016

Lorde, Audre. *Sister Outsider: Essays and Speeches*. Berkeley, California: Crossing Press, 2012.

Luis, William. "Introducción." *Autobiografía del esclavo poeta y otros escritos/Juan Francisco Manzano: Edición, introducción y notas de William Luis*, pp. 13–69 by William Luis, Madrid: Iberoamericana, 2007.

Luis, William. "Juan Francisco Manzano: Entre la oralidad y la escritura." *Del Caribe*, 2000, pp. 33–40.

Luis, William. *Literary Bondage: Slavery in Cuban Narrative*. Austin: University of Texas Press, 1990.

Luis, William. "Nicolás Azcárate's Antislavery Notebook and the Unpublished Poems of the Slave Juan Francisco Manzano." *Revista de Estudios Hispánicos*, vol. 28, 1994, pp. 331–351.

Madden, Richard Robert. *The Island of Cuba Its Resources, Progress and Prospects*. London, 1849.

Manzano, Juan Francisco. *Autobiografía del esclavo poeta y otros escritos / Juan Francisco Manzano: Edición, introducción y notas de William Luis*. Edited by William Luis. Madrid: Iberoamericana, 2007.

Manzano, Juan Francisco. *The Autobiography of a Slave = Autobiografía de un esclavo / by Juan Francisco Manzano: Introduction and Modernized Spanish Version by Ivan A. Schulman*. Edited by Ivan A. Schulman. Detroit: Wayne State University Press, 1996.

Manzano, Juan Francisco. *Juan Francisco Manzano: Esclavo poeta en la isla de Cuba*. Edited by Abdeslam Azougarh. Valencia: Ediciones Episteme, 2000.

Manzano, Juan Francisco. *The Life and Poems of a Cuban Slave: Juan Francisco Manzano, 1797–1854*. Edited by Edward Mullen, Hamden, Connecticut: Archon Books, 1981.

Manzano, Juan Francisco. *Obras de Juan Francisco Manzano*. Edited by José Luciano Franco. Havana: Instituto del Cubano Libro, 1972.

Manzano, Juan Francisco. "Mis treinta años." *Aguinaldo habanero*, edited by José Antonio Echeverría and Ramón del Palma, pp. 141–143. Havana: Imprenta de José María Palmer, 1837.

Manzano, Juan Francisco. "Un sueño: A mi segundo hermano." *El Álbum*, Edited by Ramón del Palma. Havana, vol. 7, 1838, pp. 16–17.

Martin, Kameelah. *Conjuring Moments in African American Literature: Women, Spirit Work, and Other Such Hoodoo*. New York: Palgrave Macmillan, 2012.

Martin, Kameelah. "Hoodoo Ladies and High Conjurers: New Directions for an Old Archetype" *Literary Expressions of African Spirituality*, edited by Carol P. Marsh-Lockett and Elizabeth J. West, pp. 119–144. Lanham, Maryland: Lexington Books, 2013.

Martínez-Alier, Verena. *Marriage, Class and Colour in Nineteenth Century Cuba: A Study of Racial Attitudes and Sexual Values in a Slave Society* London: Cambridge University Press, 1974.

Mbiti, John S. *African Religions and Philosophy* 2nd ed. Oxford: Heinemann Educational, 1999.

McDaniel, Lorna. "The Flying Africans: Extent and Strength of the Myth in the Americas." *New West Indian Guide/Nieuwe West-Indische Gids*, vol. 64, no.1/2, pp. 28–40. www.kitlv-journals .nl. Accessed 14 May 2019.

Mesa, M. García Garófalo. *Plácido, poeta, y mártir*. Mexico City: Acción Moderna Mercantil, 1938.

Midlo-Hall, Gwendolyn. *Social Control in Slave Plantation Societies: A Comparison of St. Domingue and Cuba*. Baton Rouge: Louisiana State University Press, 1996.

Mignolo, Walter. "Delinking: The Rhteoric of Modernity, the Logic of Coloniality, and the Grammar of De-Coloniality." *Cultural Studies*, vol. 21, no. 2, pp. 449–514. http://dx.doi.org /10.1080/09502380601162647.

Mignolo, Walter. "On Pluriversality." *Walter Mignolo*. http://waltermignolo.com/on-pluriversality/.

Milanés, José Jacinto. *José Jacinto Milanés: Obras completas tomo I*. Havana: Editorial Nacional de Cuba, 1963.

Miller, Ivor. *Voice of the Leopard: African Secret Societies and Cuba*. Jackson: University Press of Mississippi, 2009.

Miller, Marilyn. "Rebeldía narrativa: Resistencia poética y "libre" en Juan Francisco Manzano." *Revista Iberoamericana*, vol. 71, no. 211, 2005, pp. 417–436.

Millet, José. *Glosario mágico religioso cubano*. Santiago de Cuba: Editorial Oriente, 1994.

Moliner, Israel. "Manzano: La denuncia del silencio." *Obras*, pp. 226–231. Havana: Instituto Cubano del Libro, 1972.

Molloy, Sylvia. "From Serf to Self: The Autobiography of Juan Francisco Manzano." *Modern Language Notes*, vol. 104, no. 2, 1989, pp. 393–417.

Montenegro, Julia, and Del Castillo, Arcadio. "En torno a la conflictiva fecha de la batalla de Covadonga." *Anales de la Universidad de Alicante: Historia Medieval*, 1990–1991, no. 8, pp. 7–18. rua.ua.es. www.revistes.ua.es/medieval/article/view/1991-n8-en-torno-a-la-conflictiva -fecha-de-la-batalla-de-covadonga/pdf.

Moore, Carlos. *Castro, the Blacks, and Africa*. Berkeley: University of California Press, 1988.

Moore, John A. "A Note on Erasmus and Fray Luis de Granada." *Romance Notes*, vol. 9, no. 2, 1968, pp. 314–319.

Moore, Robin. "The *Teatro Bufo*: Cuban Blackface Theatre of the Nineteenth Century." *Soundscapes from the Americas: Ethnomusicological Essays on the Power, Poetics and Ontology of Performance*, edited by Donna A. Buchanan, pp. 25–42. London: Routledge, 2014.

Moore, Samuel. *Biography of Mahommah Gardo Baquaqua.* Edited by Robin Law and Paul Lovejoy. Princeton: Markus Weiner, 2007.

Morales, Sebastián Alfredo de, ed. "Prólogo." *Plácido: Gabriel de la Concepción Valdés: Poesías completas con doscientas diez composiciones inéditas su retrato y un prólogo biográfico.* Havana, 1886.

Morejón, Nancy. *Nación y mestizaje en Nicolás Guillén.* Havana: Unión de Escritores y Artistas de Cuba, 1980.

Moreno, Mario Guiral. "Bibliografía de autores de la raza de color, de Cuba." *Cuba Contemporánea: Revista Mensual*, vol. 169, 1927, pp. 30–78.

Mudimbe, Valentin. *The Invention of Africa: Gnosis, Philosophy, and the Order of Knowledge.* Bloomington: Indiana University Press, 1988.

Murphy, Joseph M. "Yeyé Cachita: Ochún in a Cuban Mirror." *Osun across the Waters: A Yoruba Goddess in Africa and the Americas,* edited by Joseph Murphy and Mei-Mei Sanford, pp. 87–101. Bloomington: Indiana University Press, 2001.

Nwankwo, Ifeoma Kiddoe. *Black Cosmopolitanism: Racial Consciousness and Transnational Identity in the Nineteenth-Century Americas.* Philadelphia: University of Pennsylvania Press, 2005.

Ochoa, Todd. *Society of the Dead: Quita Manaquita and Palo Praise in Cuba.* Berkeley: University of California Press, 2010.

Ogungbemi, Segun. "Èṣù: The Phenomenon of Existence." *Èṣù: Yoruba God, Power, and the Imaginative Frontiers,* edited by Toyin Falola, pp. 77–89. Durham: Carolina Academic Press, 2013.

Olsen, Margaret M. "Manzano's *Zafira* and the Performance of Cuban Nationhood." *Hispanic Review*, vol. 75, no. 2, pp. 135–158. JSTOR, www-jstor-org.nuncio.cofc.edu/stable/pdf /27668787.pdf?refreqid=excelsior%3A939f84be2a249d14039656131069758d. Accessed 11 Aug. 2018.

Olsen, Margaret M. *Slavery and Salvation in Colonial Cartagena de las Indias.* Gainesville: University Press of Florida, 2004.

Orta Ruiz, Jesús. *Décima y folclor.* Havana: Ediciones Union, 1980.

Ortiz, Fernando. *Los cabildos y la fiesta afro-cubanos del Día de Reyes.* Havana: Editorial de Ciencias Sociales, 1992.

Ortiz, Fernando. *Contrapunteo cubano de tabaco y azúcar.* 1940. Edited by Enrico Mario Santí. 1st ed. Madrid: Ediciones Cátedra Grupo Anaya, S.A., 2002.

Ortiz, Fernando. *Los negros brujos: Apuntes para un estudio de etnología criminal.* Miami: New House, 1973.

Ortiz, Fernando. *Los negros esclavos.* 1st reprint ed. Havana: Editorial de Ciencias Sociales, 1987.

Otero, Solimar. "Èṣù at the Transatlantic Crossroads: Locations of Crossing Over." *Èṣù: Yoruba God, Power, and the Imaginative Frontiers,* edited by Toyin Falola, pp. 191–213. Durham: Carolina Academic Press, 2013.

Otero, Solimar. "Yemayá y Ochún: Queering the Vernacular Logics of the Waters." *Yemoja: Gender, Sexuality, and Creativity in the Latina/o and Afro-Atlantic Diasporas,* edited by Solimar Otero and Toyin Falola, pp. 85–111. Albany: State University of New York Press, 2013.

Palmié, Stephan. "Ethnogenetic Processes and Cultural Transfer in Afro-American Slave Populations." *Slavery in the Americas,* edited by Wolfgang Binder, pp. 337–363. Wurzburg: Konigshausen and Neumann, 1993.

Palmié, Stephan. *Wizards and Scientists: Explorations in Afro-Cuban Modernity and Tradition*. Durham: Duke University Press, 2002.

Paquette, Robert. *Sugar Is Made with Blood: The Conspiracy of La Escalera and the Conflict between Empires over Slavery in Cuba*. Middletown, Connecticut: Wesleyan University Press, 1988.

Patterson, Orlando. *Slavery and Social Death: A Comparative Study*. Cambridge: Harvard University Press, 1982.

Payne, Stanley G. *Spanish Catholicism: An Historical Overview*. Madison: University of Wisconsin Press, 1984.

Pérez, Louis A. Jr. *Cuba: Between Reform and Revolution*. New York: Oxford University Press, 1995.

Pettway, Matthew. "The Altar, the Oath and the Body of Christ: Ritual Poetics and Cuban Racial Politics of 1844." *Black Writing, Culture and the State in Latin America*, edited by Jerome Branche, pp. 9–32, Nashville: Vanderbilt University Press, 2015.

Pettway, Matthew. "Black Femininity and the Silence of Domestic Space in "The Cemetery on the Sugar Plantation" by José del Carmen Díaz," *Zora Neale Hurston Forum*, 2013, pp. 19–46.

Pettway, Matthew. "Braggarts, Charlatans and *Curros*: Black Cuban Masculinity and Humor in the Poetry of Gabriel de la Concepción Valdés." *Breaking the Chains, Forging the Nation: The Afro-Cuban Struggle for Freedom and Equality, 1812-1912*, edited by Aisha Finch and Fannie Rushing, pp. 103–127, Baton Rouge: Louisiana State University Press, 2019.

Pettway, Matthew. "Manzano en el monte: Recuperando el sujeto perdido en 'Un sueño a mi segundo hermano.'" *Del Caribe,* no. 60, 2013, pp. 10–21.

Pettway, Matthew. "Páginas salvadas: De la historia de Santiago de Cuba." *Del Caribe*, no. 112, 2014, pp. 62–63.

Pettway, Matthew. "Ritual and Reason: Negotiating Freedom in the Literature of Juan Francisco Manzano." *PALARA*, no. 16, 2012, pp. 64–77.

Pettway, Matthew. "Sacred Ways of Meaning and Knowing: A Comparative Reading of Caribbean Literature." *American Studies Journal*, vol. 54, no. 1, 2015, pp. 115–127.

Pichardo y Tapia, Esteban. *Diccionario provincial casi razonado de vozes y frases cubanas*. 4th ed. Havana: Imprenta El Trabajo de León F. Dediot, 1875.

Pichardo y Tapia, Esteban. *Diccionario provincial de voces cubanas*. Matanzas: Imprenta de la Real Marina, 1836.

Pimienta-Bey, José. "Moorish Spain: Academic Source and Foundation for the Rise and Success of Western European Universities." *The Golden Age of the Moors*, edited by Ivan Van Sertima, pp. 182–247. Piscataway, NJ: Transaction, 1992.

Portuondo, José Antonio. *Bosquejo histórico de las letras cubanas*. Havana: Editorial Nacional de Cuba, 1962.

Pratt, Mary Louise. *Imperial Eyes: Travel Writing and Transculturation*. London: Routledge, 1992.

Pratt, Mary Louise. "Transculturation and Autoethnography: Peru, 1615/1980." *Colonial Discourse/Postcolonial Theory*, edited by Francis Barker, Peter Hulme, and Margaret Iversen, pp. 24-46. Manchester: Manchester University Press, 1994.

Price, Rachel. "Enemigo Suelo: Manzano Rewrites Cuban Romanticism." *Revista Canadiense de Estudios Hispánicos*, vol. 38, no. 3, 2014, pp. 529–554.

Purcell, Mary. *St. Anthony and His Times*. Dublin: M. H. Gill and Son, 1960.

Rama, Ángel. *Transculturación narrativa en América Latina*. 1st ed. México City: Siglo Veintiuno, 1982.

Ramos, Julio. "La ley es otra: Literatura y constitución de la persona jurídica." *Revista de Crítica Literaria Latinoamericana*, vol. 20, no. 40, 1994, pp. 305–335. *JSTOR*, http://www.jstor.org /stable/4530773. Accessed 15 May 2017.

Reis, João José. "Nagô and Mina: The Yoruba Diaspora in Brazil." *The Yoruba Diaspora in the Atlantic World*, edited by Toyin Falola and Matt Childs, pp. 77–110. Bloomington: Indiana University Press, 2004.

Rivera Pagán, Luis N. *A Violent Evangelism: The Political and Religious Conquest of the Americas*. Westminster/John Knox Press, 1992.

Rodríguez, Ileana. "Romanticismo literario y liberalismo reformista: El grupo de Domingo Delmonte." *Caribbean Studies*, vol. 20, no. 1, 1980, pp. 35–56. *JSTOR*, www.jstor.org/stable /25612885. Accessed 25 June 2013.

Román, Reinaldo L. "Governing Man-Gods: Spiritism and the Struggle for Progress in Republican Cuba." *Journal of Religion in Africa*, vol. 37, 2007, pp. 212–214.

Rosenberg, John R. *The Black Butterfly: Concepts of Spanish Romanticism*. Jackson: University of Mississippi: Romance Monographs, 1998.

Saco, José Antonio. *Memoria sobre la vagancia en la isla de Cuba*, edited by Rafael Esténger. Havana: Publicaciones del Ministerio de Educación, 1946.

Said, Edward. "The Text, the World and the Critic." *Bulletin of the Midwest Modern Language Association*, vol. 8, no. 2, 1975, pp. 1–23.

Salas y Quiroga, Jacinto de. *Viajes de D. Jacinto de Salas y Quiroga: Isla de Cuba*. Madrid, 1840.

Sanguily, Manuel. "Otra vez Plácido y Menéndez y Pelayo. Reparos a censuras apasionadas." *Acerca de Plácido*. Edited by Salvador Bueno. pp. 176-190, Havana, Editorial Letras Cubanas, 1985.

Sanguily, Manuel. "Un improvisador cubano: el poeta Plácido y el juicio de Menéndez y Pelayo." *Acerca de Plácido*. Edited by Salvador Bueno. pp. 160-175, Havana, Editorial Letras Cubanas, 1985.

Saqui, Carlos Cabrera, ed. *Francisco: El ingenio o las delicias del campo*. Havana: Ministerio de Educación Dirección de Cultura, 1947.

Schomburg, Arturo A. *Plácido: A Cuban Martyr*. New York, A.V. Bernier Printer, 1910.

Schomburg, Arturo A. "The Negro Digs Up His Past." *Survey*, pp. 670–672, 1925. http://www .unz.com/print/TheSurvey-1925mar01-00670. Accessed 14 May 2019.

Scott, James C. *Domination and the Arts of Resistance: Hidden Transcripts*. New Haven: Yale University Press, 1990.

Sekora, John, and Darwin T. Turner, eds. *The Art of Slave Narrative: Original Essays in Criticism and Theory*. Macomb: Western Illinois University Press, 1982.

Sharpe, Jenny. *The Ghosts of Slavery: A Literary Archaeology of Black Women's Lives*. Minneapolis: University of Minnesota Press, 2003.

Shepherd, Verene. *Women in Caribbean History*. Kingston: Ian Randle, 1999.

Sierra Torres, Guillermo. "El Bembé de San Lázaro (De Contramaestre a Santiago de Cuba)." *Tebeto: Anuario del Archivo Histórico Insular de Fuerteventura* (Las Canarias), no. 11, 1998, pp. 295–306. www.mdc.ulpgc.es/cdm/ref/collection/tebeto/id/220. Accessed 7 Aug. 2018.

Spillers, Hortense. "Mama's Baby, Papa's Maybe: An American Grammar Book." *Diacritics*, vol. 17. no. 2, 1987. *JSTOR*, www.jstor.org/stable/464747?origin=JSTOR-pdf&seq=1#metadata _info_tab_contents. Accessed 28 Aug. 2012.

Spillers, Hortense. "Shades of Intimacy: What the Eighteenth-Century Teaches Us." *YouTube*. www.youtube.com/watch?v=0r2s8kRYWDo. Accessed 20 Sept. 2018.

Strand, Kenneth A. "The Brethren of the Common Life: A Review Article of R. R. Post's 'The Modern Devotion.'" *Andrew University Seminary Studies.Digital Commons, Andrews*. www .digitalcommons.andrews.edu/cgi/viewcontent.cgi?referer=https://scholar.google.com /&httpsredir=1&article=1123&context=auss, 1970, pp. 65–76.

Stewart Diakaté, Dianne H., and Tracey Hucks. "Africana Religious Studies: Toward a Transdisciplinary Agenda in an Emerging Field." *Journal of Africana Religions*, vol. 1, no. 1, 2013.

Suáres, Ángel L. Fernández Guerra y Norma, ed. *Los Negros curros*. Havana: Editorial de Ciencias Sociales, 1986.

Suárez y Romero. *Francisco, el ingenio o las delicias del campo*. Seville: Editorial Doble J, 2009.

Sullivan, Shannon, and Nancy Tuana. "Introduction." *Race and Epistemologies of Ignorance*, by Sullivan and Tuana, pp. 1–10. Albany: State University of New York Press, 2007.

Surwillo, Lisa. *Monsters by Trade: Slave Traffickers in Modern Spanish Literature and Culture*. Stanford, California: Stanford University Press, 2004.

Sweeney, Fionnghuala. "Atlantic Counter Cultures and the Networked Text: Juan Francisco Manzano, R. R. Madden and the Cuban Slave Narrative." *Forum for Modern Language Studies*, vol. 40, no. 4, 2004, pp. 401–414.

Sweet, James. "The Iberian Roots of American Racist Thought." *William and Mary Quarterly*, vol. 54, no. 1, 1997, pp. 143–166. *JSTOR*, www.jstor.org/stable/2953315. Accessed 2 Aug. 2015.

Tanco y Bosmeniel, Félix. *Petrona y Rosalía*.

Thompson, Robert Farris. *Flash of the Spirit: African and Afro-American Art and Philosophy*. 1st ed. New York: Random House, 1983.

Thornton, John. *Africa and Africans in the Making of the Atlantic World, 1400–1800*. 1992. 2nd ed. Cambridge: Cambridge University Press, 1999.

Thornton, John. "African Soldiers in the Haitian Revolution." *Journal of Caribbean History*, vol. 25.1, no. 2, 1991, pp. 58–79.

Tinsley, Natasha Omise'eke. *Thiefing Sugar: Eroticism between Women in Caribbean Literature*. Duke University Press: Durham, 2010.

Torres Cuevas, Eduardo. *Félix Varela: Los orígenes de la ciencia y conciencia cubanas*. Havana: Editorial de Ciencias Sociales, 2002.

Trelles, Carlos M. "Bibliografía de autores de la raza de color, de Cuba." *Cuba Contemporánea: Revista Mensual*, vol. 43, 1927, 30–78.

Trouillot, Michel-Rolph. *Silencing the Past: Power and the Production of History*. Boston: Beacon Press, 1995.

Twinam, Ann. *Purchasing Whiteness: Pardos, Mulatos and the Quest for Social Mobility in the Spanish Indies*. Stanford: Stanford University Press, 2015.

Urbano, Carmenate. *Plácido: Bicentenario del poeta: 1809–2009*. Matanzas: Ediciones Unión, 2009.

Valdés, Gabriel de la Concepción. *Plácido: Gabriel de la Concepción Valdés: Poesías completas con doscientas diez composiciones inéditas su retrato y un prólogo biográfico*. Edited by Sebastián Alfredo de Morales. Havana, 1886.

Valdés, Gabriel de la Concepción. *Plácido: Poesías completas con doscientas diez composiciones inéditas*. Edited by José López Rodríguez. Buenos Aires: Casa Editorial Maucci Hermanos é Hijos, 1903.

Valdés, Gabriel de la Concepción. *Poesías completas de Plácido (Gabriel de la Concepción Valdés)*. Edited by Mme. C. Denné Schmitz. Paris and Mexico City, 1862.

Valdés, Gabriel de la Concepción. *Poesías de Plácido (Gabriel de la Concepción Valdés)*. Edited by Francisco Javier Vingut. New York, 1855.

Valdés, Gabriel de la Concepción. "Si a todos Arcino dices." *Poesía afroantillana y negrista (Puerto Rico—República Dominicana—Cuba)*, edited by Jorge Luis Morales, p. 149. San Juan: Editorial Universitaria, Universidad de Puerto Rico, 1976.

Valdés, Vanessa K. *Oshun's Daughters: The Search for Womanhood in the Americas*. Albany: State University of New York Press, 2014.

Varela y Morales, Félix. *Cartas a Elpidio: La impiedad, la superstición y el fanatismo en sus relaciones con la sociedad*. Havana: Editorial de la Universidad de la Habana, 1945.

Varela y Morales, Félix. "Memoria que demuestra la necesidad de extinguir la esclavitud de los negros en la Isla de Cuba." *Historia de la esclavitud de la raza africana en el nuevo mundo y en especial los países américo-hispanos.*Edited by Fernando Ortiz, Havana, Editorial de Ciencias Sociales, 1977, pp. 157–179.

Villaverde, Cirilo. *Cecilia Valdés o La Loma de Ángel.* Madrid: Cátedra, 1992.

Vitier, Cintio. "Dos poetas cubanos, Plácido y Manzano." *Bohemia,* 1973. pp. 18–21.

Wade, Peter. "Identity, Ethnicity and Race." *A Companion to Latin American History,* edited by Thomas H. Holloway. Oxford: Blackwell, 2008, pp. 480–493.

Walcott, Derek. "The Sea Is History." *Poet Derek Walcott.* http://www.poets.org/poetsorg/poem /sea-history. Accessed 28 June 2018.

Walker, Daniel E. *No More, No More: Slavery and Cultural Resistance in Havana and New Orleans.* 1st ed. Minneapolis: University of Minneapolis Press, 2004.

Warner-Lewis, Maureen. *Central Africa in the Caribbean: Transcending Time, Transforming Cultures.* Kingston: University of the West Indies Press, 2003.

Washington, Booker T. *Up from Slavery.* New York: Dover, 1995.

Williams, Claudette. *Charcoal and Cinnamon: The Politics of Color in Spanish Caribbean Literature.* Gainesville: University Press of Florida, 2000.

Williams, Claudette. "The Devil in the Details of Cuban Antislavery Narrative: Félix Tanco y Bosmeniel's 'Petrona y Rosalía.'" *Afro-Hispanic Review,* no. 2, 2006, pp. 138, 140.

Willis, Susan. "Crushed Geraniums: Juan Francisco Manzano and the Language of Slavery." *The Slave's Narrative: Texts and Contexts,* edited by Charles T. Davis and Henry Louis Gates, pp. 199–224. Oxford University Press, 1985.

Winant, Howard. *Racial Conditions: Politics, Theory, Comparisons.* Minneapolis: University of Minnesota Press, 2002.

Young, Jason R. *Rituals of Resistance: African Atlantic Religion in Kongo and the Low Country in the Era of Slavery.* Baton Rouge: Louisiana State University Press, 2011.

Zelyck, Lorne. "An Evaluation of Thomas à Kempis' The Imitation of Christ" *Journal of the Grace Angelical Soceity.* 2005, pp. 77–88.

Zimmerman, Héctor. "Del tiempo de Maricastaña." *Revista El Abasto,* www.original.revistaelabasto .com.ar/97_zimmerman_Del_tiempo_de_Maricastania.htm.

# INDEX

Abakuá, 209, 227–28
Ábásí, 209
Abasonga, 209
Abimbola, Kola, 222
Abyssinia/Ethiopia, 9, 107–8, 163–64, 204
acculturation: Herskovits on, 28; of slaves, 51–54, 56–61
Aday, Manuel T., 281
Adorno, Rolena, 73
Afolabi Ojo, G. J., 144
African Americans: autobiographies and biographies, 10, 42, 46, 64, 75–76, 277, 278; Christianity/Protestantism and, 9–10, 203–4; on Manzano and Plácido, 279–80; revolts against slavery, 203–4; spirituals, 75. *See also* slavery; spirituality, African-inspired
African Atlantic religion, 11, 38. *See also* spirituality, African-inspired
African-Cuban cultural lens: Catholic Church vs., 6–7, 18–22, 54–55; Manzano and, 14, 17, 124, 130, 169, 171; nature of, 7; Plácido and, 218–21
African Diaspora: antislavery ideology in literature of, 6; "entities of the crossroads," 146–47; ethnonyms, 23, 211; historic periods of, 11
Africans/African descendants, as term, xiii
Agamben, Giorgio, *The Sacrament of Language*, 5, 206–7
"A Jesús en la cruz" (To Jesus on the Cross) (Manzano), 71–72, 79–82, 84, 123
Akinyela, Makungu, 203
*Álbum, El* (1838) (Manzano), 17, 157–58
Alexander VI (pope): *Inter caetera*, 19–20
Alfredo de Morales, Sebastián, 108, 118
"A Lince, desde la prisión" (To Lince, from Prison) (Plácido), 112, 116

Alix, Juan Antonio, 101
*almas aparecidas* (the apparitions of souls), 125, 126
altars: in "A 'El Pan,'" 191, 195; in Bakongo-inspired conception of natural world, 4–5; in Catholicism, 4, 209–10; in "El juramento," 4, 207–10, 259, 274; as "sacred space," 4; in Yoruba-inspired spiritual practice, 26
Álvarez, Cayito, 181
Álvarez, Santiago, 232
"Ambarina, La: En los días de S. M. la Reina Gobernadora" (In the Days of Her Majesty the Regent Queen) (Plácido), 116
Ambibola, Kola, 145–46
"A la muerte de Cristo" (To the Death of Christ) (Plácido), 112–14, 116, 233
Andrés de la Flor, Don, 193–94
Andrews, George Reid, 106
*animas* (soul in purgatory), 123
antislavery aesthetic: in African Diaspora, 6, 11; African-inspired spirituality as source of power, 6–7, 10, 11–12; of Aponte, 11–12, 116, 203–5, 264; Catholic saints laboring for black freedom, 11–12, 13 (*See also* Catholic saints); as conversion of power relationship, 5; Del Monte and, 7–8, 13, 32–34, 93; Manzano-Plácido collaboration in, 10–11, 17–18, 25, 42–43; Virgin Mary laboring for black freedom, 11–12 (*See also* Virgin Mary)
antislavery movement (1844), 41–42, 83–84, 107, 195–210; *el año del cuero*, 265; antislavery rebellions prior to, 6, 238, 251, 253, 257; arrest and imprisonment of Manzano and Plácido, 5, 237–40; Black Eagle Conspiracy, 193–94; in bridging divisions among blacks, 272–81;

# ABOUT THE AUTHOR

Matthew Pettway is Assistant Professor of Spanish at the University of South Alabama, where he is associated with the Africana Studies Program. He teaches Afro-Latin American, Caribbean, and Spanish literatures. He was a Visiting Scholar in the LLILAS Benson Latin American Studies Collections at the University of Texas in Austin in 2014. And, in 2013, the University of Kansas named him the Langston Hughes Visiting Professor. At Kansas he offered a graduate seminar on blacks in Cuban literature and delivered a public lecture on his research. Moreover, the U.S. Department of Education awarded him the Foreign Language Area Studies Fellowship (FLAS) to study Brazilian Portuguese in Salvador da Bahia in summer 2005.

Pettway has a keen interest in how Afro-Latin Americans that endured extreme trauma in the colonial era took hold of the aesthetic and spiritual tools available to them to conceive a poetics of emancipation. His research examines race, slavery, and African ideas of spirit and cosmos in nineteenth-century black Cuban literature. His work is part of a broader project of literary and historical recovery, akin to what Toni Morrison has termed "a kind of literary archaeology." And he has published peer-reviewed articles, book chapters, and encyclopedia entries on Cuban writers of African descent such as Juan Francisco Manzano, Plácido, José del Carmen Díaz, and Ambrosio Echemendía.

His first book, *Cuban Literature in the Age of Black Insurrection: Manzano, Plácido and Afro-Latino Religion*, is part of the Caribbean Studies series of the University Press of Mississippi.

Pettway's peer-reviewed articles "Ritual and Reason: Negotiating Freedom in the Literature of Juan Francisco Manzano" and "Black Femininity and the Silence of Domestic Space in 'The Cemetery on the Sugar Plantation' by José del Carmen Díaz" appeared in *PALARA* (2012) and *The Zora Neale Hurston Forum* (2013), respectively. In the Cuban journal *Del Caribe*, he published two pieces: "Manzano en el monte: Recuperando el sujeto perdido en 'Un sueño a mi segundo hermano'" (2013) and "Páginas salvadas de la historia de Santiago de Cuba" (2014). His review essay in *American Studies Journal* examines *Caribbean Literature and the Public Sphere: From the Plantation to the Postcolonial* (2011) by Raphael Dalleo and *Oshun's Daughters: The Search for Womanhood in the Americas* (2014) by Vanessa Valdés. Furthermore, he published "The Altar, The Oath and the Body of Christ: Ritual Poetics and Cuban Racial Politics of 1844," the inaugural chapter in *Black Writing, Culture and the State in Latin America*, an anthology edited by Jerome Branche and published by Vanderbilt University Press (2015). He also contributed four biographical articles to *The Dictionary of Caribbean and Afro-Latin American Biography* that Oxford University Press released in 2016. Pettway's latest piece, "Braggarts, Charlatans, and Curros: Black Cuban Masculinity and Humor in the Poetry of Gabriel de la Concepción Valdés" appears in *Breaking the Chains, Forging the Nation: The Afro-Cuban Fight for Freedom and Equality, 1812-1912*, an anthology edited by Aisha Finch and Fannie Rushing and published by Louisiana State University Press.

Matthew Pettway is a native of Detroit, Michigan.

CPSIA information can be obtained
at www.ICGtesting.com
Printed in the USA
BVHW031720271119
564909BV00004B/8/P

9 781496 825018